AQA Chemistry

Exclusively endorsed by AQA

A2

Ted Lister
Janet Renshaw

Nelson Thornes

Published in 2009 by:
Nelson Thornes Ltd
Delta Place
27 Bath Road
CHELTENHAM
GL53 7TH
United Kingdom

09 10 11 12 13 / 10 9 8 7 6 5 4 3 2 1

A catalogue record for this book is available from the British Library

ISBN 978 0 7487 8279 6

Cover photograph by Photolibrary
Illustrations include artwork drawn by GreenGate Publishing
Page make-up by GreenGate Publishing, Kent

Printed in Croatia by Zrinski

Acknowledgements

The authors and publisher are grateful to the following for permission to reproduce photographs and other copyright material in this book.

Photograph acknowledgements

Alamy/Dburke: p 211; **Alamy/Mark Boulton:** p 100; **Alamy/Richard Wareham Fotografie:** p 63 (both); **Alamy/Robert Clay:** p 119; **Allsport: Agence Vandystadt/Jean-Marc Labout:** p 117 (bottom); **Argonaut Technologies:** p 107; **Corel (NT):** p 46 (top), p 112; **Fotolia/ Katrina Brown:** p 152 (bottom); **Fotolia/©Potis:** p 152 (top); **©garteneidechse:** p 77; **Hutton Getty:** p 90; **iStockphoto:** p 115 (both); **Martyn Chillmaid:** p 39 (left), p 62, p 69 (both), p 89, p 95, p 113, p 187 (top), p 210, p 215; **Oxford Scientific Films/Densey Clyne:** p 36; **Proctor and Gamble:** p 46 (bottom); **Science Photo Library:** p 25, p 27, p 235 (top and middle); **Science Photo Library/Andrew Lambert Photography:** p 20, p 30, p 39 (right), p 72, p 163, p 187 (bottom), p 240, p242; **Science Photo Library/Charles D. Winters:** p 117 (top), p 153, p 188, p 227; **Science Photo Library/Equinox Graphics:** p106; **Science Photo Library/Lawrence Berkeley National Laboratory:** p 235 (bottom); **Science Photo Library/ Martyn Chillmaid:** p 3, p 75; **Science Photo Library/Mauro Fermariello:** p 143; **Science Photo Library/Tek image:** p 154.

Every effort has been made to trace and contact all copyright holders and we apologise if any have been overlooked. The publisher will be pleased to make the necessary arrangements at the first opportunity.

Contents

Introduction

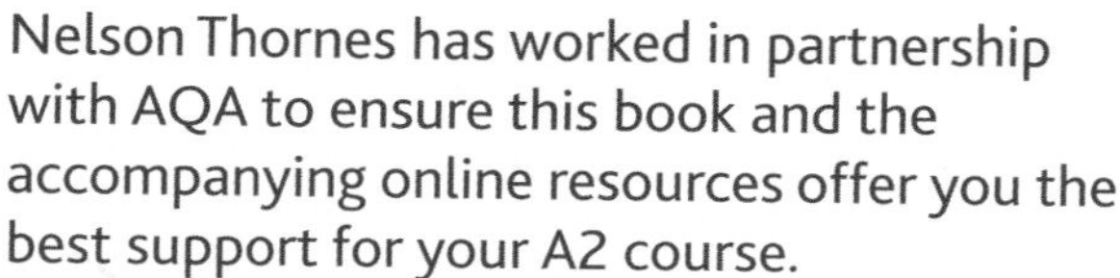

Nelson Thornes has worked in partnership with AQA to ensure this book and the accompanying online resources offer you the best support for your A2 course.

All resources have been approved by senior AQA examiners so you can feel assured that they closely match the specification for this subject and provide you with everything you need to prepare successfully for your exams.

These print and online resources together **unlock blended learning**; this means that the links between the activities in the book and the activities online blend together to maximise your understanding of a topic and help you achieve your potential.

These online resources are available on kerboodle! which can be accessed via the internet at **http://www.kerboodle.com/live**, anytime, anywhere. If your school or college subscribes to this service you will be provided with your own personal login details. Once logged in, access your course and locate the required activity.

For more information and help visit **http://www.kerboodle.com**

Icons in this book indicate where there is material online related to that topic. The following icons are used:

Learning activity

These resources include a variety of interactive and non-interactive activities to support your learning:

- Animations
- Simulations
- Maths skills
- Key diagrams
- Glossary

Progress tracking

These resources include a variety of tests which you can use to check your knowledge on particular topics (Test yourself) and a range of resources that enable you to analyse and understand examination questions (On your marks…).

You will also find the answers to the examination-style questions online.

Research support

These resources include WebQuests, in which you are assigned a task and provided with a range of web links to use as source material for research.

These are designed as stretch and challenge resources to stretch you and broaden your learning, in order for you to attain the highest possible marks in your exams.

Web links

Our online resources feature a list of recommended weblinks, split by chapter. This will give you a head start, helping you to navigate to the best websites that will aid your learning and understanding of the topics in your course.

How science works

These resources are a mixtures of interactive and non-interactive activities to help you learn the skills required for success in this new area of the specification.

Practical

This icon signals where there is a relevant practical activity to be undertaken, and support is provided online.

When you see an icon, go to **http://www.kerboodle.com/live**, enter your access details and select your course. The materials are arranged in the same order as the topics in the book, so you can easily find the resources you need.

How to use this book

This book covers the specification for your course and is arranged in a sequence approved by AQA.

The textbook will cover all three of the Assessment Objectives required in your AQA A Level Chemistry course.

The main text of the book will cover AO1 – Knowledge and understanding. This consists of the main factual content of the specification. The other Assessment Objectives (AO2 – Application of knowledge and understanding and AO3 – How science works) make up around 50% of the assessment weighting of the specification, and as such will be covered in the textbook in the form of the features 'Applications and How science works' (see below).

The book content is divided into the two theory units of the AQA Chemistry A2 specification: Unit 4 (Kinetics, Equilibria and Organic Chemistry) and Unit 5 (Energetics, Redox and Inorganic chemistry).

Units are then further divided into chapters, and then topics, making the content clear and easy to use.

Unit openers give you a summary of the content you will be covering.

The features in this book include:

Learning objectives

At the beginning of each section you will find a list of learning objectives that contain targets linked to the requirements of the specification. The relevant specification reference is also provided.

Key terms

Terms that you will need to be able to define and understand are highlighted in bold blue type within the text, e.g. **isomer**. You can look up these terms in the Glossary.

Hint

Hints to aid your understanding of the content.

Link

Synoptic links are highlighted in the margin near the relevant text using the link icon accompanied by brief notes which include references to where the linked topics are to be found in this book or the AS book.

Applications and How science works

This feature may cover either or both of the assessment objectives AO2 – Application of knowledge and understanding and AO3 – How science works, both key parts of the new specification.

As with the specification, these objectives are integrated throughout the content of the book. This feature highlights opportunities to apply your knowledge and understanding and draws out aspects of 'How science works' as they occur within topics, so that it is always relevant to what you are studying. The ideas provided in these features intend to teach you the skills you will need to tackle this part of the course, and give you experience that you can draw upon in the examination. You will **not be examined** on the exact information provided in this book with relation to Application and How science works.

For more information, see the 'How science works' spread on page 1 for more detail.

Summary questions

Short questions that test your understanding of the subject and allow you to apply the knowledge and skills you have acquired to different scenarios. Answers are supplied at the back of the book.

AQA Examiner's tip

Hints from AQA examiners to help you with your studies and to prepare you for your exam.

AQA Examination-style questions

Questions in the style that you can expect in your exam, including the new 'How science works' strand. These occur at the end of each chapter to give practice in examination-style questions for a particular topic. They also occur at the end of each unit; the questions here may cover any of the content of the unit.

Synopticity

Synoptic questions or part-questions are a key feature of your A2 examination papers. Such a question may require you to draw on knowledge, understanding and skills from AS Level that underpin the A2 topic which the question is about. They link knowledge, understanding and skills from topics in the A2 theory unit on which the question is set, perhaps in a new context, which is described in the question.

Stretch and challenge

Some of the questions in the papers for Units 4 and 5 are designed to test the depth of your knowledge and understanding of the subject. Such questions may require you to solve a problem where you have to decide on a suitable strategy and appropriate methods, possibly linking different ideas from within the unit, discuss in an extended written answer a controversial issue involving chemistry, perhaps in terms of advantages and disadvantages, that affects people or society at large.

The questions test your ability to think deeply and clearly about chemistry and to provide solutions and answers that are coherent and clear.

Answers to these questions are supplied online.

AQA examination questions are reproduced by permission of the Assessment and Qualifications Alliance.

Nelson Thornes is responsible for the solution(s) given and they may not constitute the only possible solution(s).

Web links in the book

Because Nelson Thornes is not responsible for third party content online, there may be some changes to this material that are beyond our control. In order for us to ensure that the links referred to in the book are as up-to-date and stable as possible, the websites provided are usually homepages with supporting instructions on how to reach the relevant pages if necessary.

Please let us know at **kerboodle@nelsonthornes.com** if you find a link that doesn't work and we will do our best to correct this at reprint, or to list an alternative site.

Studying A2 Chemistry

The successful study of any subject at A level requires commitment and determination to gain the knowledge and understanding of the subject matter. This is certainly true of chemistry. Students should commit their time and effort to gain a knowledge of the principles and theories to form the base on which understanding is built. The rewards for this effort will be repaid many times over, both for those who continue to study the subject at a higher level and those who decide to end their formal study of the subject at A level.

This A2 course builds on a knowledge and understanding of chemistry gained during a study of the subject during your AS course. Topics are revisited and further developed and new concepts are introduced. This textbook leads you through the new information and helps you to recognise the underlining patterns and to gain an understanding of the concepts involved. Questions are included at the end of each chapter to help you check that you have gained the required knowledge and understanding.

During this course you will perform many experiments which will help you develop your ability to make accurate observations and measurements. With guidance from your teachers you will be challenged to interpret the results and to suggest additional experiments. The results of some experiments will not fit an expected pattern and you will need to search for reasons why this is the case.

The assessment of practical and investigative skills forms part of the A2 course. Practical skills will be assessed by your teacher who will observe your work throughout the course checking it using guidelines provided by the Examination Board. Investigative skills will be assessed using exercises devised by the Examination Board which will be marked either by your teachers, the PSA + ISA route, or by an external board appointed examiner, the EMPA route. Both routes form 10% of the total A Level assessment.

This textbook contains a wealth of information and guidance to help you to develop your understanding of chemistry. Delight in the subject can be achieved when you have gained both knowledge and understanding of the basic principles. The rewards are certainly worthy of the effort required.

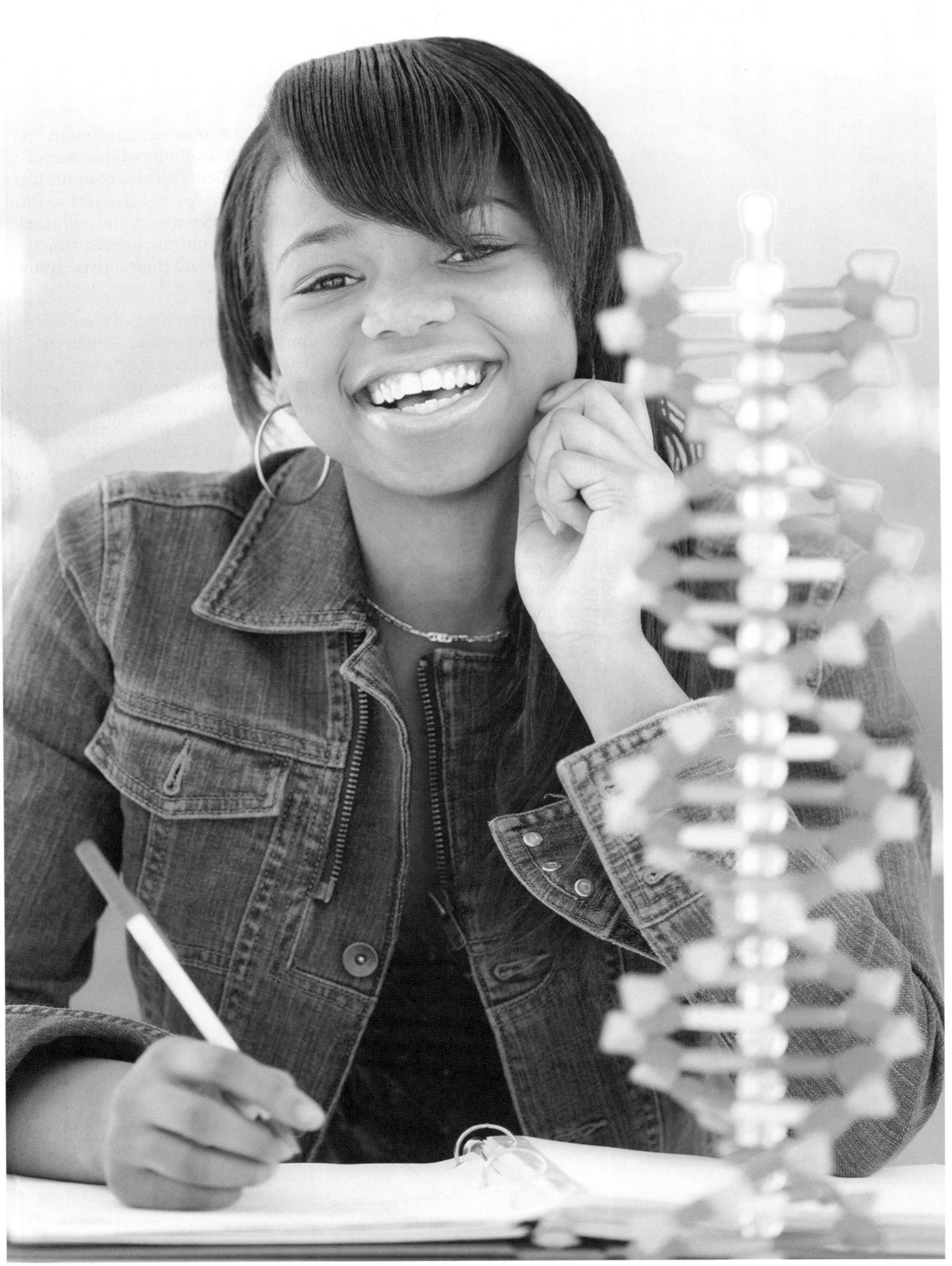

How science works

This book also contains many sections headed 'How science works' which build on ideas introduced during your GCSE and AS courses. The issues considered here will help you recognise how the interpretation of experimental results obtained by research scientists lead to theories and predictions which can be tested by further experiments. In some cases the results obtained from one series of experiments conflict with those obtained from related experiments performed by other scientists. In these cases you will see that there is insufficient experimental evidence for a firm theory to be made.

Your study of chemistry and the 'How science works' issues included in this and the resources online will help you to choose and carry out experimental and investigative activities to answer scientific questions and solve scientific problems. They should further develop your ability to think as a chemist. You will develop the ability to analyse and to question the validity of information given to you. You will be able to appreciate the contribution that chemists have made, and continue to make to our society and understand why it is necessary for chemists to be involved in decisions which affect our society.

Your understanding of the concepts and principles included in these sections will be assessed in the examination. Some questions will build on topics included in the specification content but in other cases you may be given information from which you will be required to make deductions.

By the end of the course you should be able to use scientific logic to assess critically a wide range of ideas presented in newspapers, books and in television and radio programmes.

UNIT 4

Kinetics, equilibria and organic chemistry

Chapters in this unit

This unit returns to physical chemistry and organic chemistry, extending some of the themes covered at AS level.

Kinetics is about rates of reactions. The rate equation is an expression that links the rate of a reaction to the concentration of different reactants. The importance of a rate-determining step is introduced.

Equilibria looks at reactions that reach equilibrium and derives expressions that will predict the position of equilibrium. The effect of temperature on these equilibria is studied.

Acids, bases and buffers extends the definition of acids and bases. An expression to find the pH of a solution is derived and the idea of weak acids and bases introduced and applied quantitatively. Titrations between strong and weak acids and bases as well as buffers are examined.

Nomenclature and isomerism in organic chemistry extends the IUPAC rules for naming compounds to include more functional groups and benzene. It introduces optical (mirror image) isomers and looks at their properties.

Compounds containing the carbonyl group all contain the $C{=}O$ functional group. They include aldehydes, ketones, carboxylic acids and esters. This chapter looks at their structures, the mechanism of their reactions and some of their uses in today's world.

Aromatic chemistry introduces benzene, C_6H_6. Its structure is explained, together with the properties that follow from its unique bonding. Some of the more important reactions of benzene are covered and their mechanisms explained.

Amines are organic compounds containing the NH_2 functional group. They are bases and in this chapter are compared with ammonia. Their substitution reactions are covered as well as methods of preparing them.

Amino acids: all proteins, the building blocks of life, are made up of just 20 different amino acids. This chapter describes the properties of amino acids and how they link together to form proteins.

Polymerisation looks again at addition polymers and also introduces condensation polymers. It deals with biodegradability and the economics of recycling polymers.

Organic synthesis and analysis is about working out a series of reactions for building a given molecule using the organic reactions covered earlier. It also looks at the ways organic functional groups can be identified using these reactions.

Structure determination: mass spectrometry, infra-red spectrometry and nuclear magnetic resonance are used to identify different aspects of organic molecules, such as their molecular masses and the functional groups they contain. The use of chromatography to separate similar organic compounds is illustrated.

What you already know

The material in this Unit builds upon knowledge and understanding that you have developed at AS level, in particular the following:

- The rates of chemical reactions are governed by collisions between particles which occur with sufficient energy.
- Reversible reactions may reach equilibrium.
- Le Châtelier's principle can be used to make predictions about the position of equilibrium.
- The IUPAC system is used for naming organic compounds.
- Alkanes, alkenes, haloalkanes and alcohols are examples of families of organic compounds with characteristic reactions.
- Addition polymerisation, the uses and disposal of polymers.
- Mass spectrometry and infra-red spectrometry are analytical techniques used to determine the structures of molecules.

1 Kinetics

1.1 The rate of chemical reactions

Learning objectives:

- What is the meaning of 'the rate of a reaction'?

Specification reference: 3.4.1

Link

You will need to know the kinetics studied in *AQA AS Chemistry*, Chapter 8.

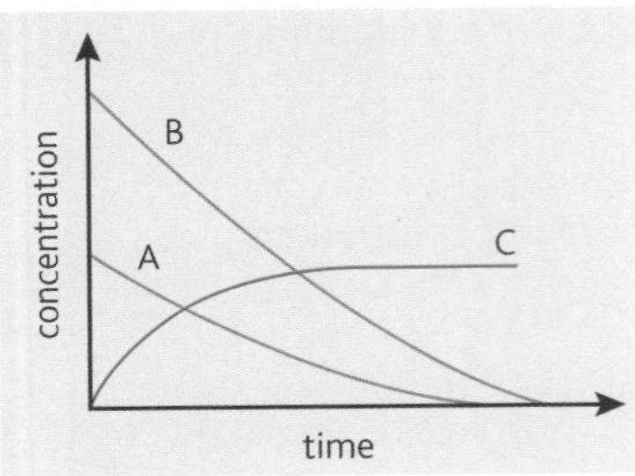

Figure 1 *Changes of concentration with time for A, B and C*

Hint

Square brackets round a chemical symbol, [ ], are used to indicate its concentration in $mol\,dm^{-3}$.

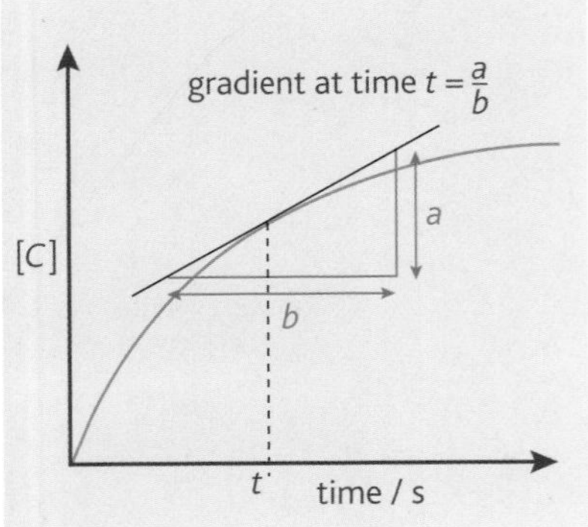

Figure 2 *The rate of change of [C] at time t, is the gradient of the concentration–time graph at t*

The main factors that affect the rate of chemical reactions are: temperature, concentration, pressure, surface area and catalysts. In this topic we will look at the measurement of reaction rates.

What is a reaction rate?

As the reaction: $A + 2B \longrightarrow C$ takes place, the concentrations of the reactants A and B decrease with time and that of the product C increases with time. We could measure the concentration of A, B or C with time and plot the results as shown in Figure 1.

The **rate of the reaction** is defined as the change in concentration (of any of the reactants or products) with unit time. But notice how different the graphs are for A, B and C. Note that as [C] (the product) increases, [A] and [B] (the reactants) decrease. However, as the equation tells us, for every A that reacts there are two of B, so [B] decreases twice as fast as [A]. For this reason it is important to state whether we are following A, B or C. We usually assume that a rate is measured by following the concentration of a product(s) C, because the concentration of the product increases with time.

The rate of reaction at any instant

We are often interested in the rate *at a particular instant* in time rather than over a period of time. To find the rate of change of [C] at a particular instant we draw a tangent to the curve at that time and then find its gradient (slope), Figure 2.

Application

Measuring a reaction rate

To measure a reaction rate, we need a method of measuring the concentration of one of the reactants or products over a period of time (keeping the temperature constant, because rate varies with temperature). The method we choose will depend on the substance whose concentration is being measured and also on the speed of the reaction.

Reaction rates are measured in the units moles per cubic decimetre per second, i.e.:

$$mol\,dm^{-3}\,s^{-1}.$$

For example, in the reaction between bromine and methanoic acid the solution starts off brown (from the presence of bromine) and ends up colourless:

$$Br_2(aq) + HCO_2H(aq) \longrightarrow 2Br^-(aq) + 2H^+(aq) + CO_2(g)$$

So, we can use a colorimeter to measure the decreasing concentration of Br_2. The reaction is slow enough to enable us to read the colorimeter every half a minute and write down the measurements. We could use a computer or data logger to measure the readings and indeed this may be essential for faster reactions.

Table 1 shows some typical results.

In order to find the reaction rate at different times, we plot the results on a graph and then measure the gradients of the tangents at the times required, see Figure 3. For example, when $t = 0$, 300 and 600 s.

$$\text{At } t = 0\,\text{s, rate of reaction} = \frac{0.010}{240} = 0.000\,041\,6\,\text{mol}\,\text{dm}^{-3}\,\text{s}^{-1}$$

$$\text{At } t = 300\,\text{s, rate of reaction} = \frac{0.0076}{540} = 0.000\,014\,\text{mol}\,\text{dm}^{-3}\,\text{s}^{-1}$$

$$\text{At } t = 600\,\text{s, rate of reaction} = \frac{0.0046}{840} = 0.000\,005\,5\,\text{mol}\,\text{dm}^{-3}\,\text{s}^{-1}$$

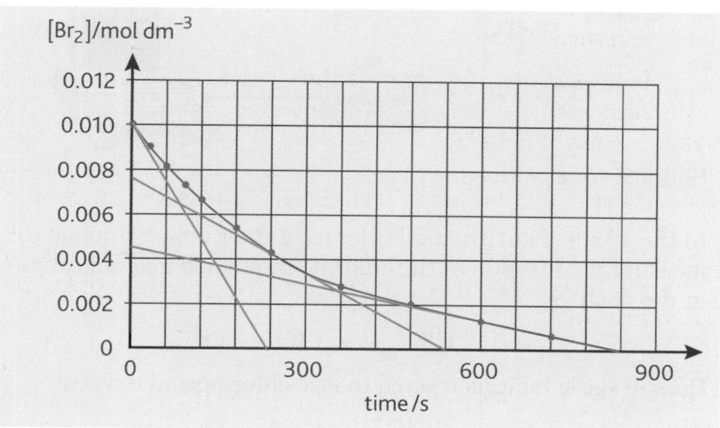

Figure 3 *Finding the rate of reaction at t = 0, t = 300 and t = 600 s*

Table 1 *[Br_2] measured over time*

Time / s	[Br_2] / mol dm^{-3}
0	0.0100
30	0.0090
60	0.0081
90	0.0073
120	0.0066
180	0.0053
240	0.0044
360	0.0028
480	0.0020
600	0.0013
720	0.0007

How science works

'Damn fast reactions indeed'

English chemist, Ronnie Bell, was asked at a scientific meeting by the German Manfred Eigen how the English language would describe reactions that were faster than fast. His reply was as follows. 'Damn fast reactions, Manfred, and if they get faster than that, the English language will not fail you, you can call them damn fast reactions indeed!'

Measuring the rate of a chemical reaction requires the experimenter to measure the concentration of one of the reactants or products several times over the course of the reaction. This is fine for reactions that take a few hours or a few minutes – we can sample the reaction mixture every so often and do a titration to find the concentration of one of the components, for example. But how can we follow a reaction that is over in a few seconds or less?

The British chemists George Porter and Ronald Norrish received the 1967 chemistry Nobel Prize for devising a technique to follow reactions that are over in a microsecond (10^{-6} s). They shared the prize with Manfred Eigen. Their method is called 'flash photolysis' and involves starting a reaction by firing a powerful pulse of light (the photolysis flash) into a reaction mixture. This breaks chemical bonds and produces highly reactive free radicals which react rapidly with each other and with other molecules. Shortly after the first flash, further flashes of light (the probe flashes) are shone through the reaction vessel at carefully timed intervals down to as little as a microsecond (the timing is done electronically). The probe flashes are used to record the amount of light absorbed by one of the species involved in the reaction and thereby measure its concentration.

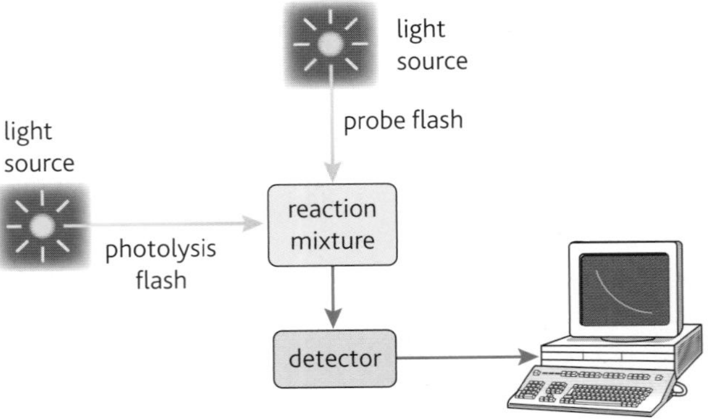

Figure 5 *Flash photolysis*

In the 1950s, Norrish and Porter used their new technique to measure the reaction of the chlorine monoxide free radical produced in the flash:

$$ClO_2 \longrightarrow ClO^{\bullet} + O^{\bullet}$$

Pairs of these radicals reacted to give chlorine and oxygen:

$$2ClO^{\bullet} \longrightarrow Cl_2 + O_2$$

At the time, this reaction (over in about $\frac{1}{1000}$ s) was thought to be of academic interest only. However, 30 years on, it was realised that it was involved in the breakdown of ozone in the atmosphere catalysed by chlorine resulting from CFC molecules in aerosol propellants, etc. Thus Norrish and Porter's work has come to have immense practical importance in enabling us to understand this environmental problem.

In recent years, the use of lasers for the flashes has allowed chemists to measure even faster reactions, down to picoseconds and less (a picosecond is 10^{-12} s). Truly 'damn fast reactions indeed!'

Summary questions

Answer the following questions about the reaction rate graph below.

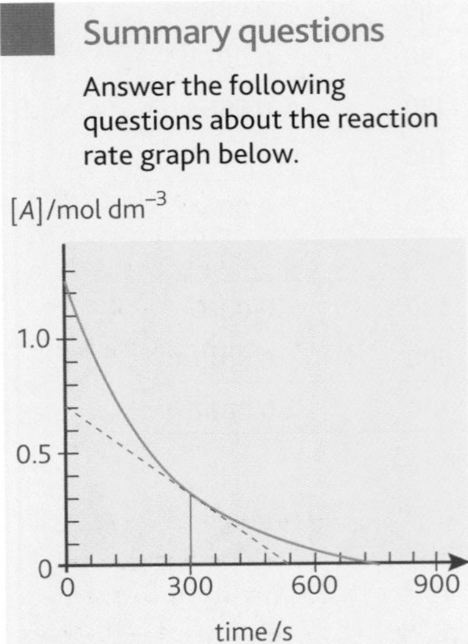

Figure 4

1. Is the concentration being plotted that of a reactant or a product? Explain your answer.
2. The tangent to the curve at the time 300 seconds is drawn on the graph. Find the gradient of the tangent: remember to include units.
3. What does this gradient represent?
4. Without drawing tangents, what can be said about the gradients of the tangents at time 0 seconds and time 600 seconds?
5. Explain your answer to question 4.

1.2 The rate expression and order of reaction

Learning objectives:

- What are the definitions of the terms 'order of reaction' and 'overall order of reaction'?
- What is a rate equation?
- What is the rate constant of a rate equation?

Specification reference: 3.4.1

'Species', in chemistry, is a general term that includes molecules, ions and atoms that might be involved in a chemical reaction.

Hint

When X ∝ Y, if X is doubled then Y also doubles.

The rate of a chemical reaction depends on the concentrations of some or all of the species in the reaction vessel: reactants and catalysts. But, these do not necessarily all make the same contribution to how fast the reaction goes. The **rate expression** tells us about the contributions of the species that do affect the reaction rate.

For example, in the reaction $X + Y \longrightarrow Z$, the concentration of X, [X], may have more effect than the concentration of Y, [Y]. Or, it may be that [X] has no effect on the rate and only [Y] matters. The detail of how each species contributes to the rate of the reaction can only be found out by experiment. A species that does not appear in the chemical equation may also affect the rate – a catalyst for example.

The rate expression

The rate expression is the result of experimental investigation. It is an equation that describes how the rate of the reaction at a particular temperature depends on the concentration of species involved in the reaction. It is quite possible that one (or more) of the species that appear in the chemical equation will not appear in the rate expression. This means that they do not affect the rate. For example, the reaction:

$$X + Y \longrightarrow Z$$

might have the rate expression

$$\text{rate} \propto [X][Y]$$

where the symbol ∝ means 'proportional to'.

This would mean that both [X] and [Y] have an equal effect on the rate. Doubling either [X] or [Y] would double the rate of the reaction. Doubling the concentration of both would quadruple the rate.

But it might be that the rate expression for the reaction is:

$$\text{rate} \propto [X][Y]^2$$

This would mean that doubling [X] would double the rate of the reaction, but doubling [Y] would quadruple the rate.

A species that is not in the chemical equation may appear in the rate equation.

The rate constant *k*

We can get rid of the proportionality sign if we introduce a constant to this expression. For example, suppose the rate expression were:

$$\text{rate} \propto [X][Y]^2$$

This can be written:

$$\text{rate} = k[X][Y]^2$$

and k is called the **rate constant** for the reaction. k is different for every reaction and varies with temperature, so the temperature at which it was measured needs to be stated. If the concentrations of all the species in the rate equation are 1 mol dm^{-3}, then the rate of reaction is equal to the value of k.

The order of a reaction

Suppose the rate expression for a reaction is:

$$\text{rate} = k[\text{X}][\text{Y}]^2$$

This means that [Y], which is raised to the power of 2, has double the effect on the rate than that of [X]. The **order of reaction**, with respect to one of the species, is the *power* to which the concentration of that species is raised in the rate expression. It tells us how the rate depends on the concentration of that species.

So, for rate $= k[\text{X}][\text{Y}]^2$ the order with respect to X is *one*, ([X] and $[\text{X}]^1$ are the same thing) and the order with respect to Y is *two*.

The overall order of the reaction is the sum of the orders of all the species, which appear in the rate expression. In this case the overall order is *three*. So this reaction is said to be *first order* with respect to X, *second order* with respect to Y and *third order* overall.

So : if the rate expression for a reaction is rate $= k[\text{A}]^m[\text{B}]^n$ where m and n are the orders of the reaction with respect to A and B, the overall order of the reaction is $m + n$.

AQA Examiner's tip

Remember that the rate expression is entirely derived from experimental evidence and that it *cannot* be predicted from the chemical equation for the reaction. It is therefore quite unlike the equilibrium law expression that you will meet in Chapter 2 (although it looks similar to it at first sight).

The chemical equation and the rate expression

The rate expression tells us about the species that affect the rate. Species that appear in the chemical equation do not necessarily appear in the rate equation. Also, the coefficient of a species in the chemical equation – the number in front of it – has no relevance to the rate expression. But, catalysts, which do not appear in the chemical equation, *may* appear in the rate expression.

For example, in the reaction

$$\underset{\text{propanone}}{CH_3COCH_3(aq)} + \underset{\text{iodine}}{I_2(aq)} \xrightarrow{H^+ \text{ catalyst}} \underset{\text{iodopropanone}}{CH_2ICOCH_3(aq)} + \underset{\text{hydrogen iodide}}{HI(aq)}$$

The rate expression has been found *by experiment* to be:

$$\text{rate} = k[CH_3COCH_3(aq)][H^+(aq)]$$

So the reaction is first order with respect to propanone, first order with respect to H^+ ions and second order overall. The rate does not depend on $[I_2\ (aq)]$, so we can say the reaction is *zero* order with respect to iodine. The H^+ ions act as a catalyst in this reaction.

Link

You will need to know the influence of carbon–halogen bond enthalpy on the rate of hydrolysis of haloalkanes and the mechanism of substitution and elimination reactions covered in *AQA AS Chemistry*, Chapter 14.

Units of the rate constant, *k*

The units of rate constant vary depending on the overall order of the reaction.

For a first order reaction where:

$$\text{rate} = k[\text{A}]$$

the units of rate are $\text{mol}\,\text{dm}^{-3}\,\text{s}^{-1}$ and the units of [A] are $\text{mol}\,\text{dm}^{-3}$ so the units of k are s^{-1}, obtained by cancelling:

$$\cancel{\text{mol}\,\text{dm}^{-3}}\,\text{s}^{-1} = k\,\cancel{\text{mol}\,\text{dm}^{-3}}$$

Therefore the unit of k for a first order reaction is s^{-1}.

For a second order reaction where:

$$\text{rate} = k[\text{B}][\text{C}]$$

the units of rate are $mol\,dm^{-3}\,s^{-1}$ and the units of both [A] and [B] are $mol\,dm^{-3}$ so, by cancelling :

$$\cancel{mol\,dm^{-3}}\,s^{-1} = k\,\cancel{mol\,dm^{-3}} \times mol\,dm^{-3}$$

Therefore the units of k for a second order reaction are $mol^{-1}\,dm^{3}\,s^{-1}$.

Hint

It is best to work out the units rather than try to remember them.

AQA Examiner's tip

Make sure you understand the terms 'rate of reaction' and 'rate constant'.

Summary questions

1 Write down the rate expression for a reaction that is first order with respect to [A], first order with respect to [B] and second order with respect to [C].

2 For the reaction:

$$BrO_3^-(aq) + 5Br^-(aq) + 6H^+(aq) \longrightarrow 3Br_2(aq) + 3H_2O(l)$$

bromate ions	bromide ions	hydrogen ions	bromine	water

the rate expression is:

$$\text{rate} = k[BrO_3^-(aq)][Br^-(aq)][H^+(aq)]^2$$

a What is the order with respect to:

i $BrO_3^-(aq)$ ii $Br^-(aq)$ iii $H^+(aq)$?

b What would happen to the rate if we doubled the concentration of:

i $BrO_3^-(aq)$ ii $Br^-(aq)$ iii $H^+(aq)$?

c What are the coefficients of the following in the chemical equation above?

i $BrO_3^-(aq)$ ii $Br^-(aq)$ iii $H^+(aq)$

iv $Br_2(aq)$ v $H_2O(l)$

d Work out the units for the rate constant.

3 In the reaction $L + M \longrightarrow N$ the rate expression is found to be:

$$\text{rate} = k[L]^2[H^+]$$

a What is k?

b What is the order of the reaction with respect to:

i L ii M iii N iv H^+?

c What is the overall order of the reaction?

d The rate is measured in $mol\,dm^{-3}\,s^{-1}$. What are the units of k?

e Suggest the function of H^+ in the reaction.

4 In the reaction $G + 2H \longrightarrow I + J$, which is the correct rate expression?

A Rate = $k[G][H]^2$

B Rate = $\dfrac{k[G][H]}{[I][J]}$

C Rate = $k[G][H]$

D It is impossible to tell without experimental data.

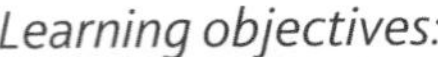

1.3 Determining the rate equation

Learning objectives:

- How is the order of a reaction with respect to a reagent found experimentally?
- How does a change in concentration affect the value of the rate constant?
- How does a change in temperature affect the value of the rate constant?

Specification reference: 3.4.1

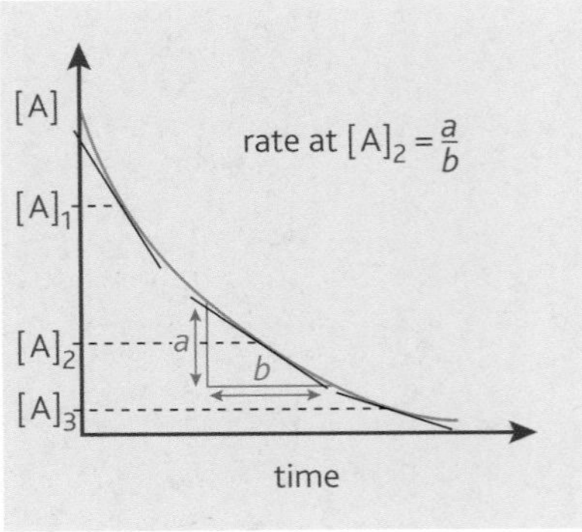

Figure 1 *Finding the rates of reaction for different values of [A]*

The rate expression tells us how the rate of a reaction depends on the concentration of the species involved. It only includes the species that affect the rate of the reaction, see Topic 1.2.

- If the rate is not affected by the concentration of a species, the reaction is *zero order* with respect to that species. We do not include this species in the rate expression.
- If the rate is directly proportional to the concentration of the species, the reaction is *first order* with respect to that species.
- If the rate is proportional to the square of the concentration of the species, the reaction is *second order* with respect to that species, and so on.

Finding the order of a reaction by using rate–concentration graphs

One method of finding the order of a reaction with respect to a particular species A is by plotting a graph of rate against concentration.

We start with the original graph of [A] against time, and draw tangents at different values of [A]. The gradients of these tangents are the reaction rates (the changes in concentration over time) at different concentrations, see Figure 1. The values for these rates can then be used to construct a second graph of rate against concentration, see Figure 2.

- If the graph is a horizontal straight line (Figure 2a), this means that the rate is unaffected by [A] so the order is zero.
- If the graph is a sloping straight line through the origin (Figure 2b) then rate $\propto [A]^1$ so the order is 1.
- If the graph is not a straight line (Figure 2c), we cannot find the order directly – it could be 2. Try plotting rate against $[A]^2$. If this is a straight line, then the order is 2.

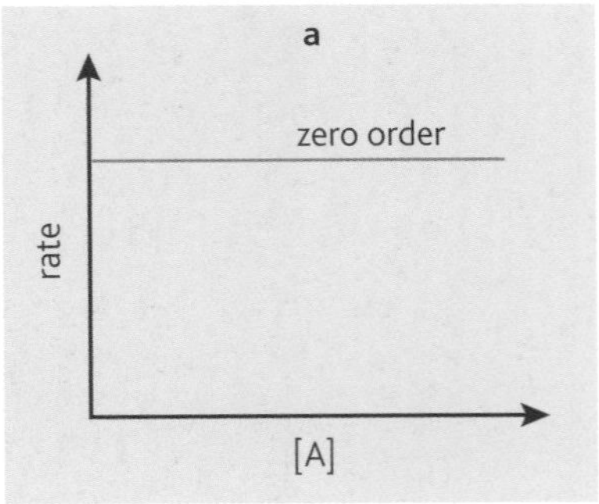

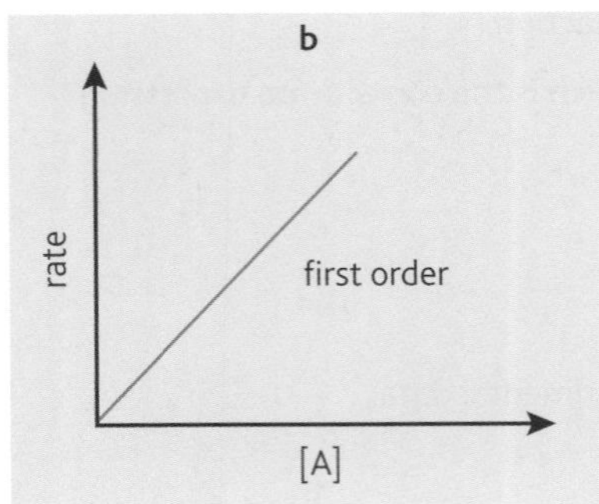

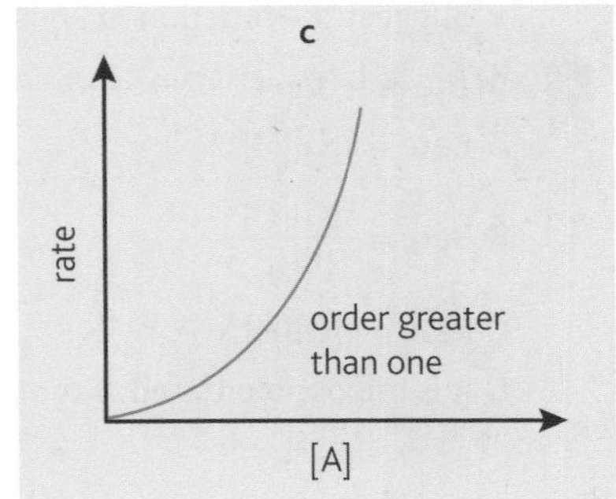

Figure 2 *Graphs of rate against concentration*

The initial rate method

With the initial rate method, a series of experiments is carried out at constant temperature. Each experiment starts with a different combination of initial concentrations of reactants, catalyst, etc. The experiments are planned so that, between any pair of experiments, the concentration of only one species varies – the rest stay the same. Then, for each experiment, the concentration of one reactant is followed and a concentration–time graph plotted, Figure 3. The tangent to the graph at time = 0 is drawn. The gradient of this tangent is the initial rate. The beauty of measuring the *initial* rate is that the concentrations of all substances in the reaction mixture are known *exactly* at this time.

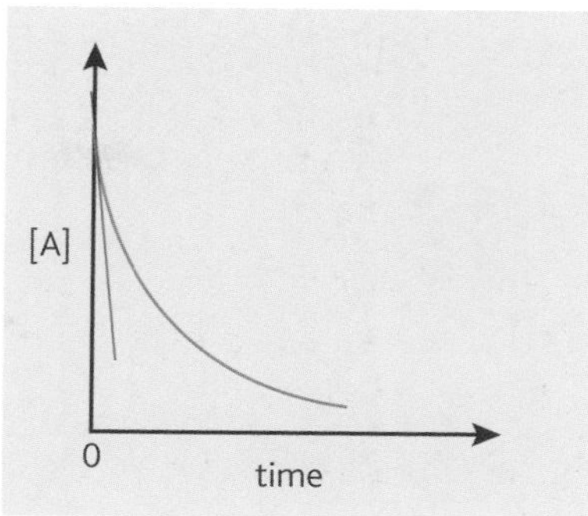

Figure 3 *Finding the initial rate of a reaction. The initial rate is the gradient at time = 0*

Comparing the initial concentration and the initial rates for pairs of experiments allows the order with respect to each reactant to be found. For example, for the reaction:

$$2NO(g) + O_2(g) \longrightarrow 2NO_2(g)$$

nitrogen monoxide   oxygen   nitrogen dioxide

The initial rates are shown in Table 1:

Table 1 *Results obtained for the reaction: $2NO(g) + O_2(g) \longrightarrow 2NO_2(g)$*

Experiment number	Initial [NO] / $mol\,dm^{-3}$	Initial $[O_2]$ / $mol\,dm^{-3}$	Initial rate / $mol\,dm^{-3}\,s^{-1}$
1	1.0×10^{-3}	1.0×10^{-3}	7×10^{-4}
2	2.0×10^{-3}	1.0×10^{-3}	28×10^{-4}
3	3.0×10^{-3}	1.0×10^{-3}	63×10^{-4}
4	2.0×10^{-3}	2.0×10^{-3}	56×10^{-4}
5	3.0×10^{-3}	3.0×10^{-3}	189×10^{-4}

Comparing Experiment 1 with Experiment 2, [NO] is doubled while $[O_2]$ stays the same. The rate quadruples (from $7 \times 10^{-4}\,mol\,dm^{-3}\,s^{-1}$ to $28 \times 10^{-4}\,mol\,dm^{-3}\,s^{-1}$) which suggests rate $\propto [NO]^2$. This is confirmed by considering Experiments 1 and 3 where [NO] is trebled while $[O_2]$ stays the same. Here the rate is increased ninefold, as would be expected if rate $\propto [NO]^2$. So the order with respect to NO is two.

Now compare Experiment 2 with Experiment 4. Here [NO] is constant but $[O_2]$ doubles. The rate doubles (from $28 \times 10^{-4}\,mol\,dm^{-3}\,s^{-1}$ to $56 \times 10^{-4}\,mol\,dm^{-3}\,s^{-1}$) so it looks as if rate $\propto [O_2]$. This is confirmed by considering Experiments 3 and 5. Again [NO] is constant, but $[O_2]$ triples. The rate triples too, confirming that the order with respect to O_2 is 1.

So rate $\propto [NO]^2$

rate $\propto [O_2]^1$

i.e. rate $\propto [NO]^2[O_2]^1$

Provided that no other species affect the reaction rate, the overall order is 3 and the rate expression is:

$$\text{rate} = k[NO]^2[O_2]^1$$

Hint

It is easier to apply the technique to problems than to read about it. However, you can always work out the answer mathematically.

We know that in the above example, rate is $= k[NO]^x[O_2]^y$, where x is the order with respect to NO and y is the order with respect to O_2.

So, $\frac{\text{rate of experiment 2}}{\text{rate of experiment 1}} = \frac{k[NO]_2^x[O_2]_2^y}{k[NO]_1^x[O_2]_1^y}$

Putting in the numbers from the table,

$$\frac{28 \times 10^{-4}}{7 \times 10^{-4}} = \frac{k[2.0 \times 10^{-3}]_2^x[1.0 \times 10^{-3}]_2^y}{k[1.0 \times 10^{-3}]_1^x[1.0 \times 10^{-3}]_1^y}$$

$$\frac{28 \times 10^{-4}}{7 \times 10^{-4}} = \frac{\cancel{k}[2.0 \times 10^{-3}]_2^x\cancel{[1.0 \times 10^{-3}]_2^y}}{\cancel{k}[1.0 \times 10^{-3}]_1^x\cancel{[1.0 \times 10^{-3}]_1^y}}$$

$$4 = 2^x$$

$$x = 2$$

So the order with respect to NO is 2.

Finding the rate constant, *k*

To find k in the equation above, we simply substitute any set of values of rate, [NO] and $[O_2]$ in the equation.

Taking the values for Experiment 2:

$$28 \times 10^{-4} = k(2 \times 10^{-3})^2 \times 1 \times 10^{-3}$$

$$28 \times 10^{-4} = k \times 4 \times 10^{-9}$$

$$k = \frac{28}{4} \times 10^5$$

$$k = 7 \times 10^5$$

But we need to work out the units for k, as these are different for reactions of different overall order. Putting in the units gives:

$$28 \times 10^{-4}\,\text{mol dm}^{-3}\,\text{s}^{-1} = k\,(2 \times 10^{-3})^2\,(\text{mol dm}^{-3})\,(\text{mol dm}^{-3}) \times 1 \times 10^{-3}\,\text{mol dm}^{-3}$$

Units can be cancelled in the same way as numbers, so cancelling the units where we can gives:

$$28 \times 10^{-4}\,\cancel{\text{mol dm}^{-3}}\,\text{s}^{-1} =$$

$$k\,(4 \times 10^{-6})\,(\cancel{\text{mol dm}^{-3}})\,(\text{mol dm}^{-3}) \times 1 \times 10^{-3}\,\text{mol dm}^{-3}$$

$$28 \times 10^{-4} = k \times 4 \times 10^{-9}\,\text{mol}^2\,\text{dm}^{-6}\,\text{s}^1$$

$$k = 28/4 \times 10^5\,\text{mol}^{-2}\,\text{dm}^6\,\text{s}^{-1}$$

$$k = 7 \times 10^5\,\text{mol}^{-2}\,\text{dm}^6\,\text{s}^{-1}$$

Since the units of k vary for reactions of different orders, it is important to put the units for rate and the concentrations in and then cancel them to make sure you have the correct units for k.

Hint

You should get the same value of k using the figures for any of the experiments.

The effect of temperature on *k*

Small changes in temperature produce large changes in reaction rates. A rough rule of thumb is that for every 10 K rise in temperature, the rate of a reaction doubles. Suppose the rate expression for a reaction is rate = k[A][B]. We know that [A] and [B] do not change with temperature, so the rate constant, k, must increase with temperature.

In fact, the rate constant, k, allows us to compare the speeds of different reactions at a given temperature. It is an inherent property of a particular reaction. It is the rate of the reaction at a particular temperature when the concentrations of all the species in the rate expression are 1 mol dm^{-3}. The larger the value of k, the faster is the reaction. Look at Table 2. You can see that the value of k increases with temperature. This is true for all reactions.

Table 2 *The values of the rate constant, k, at different temperatures for the reaction:* $2HI(g) \longrightarrow I_2(g) + H_2(g)$

Temperature / K	k / mol^{-1} dm^3 s^{-1}
633	0.0178×10^{-3}
666	0.107×10^{-3}
697	0.501×10^{-3}
715	1.05×10^{-3}
781	15.1×10^{-3}

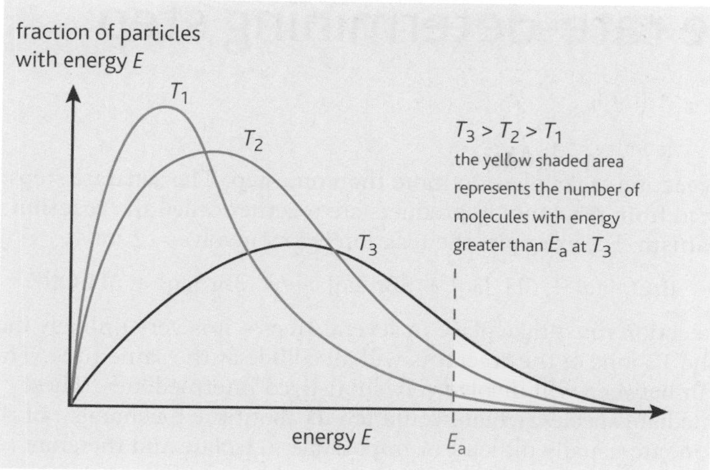

Figure 4 *The distribution of molecular energies at three temperatures*

Why the rate constant depends on temperature

Temperature is a measure of the average kinetic energy. Particles will only react together if their collisions have enough energy to start bond breaking. This energy is called the activation energy, E_a (see *AQA AS Chemistry,* Topic 8.1). Figure 4 shows how the energies of the particles in a gas (or in a solution) are distributed at three different temperatures. Only molecules with energy greater than E_a can react.

The shape of the graph changes with temperature. As the temperature increases, a greater proportion of molecules have enough energy to react. This is the main reason for the increase in reaction rate with temperature.

AQA Examiner's tip

- Make sure you can work out the units for a rate constant.
- Remember: increasing temperature always increases the rate of reaction and the value of the rate constant, k.

Summary questions

1 For the reaction $A + B \longrightarrow C$, the following data were obtained:

Initial [A] / $mol\,dm^{-3}$	Initial [B] / $mol\,dm^{-3}$	Initial rate / $mol\,dm^{-3}\,s^{-1}$
1	1	3
1	2	12
2	2	24

a What is the order of reaction with respect to:

i A

ii B?

b What is the overall order?

c What would be the initial rate if the initial [A] were $1\,mol\,dm^{-3}$ and [B] were $3\,mol\,dm^{-3}$?

d What do these results suggest is the rate expression for this reaction?

e Can we be certain that this is the full rate expression? Explain your answer.

1.4 The rate-determining step

Learning objectives:

- What is the rate-determining step of a reaction?
- What is the connection between the rate equation for a reaction and the reaction mechanism?

Specification reference: 3.4.1

Most reactions take place in more than one step. The separate steps that lead from reactants to products are together called the **reaction mechanism**. For example, the reaction below involves 12 ions:

$$BrO_3^-(aq) + 6H^+(aq) + 5Br^-(aq) \longrightarrow 3Br_2(aq) + 3H_2O(l)$$

This reaction *must* take place in several steps – it is very unlikely indeed that the 12 ions of the reactants will all collide at the same time. The steps in-between will involve very short-lived intermediates. These intermediate species, which would tell us about the mechanism of the reaction, are usually difficult or impossible to isolate and therefore identify. So, we must use other ways of working out the mechanism of the reaction.

The rate-determining step

In a multi-step reaction, the steps nearly always follow *after* each other, so that the product(s) of one step is/are the starting material(s) for the next. Therefore the rate of the slowest step may govern the rate of the whole process. The slowest step may form a 'bottleneck', called the **rate-determining step** or **rate-limiting step**. Suppose you had everything you needed to make a cup of coffee, starting with cold water. The rate of getting your drink will be governed by the slowest step – waiting for the kettle to boil, no matter how quickly you get the cup out of the cupboard and the coffee out of the jar.

In a chemical reaction, any step that occurs *after* the rate-determining step will not affect the rate, provided that it is fast compared with the rate-determining step. So species that are involved in the mechanism after the rate-determining step do not appear in the rate expression. For example, the reaction:

$$A + B + C \longrightarrow Y + Z$$

might occur in the following steps:

1. $A + B \xrightarrow{\text{fast}} D$ (first intermediate)

2. $D \xrightarrow{\text{slow}} E$ (second intermediate)

3. $E + C \xrightarrow{\text{fast}} Y + Z$

Step 2 is the slowest step and so determines the rate. Then, as soon as some E is produced, it rapidly reacts with C to produce Y and Z.

But the rate of Step 1 might affect the overall rate – the concentration of D depends on this. So, any species involved in or *before* the rate-determining step could affect the overall rate and therefore appear in the rate expression.

The reaction between iodine and propanone shows this. (You will not be expected to recall details for an examination.)

The overall reaction is:

```
   H  O  H                                   H  O  H
   |  ‖  |                 H+                |  ‖  |
H—C—C—C—H  +  I2 [aq]  ————————→  I—C—C—C—H  +  HI [aq]
   |     |              catalyst             |     |
   H     H                                   H     H

  propanone          iodine               iodopropane
```

and the rate expression is found to be rate = $k[CH_3COCH_3][H^+]$

The mechanism is:

```
                                               H
                                              /
   H  O                                 H  O
   |  ‖               slow              |  |
H—C—C—CH3  +  H+   ————————→        H—C—C—CH3
   |                                    |  +
   H                                    H

          H
         /
   H  O                              H          O—H
   |  |              fast             \        /
H—C—C—CH3          ————————→           C=C                + H+
   |  +                               /        \
   H                                 H          CH3

                                                 H
                                                /
H          O—H                            H  O
 \        /                 fast          |  |
  C=C          + I2      ————————→     H—C—C—CH3
 /        \                               |  |
H          CH3                            I  I

          H
         /
   H  O                               H  O
   |  |              fast             |  ‖
H—C—C—CH3          ————————→      H—C—C—CH3  +  H+  +  I−
   |  |                               |
   I  I                               I
```

The rate-determining step is the first one, which explains why I_2 does *not* appear in the rate expression.

Using the order of a reaction to find the rate-determining step

Here is a simple example. The three structural isomers with formula C_4H_9Br, all react with alkali. The overall reaction is represented by the following equation:

$$C_4H_9Br + OH^- \longrightarrow C_4H_9OH + Br^-$$

Two mechanisms are possible.

a A two-step mechanism:

Step 1: $C_4H_9Br \xrightarrow{\text{slow}} C_4H_9^+ + Br^-$

followed by Step 2: $C_4H_9^+ + OH^- \xrightarrow{\text{fast}} C_4H_9OH$

The slow step involves breaking the C—Br bond while the second (fast) step is a reaction between oppositely charged ions.

b A one-step mechanism:

$$C_4H_9Br + OH^- \xrightarrow{\text{slow}} C_4H_9OH + Br^-$$

The C—Br bond breaks at the same time as the C—OH bond is forming.

The three isomers of formula C_4H_9Br are:

```
    H   H   H   H
    |   |   |   |
H — C — C — C — C — Br
    |   |   |   |
    H   H   H   H
```

1-bromobutane

```
        CH3
    H    |   H
    |    |   |
H — C —  C — C — H
    |    |   |
    H   Br   H
```

2-bromo-2-methylpropane

```
    H   H   H   H
    |   |   |   |
H — C — C — C — C — H
    |   |   |   |
    H   H   Br  H
```

2-bromobutane

AQA Examiner's tip

The species in the rate equation are the reactants involved in reactions occurring before the rate-determining step.

Experiments show that 1-bromobutane reacts by a second order mechanism:

$$\text{rate} = k[C_4H_9Br][OH^-]$$

The rate depends on the concentration of *both* the bromobutane *and* the OH^- ions, suggesting mechanism (b), a one-step reaction.

Experiments show that 2-bromo-2-methylpropane reacts by a first order mechanism:

$$\text{rate} = k[C_4H_9Br]$$

This suggests mechanism (a) in which a slow step, breaking the C—Br bond, is followed by a rapid step in which two oppositely charged ions react together. So, the breaking of the C—Br bond is the rate-determining step.

The compound 2-bromobutane reacts by a mixture of both mechanisms and has a more complex rate expression.

Summary questions

1 The following reaction schemes show possible mechanisms for the overall reaction:

$$A + E \xrightarrow{\text{catalyst}} G$$

Scheme 1	Scheme 2	Scheme 3
(i) $A + B \xrightarrow{\text{slow}} C$	(i) $A + B \xrightarrow{\text{fast}} C$	(i) $A + B \xrightarrow{\text{fast}} C$
(ii) $C \xrightarrow{\text{fast}} D + B$	(ii) $C \xrightarrow{\text{fast}} D + B$	(ii) $C \xrightarrow{\text{slow}} D + B$
(iii) $D + E \xrightarrow{\text{fast}} F$	(iii) $D + E \xrightarrow{\text{slow}} F$	(iii) $D + E \xrightarrow{\text{fast}} F$
(iv) $F \xrightarrow{\text{fast}} G$	(iv) $F \xrightarrow{\text{slow}} G$	(iv) $F \xrightarrow{\text{fast}} G$

a In scheme 2, which species is the catalyst?

b Which species *cannot* appear in the rate expression for scheme 1?

c Which is the rate-determining step in scheme 3?

AQA Examination-style questions

1 (a) The following data were obtained by studying the reaction between compounds **A**, **B** and **C** at a constant temperature.

Experiment	Initial concentration of A / mol dm^{-3}	Initial concentration of B / mol dm^{-3}	Initial concentration of C / mol dm^{-3}	Initial rate / mol dm^{-3} s^{-1}
1	0.20	0.10	0.40	0.80×10^{-3}
2	0.20	0.40	0.40	3.20×10^{-3}
3	0.10	0.80	0.40	1.60×10^{-3}
4	0.10	0.30	0.20	0.60×10^{-3}

(i) Deduce the order of reaction with respect to **A**.

(ii) Deduce the order of reaction with respect to **B**.

(iii) Deduce the order of reaction with respect to **C**. *(3 marks)*

(b) The rate equation for the reaction between compounds **D** and **E** at a given temperature is

$$\text{rate} = k[\text{D}]^2[\text{E}]$$

The initial rate of reaction is 8.36×10^{-4} mol dm^{-3} s^{-1} when the initial concentration of **D** is 0.84 mol dm^{-3} and the initial concentration of **E** is 1.16 mol dm^{-3}.

Calculate a value for the rate constant, k, at this temperature and deduce its units. *(3 marks)*

AQA, 2007

2 (a) The initial rate of the reaction between compounds **X** and **Y** was measured in a series of experiments at a fixed temperature. The following rate equation was deduced.

$$\text{rate} = k[\mathbf{X}]^2[\mathbf{Y}]^0$$

(i) Complete the table of data below for the reaction between **X** and **Y**.

Experiment	Initial [X] / mol dm^{-3}	Initial [Y] / mol dm^{-3}	Initial rate / mol dm^{-3} s^{-1}
1	1.20×10^{-3}	3.30×10^{-3}	2.68×10^{-4}
2	1.20×10^{-3}	6.60×10^{-3}	
3	2.40×10^{-3}	6.60×10^{-3}	
4		9.90×10^{-3}	8.04×10^{-4}

(ii) Using the data for experiment 1, calculate a value for the rate constant, k, and state its units. *(6 marks)*

(b) Sketch a graph to show how the value of the rate constant varies with temperature. *(1 mark)*

AQA, 2008

3 (a) The rate equation for the reaction between compounds **C** and **D** is

$$\text{rate} = k[\mathbf{C}][\mathbf{D}]^2$$

(i) In an experiment where the initial concentration of **C** is 0.15 mol dm^{-3} and the initial concentration of **D** is 0.24 mol dm^{-3}, the initial rate of reaction is 0.65 mol dm^{-3} s^{-1} at a given temperature. Calculate a value for the rate constant, k, at this temperature and deduce its units.

(ii) The reaction between **C** and **D** is repeated in a second experiment at the same temperature, but the concentrations of both **C** and **D** are half of those in part (a)(i). Calculate the initial rate of reaction in this second experiment. *(4 marks)*

(b) The following data were obtained in a series of experiments on the rate of the reaction between compounds **E** and **F** at a constant temperature.

Experiment	**Initial concentration of E/mol dm^{-3}**	**Initial concentration of F/mol dm^{-3}**	**Initial rate/ mol dm^{-3} s^{-1}**
1	0.24	0.64	0.80×10^{-2}
2	0.36	0.64	1.80×10^{-2}
3	0.48	0.32	3.20×10^{-2}

(i) Deduce the order of reaction with respect to **E**.

(ii) Deduce the order of reaction with respect to **F**. *(2 marks)*

AQA, 2007

4 (a) The following table shows the results of three experiments carried out at the same temperature to investigate the rate of the reaction between compounds **P** and **Q**.

	Experiment 1	**Experiment 2**	**Experiment 3**
Initial concentration of **P** / mol dm^{-3}	0.50	0.25	0.25
Initial concentration of **Q** / mol dm^{-3}	0.36	0.36	0.72
Initial rate / mol dm^{-3} s^{-1}	7.6×10^{-3}	1.9×10^{-3}	3.8×10^{-3}

Use the data in the table to deduce the order with respect to **P** and the order with respect to **Q**. *(2 marks)*

(b) In a reaction between **R** and **S**, the order of reaction with respect to **R** is one, the order of reaction with respect to **S** is two and the rate constant at temperature T_1 has a value of 4.2×10^{-4} mol^{-2} dm^{6} s^{-1}.

(i) Write a rate equation for the reaction. Calculate a value for the initial rate of reaction when the initial concentration of **R** is 0.16 mol dm^{-3} and that of **S** is 0.84 mol dm^{-3}.

(ii) In a second experiment performed at a different temperature, T_2, the initial rate of reaction is 8.1×10^{-5} mol dm^{-3} s^{-1} when the initial concentration of **R** is 0.76 mol dm^{-3} and that of **S** is 0.98 mol dm^{-3}. Calculate the value of the rate constant at temperature T_2.

(iii) Deduce which of T_1 and T_2 is the higher temperature. *(6 marks)*

AQA, 2005

5 (a) The following data were obtained in a series of experiments on the rate of the reaction between compounds **A** and **B** at a constant temperature.

Experiment	Initial concentration of A / mol dm^{-3}	Initial concentration of B / mol dm^{-3}	Initial rate / mol dm^{-3} s^{-1}
1	0.12	0.15	0.32×10^{-3}
2	0.36	0.15	2.88×10^{-3}
3	0.72	0.30	11.52×10^{-3}

(i) Deduce the order of reaction with respect to **A**.

(ii) Deduce the order of reaction with respect to **B**. *(2 marks)*

(b) The following data were obtained in a series of experiments on the rate of the reaction between NO and O_2 at a constant temperature.

Experiment	Initial concentration of NO / mol dm^{-3}	Initial concentration of O_2 / mol dm^{-3}	Initial rate / mol dm^{-3} s^{-1}
4	5.0×10^{-2}	2.0×10^{-2}	6.5×10^{-4}
5	6.5×10^{-2}	3.4×10^{-2}	To be calculated

The rate equation for this reaction is

$$rate = k[NO]^2[O_2]$$

(i) Use the data from experiment 4 to calculate a value for the rate constant, k, at this temperature, and state its units.

(ii) Calculate a value for the initial rate in experiment 5. *(4 marks)*

AQA, 2004

2 Equilibria

2.1 Chemical equilibrium

Learning objectives:

- What is meant by a 'reversible reaction'?
- What is chemical equilibrium?
- What is an equilibrium constant and how is it determined?

Specification reference: 3.4.2

Link

You will need to know the equilibria studied in *AQA AS Chemistry*, Chapter 9.

Figure 1 *Titrating the ethanoic acid to investigate the equilibrium position*

Hint

The concentration of a solution is the number of moles of solute dissolved in 1 dm^3 of solution. A square bracket around a formula is shorthand for 'concentration of that substance in $mol\,dm^{-3}$'.

Many reactions are reversible and do not go to completion, but instead end up as an equilibrium mixture of reactants and products. A reversible reaction that can reach equilibrium is indicated by the symbol $\rightleftharpoons$. In this topic we see how we can tackle equilibrium reactions mathematically. We will deal only with homogeneous systems: those where all the reactants and products are in the same phase, for example all liquids.

Equilibrium reactions

Many reactions are reversible and will reach equilibrium with time. The reaction between ethanol, C_2H_5OH, and ethanoic acid, CH_3CO_2H, to produce ethyl ethanoate, $CH_3CO_2C_2H_5$ (an ester), and water is typical.

If ethanol and ethanoic acid are mixed in a flask (stoppered to prevent evaporation) and left for several days with a strong acid catalyst, an equilibrium mixture is obtained in which *all four* substances are present. We can write:

$$\underset{\text{ethanol}}{C_2H_5OH\,(l)} + \underset{\text{ethanoic acid}}{CH_3CO_2H\,(l)} \rightleftharpoons \underset{\text{ethyl ethanoate}}{CH_3CO_2C_2H_5(l)} + \underset{\text{water}}{H_2O(l)}$$

The mixture may be analysed by titrating the ethanoic acid with standard alkali (allowing for the amount of acid catalyst added). It is possible to do this without significantly disturbing the equilibrium mixture because the reversible reaction is much slower than the titration reaction.

The titration allows us to work out the number of moles of ethanoic acid in the equilibrium mixture. From this we can calculate the number of moles of the other components (and from this their concentrations, if the total volume of the mixture is known).

If several experiments are done with different quantities of starting materials, it is always found that the ratio:

$$\frac{[CH_3CO_2C_2H_5(l)]_{eqm}\,[H_2O(l)]_{eqm}}{[CH_3CO_2H(l)]_{eqm}\,[C_2H_5OH(l)]_{eqm}}$$

has a constant value, provided the experiments are done at the same temperature. The subscript 'eqm' means that the concentrations have been measured when equilibrium has been reached.

The equilibrium constant, K_c

For *any* reaction that reaches an equilibrium we can write the equation in the form:

$$aA + bB + cC \rightleftharpoons xX + yY + zZ$$

Then the expression $\frac{[X]_{eqm}{}^{x}\,[Y]_{eqm}{}^{y}\,[Z]_{eqm}{}^{z}}{[A]_{eqm}{}^{a}\,[B]_{eqm}{}^{b}\,[C]_{eqm}{}^{c}}$ is constant, provided the temperature is constant. We call this constant, K_c.This expression can be applied to *any* reversible reaction. K_c is called the **equilibrium constant** and is different for different reactions. It changes with temperature. The units of K_c vary, and you must work them out for each reaction by cancelling out the units of each term, for example:

$$2A + B \rightleftharpoons 2C \qquad K_c = \frac{[C]^2}{[A]^2[B]}$$

Units are: $$\frac{\cancel{(mol\,dm^{-3})^2}}{\cancel{(mol\,dm^{-3})^2}\,(mol\,dm^{-3})} = \frac{1}{mol\,dm^{-3}} = mol^{-1}\,dm^3$$

The value of K_c is found by experiment for any particular reaction at a given temperature.

AQA Examiner's tip

Make sure that you are able to calculate K_c from given data.

To find the value of K_c for the reaction between ethanol and ethanoic acid

0.10 mol of ethanol is mixed with 0.10 mol of ethanoic acid and allowed to reach equilibrium. The total volume of the system is made up to 20.0 cm³ (0.020 dm³) with water. We find by titration that 0.033 mol ethanoic acid is present once equilibrium is reached.

From this we can work out the number of moles of the other components present at equilibrium:

AQA Examiner's tip

It is acceptable to omit the 'eqm' subscripts unless they are specifically asked for.

At start

$$C_2H_5OH\,(l) + CH_3CO_2H\,(l) \rightleftharpoons CH_3CO_2C_2H_5(l) + H_2O(l)$$

0.10 mol   0.10 mol   0 mol   0 mol

We know that there are 0.033 mol of CH_3CO_2H at equilibrium. This means that:

- There must also be 0.033 mol of C_2H_5OH at equilibrium. (The equation tells us that they react 1:1 and we know we started with the same number of moles of each.)
- (0.10 – 0.033) = 0.067 mol of CH_3CO_2H has been used up. The equation tells us that when 1 mol of CH_3CO_2H is used up, 1 mol each of $CH_3CO_2C_2H_5$ and H_2O are produced. So, there must be 0.067 mol of each of these.

At equilibrium

$$C_2H_5OH\,(l) + CH_3CO_2H\,(l) \rightleftharpoons CH_3CO_2C_2H_5(l) + H_2O(l)$$

0.033 mol   0.033 mol   0.067 mol   0.067 mol

We need the *concentrations* of the components at equilibrium. As the volume of the system is 0.020 dm³ these are:

$$C_2H_5OH\,(l) + CH_3CO_2H\,(l) \rightleftharpoons CH_3CO_2C_2H_5(l) + H_2O(l)$$

$$\frac{0.033}{0.020}\,mol\,dm^{-3} \quad \frac{0.033}{0.020}\,mol\,dm^{-3} \quad \frac{0.067}{0.020}\,mol\,dm^{-3} \quad \frac{0.067}{0.020}\,mol\,dm^{-3}$$

We enter the concentrations into the equilibrium equation:

$$K_c = \frac{[CH_3CO_2C_2H_5(l)][H_2O(l)]}{[CH_3CO_2H(l)][C_2H_5OH(l)]}$$

$$K_c = \frac{[0.067/0.020\,mol\,dm^{-3}][0.067/0.020\,mol\,dm^{-3}]}{[0.033/0.020\,mol\,dm^{-3}][0.033/0.020\,mol\,dm^{-3}]} = 4.1$$

The units all cancel out, and the volumes (0.020 dm³) cancel out, so in this case we didn't need to know the volume of the system, so $K_c = 4.1$. In this case, K_c has no units.

Summary questions

1 Write down the expressions for the equilibrium constant for the following:

a $A + B \rightleftharpoons C$

b $2A + B \rightleftharpoons C$

c $2A + 2B \rightleftharpoons 2C$

2 Work out the units for K_c for question **1a** to **c**.

3 For the reaction between ethanol and ethanoic acid, at a different temperature to the example above, the equilibrium mixture was found to contain 0.117 mol of ethanoic acid, 0.017 mol of ethanol, 0.083 mol ethyl ethanoate and 0.083 mol of water.

a Calculate K_c

b Why do you not need to know the volume of the system to calculate K_c in this example?

c Is the equilibrium further to the right or to the left compared with the worked example above?

2.2 Calculations using equilibrium constant expressions

Learning objectives:

- How is K_c used to work out the composition of an equilibrium mixture?

Specification reference: 3.4.2

A reaction that has reached equilibrium at a given temperature will be a mixture of reactants and products. We can use the equilibrium expression to calculate the composition of this mixture.

Calculating the composition of a reaction mixture

Example

The reaction of ethanol and ethanoic acid is:

$$C_2H_5OH\,(l) + CH_3CO_2H\,(l) \rightleftharpoons CH_3CO_2C_2H_5(l) + H_2O(l)$$

ethanol — ethanoic acid — ethyl ethanoate — water

We know that at equilibrium:

$$K_c = \frac{[CH_3CO_2C_2H_5(l)][H_2O(l)]}{[CH_3CO_2H(l)][C_2H_5OH(l)]}$$

Suppose that $K_c = 4.0$ at the temperature of our experiment and we want to know how much ethyl ethanoate we could produce by mixing 1 mol of ethanol and 1 mol of ethanoic acid. Set out the information as shown below:

Equation:	$C_2H_5OH\,(l)$ +	$CH_3CO_2H\,(l)$ $\rightleftharpoons$	$CH_3CO_2C_2H_5(l)$ +	$H_2O(l)$
	ethanol	ethanoic acid	ethyl ethanoate	water
At start:	1 mol	1 mol	0 mol	0 mol
At equilibrium:	$(1 - x)$ mol	$(1 - x)$ mol	x mol	x mol

We do not know how many moles of ethyl ethanoate will be produced, so we call this x. The equation tells us that x mol of water will also be produced and, in doing so, x mol of both ethanol and ethanoic acid will be used up. So the amount of each of these remaining at equilibrium is $(1 - x)$ mol.

These figures are in moles, but we need concentrations in mol dm^{-3} to substitute in the equilibrium law expression. Suppose the volume of the system at equilibrium was V dm^{-3}. Then :

$$[C_2H_5OH(l)]_{eqm} = \frac{(1-x)}{V}\,\text{mol dm}^{-3}$$

$$[CH_3CO_2H(l)]_{eqm} = \frac{(1-x)}{V}\,\text{mol dm}^{-3}$$

$$[CH_3CO_2C_2H_5(l)]_{eqm} = \frac{x}{V}\,\text{mol dm}^{-3}$$

$$[H_2O(l)]_{eqm} = \frac{x}{V}\,\text{mol dm}^{-3}$$

These figures may now be put into the expression for K_c:

$$K_c = \frac{x/\cancel{V} \times x/\cancel{V}}{(1-x)/\cancel{V} \times (1-x)/\cancel{V}}$$

The V's cancel, so *in this case* we do not need to know the actual volume of the system.

$$4.0 = \frac{x \times x}{(1-x) \times (1-x)}$$

$$4.0 = \frac{x^2}{(1-x)^2}$$

Taking the square root of both sides, we get:

$$2 = \frac{x}{(1-x)}$$

$$2\,(1-x) = x$$

$$2 - 2x = x$$

$$2 = 3x$$

$$x = \frac{2}{3}$$

So $\frac{2}{3}$mol of ethyl ethanoate and $\frac{2}{3}$mol of water is produced if the reaction reaches equilibrium, and the composition of the equilibrium mixture would be: ethanol $\frac{1}{3}$mol, ethanoic acid $\frac{1}{3}$mol, ethyl ethanoate $\frac{2}{3}$mol, water $\frac{2}{3}$mol.

Calculating the amount of a reactant needed

We can also use K_c to find the amount of a reactant needed to give a required amount of product.

Example

For the following reaction in ethanol solution, $K_c = 30.0\,mol^{-1}\,dm^3$:

$$CH_3COCH_3 + HCN \rightleftharpoons CH_3C(CN)(OH)CH_3$$

propanone   hydrogen cyanide   2-hydroxy-2-methylpropanenitrile

$$K_c = \frac{[CH_3C(CN)(OH)CH_3]}{[CH_3COCH_3][HCN]} = 30.0\,mol^{-1}\,dm^3$$

Suppose we are carrying out this reaction in 2.00 dm^3 of ethanol. How much hydrogen cyanide is required to produce 1.00 mol of product if we start with 4.00 mol of propanone? Set out as before with the quantities at the start and at equilibrium.

At equilibrium, we want 1 mol of product. Let x be the number of moles of HCN required.

Equation:	CH_3COCH_3 +	$HCN \rightleftharpoons$	$CH_3C(CN)(OH)CH_3$
At start:	4.00 mol	x mol	0 mol
At equilibrium:	(4.00 – 1.00) mol	(x – 1.00) mol	1.00 mol
	3.00 mol	(x – 1.00) mol	1.00 mol

These are the numbers of moles, but we need the *concentrations* to put in the equilibrium law expression. The volume of the solution is 2.00 dm^3 and the units for concentration are mol dm^{-3} so we next divide each quantity by 2.00 dm^3.

AQA Examiner's tip

The volume of the reaction mixture will cancel for all systems with equal numbers of moles of products and reactants, so V is sometimes omitted. But, it is always better to include V and cancel it out later, so you will not forget it for systems where the Vs do not cancel out.

So, at equilibrium

$$[CH_3COCH_3]_{eqm} = \frac{3.00}{2.00}\,\text{mol dm}^{-3}$$

$$[HCN]_{eqm} = \frac{(x - 1.00)}{2.00}\,\text{mol dm}^{-3}$$

$$[CH_3C(CN)(OH)CH_3]_{eqm} = \frac{1.00}{2.00}\,\text{mol dm}^{-3}$$

Putting the figures into the equilibrium expression:

$$30.0\ ^3\text{mol}^{-1}\,\text{dm}^3 = \frac{1.00/2.00\,\cancel{\text{mol dm}^{-3}}}{3.00/2.00\,\cancel{\text{mol dm}^{-3}} \times (x - 1.00)/2.00\,\text{mol dm}^{-3}}$$

Cancelling through and rearranging we have:

$$30\left(\frac{3/2\,(x-1)}{2}\right) = \frac{1}{2}$$

$$45(x - 1) = 1$$

$$45x = 46$$

$$x = \frac{46}{45} = 1.02$$

So, to obtain 1 mol of product we must start with 1.02 mol hydrogen cyanide, if the volume of the system is 2.00 dm^3.

In this example the volume of the system *does* make a difference, because this reaction does not have the same number of moles of products and reactants.

Summary questions

1 Try reworking the problem above with the same conditions but:

a with a volume of 1.00 dm^3 of ethanol

b starting with 2.0 mol of propanone

c to produce 2.0 mol of product.

2.3 The effect of changing conditions on equilbria

Learning objectives:

- How does Le Châtelier's principle predict how changes in conditions affect the position of equilibrium?
- How is the equilibrium constant affected by changing the conditions of a reaction?

Specification reference: 3.4.2

Figure 1 *Henri Louis Le Châtelier put forward his principle in 1888*

Link

See *AQA AS Chemistry*, Topic 9.2.

AQA Examiner's tip

When the value for ΔH is given for a reversible reaction, it is taken to refer to the forward reaction, i.e. left to right.

Le Châtelier's principle states that when a system at equilibrium is disturbed, the equilibrium position moves in the direction that will reduce the disturbance. We can use Le Châtelier's principle to predict the qualitative effect of changing temperature and concentration on the position of equilibrium. For reactions involving gases, changing the overall pressure has the same effect as changing the concentration of all the gases involved because it squeezes more gas molecules into the same volume.

So, for example, if we increase the pressure on a gas phase equilibrium reaction it predicts that the equilibrium moves towards the side with fewest molecules. If we decrease the temperature of a reaction, it will move in the exothermic direction (in which heat is given out). In this topic we look at what underlies this.

The effect of changing temperature on the equilibrium constant

Changing the temperature changes the value of the equilibrium constant, K_c. Whether K_c increases or decreases depends on whether the reaction is exothermic or endothermic. What happens is summarised in Table 1.

Table 1 *The effect of changing temperature on equilibria*

Type of reaction	Temperature change	Effect on K_c	Effect on products	Effect on reactants	Direction of change of equilibrium
endothermic	decrease	decrease	decrease	increase	moves left
endothermic	increase	increase	increase	decrease	moves right
exothermic	increase	decrease	decrease	increase	moves left
exothermic	decrease	increase	increase	decrease	moves right

If the equilibrium constant K_c increases in value, the equilibrium moves to the right, i.e. the forward direction (more product). If it decreases in value, the equilibrium moves to the left, i.e. the backward direction (less product).

This is because the expression for K_c is always of the form $\frac{[\text{products}]}{[\text{reactants}]}$.

The general rule is that:

- For an exothermic reaction (ΔH is negative) increasing the temperature decreases the equilibrium constant.
- For an endothermic reaction (ΔH is positive) increasing the temperature increases the equilibrium constant.

So for an exothermic reaction, increasing the temperature will move the equilibrium to the left; for an endothermic reaction, increasing the temperature will move the equilibrium to the right.

The effect of changing concentration on the position of equilibrium

First remember that the equilibrium constant does not change unless the temperature changes.

Make sure that you know how to apply Le Châtelier's principle for all changes in conditions.

Look at the following example:

$$C_2H_5OH\,(l) + CH_3CO_2H\,(l) \rightleftharpoons CH_3CO_2C_2H_5(l) + H_2O(l)$$

ethanol ethanoic acid ethyl ethanoate water

Le Châtelier's principle tells us that the equilibrium will react to any disturbance by moving in such a way as to reduce the disturbance.

Imagine we add more ethanol, thereby increasing its concentration. The only way this concentration can be reduced is by some of the ethanol reacting with ethanoic acid producing more ethyl ethanoate and water. Eventually a new equilibrium will be set up with relatively more of the products. We say that the equilibrium has moved to the right (or in the forward direction).

Let us see how this works mathematically.

We know that:

$$K_c = \frac{[CH_3CO_2C_2H_5(l)][H_2O(l)]}{[CH_3CO_2H(l)][C_2H_5OH(l)]}$$

Remember that K_c remains constant, provided that temperature remains constant. Adding ethanol makes the bottom line of the **equilibrium law expression** larger. To restore the situation, some of the ethanol reacts with ethanoic acid reducing both the concentrations in the bottom line of the fraction. This produces more ethyl ethanoate and water, thus increasing the value in the top line of the fraction. The combined effect is to restore the fraction to the original value of K_c.

K_c and the position of equilibrium

The size of the equilibrium constant, K_c, can tell us about the composition of the equilibrium mixture. The equilibrium expression is always of the general form $\frac{\text{products}}{\text{reactant}}$. So:

- If K_c is much greater than 1, products predominate over reactants. We usually say that the equilibrium is over to the right.
- If K_c is much less than 1, reactants predominate, and the equilibrium position is over to the left.

Reactions where the equilibrium constant is greater than 10^{10} are usually regarded as going to completion; while those with an equilibrium constant of less than 10^{-10} are regarded as not taking place at all.

Catalysts and the value of K_c

Catalysts have no effect whatsoever on the value of K_c and therefore the position of equilibrium. This is because they affect the rates of both forward and back reactions equally. They do this by reducing the activation energy for the reactions (see *AQA AS Chemistry*, Topic 8.1). They do however affect the *rate* at which equilibrium is attained: this is important in industrial processes.

How science works

The development of the Haber process

Nitrogen constitutes 80% of the Earth's atmosphere: about 4 quadrillion (4×10^{15}) tonnes of it! So it might be surprising at first sight that any country could have difficulty in getting hold of nitrogen compounds. The problem is 'persuading' nitrogen molecules, N≡N, to break apart and allow the atoms to combine with anything else. This is partly due to the great strength of the nitrogen–nitrogen triple bond, nearly 1000 kJ mol^{-1}, one of the strongest chemical bonds.

Shortage of nitrogen compounds to make fertilisers (such as ammonium nitrate, $NaNO_3$) and explosives (such as TNT, $C_7H_5O_6N_3$) was a serious problem in Germany in the early 1900s. At the time, the main source of nitrogen that could be turned into other compounds was sodium nitrate imported by sea from deposits in South America. Germany was renowned for its chemistry research and industry. Could her chemists devise a way of 'fixing' nitrogen from the air to reduce Germany's dependence on seaborne imports which would be vulnerable in the event of a war?

As early as 1900 Wilhelm Ostwald, who won a Nobel Prize for his work on chemical equilibria, claimed to have mixed nitrogen and hydrogen with an iron catalyst and obtained traces of ammonia, NH_3. He took out a patent, only to have to embarrassingly withdraw it after a young chemical engineer, Carl Bosch, debunked his results.

Figure 2 *Carl Bosch (1874–1940)*

Fritz Haber, a chemistry professor at Karlsruhe University, then took up the challenge. It was realised that the reaction of nitrogen and hydrogen was a reversible one and that it was extremely slow at room temperature:

$$N_2 + 3H_2 \rightleftharpoons 2NH_3$$

Speeding up the reaction by heating it to high temperatures merely caused any ammonia formed to decompose. Clearly a catalyst was required so that a lower temperature could be used. What about the effect of pressure? Would increasing this have the effect of forcing the nitrogen and hydrogen molecules to stay combined as ammonia? The problem was that the equilibrium constant for the reaction was not known and nor was the effect of temperature on its value. There were also public disagreements between Haber and another distinguished chemist, Walther Nernst, about the validity of Haber's results.

Eventually, Haber juggled the effects of pressure and temperature and began a trial-and-error search for a catalyst through a variety of metals, including platinum, uranium and osmium as well as iron. Eventually Haber built a laboratory-scale apparatus capable of producing 2 cm^3 ammonia per minute and convinced the BASF chemical company of the process's feasibility. The task of working the process up to an industrial scale fell to Carl Bosch, the same Bosch who had earlier debunked Ostwald. Bosch's task involved building a plant that would stand up to the high pressures and temperatures required and developing additives for the iron catalyst.

By 1914, Gemany had factories producing ammonia, which meant that she was not dependent on imported nitrates to make explosives and fertilisers and was therefore capable of waging war.

During the First World War, Haber was instrumental in developing the use of poison gas which many find abhorrent. Haber, a highly patriotic German, saw this as simply using his skills in the interests of his country.

In the Second World War, the Germans produced methanol for motor fuel by another equilibrium reaction, see *AQA AS Chemistry*, Topic 9.3.

Summary questions

1 Using Le Châtelier's principle, predict the effect of increasing: (i) the pressure and (ii) the temperature on the following reactions:

a $2SO_2(g) + O_2(g) \rightleftharpoons 2SO_3(g)$ $\Delta H = -197\ \text{kJ mol}^{-1}$

b $N_2O_4(g) \rightleftharpoons 2NO_2(g)$ $\Delta H = +58\ \text{kJ mol}^{-1}$

c $H_2(g) + CO_2(g) \rightleftharpoons H_2O(g) + CO(g)$ $\Delta H = +40\ \text{kJ mol}^{-1}$

2 $A + B \rightleftharpoons C + D$ represents an exothermic reaction and $K_c = \dfrac{[C][D]}{[A][B]}$

In the above expression, what would happen to K_c:

a if the temperature were decreased

b if more A were added to the mixture

c if a catalyst were added?

AQA Examination-style questions

1 Under suitable conditions the equilibrium represented below was established.

$$2CH_4(g) \rightleftharpoons 3H_2(g) + C_2H_2(g) \qquad \Delta H^\ominus = +377\,kJ\,mol^{-1}$$

(a) Write an expression for the equilibrium constant, K_c, for this reaction. *(1 mark)*

(b) At a given temperature and pressure, the equilibrium mixture contained 0.44 mol of methane, 0.28 mol of hydrogen and 0.12 mol of ethyne (C_2H_2) in a container of volume 0.25 dm^3.

Calculate the value of K_c under these conditions and give its units. *(4 marks)*

(c) State the effect of an increase in temperature on the position of this equilibrium and on the value of K_c for this reaction. *(2 marks)*

(d) State the effect of an increase in pressure on the position of this equilibrium and on the value of K_c for this reaction. *(2 marks)*

2 Tetrafluoroethene, C_2F_4, is obtained from chlorodifluoromethane, $CHClF_2$, according to the equation:

$$2CHClF_2(g) \rightleftharpoons C_2F_4(g) + 2HCl(g) \qquad \Delta H^\ominus = +128\,kJ\,mol^{-1}$$

(a) A 1.0 mol sample of $CHClF_2$ is placed in a container of volume 18.5 dm^3 and heated. When equilibrium is reached, the mixture contains 0.20 mol of $CHClF_2$

(i) Calculate the number of moles of C_2F_4 and the number of moles of HCl present at equilibrium.

(ii) Write an expression for K_c for the equilibrium.

(iii) Calculate a value for K_c and give its units. *(6 marks)*

(b) (i) State how the temperature should be changed at constant pressure to increase the equilibrium yield of C_2F_4

(ii) State how the total pressure should be changed at constant temperature to increase the equilibrium yield of C_2F_4 *(2 marks)*

AQA, 2005

3 Nitrogen dioxide dissociates according to the following equation.

$$2NO_2(g) \rightleftharpoons 2NO(g) + O_2(g)$$

When 21.3 g of nitrogen dioxide were heated to a constant temperature, T, in a flask of volume 11.5 dm^3, an equilibrium mixture was formed which contained 7.04 g of oxygen.

(a) (i) Calculate the number of moles of oxygen present in this equilibrium mixture and deduce the number of moles of nitrogen monoxide also present in this equilibrium mixture.

(ii) Calculate the number of moles in the original 21.3 g of nitrogen dioxide and hence calculate the number of moles of nitrogen dioxide present in this equilibrium mixture. *(4 marks)*

(b) Write an expression for the equilibrium constant, K_c, for this reaction. Calculate the value of this constant at temperature T and give its units. *(4 marks)*

(c) The total number of moles of gas in the flask is 0.683. Use the ideal gas equation to determine the temperature T at which the total pressure in the flask is 3.30×10^5 Pa. (The gas constant $R = 8.31\,J\,K^{-1}\,mol^{-1}$) *(3 marks)*

(d) State the effect on the equilibrium yield of oxygen and on the value of K_c when the same mass of nitrogen dioxide is heated to the same temperature T, but in a different flask of greater volume. *(2 marks)*

AQA, 2003

4 (a) The expression for an equilibrium constant, K_c, for a homogeneous equilibrium reaction is given below.

$$K_c = \frac{[A]^2[B]}{[C][D]^3}$$

(i) Write an equation for the forward reaction.

(ii) Deduce the units of K_c

(iii) State what can be deduced from the fact that the value of K_c is larger when the equilibrium is established at a lower temperature. *(3 marks)*

(b) A 36.8 g sample of N_2O_4 was heated in a closed flask of volume 16.0 dm^3. An equilibrium was established at a constant temperature according to the following equation.

$$N_2O_4(g) \rightleftharpoons 2NO_2(g)$$

The equilibrium mixture was found to contain 0.180 mol of N_2O_4

(i) Calculate the number of moles of N_2O_4 in the 36.8 g sample.

(ii) Calculate the number of moles of NO_2 in the equilibrium mixture.

(iii) Write an expression for K_c and calculate its value under these conditions.

(iv) Another 36.8 g sample of N_2O_4 was heated to the same temperature as in the original experiment, but in a larger flask. State the effect, if any, of this change on the position of equilibrium and on the value of K_c compared with the original experiment. *(9 marks)*

AQA, 2006

5 (a) **Figure 1** shows the effect of temperature and pressure on the equilibrium yield of the product in a gaseous equilibrium.

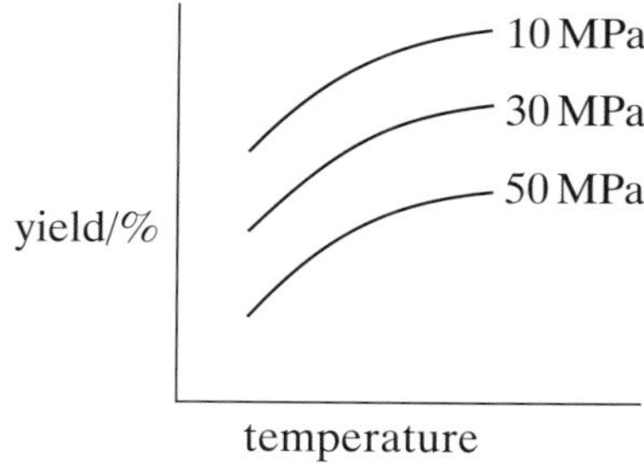

Figure 1

(i) Use the diagram to deduce whether the forward reaction involves an increase or a decrease in the number of moles of gas. Explain your answer.

(ii) Use the diagram to deduce whether the forward reaction is exothermic or endothermic.
Explain your answer. *(6 marks)*

(b) When a 0.218 mol sample of hydrogen iodide was heated in a flask of volume V dm^3, the following equilibrium was established at 700 K.

$$2HI(g) \rightleftharpoons H_2(g) + I_2(g)$$

The equilibrium mixture was found to contain 0.023 mol of hydrogen.

(i) Calculate the number of moles of iodine and the number of moles of hydrogen iodide in the equilibrium mixture.

(ii) Write an expression for K_c for the equilibrium.

(iii) State why the volume of the flask need not be known when calculating a value for K_c.

(iv) Calculate the value of K_c at 700 K.

(v) Calculate the value of K_c at 700 K for the equilibrium

$$H_2(g) + I_2(g) \rightleftharpoons 2HI(g)$$

(7 marks)

AQA, 2006

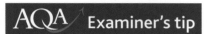

3 Acids, bases and buffers

3.1 Defining an acid

Learning objectives:

- What are the Brønsted–Lowry definitions of an acid and a base?
- What happens in Brønsted–Lowry acid–base reactions?
- What is the expression for the ionic product of water, K_w?

Specification reference: 3.4.3

AQA Examiner's tip

Water-soluble bases are called alkalis and produce OH^- ions in aqueous solution.

Link

You will need to know hydrogen halides are formed when solid sodium halides react with concentrated sulfuric acid (see *AQA AS Chemistry*, Topic 11.3) and the relative solubilities of the hydroxides of the elements Mg – Ba and their uses (see *AQA AS Chemistry*, Topic 12.1).

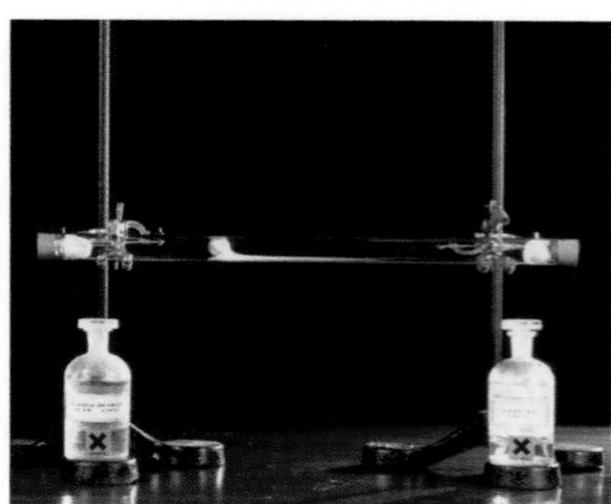

Figure 1 *The white ring of ammonium chloride is formed when hydrogen chloride(left) and ammonia (right) react*

The Brønsted–Lowry description of acidity (developed in 1923 by Thomas Lowry and Johannes Brønsted independently) is the most generally useful current theory of acids and bases.

An acid is a substance that can donate a proton (H^+ ion) and a base is a substance that can accept a proton.

Proton transfer

Hydrogen chloride gas and ammonia gas react together to form ammonium chloride – a white ionic solid:

$$\underset{\text{hydrogen chloride}}{HCl(g)} + \underset{\text{ammonia}}{NH_3(g)} \longrightarrow \underset{\text{ammonium chloride}}{NH_4Cl(s)}$$

Here, hydrogen chloride is acting as an acid by donating a proton to ammonia. Ammonia is acting as a base by accepting a proton. Acids and bases can only react in pairs – one acid and one base.

So, we could think of the reaction in these terms:

$$\underset{\text{acid}}{HCl(g)} + \underset{\text{base}}{NH_3(g)} \longrightarrow [NH_4^+Cl^-](s)$$

Another example is a mixture of concentrated sulfuric acid and concentrated nitric acid. They behave as an acid–base pair:

$$H_2SO_4 + HNO_3 \longrightarrow H_2NO_3^+ + HSO_4^-$$

H_2SO_4 donates a proton to HNO_3, so is acting as the acid, while in this example HNO_3 is acting as a base. In fact, whether a species is acting as an acid or a base depends on the reactants. Water is a good example of this.

Water as an acid and a base

HCl can donate a proton to water, so that water acts as a base:

$$HCl + H_2O \longrightarrow H_3O^+ + Cl^-$$

H_3O^+ is called the **oxonium ion,** but the names hydronium ion and hydroxonium ion are also used.

Water may also act as an acid. For example:

$$H_2O + NH_3 \longrightarrow OH^- + NH_4^+$$

Here water is donating a proton to ammonia.

The proton in aqueous solution

It is important to realise that the H^+ ion is just a proton. The hydrogen atom has only one electron and if this is lost all that remains is a proton (the hydrogen nucleus). This is about 10^{-15} m in diameter, compared to 10^{-10} m or more for any other chemical entity. This extremely small size and consequent intense electric field cause it to have unusual properties compared with other positive ions. It is never found isolated. In aqueous solutions it is always bonded to at least one water molecule to form the ion H_3O^+. For simplicity, we shall represent a proton in an aqueous solution by $H^+(aq)$ rather than $H_3O^+(aq)$.

Since the H^+ ion has no electrons of its own, it can only form a bond with another species that has a lone pair of electrons.

The ionisation of water

Water is slightly ionised:

$$H_2O(l) \rightleftharpoons H^+(aq) + OH^-(aq)$$

or this may be written:

$$H_2O(l) + H_2O(l) \rightleftharpoons H_3O^+(aq) + OH^-(aq)$$

to emphasise that this is an acid–base reaction in which one water molecule donates a proton to another.

This equilibrium is established in water and all aqueous solutions:

$$H_2O(l) \rightleftharpoons H^+(aq) + OH^-(aq)$$

and we can write an equilibrium expression, see Topic 2.1:

$$K_c = \frac{[H^+(aq)][OH^-(aq)]}{[H_2O(l)]}$$

The concentration of water, $[H_2O(l)]$, is constant and is incorporated into a modified equilibrium constant K_w, where $K_w = K_c \times [H_2O(l)]$.

So,
$$K_w = [H^+(aq)]_{eqm}\,[OH^-(aq)]_{eqm}$$

K_w is called the **ionic product** of water and at 298 K it is equal to $1.0 \times 10^{-14}\,mol^2\,dm^{-6}$. Each H_2O that dissociates (splits up) gives rise to one H^+ and one OH^- so, in pure water, at 298 K:

$$[OH^-(aq)] = [H^+(aq)]$$

So
$$1.0 \times 10^{-14} = [H^+(aq)]^2$$

$$\mathbf{[H^+(aq)] = 1.0 \times 10^{-7}\,mol\,dm^{-3} = [OH^-(aq)]}$$

AQA Examiner's tip

The important point to remember at this stage is that the product of $[H^+(aq)]_{eqm}$ and $[OH^-(aq)]_{eqm}$ is constant so that if the concentration of one of these ions increases, the other must decrease proportionately.

Summary questions

1 Identify which reactant is an acid and which a base in the following:

a $HNO_3 + OH^- \longrightarrow NO_3^- + H_2O$

b $CH_3COOH + H_2O \longrightarrow CH_3COO^- + H_3O^+$

2 At 298 K in an acidic solution, $[H^+]$ is $1 \times 10^{-4}\,mol\,dm^{-3}$. What is $[OH^-(aq)]$?

3 What species are formed when the following bases accept a proton?

a OH^- b NH_3 c H_2O d Cl^-

3.2 The pH scale

Learning objectives:

- What is the definition of pH?
- Why is a logarithmic scale used?
- How is pH measured?
- How is the pH of a solution used to find the concentration of $H^+(aq)$ and $OH^-(aq)$ ions?
- How is the pH of a solution calculated from the concentration of $H^+(aq)$ ions?

Specification reference: 3.4.3

AQA Examiner's tip

Always give pH values to two decimal places.

How science works

How the pH scale was invented

Did you know that the pH scale was first introduced by a brewer? In 1909, the Danish biochemist Søren Sørenson was working for the Carlsberg company studying the brewing of beer. Brewing requires careful control of acidity to produce conditions in which yeast (which aids the fermentation process) will grow but unwanted bacteria will not. The concentrations of acid with which Sørenson was working were very small, such as one ten-thousandth of a mole per litre, and so he looked for a way to avoid using numbers such as 0.0001 (1×10^{-4}). Taking the $\log_{10}$ of this number gave –4, and for further convenience he took the negative of it giving 4. So the pH scale was born.

The acidity of a solution depends on the concentration of $H^+(aq)$ and is measured on the pH scale.

pH is defined as $-\log_{10}[H^+(aq)]$

Remember that square brackets, [ ], mean the concentration in $mol\,dm^{-3}$.

This expression is more complicated than simply stating the concentration of $H^+(aq)$. However, using the logarithm of the concentration does away with awkward numbers like 10^{-13}, etc., which occur because the concentration of $H^+(aq)$ in most aqueous solutions is so small. The minus sign makes almost all pH values positive (because the logs of numbers less than 1 are negative).

On the pH scale:

- The *smaller* the pH, the *greater* the concentration of $H^+(aq)$.
- A difference of *one* pH number means a *tenfold* difference in $[H^+]$ so that, for example, pH 2 has ten times the H^+ concentration of pH 3.

Remember that, at 298 K, $K_w = [H^+(aq)][OH^-(aq)] = 1.0 \times 10^{-14}\ mol^2\,dm^{-6}$. This means that in neutral aqueous solutions:

$$[H^+(aq)] = [OH^-(aq)] = 1.0 \times 10^{-7}\ mol\,dm^{-3}$$

$$pH = -\log_{10}[H^+(aq)] = -\log_{10}[1.0 \times 10^{-7}] = 7.00$$

so the pH is 7.00.

pH and temperature

The equilibrium reaction

$$H_2O(l) \rightleftharpoons H^+(aq) + OH^-(aq) \qquad \Delta H = +57.3\ kJ\,mol^{-1}$$

is endothermic in the forward direction, and therefore the value of K_w increases with temperature (see Topic 2.3) and the pH of water is different at different temperatures – see Table 1. So, for example, at 373 K (boiling point), the pH of water is about 6. This does not mean that water is acidic (water is always neutral because it always has an equal number of H^+ ions and OH^- ions) but merely that the neutral value for the pH is 6 at this temperature, rather than the 7 that we are familiar with. So in boiling water $[H^+]$ (and $[OH^-]$) are both about 1×10^{-6} mol dm^{-3}.

Table 1 *The effect of temperature on the pH of water*

T / K	K_w / mol^2 dm^{-6}	pH (neutral)
273	0.114×10^{-14}	7.47
283	0.293×10^{-14}	7.27
293	0.681×10^{-14}	7.08
298	1.008×10^{-14}	7.00
303	1.471×10^{-14}	6.92
313	2.916×10^{-14}	6.77
323	5.476×10^{-14}	6.63
373	51.3×10^{-14}	6.14

The table shows that the pH of sea water at the poles and at the Equator will be different – you can estimate the values from the table.

pH measures alkalinity as well as acidity, because as $[H^+(aq)]$ goes up, $[OH^-(aq)]$ goes down. At 298 K, if a solution contains more $H^+(aq)$ than $OH^-(aq)$, its pH will be less than 7 and we call it acidic. If a solution contains more $OH^-(aq)$ than $H^+(aq)$, its pH will be greater than 7 and we call it alkaline, see Figure 2.

$[OH^-]$	pH	$[H^+]$/mol dm^{-3}
1×10^{-14}	0	1
1×10^{-13}	1	1×10^{-1}
	2	
	3	
	4	
	5	
1×10^{-8}	6	1×10^{-6}
1×10^{-7}	7	1×10^{-7}
1×10^{-6}	8	1×10^{-8}
	9	
	10	
	11	
	12	
1×10^{-1}	13	1×10^{-13}
1	14	1×10^{-14}

Figure 2 *The pH scale. What is the concentration of stomach acid (hydrochloric acid) which has a pH of 2?*

How science works

Measuring pH

pH can be measured using an indicator paper or a solution, such as universal indicator. This is made from a mixture of dyes that change colour at different $[H^+(aq)]$, see Topic 3.5. This is fine for measurements to the nearest whole number, but for more precision we use a pH meter. A pH meter has an electrode which dips into a solution and produces a voltage related to $[H^+(aq)]$. The pH readings can then be read directly on the meter or fed into a computer or data logger, for continuous monitoring of a chemical process or medical procedure, for example.

Figure 1 *Using a pH meter*

A solution is neutral when $[H^+] = [OH^-]$.

Working with the pH scale

Finding $[H^+(aq)]$ from pH

We can work out the concentration of hydrogen ions, $[H^+]$, in an aqueous solution if we know the pH. It is the antilogarithm of the pH value.

For example, an acid has a pH of 3.00:

$$\begin{aligned} pH &= -\log_{10}[H^+(aq)] \\ 3.00 &= -\log_{10}[H^+(aq)] \\ -3.00 &= \log_{10}[H^+(aq)] \end{aligned}$$

Take the antilog of both sides:

Note: To find the antilog of a number, press INV and then the $\log_{10}$ button on your calculator. (Make sure you know how the $\log_{10}$ button is represented on your calculator.)

So, $$[H^+(aq)] = 1.0 \times 10^{-3}\,mol\,dm^{-3}$$

Finding $[OH^-(aq)]$ from pH

With bases, we need two steps. Suppose the pH of a solution is 10.00:

$$\begin{aligned} pH &= -\log_{10}[H^+(aq)] \\ 10.00 &= -\log_{10}[H^+(aq)] \\ -10.00 &= \log_{10}[H^+(aq)] \end{aligned}$$

Take the antilog of both sides:

So, $$[H^+(aq)] = 1.0 \times 10^{-10}$$

We know $$[H^+(aq)]\,[OH^-(aq)] = 1.0 \times 10^{-14}\,mol^2\,dm^{-6}$$

Substituting our value for $[H^+(aq)] = 1.0 \times 10^{-10}$ into the equation:

$$[1.0 \times 10^{-10}]\,[OH^-(aq)] = 1.0 \times 10^{-14}\,mol^2\,dm^{-6}$$

So, $$[OH^-(aq)] = \frac{1.0 \times 10^{-14}}{1.0 \times 10^{-10}} = 1.0 \times 10^{-4}\,mol\,dm^{-3}$$

Hint

To find the $\log_{10}$ of a number, simply enter the number into your calculator and press the $\log_{10}$ button.

The pH of strong acid solutions

HCl dissociates completely in dilute aqueous solution to $H^+(aq)$ ions and $Cl^-(aq)$ ions, i.e. the reaction:

$$HCl(aq) \longrightarrow H^+(aq) + Cl^-(aq)$$

goes to completion. Acids that dissociate completely like this are called **strong acids**.

So in $1.00\,mol\,dm^{-3}$ HCl:

$$\begin{aligned} [H^+(aq)] &= 1.00\,mol\,dm^{-3} \\ \log[H^+(aq)] &= \log 1.00 = 0.00 \\ -\log[H^+(aq)] &= 0.00 \end{aligned}$$

so the pH of $1\,mol\,dm^{-3}$ HCl $= 0.00$

In a 0.160 mol dm^{-3} solution of HCl:

$$[H^+(aq)] = 0.160\ mol\ dm^{-3}$$
$$\log [H^+(aq)] = \log 0.160 = -0.796$$
$$-\log[H^+(aq)] = 0.796$$

So the pH of 0.160 mol dm^{-3} HCl = 0.80 to 2 dp

The pH of alkaline solutions

In alkaline solutions, it takes two steps to calculate $[H^+(aq)]$.

To find the $[H^+(aq)]$ of an alkaline solution at 298 K:

- Calculate $[OH^-(aq)]$.
- Then use: $[H^+(aq)]\ [OH^-(aq)] = 1.00 \times 10^{-14}\ mol^2\ dm^{-6}$ to calculate $[H^+(aq)]$.

The pH can then be calculated.

For example, to find the pH of 1.00 mol dm^{-3} sodium hydroxide solution:

Sodium hydroxide is fully dissociated in aqueous solution – we call this a strong alkali, see Topic 3.3.

$$NaOH(aq) \longrightarrow Na^+(aq) + OH^-(aq)$$
$$[OH^-(aq)] = 1.00\ mol\ dm^{-3}$$

but
$$[OH^-(aq)]\ [H^+(aq)] = 1.00 \times 10^{-14}\ mol\ dm^{-3}$$
$$[H^+(aq)] = 1.00 \times 10^{-14}\ mol\ dm^{-3}$$

and
$$[H^+(aq)] = -\log(1.00 \times 10^{-14})$$
$$pH = 14.00$$

In a 0.100 mol dm^{-3} sodium hydroxide solution:

$$[OH^-(aq)] = 1.00 \times 10^{-1}\ mol\ dm^{-3}$$
$$[OH^-(aq)]\ [H^+(aq)] = 1.00 \times 10^{-14}\ mol\ dm^{-3}$$
$$[H^+(aq)] \times 10^{-1} = 1.00 \times 10^{-14}\ mol\ dm^{-3}$$
$$[H^+(aq)] = 1.00 \times 10^{-13}\ mol\ dm^{-3}$$
$$\log[H^+(aq)] = -13.00$$
$$pH = 13.00$$

Summary questions

1. What is the pH of a solution in which $[H^+]$ is 1.00×10^{-2} mol dm^{-3}?
2. What is $[H^+]$ in a solution of pH = 6.00?
3. At 298 K what is $[OH^-]$ in a solution of pH = 9.00?
4. Calculate the pH of a 0.0200 mol dm^{-3} solution of HCl.
5. Calculate the pH of 0.200 mol dm^{-3} sodium hydroxide.

AQA Examiner's tip

In concentrated solution even strong acids are not fully ionised.

AQA Examiner's tip

The pH of solutions of strong acids which have a concentration greater than 1 mol dm^{-3} is negative. The pH of solutions of strong bases which have concentration greater than 1 mol dm^{-3} is larger than 14.00.

AQA Examiner's tip

When writing out calculations on pH it is acceptable to omit the 'eq' in expressions such as $[H^{+}(aq)]$, so we could write simply pH = $-\log_{10}[H^+]$.

3.3 Finding the pH of weak acids and bases

Learning objectives:

- What is meant by the terms 'weak acid' and 'weak base'?
- How is the pH of a weak acid calculated?

Specification reference: 3.4.3

In Topic 3.2 we found the pH of acids such as hydrochloric acid which, when dissolved in water, dissociate completely into ions. Acids that completely dissociate into ions in aqueous solutions are called **strong acids**. The word 'strong' refers only to the extent of dissociation and not in any way to the concentration. So it is perfectly possible to have a very dilute solution of a strong acid.

The same arguments apply to bases. Strong bases are completely dissociated into ions in aqueous solutions. For example, sodium hydroxide is a strong base:

$$NaOH(aq) \longrightarrow Na^+(aq) + OH^-(aq)$$

In this topic we look at weak acids and bases and see how to find their pHs.

Hint

Although in the gas phase, hydrogen chloride, HCl, is a covalent molecule, a solution of it in water is wholly ionic (that is, $H^+(aq) + Cl^-(aq)$). We can assume that there are no molecules remaining, so hydrochloric acid is a strong acid.

Weak acids and bases

Many acids and bases are not fully dissociated when dissolved in water. Ethanoic acid (the acid in vinegar, also known as acetic acid) is a typical example. In a 1 mol dm^{-3} solution of ethanoic acid, only about 4 in every thousand ethanoic acid molecules are dissociated into ions (so the degree of dissociation is $\frac{4}{1000}$); the rest remain dissolved as wholly covalently bonded molecules. In fact an equilibrium is set up:

$$CH_3COOH(aq) \rightleftharpoons H^+(aq) + CH_3COO^-(aq)$$

	ethanoic acid	hydrogen ions	ethanoate ions
Before dissociation:	1000	0	0
At equilibrium:	996	4	4

AQA Examiner's tip

The *strength* of an acid and its *concentration* are completely independent, so use the two different words carefully.

Acids like this are called **weak acids**. Again note that 'weak' refers only to the degree of dissociation. In a 5 mol dm^{-3} solution, ethanoic acid is still a weak acid, while in a 10^{-4} mol dm^{-3} solution, hydrochloric acid is still a strong acid.

When we dissolve ammonia in water, it forms an alkaline solution. The equilibrium lies well to the left and is weakly basic:

$$NH_3(aq) + H_2O(l) \rightleftharpoons NH_4^+(aq) + OH^-(aq)$$

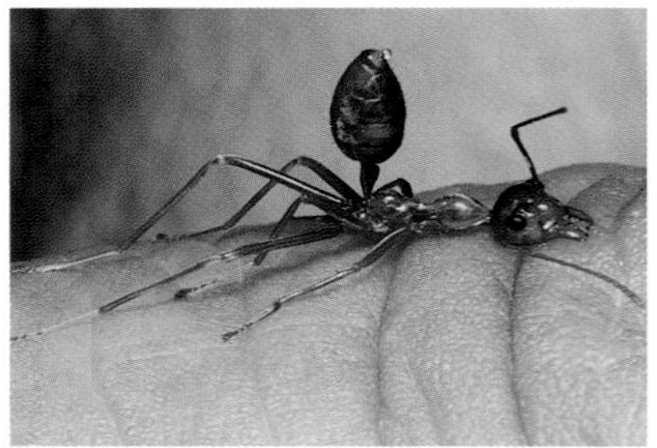

Figure 1 *Formic acid (methanoic acid) is quite concentrated when used as a weapon by the stinging ant and, although it is a weak acid, being sprayed with it can be a painful experience*

The dissociation of weak acids

Weak acids

Imagine a weak acid HA which dissociates:

$$HA(aq) \rightleftharpoons H^+(aq) + A^-(aq)$$

The equilibrium constant is given by:

$$K_c = \frac{[H^+(aq)]_{eqm}[A^-(aq)]_{eqm}}{[HA(aq)]_{eqm}}$$

For a weak acid, this is usually given the symbol K_a and called the **acid dissociation constant**.

$$K_a = \frac{[H^+(aq)]_{eqm}[A^-(aq)]_{eqm}}{[HA(aq)]_{eqm}}$$

The larger the value of K_a, the further the equilibrium is to the right, the more the acid is dissociated and the stronger it is. Acid dissociation constants for some acids are given in Table 1.

K_a has units and it is important to state these. They are found by multiplying and cancelling the units in the expression for K_a.

$$K_a = \frac{\cancel{\text{mol dm}^{-3}} \times \text{mol dm}^{-3}}{\cancel{\text{mol dm}^{-3}}} = \text{mol dm}^{-3}$$

Table 1 *Values of K_a for some weak acids*

Acid	K_a / mol dm^{-3}
chloroethanoic	1.3×10^{-3}
benzoic	6.3×10^{-5}
ethanoic	1.7×10^{-5}
hydrocyanic	4.9×10^{-10}

Calculating the pH of solutions

Weak acids

In Topic 3.2 we calculated the pH of solutions of strong acids, by assuming that they are fully dissociated. For example, in a 1.00 mol dm^{-3} solution of nitric acid, $[H^+] = 1.00$ mol dm^{-3}. In weak acids this is no longer true, and we must use the acid dissociation expression to calculate $[H^+]$.

Calculating the pH of 1.00 mol dm^{-3} ethanoic acid:

Using the same method as in Topic 2.2 for equilibrium calculations, the concentrations in mol dm^{-3} are:

	$CH_3COOH(aq)$	$\rightleftharpoons$	$CH_3COO^-(aq)$	+	$H^+(aq)$
Before dissociation:	1.00		0		0
At equilibrium:	$1.00 - [CH_3COO^-(aq)]$		$[CH_3COO^-(aq)]$		$[H^+(aq)]$

$$K_a = \frac{[CH_3COO^-(aq)][H^+(aq)]}{[CH_3COOH(aq)]}$$

But as each CH_3COOH molecule that dissociates produces one CH_3COO^- ion and one H^+ ion:

$$[CH_3COO^-(aq)] = [H^+(aq)]$$

Since the degree of dissociation of ethanoic acid is so small (it is a weak acid), $[H^+(aq)]_{eqm}$ is very small and to a good approximation, $1.00 - [H^+(aq)] \approx 1.00$.

so $$K_a = \frac{[H^+(aq)]^2}{1.00}$$

From Table 1, $$K_a = 1.7 \times 10^{-5}\ \text{mol dm}^{-3}$$

so $$1.7 \times 10^{-5} = [H^+(aq)]^2$$

$$[H^+(aq)] = \sqrt{1.75 \times 10^{-5}}$$

$$[H^+(aq)] = 4.12 \times 10^{-3}\ \text{mol dm}^{-3}$$

Taking logs: $$\log [H^+(aq)] = -2.385$$

AQA Examiner's tip

It is acceptable to omit the 'eqm' subscripts unless they are specifically asked for.

AQA Examiner's tip

The general expression for the weak acid HA

$$K_a = \frac{[H^+]^2}{[HA]}$$

does not apply to buffer solutions (see page 45).

so $\mathrm{pH} = 2.385 = 2.39$ to 2 dp

Calculating the pH of $0.100\,\mathrm{mol\,dm^{-3}}$ ethanoic acid:

Using the same method, we get:

$$K_a = \frac{[\mathrm{H^+(aq)}]^2}{0.10 - [\mathrm{H^+(aq)}]}$$

Again, $0.100 - [\mathrm{H^+(aq)}] \approx 0.10$

so: $1.70 \times 10^{-5} = \dfrac{[\mathrm{H^+(aq)}]^2}{0.10}$

$$1.70 \times 10^{-6} = [\mathrm{H^+(aq)}]^2$$

$$[\mathrm{H^+(aq)}] = 1.30 \times 10^{-3}\,\mathrm{mol\,dm^{-3}}$$

$$\mathrm{pH} = 2.89 \text{ to 2 dp}$$

pK_a

For a weak acid we often refer to pK_a. This is defined as:

$$\mathrm{p}K_a = -\log_{10} K_a$$

Think of 'p' as meaning '$-\log_{10}$ of'.

pK_a can be useful in calculations, see Table 2. It gives a measure of how strong a weak acid is – the smaller the value of pK_a, the stronger the acid.

Table 2 *Values of K_a and pK_a for some weak acids*

Acid	K_a/mol dm^{-3}	pK_a
chloroethanoic	1.3×10^{-3}	2.88
benzoic	6.3×10^{-5}	4.20
ethanoic	1.7×10^{-5}	4.77
hydrocyanic	4.9×10^{-10}	9.31

Summary questions

1 Which is the strongest acid in Table 2?

2 What can you say about the concentration of H^+ ions compared with concentration of ethanoate ions in all solutions of ethanoic acid?

3 Calculate the pH of the following solutions:

a $0.100\,\mathrm{mol\,dm^{-3}}$ chloroethanoic acid

b $0.0100\,\mathrm{mol\,dm^{-3}}$ benzoic acid

3.4 Acid–base titrations

Learning objectives:

- How is pH determined experimentally?
- What are the shapes of the pH curves for acid–base titrations?
- What is the equivalence point?

Specification reference: 3.4.3

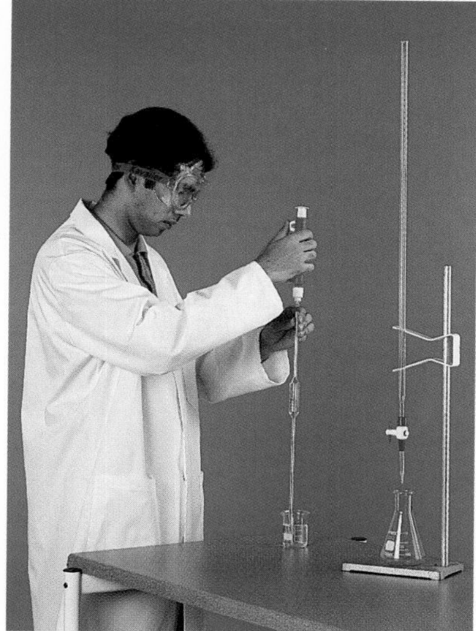

Figure 1 *An acid–base titration, to find the concentration of a base. A pipette is used to deliver an accurately measured volume of base of unknown concentration into the flask. The acid of known concentration is in the burette*

A titration is used to find the concentration of a solution by gradually adding to it a second solution with which it reacts. One of the solutions is of known concentration. To use a titration, we must know the equation for the reaction.

pH changes during acid–base titrations

In an acid–base titration, an acid of known concentration is added from a burette to a measured amount of a solution of a base (an alkali) until an indicator shows that the base has been neutralised, or the base is added to the acid until the acid is neutralised. We can then calculate the concentration of the alkali from the volume of acid used.

We can also follow a neutralisation reaction by measuring the pH with a pH meter, see Figure 2b, in which case we do not need an indicator. The pH meter is calibrated by placing the probe in a buffer solution of a known pH (see Topic 3.6).

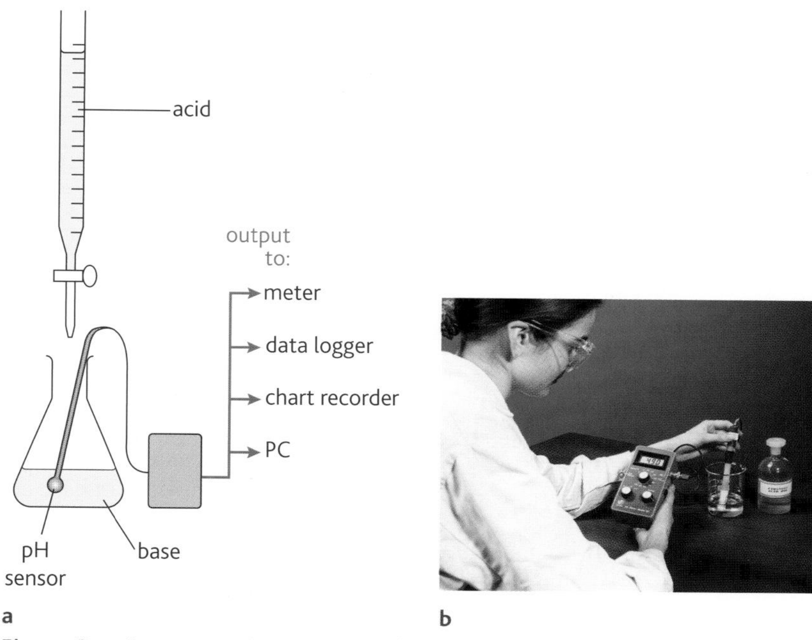

Figure 2 **a** *Apparatus to investigate pH changes during a titration* **b** *A pH meter*

Titration curves

Figures 3 a, b, c, and d, show the results obtained for four cases using monoprotic acids. Notice that in these cases the *base* is added from the burette and the acid has been accurately measured into a flask. The shape of each titration curve is typical for the type of acid–base titration.

AQA Examiner's tip

A monoprotic acid has only one acidic hydrogen (i.e. one that can be donated to a base). Hydrochloric acid, HCl, is monoprotic, whereas sulfuric acid H_2SO_4, is diprotic.

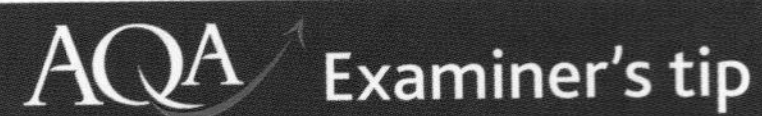

The equivalence point is also called the stoichiometric point.

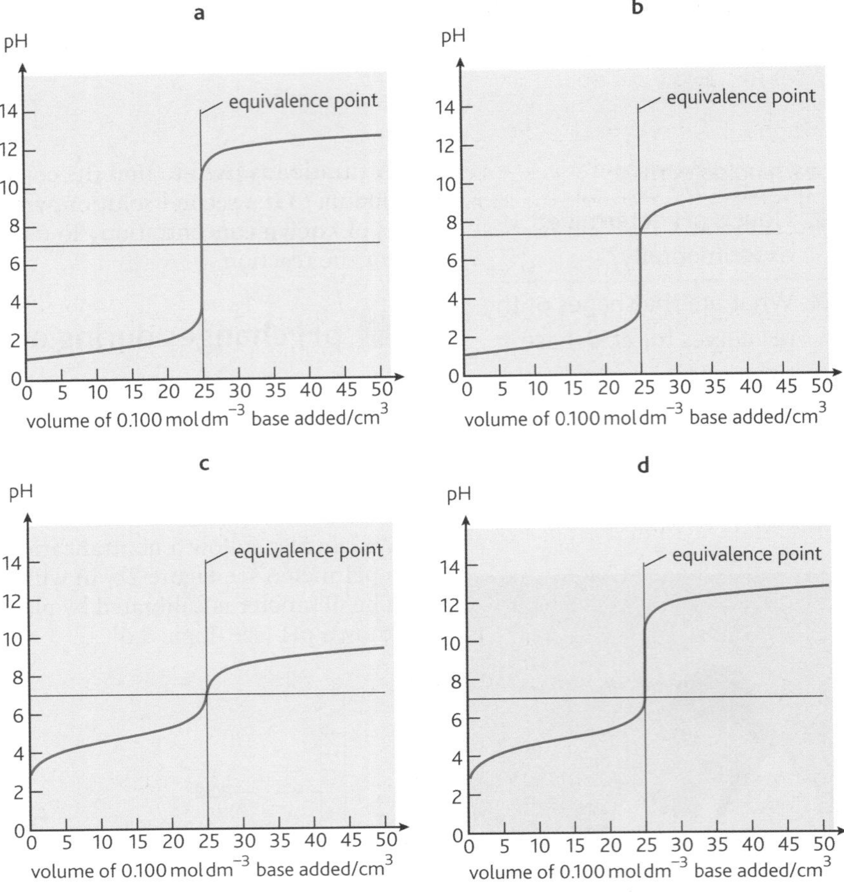

Figure 3 *Graphs of pH changes for titrations of different acids and bases.* **a** *strong acid and strong base,* **b** *strong acid and weak base,* **c** *weak acid and weak base,* **d** *weak acid and strong base*

The first thing to notice about these curves is that the pH does not change in a linear manner as the base is added. Each curve has almost horizontal sections where a lot of base can be added without changing the pH much. There is also a very steep portion of each curve, except weak acid–weak base, where a single drop of base changes the pH by several units.

In a titration, the **equivalence point** is the point at which sufficient base has been added to just neutralise the acid (or vice-versa). In each of the titrations in Figure 3 the equivalence point is reached after 25.0 cm^3 of base has been added. However, the pH at the equivalence point is not always exactly 7.

Notice that in each case, except the weak acid–weak base titration, there is a large and rapid change of pH at the equivalence point (i.e. the curve is almost vertical) even though this is may not be centred on pH 7. This is relevant to the choice of indicator for a particular titration (see Topic 3.5).

Notice that we can add the acid to the base for these pH curves and the shape will be flipped around the pH 7 line. For example, Figure 4 shows a strong acid–strong base curve.

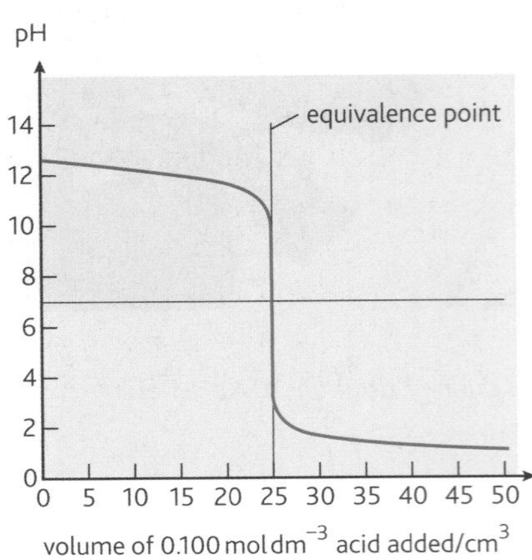

Figure 4 *Titration of a strong base–strong acid, adding 0.100 mol dm^{-3} HCl(aq) to 25.0 cm^3 of 0.100 mol dm^{-3} NaOH(aq)*

Working out concentrations

We can use the equivalence point to work out the concentration of the unknown acid (or base).

Example 1: a monoprotic acid

In a titration, we find that the equivalence point is reached when 25.0 cm³ of 0.0150 mol dm⁻³ sodium hydroxide is neutralised by 15.0 cm³ hydrochloric acid. What is the concentration of the acid?

$$HCl(aq) + NaOH(aq) \longrightarrow NaCl(aq) + H_2O(l)$$

The equivalence point shows that 15.0 cm³ hydrochloric acid of concentration *A* contains the same number of moles as 25.0 cm³ of 0.0150 mol dm⁻³ sodium hydroxide.

$$\text{number of moles in solution} = M \times \frac{V}{1000}$$

where M = concentration in mol dm⁻³ and V = volume in cm³

From the equation, number of moles HCl = number of moles NaOH

So $$25.0 \times \frac{0.0150}{1000} = 15.0 \times \frac{A}{1000}$$

$$A = 0.025$$

So, the concentration of the acid is 0.0250 mol dm⁻³.

Example 2: a diprotic acid

In a titration, we find that the equivalence point is reached when 20.0 cm³ of 0.0100 mol dm⁻³ sodium hydroxide is neutralised by 15.0 cm³ sulfuric acid. What is the concentration of the acid?

$$H_2SO_4(aq) + 2NaOH(aq) \longrightarrow Na_2SO_4(aq) + 2H_2O(l)$$

The equivalence point shows that 15.0 cm³ sulfuric acid of concentration *B* contains the same number of moles as 20.0 cm³ of 0.0100 mol dm⁻³ ³ sodium hydroxide.

$$\text{number of moles in solution} = M \times \frac{V}{1000}$$

where M = concentration in mol dm⁻³ and V = volume in cm³.

$$\text{Number of moles of NaOH} = 20.0 \times \frac{0.0100}{1000} = \frac{0.2}{1000}$$

From the equation, number of moles $H_2SO_4 = \frac{1}{2}$ number of moles NaOH

$$\text{So number of moles of } H_2SO_4 = \frac{0.1}{1000}$$

$$\text{Number of moles of } H_2SO_4 = 15.0 \times \frac{B}{1000} = \frac{0.1}{1000}$$

So, the concentration, *B*, of the acid is 0.006 67 mol dm⁻³.

Summary questions

1 25.0 cm³ sodium hydroxide is neutralised by 15.0 cm³ sulfuric acid, H_2SO_4, of concentration 0.100 mol dm⁻³.

a Write the equation for this reaction.

b From the equation, how many moles of sulfuric acid will neutralise 1.00 mol of sodium hydroxide?

c How many moles of sulfuric acid are used in the neutralisation?

d What is the concentration of the sodium hydroxide?

2 The graph below shows two titration curves of two acids labelled A and B with a base.

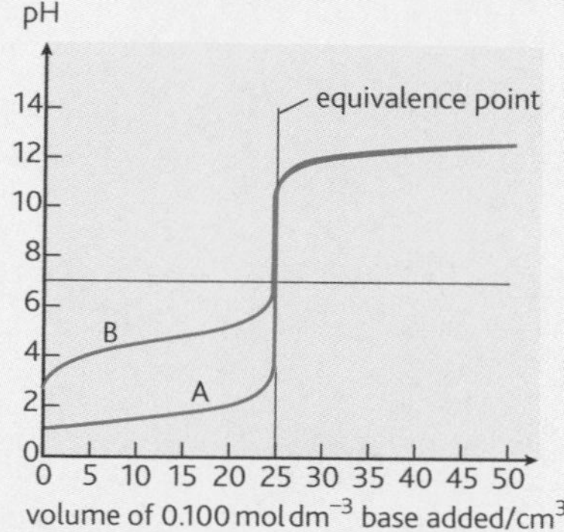

Figure 5

a Which represents that for:

i a strong acid

ii a weak acid?

b Which one could represent:

i ethanoic acid, CH_3COOH

ii hydrochloric acid, HCl?

c Was the base strong or weak? Explain your answer.

3.5 Choice of indicators for titrations

Learning objectives:

- How can pH curves be used to select a suitable indicator?
- How can the end point be found from the curves?
- What is the significance of the half-neutralisation point on these curves?

Specification reference: 3.4.3

An acid–base titration uses an indicator to find the concentration of a solution of an acid or alkali. The equivalence point is the volume at which exactly the same number of moles of hydrogen ions (or hydroxide ions) has been added as there are moles of hydroxide ions (or hydrogen ions). The **end point** is the volume of alkali or acid added when the indicator just changes colour. Unless we choose the right indicator, the equivalence point and the end point may not always give the same answer.

A suitable indicator for a particular titration needs the following properties:

- The colour change must be sharp rather than gradual at the end point, i.e. no more than one drop of acid (or alkali) is needed to give a complete colour change. An indicator that changes colour gradually over several cubic centimetres would be unsuitable and would not indicate a correct end point.
- The end point of the titration given by the indicator must be the same as the equivalence point, otherwise the titration will give us the wrong answer.
- The indicator should give a distinct colour change. For example, the colourless to pink change of phenolphthalein is easier to see than the red to yellow of methyl orange.

Some common indicators are given in Figure 1 with their approximate colour changes. Notice that the colour change of most indicators takes place over a pH range of around 2 units, centred around the value of pK_a for the indicator. For this reason, not all indicators are suitable for all titrations. Universal indicator is not suitable for any titration because of its gradual colour changes.

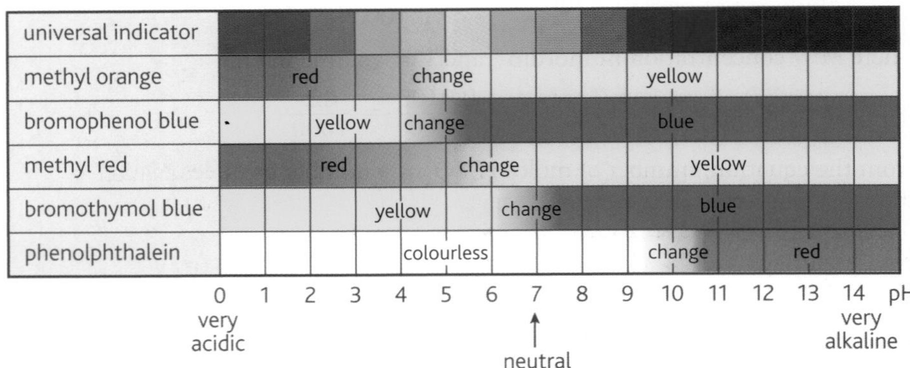

Figure 1 *Some common indicators. Universal indicator is a mixture of indicators that change colour at different pHs*

The following examples compare the suitability of two common indicators, phenolphthalein and methyl orange, for four different types of acid–base titration. In each case, the base is being added to the acid.

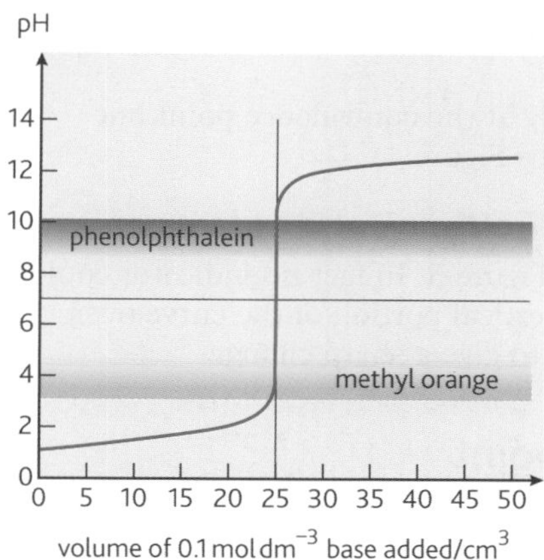

Figure 2 *Titration of a strong acid–strong base, adding 0.1 mol dm^{-3} NaOH(aq) to 25 cm^3 of 0.1 mol dm^{-3} HCl(aq)*

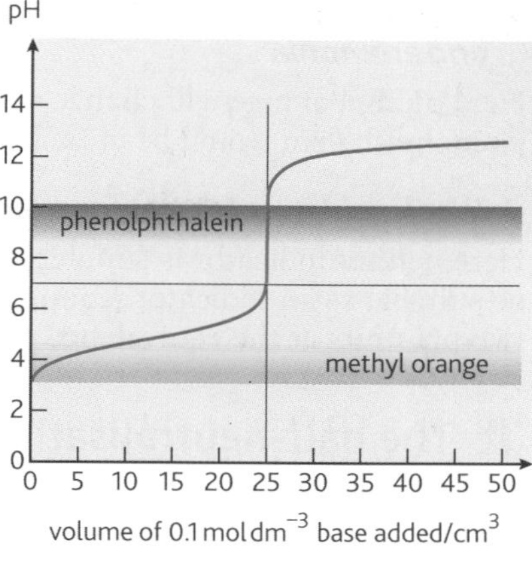

Figure 3 *Titration of a weak acid–strong base, adding 0.1 mol dm^{-3} NaOH(aq) to 25 cm^3 of 0.1 mol dm^{-3} CH_3COOH(aq)*

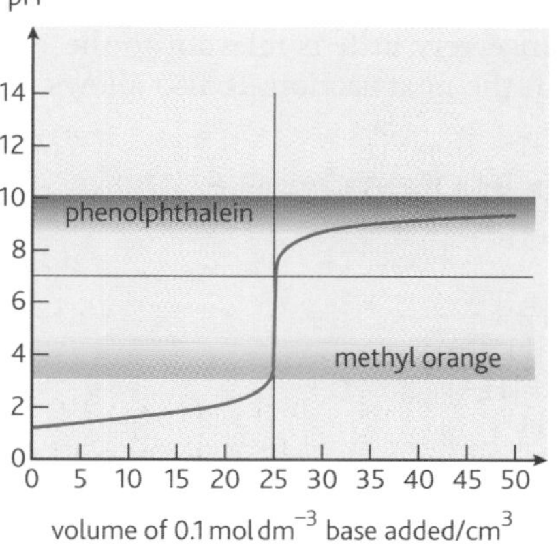

Figure 4 *Titration of a strong acid–weak base, adding 0.1 mol dm^{-3} NH_3(aq) to 25 cm^3 of 0.1 mol dm^{-3} HCl(aq)*

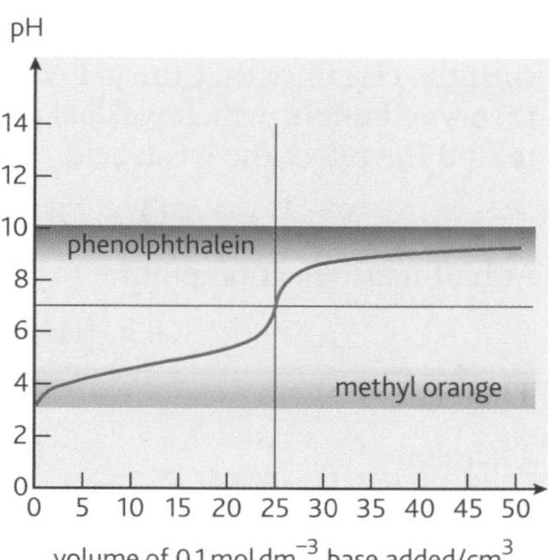

Figure 5 *Titration of a weak acid–weak base, adding 0.1 mol dm^{-3} NH_3(aq) to 25 cm^3 of 0.1 mol dm^{-3} CH_3COOH(aq)*

Make sure that you know how to use a pH curve to select a suitable indicator.

1 Strong acid–strong base, for example hydrochloric acid and sodium hydroxide

Figure 2 is the graph of pH against volume of base added. The pH ranges, over which two indicators change colour, are shown. To fulfil the first two criteria above, the indicator must change within the vertical portion of the pH curve. Here either indicator would be suitable, but phenolphthalein is usually preferred because of its more easily seen colour change.

2 Weak acid–strong base titration, for example ethanoic acid and sodium hydroxide

Methyl orange is not suitable, see Figure 3. It does not change in the vertical portion of the curve and will change colour in the 'wrong' place and over the addition of many cubic centimetres of base. Phenolphthalein will change sharply at exactly 25 cm^3, the equivalence point, and would therefore be a good choice.

3 Strong acid–weak base titration, for example hydrochloric acid and ammonia

Here methyl orange will change sharply at the equivalence point but phenolphthalein would be of no use, see Figure 4.

4 Weak acid–weak base, for example ethanoic acid and ammonia

Here neither indicator is suitable, see Figure 5. In fact no indicator could be suitable as an indicator requires a vertical portion of the curve over two pH units at the equivalence point to give a sharp change.

The half-neutralisation point

AQA Examiner's tip

This provides a method of determining pK_a values experimentally.

If we look at the titration curves we can see that there is always a very gently sloping, almost horizontal, part to the curve before we reach the steep line on which the equivalence point lies. As we add acid (or base), there is very little change to the pH, almost up to the volume of the equivalence point. The point half-way between the zero and the equivalence point is the **half-neutralisation point**. This is significant because the knowledge that we can add acid (or base) up to this point with the certainty that the pH will change very little is relevant to the theory of buffers, which we deal with in the next section. It also allows us to find the pK_a of the weak acid.

$$HA + OH^- \longrightarrow H_2O + A^-$$

At half-neutralisation point:

$$[HA] = [A^-]$$

Therefore $$K_a = \frac{[H^+][\cancel{A^-}]}{[\cancel{HA}]}$$

Therefore $$K_a = [H^+]$$

And $$-\log_{10} K_a = -\log_{10} [H^+]$$

i.e. $$pK_a = pH$$

Summary questions

1 The indicator bromocresol purple changes colour between pH 5.2 and 6.8. For which of the following titration types would it be suitable:

a weak acid–weak base

b strong acid–weak base

c weak acid–strong base

d strong acid–strong base?

2 For which of the above titrations would bromophenol blue be suitable?

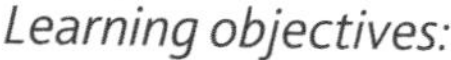

3.6 Buffer solutions

Learning objectives:

- What is a buffer?
- How do buffers work?
- How can the pH of an acidic buffer solution be calculated?
- What are buffers used for?

Specification reference: 3.4.3

Buffers are solutions that can resist changes of acidity or alkalinity. When small amounts of acid or alkali are added to them, their pH remains almost constant.

How buffers work

Buffers are designed to keep the concentration of hydrogen ions and hydroxide ions almost unchanged. They are based on an equilibrium reaction which will move in the direction to remove either additional hydrogen ions or hydroxide ions if these are added.

Acidic buffers

Acidic buffers are made from weak acids. They work because the dissociation of a weak acid is an equilibrium reaction.

Consider a weak acid HA. It will dissociate in solution:

$$HA(aq) \rightleftharpoons H^+(aq) + A^-(aq)$$

From the equation, $[H^+(aq)] = [A^-(aq)]$, and as it is a weak acid, $[H^+(aq)]$ (and $[A^-(aq)]$) are both very small because most of the HA is undissociated.

Adding alkali

If a little alkali is added, the OH^- ions will react with HA to produce water molecules and A^-:

$$HA(aq) + OH^-(aq) \longrightarrow H_2O(aq) + A^-(aq)$$

This removes the added OH^- so the pH tends to remain almost the same.

Adding acid

If H^+ is added, the equilibrium shifts to the left, H^+ ions combining with A^- ions to produce undissociated HA. But, since $[A^-]$ is small, the supply of A^- soon runs out and there is no A^- left to 'mop up' the added H^+. So we don't have a buffer.

However, we can add to the solution a supply of extra A^- by adding a soluble salt of HA, which fully ionises, such as Na^+A^-. This increases the supply of A^- so that more H^+ can be used up. Thus there is a way in which both added H^+ and OH^- can be removed. So:

An acidic buffer is made from a mixture of a weak acid and a soluble salt of that acid. It will maintain a pH of below 7 (acidic).

The function of the weak acid component of a buffer is to act as a source of HA which can remove any added OH^-:

$$HA(aq) + OH^-(aq) \longrightarrow A^-(aq) + H_2O(l)$$

The function of the salt component of a buffer is to act as a source of A^- ions which can remove any added H^+ ions:

$$A^-(aq) + H^+(aq) \longrightarrow HA(aq)$$

AQA Examiner's tip

Make sure you can write equations to explain how a buffer solution reacts when small amounts of acid or base are added.

Buffers do not ensure that *no* change in pH occurs. The addition of acid or alkali will still change the pH, but only slightly and by far less than the change that adding the same amount to a non-buffer would cause. It is also possible to 'saturate' a buffer – to add so much acid or alkali that all of the available HA or A^- is used up.

Another way of achieving a mixture of weak acid and its salt is by neutralising some of the weak acid with an alkali such as sodium hydroxide. In fact if we neutralise half the acid, see Topic 3.5, we end up with a buffer whose pH is equal to the pK_a of the acid.

At half-neutralisation: $pH = pK_a$

This is a very useful buffer because it is equally efficient at resisting a change in pH whether acid or alkali is added.

Basic buffers

Basic buffers also resist change but maintain a pH at above 7. They are made from a mixture of a weak base and a salt of that base.

A mixture of aqueous ammonia and ammonium chloride ($NH_4^+Cl^-$) acts as a basic buffer. In this case:

- The aqueous ammonia removes added H^+:
  $NH_3(aq) + H^+(aq) \longrightarrow NH_4^+(aq)$
- the ammonium ion, NH_4^+, removes added OH^-:
  $NH_4^+(aq) + OH^-(aq) \longrightarrow NH_3(aq) + H_2O(l)$

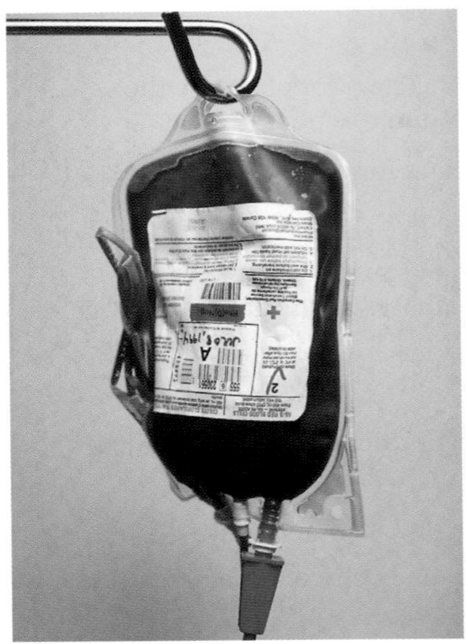

Figure 1 *Blood is buffered to a pH of 7.40*

Examples of buffers

An important example of a system involving a buffer is blood, the pH of which is maintained at approximately 7.4. A change of as little as 0.5 of a pH unit may well be fatal.

Blood is buffered to a pH of 7.4 by a number of mechanisms. The most important is:

$$H^+(aq) + HCO_3^-(aq) \rightleftharpoons CO_2(aq) + H_2O(l)$$

Addition of extra H^+ ions moves this equilibrium to the right, thus removing the added H^+. Addition of extra OH^- ions removes H^+ by reacting to form water. The equilibrium above moves to the left releasing more H^+ ions. (The same equilibrium reaction acts to buffer the acidity of soils.)

There are many examples of buffers in everyday products, such as detergents and shampoos. If either of these substances become too acidic or too alkaline, they could damage fabric (or skin and hair).

Figure 2 *Most shampoos are buffered so that they are slightly alkaline*

Calculations on buffers

Different buffers can be made which will maintain different pHs. When a weak acid dissociates:

$$HA(aq) \rightleftharpoons H^+(aq) + A^-(aq)$$

we can write the expression:

$$K_a = \frac{[H^+(aq)][A^-(aq)]}{[HA(aq)]}$$

We can use this expression to calculate the pH of buffers.

Example 1

A buffer consists of 0.100 mol dm^{-3} ethanoic acid and 0.100 mol dm^{-3} sodium ethanoate, see Figure 3. (K_a for ethanoic acid is 1.7×10^{-5}, $pK_a = 4.77$.) What is the pH of the buffer?

We do this by calculating [H$^+$(aq)] from the equation.

$$K_a = \frac{[H^+(aq)][A^-(aq)]}{[HA(aq)]}$$

Sodium ethanoate is fully dissociated, so $[A^-(aq)] = 0.100\,mol\,dm^{-3}$

Ethanoic acid is almost undissociated, so $[HA(aq)] = 0.100\,mol\,dm^{-3}$

$$1.7 \times 10^{-5} = [H^+(aq)] \times \frac{0.100}{0.100}$$

$$1.7 \times 10^{-5} = [H^+(aq)] \text{ and } pH = -\log_{10}[H^+(aq)]$$

$$pH = 4.77$$

Note that when we have equal concentrations of acid and salt, pH of the buffer = pK_a of acid used, and this is exactly the same situation as the half-neutralisation point we referred to above.

Changing the concentration of HA or A^- will affect the pH of the buffer. If we use 0.200 mol dm^{-3} ethanoic acid and 0.100 mol dm^{-3} sodium ethanoate, the pH will be 4.50. Check that you can do this by doing a calculation like the one above.

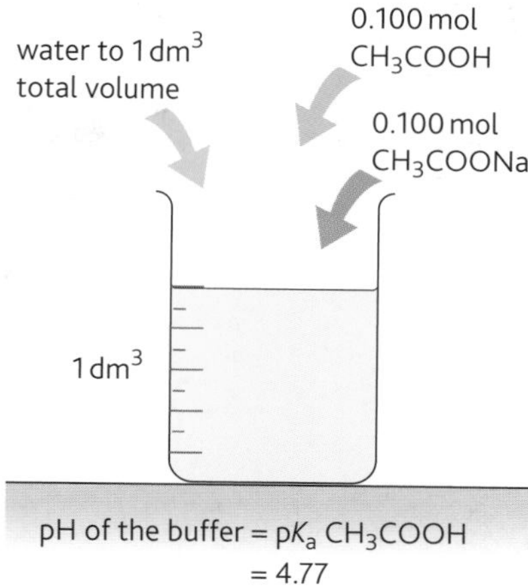

Figure 3 *Making a buffer*

AQA Examiner's tip

In a buffer solution $[H^+] \neq [A^-]$ so do *not* use the simplified expression

$$K_a = \frac{[H^+]^2}{[HA]}$$

Example 2

Calculate the pH of the buffer formed when 500 cm^3 of 0.400 mol dm^{-3} NaOH is added to 500 cm^3 1.00 mol dm^{-3} HA. $K_a = 6.25 \times 10^{-5}$.

Some of the weak acid is neutralised by the sodium hydroxide leaving a solution containing A^- and HA, which will act as a buffer.

$$\text{Moles HA} = M \times \frac{V}{1000} = 1.00 \times \frac{500}{1000} = 0.500\,mol$$

$$\text{Moles NaOH} = \text{moles } OH^- = M \times \frac{V}{1000} = 0.400 \times \frac{500}{1000} = 0.200\,mol$$

Equation:	HA	+ NaOH	$\longrightarrow$ H_2O	+ NaA
Initially:	0.500 mol	0.200 mol		0
Finally:	0.300 mol	0 mol		0.200 mol

This leaves 1000 cm^3 of a solution containing 0.300 mol HA and 0.200 mol A^- since all the NaA is dissociated to give A^-.

The concentrations are: $[HA] = 0.300\,mol\,dm^{-3}$ and $[A^-] = 0.200\,mol\,dm^{-3}$

$$K_a = \frac{[H^+(aq)][A^-(aq)]}{[HA(aq)]}$$

$$6.25 \times 10^{-5} = [H^+(aq)] \times \frac{0.200}{0.300}$$

$$[H^+(aq)] = 6.25 \times 10^{-5} \times \frac{3}{2} = 9.375 \times 10^{-5}$$

$$\text{So pH} = -\log[H^+(aq)] = 4.03$$

The pH change when an acid or a base is added to a buffer

Adding acid

We can calculate how the pH changes when acid is added to a buffer:

Suppose we start with 1.00 dm^3 of a buffer solution of ethanoic acid at concentration 0.10 mol dm^{-3} and sodium ethanoate at concentration 0.10 mol dm^{-3}. K_a is 1.7×10^{-5}. This has a pH of 4.77, as shown in the calculation previously.

Now we add 10.0 cm^3 of hydrochloric acid of concentration 1.00 mol dm^{-3} to this buffer. Virtually all the added H^+ ions will react with the ethanoate ions, $[A^-]$, to form molecules of ethanoic acid, [HA].

Before adding the acid:

- Number of moles of ethanoic acid = 0.10
- Number of moles of sodium ethanoate = 0.10

No. of moles of hydrochloric acid added is $M \times \frac{V}{1000}$.

$$1.00 \times \frac{10.0}{1000} = 0.010$$

After adding the acid, this means:

- The amount of acid is increased by 0.010 mol to 0.110 mol.
- The amount of salt is decreased by 0.010 mol to 0.090 mol.

So, the concentration of acid [HA] is now $\frac{0.110}{1000}$ mol dm^{-3}.

And, the concentration of salt $[A^-]$ is now $\frac{0.090}{1000}$ mol dm^{-3}.

In calculating these concentrations we have ignored the volume of the added hydrochloric acid: 10 cm^3 in 1000 cm^3, only a 1% change.

$$K_a = \frac{[H^+(aq)][A^-(aq)]}{[HA(aq)]}$$

So

$$1.7 \times 10^{-5} = [H^+(aq)]\frac{0.090/1000}{0.110/1000}$$

$$[H^+(aq)] = 1.7 \times 10^{-5} \times \frac{0.110}{0.090} = 2.08 \times 10^{-5}$$

$$pH = 4.68$$

Note how small the pH change is (from 4.77 to 4.68).

Adding base

If we add 10 cm^3 of 0.10 mol dm^{-3} sodium hydroxide to the original buffer, it will react with the H^+ ions and more HA will ionise, so this time we decrease the concentration of the acid [HA] by 0.010 and increase the concentration of ethanoate ions by 0.010.

Using similar steps to those above, gives the new pH as 4.89. Check that you agree with this answer.

Note how small the pH change is (from 4.77 to 4.89).

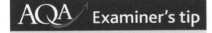

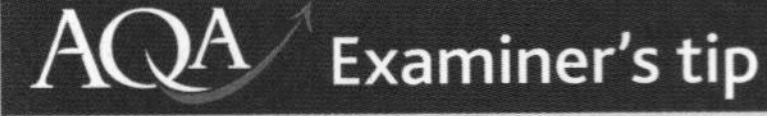

Always quote pH values to two decimal places.

Summary questions

1 Find the pH of the following buffers:

a Using [ethanoic acid] = 0.10 mol dm^{-3}, [sodium ethanoate] = 0.20 mol dm^{-3} (K_a of ethanoic acid = 1.7×10^{-5}).

b Using [benzoic acid] = 0.10 mol dm^{-3}, [sodium benzoate] = 0.10 mol dm^{-3} (K_a of benzoic acid = 6.3×10^{-5}).

AQA Examination-style questions

1 In this question, give all pH values to 2 decimal places.

(a) (i) Write expressions for the ionic product of water, K_w, and for pH.

(ii) At 318 K, the value of K_w is $4.02 \times 10^{-14}\ mol^2\,dm^{-6}$ and hence the pH of pure water is 6.70

State why pure water is not acidic at 318 K.

(iii) Calculate the number of moles of sodium hydroxide in $2.00\ cm^3$ of $0.500\ mol\,dm^{-3}$ aqueous sodium hydroxide.

(iv) Use the value of K_w given above and your answer to part (a)(iii) to calculate the pH of the solution formed when $2.00\ cm^3$ of $0.500\ mol\,dm^{-3}$ aqueous sodium hydroxide are added to $998\ cm^3$ of pure water at 318 K. *(6 marks)*

(b) At 298 K, the acid dissociation constant, K_a, for propanoic acid, CH_3CH_2COOH, has the value $1.35 \times 10^{-5}\ mol\,dm^{-3}$.

(i) Write an expression for K_a for propanoic acid.

(ii) Calculate the pH of $0.125\ mol\,dm^{-3}$ aqueous propanoic acid at 298 K. *(4 marks)*

(c) Sodium hydroxide reacts with propanoic acid as shown in the following equation.

$$NaOH + CH_3CH_2COOH \longrightarrow CH_3CH_2COONa + H_2O$$

A buffer solution is formed when sodium hydroxide is added to an excess of aqueous propanoic acid.

(i) Calculate the number of moles of propanoic acid in $50.0\ cm^3$ of $0.125\ mol\,dm^{-3}$ aqueous propanoic acid.

(ii) Use your answers to part (a)(iii) and part (c)(i) to calculate the number of moles of propanoic acid in the buffer solution formed when $2.00\ cm^3$ of $0.500\ mol\,dm^{-3}$ aqueous sodium hydroxide are added to $50.0\ cm^3$ of $0.125\ mol\,dm^{-3}$ aqueous propanoic acid.

(iii) Hence calculate the pH of this buffer solution at 298 K. *(6 marks)*

AQA, 2006

2 In this question give all values of pH to 2 decimal places.

The acid dissociation constant, K_a, for propanoic acid has the value $1.35 \times 10^{-5}\ mol\,dm^{-3}$ at 25 °C.

$$K_a = \frac{([H^+][CH_3CH_2COO^-])}{([CH_3CH_2COOH])}$$

(a) Calculate the pH of a $0.169\ mol\,dm^{-3}$ solution of propanoic acid. *(3 marks)*

(b) A buffer solution contains 0.250 mol of propanoic acid and 0.190 mol of sodium propanoate in $1000\ cm^3$ of solution.

A 0.015 mol sample of solid sodium hydroxide is then added to this buffer solution.

(i) Write an equation for the reaction of propanoic acid with sodium hydroxide.

(ii) Calculate the number of moles of propanoic acid and of propanoate ions present in the buffer solution after the addition of the sodium hydroxide.

(iii) Hence, calculate the pH of the buffer solution after the addition of the sodium hydroxide. *(6 marks)*

AQA, 2008

3 In this question give all values of pH to 2 decimal places.

(a) The dissociation of water can be represented by the following equilibrium.

$$H_2O(l) \rightleftharpoons H^+(aq) + OH^-(aq)$$

(i) Write an expression for the ionic product of water, K_w

(ii) The pH of a sample of pure water is 6.63 at 50 °C.
Calculate the concentration in mol dm^{-3} of H^+ ions in this sample of pure water.

(iii) Deduce the concentration in mol dm^{-3} of OH^- ions in this sample of pure water.

(iv) Calculate the value of K_w at this temperature. *(4 marks)*

(b) At 25 °C the value of K_w is 1.00×10^{-14} mol^2 dm^{-6}.
Calculate the pH of a 0.136 mol dm^{-3} solution of KOH at 25 °C. *(2 marks)*

AQA, 2008

4 (a) (i) Write an expression for the term pH.

(ii) Calculate the concentration of hydrochloric acid which has a pH value of 0.36 *(2 marks)*

(b) The curve below shows how the pH changes when hydrochloric acid is added to an aqueous solution of sodium carbonate.

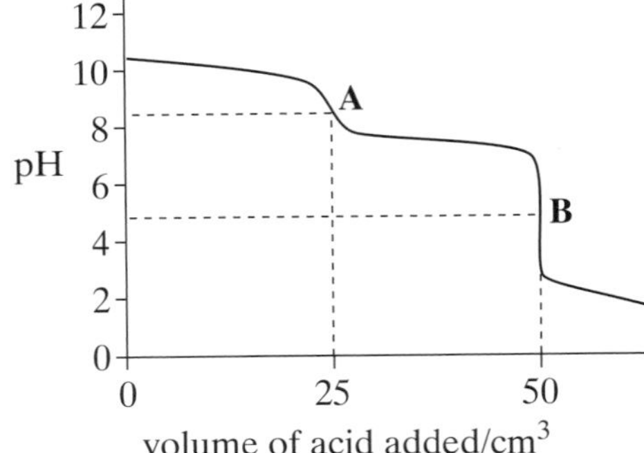

(i) Write an equation for the reaction which occurs before equivalence point **A** and an equation for the reaction which occurs between equivalence points **A** and **B**.

(ii) A list of indicators is shown in the table below.

Indicator	**pH range**
trapeolin	1.3 – 3.0
bromophenol blue	3.0 – 4.6
phenol red	6.8 – 8.4
metacresol purple	7.6 – 9.2
thymophthalein	9.3 – 10.5
nitramine	10.8 – 13.0

Select from the list the best indicator for the equivalence point **A** and, in a separate experiment, the best indicator for the equivalence point **B**.

(iii) This pH curve was obtained when a 40.0 cm^3 sample of 0.150 mol dm^{-3} aqueous sodium carbonate was used. Calculate the number of moles of sodium carbonate in this sample.

(iv) Use the volume of hydrochloric acid which has been added at the equivalence point **B** to calculate the concentration of the hydrochloric acid. *(7 marks)*

AQA, 2007

5 When answering this question, assume that the temperature is 298 K and give all pH values to 2 decimal places.

The acid dissociation costant, K_a, of propanoic acid, CH_3CH_2COOH, has the value 1.35×10^{-5} mol dm^{-3}.

$$K_a = \frac{[H^+][CH_3CH_2COO^-]}{[CH_3CH_2COOH]}$$

(a) Calculate the pH of a 0.550 mol dm^{-3} solution of propanoic acid. *(3 marks)*

(b) A buffer solution is formed when 10.0 cm^3 of 0.230 mol dm^{-3} aqueous sodium hydroxide are added to 30.0 cm^3 of 0.550 mol dm^{-3} aqueous propanoic acid.

(i) Calculate the number of moles of propanoic acid originally present.

(ii) Calculate the number of moles of sodium hydroxide added.

(iii) Hence, calculate the number of moles of propanoic acid present in the buffer solution.

(iv) Hence, calculate the pH of the buffer solution. *(6 marks)*

AQA, 2007

6 (a) A sample of hydrochloric acid has a pH of 2.34

Write an expression for pH and calculate the concentration of this acid. *(2 marks)*

(b) A 0.150 mol dm^{-3} solution of a weak acid, HX, also has a pH of 2.34

(i) Write an expression for the acid dissociation constant, K_a, for the acid HX.

(ii) Calculate the value of K_a for this acid and state its units.

(iii) Calculate the value of pK_a for the acid HX. Give your answer to two decimal places. *(5 marks)*

(c) A 30.0 cm^3 sample of a 0.480 mol dm^{-3} solution of potassium hydroxide was partially neutralised by the addition of 18.0 cm^3 of a 0.350 mol dm^{-3} solution of sulfuric acid.

(i) Calculate the initial number of moles of potassium hydroxide.

(ii) Calculate the number of moles of sulfuric acid added.

(iii) Calculate the number of moles of potassium hydroxide remaining in excess in the solution formed.

(iv) Calculate the concentration of hydroxide ions in the solution formed.

(v) Hence calculate the pH of the solution formed. Give your answer to two decimal places. *(6 marks)*

AQA, 2006

4 Nomenclature and isomerism in organic chemistry

4.1 Naming organic compounds

Learning objectives:

- How are IUPAC rules used for naming organic compounds?

Specification reference: 3.4.4

Link.

You will need to know the nomenclature and isomerism studied in *AQA AS Chemistry*, Topics 5.2 and 5.3 and the shapes and bond angles in simple molecules in Topic 3.9.

We met the system we use for naming compounds in *AQA AS Chemistry*, Topic 5.2. It was developed by the International Union of Pure and Applied Chemistry (**IUPAC**) and uses systematic names that tell us about the structures of the compounds rather than just the formulae. The material that follows revises and enlarges on this earlier topic.

Roots

A systematic name has a root that tells us the longest unbranched hydrocarbon chain or ring, see Table 1.

Table 1 *The roots used in naming organic compounds*

Number of carbons	Root
1	meth
2	eth
3	prop
4	but
5	pent
6	hex

The syllable after the root tells us whether there are any double bonds:

- -ane means no double bonds, for example ethane

$$\begin{array}{ccccccc} & & H & & H & & \\ & & | & & | & & \\ H & - & C & - & C & - & H \\ & & | & & | & & \\ & & H & & H & & \end{array}$$

has two carbon atoms and no double bond.

- -ene means there is a double bond, for example ethene

$$\begin{array}{ccccc} H & & & & H \\ & \diagdown & & \diagup & \\ & & C=C & & \\ & \diagup & & \diagdown & \\ H & & & & H \end{array}$$

has two carbon atoms and one double bond

- -yne means there is a triple bond, for example propyne

$$\begin{array}{ccccccccc} & & H & & & & & & \\ & & | & & & & & & \\ H & - & C & - & C & \equiv & C & - & H \\ & & | & & & & & & \\ & & H & & & & & & \end{array}$$

Prefixes and suffixes

Prefixes and suffixes describe the changes that have been made to the root molecule.

- Prefixes are added to the beginning of the root, for example *chloro*ethane.
- A suffix is added to the end of the root, for example ethan*ol*.

Side chains are shown by a prefix; the name tells us the number of carbons:

methyl, $CH_3—$

ethyl, $C_2H_5—$

We often call these alkyl groups R, or R′ (if there is more than one) if we are using a general formula.

For example
```
          H
          |
        H-C-H
    H  H  |  H
    |  |  |  |
  H-C--C--C--C-H
    |  |  |  |
    H  H  H  H
```
is called methylbutane.

The longest unbranched chain, four carbons long, gives us butane and there is a side chain of one methyl group. Notice that wherever the methyl group is located as a branch we have the same molecule.

Functional groups

Reactive groups of atoms attached to a hydrocarbon chain are called **functional groups.** They are named by using a suffix or prefix as shown in Table 2.

Table 2 *The suffixes and prefixes of some functional groups*

Family	Formula	Suffix	Prefix	Example
alkenes	$RCH{=}CH_2$	-ene		propene
alkynes	$RC{\equiv}CH$	-yne		propyne
haloalkanes	R—X (X is F, Cl, Br or I)		halo- (fluoro-, chloro-, bromo-, iodo-)	chloromethane CH_3Cl
carboxylic acids	RCOOH	-oic acid		ethanoic acid CH_3COOH
anhydrides	RCOOCOR′	-anhydride		ethanoic anhydride
esters	RCOOR′	-oate*		propyl ethanoate $CH_3COOC_3H_7$
acyl chlorides	RCOCl	-oyl chloride		ethanoyl chloride CH_3COCl
amides	$RCONH_2$	-amide		ethanamide CH_3CONH_2
nitriles	$RC{\equiv}N$	-nitrile		ethanenitrile $CH_3C{\equiv}N$
aldehydes	RCHO	-al		ethanal CH_3CHO
ketones	RCOR′	-one		propanone CH_3COCH_3
alcohols	ROH	-ol	hydroxy-	ethanol C_2H_5OH
amines	RNH_2	-amine	amino-	ethylamine $CH_3CH_2NH_2$
arenes	C_6H_5R			methylbenzene

*Esters are named from their parent alcohol and acid, so propyl ethanoate is derived from propanol and ethanoic acid.

Some functional groups may be identified by either a prefix or a suffix. For example, alcohols have the suffix –ol and the prefix hydroxy. The suffix is used if it is the only functional group. When there are two (or more) functional groups, the IUPAC rules have a comprehensive system of priority which you do not need to know. In Table 2 the higher in the list is a suffix and the lower a prefix. So the amino acid alanine (see below) which is both a carboxylic acid and an amine has the systematic name 2-aminopropanoic acid.

```
        NH2
        |
  H3C — C — COOH
        |
        H
```

Numbering the chain

We sometimes need to say where a side chain or a functional group is located on the main chain. For example, in the haloalkanes, the first example is 1-chlorobutane, the second 2-chlorobutane.

```
    H   H   H   H                 H   H   Cl  H
    |   |   |   |                 |   |   |   |
H — C — C — C — C — Cl    or  H — C — C — C — C — H
    |   |   |   |                 |   |   |   |
    H   H   H   H                 H   H   H   H
```

We may need more than one number:

```
    I   Br  H
    |   |   |
H — C — C — C — H        2-bromo-1-iodopropane
    |   |   |
    H   H   H
```

Bromo- is written before iodo-, because we put the substituting groups in alphabetical order.

Branched chain alkanes

```
            H
            |
        H — C — H
            |
    H   H   |   H   H
    |   |   |   |   |
H — C — C — C — C — C — H
    |   |   |   |   |
    H   H   |   H   H
            |
        H — C — H
            |
            H
```

is 3,3-dimethylpentane.

```
                        H
                        |
                    H — C — H
                        |
    H   H   H           |   H
    |   |   |           |   |
H — C — C — C     —     C — C — H
    |   |   |           |   |
    H   |   H           H   H
        |
    H — C — H
        |
        H
```

is 2,3-dimethylpentane.

AQA Examiner's tip

In chemical names, strings of numbers are separated by commas. A hyphen is placed between words and numbers.

Table 3 *Examples of systematic naming of organic compounds. Try covering up the name or structure to test yourself*

Structural formula	Name	Notes
H Br H H—C—C—C—H H Br H	2,2-dibromopropane	
H H H H H—C—C—C—C—OH H H Br H	2-bromobutan-1-ol	The suffix -ol defines the end of the chain we count from
H H OH H H—C—C—C—C—H H H H H	butan-2-ol	
H H H H C=C—C—C—H H H H	but-1-ene	Not but-2-ene, but-3-ene or but-4-ene as we use the smallest locant possible
H H H C H H—C C—H H—C C—H H C H H H	cyclohexane	Cyclo- is used to indicate a ring
H H H H H—C—C—C—C—H H H H H—C—H H	methylbutane	There is no need to use a number to locate the side chain because it must be on carbon number 2.
H H H H H—C—C—C—C—H H H H H—C—H H—C—H H	3-methylpentane	This is not 2-ethylbutane. The rule is to base the name on the longest unbranched chain, in this case pentane (picked out in red). Remember the bond angles are 109.5° not 90°
H H H H H—C—C—C—C—H H H—C—H H H H—C—H H—C—H H	2,3-dimethylpentane	Again remember the root is based on the longest unbranched chain

Hint

Sometimes hydrocarbon molecules form rings. These are indicated by the prefix cyclo- for example, cyclohexane,

```
       H   H
  H     \ /     H
   \     C     /
    \  /   \  /
 H—C         C—H
    |        |
 H—C         C—H
   /  \    /  \
  H     C      H
       / \
      H   H
```

What is the molecular formula of cyclohexane? Why is it different from that of hexane?

AQA Examiner's tip

Compounds are named according to the longest hydrocarbon chain. When the molecule is branched, look at it carefully and count the longest chain before you start numbering the carbon atoms.

How science works

The International Union of Pure and Applied Chemistry (IUPAC)

According to its website, the International Union of Pure and Applied Chemistry (IUPAC) 'serves to advance the worldwide aspects of the chemical sciences and to contribute to the application of chemistry in the service of mankind. As a scientific, international, non-governmental and objective body, IUPAC can address many global issues involving the chemical sciences.'

One of its services to the world of chemistry is to have developed a systematic naming system for organic chemicals, the full rules for which are held in a publication known as the 'Red Book'. There is a companion 'Blue Book' for inorganic chemistry.

This means that any organic chemical can be given a name which can be recognised and used by chemists throughout the world. This can obviously reduce confusion. For example one well-respected database lists a total of 28 names that are in use for the compound butanone, a relatively simple compound:

```
                 O
                 ‖
 H3C            C
     \       /     \
        C              CH3
        H2
```

butanone

IUPAC also rules on the naming of newly discovered elements. An element 'can be named after a mythological concept, a mineral, a place or country, a property, or a scientist' and the discoverer has the right to propose a name and symbol.

Summary questions

1 Draw the displayed formula of:

a 3-ethyl-3-methylhexane

b 2,4-dimethylpentane.

2 What is the name of :

a $CH_3CH_2CH_2OH$

b $CH_3CH(Cl)CH_3$

c $CH_3CH_2CH{=}CHCH_2CH_3$

d CH_3CH_2OH

e C_4H_9COOH?

4.2 Stereoisomerism

Learning objectives:

- What type of molecules show *E-Z* isomerism?
- What type of molecules show optical isomerism?

Specification reference: 3.4.4

Isomers are compounds with the same molecular formula but a different arrangement of atoms in space. Organic chemistry provides many examples of isomerism. You met with structural isomerism in *AQA AS Chemistry*, Topic 5.3. These isomers:

- Have different functional groups (see Figure 1a)
- The functional groups are attached to the main chain at different points (see Figure 1b) or
- they have a different arrangement of carbon atoms in the skeleton of the molecule (see Figure 1c).

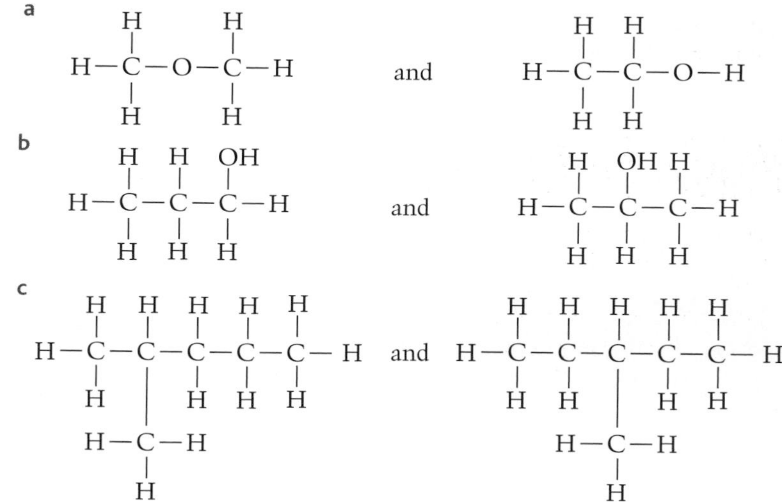

Figure 1 ***a***, ***b*** and ***c*** *are all pairs of structural isomers*

Stereoisomerism

Stereoisomerism is where two (or more) compounds have the same structural formula. They differ in the *arrangement* of the bonds in space. There are two types:

- *E-Z* isomerism and
- optical isomerism.

E-Z isomerism

E-Z isomerism tells us about the positions of substituents at either side of a carbon–carbon double bond. Two substituents may either be on the same side of the bond *Z* (*cis*) or on opposite sides *E* (*trans*).

Z-1,2-dichloroethene E-1,2-dichloroethene

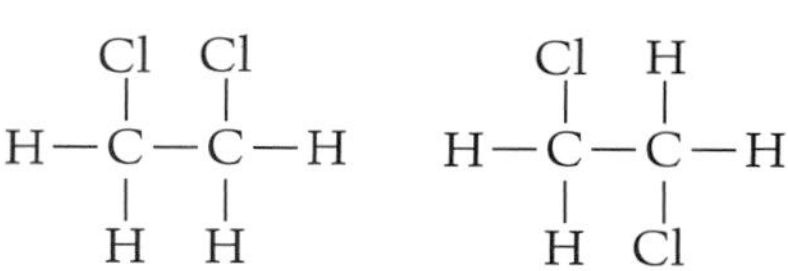

Figure 2 *Groups can rotate around a single bond. These are representations of the same molecule and are not isomers*

Substituted groups joined by a single bond can rotate around the single bond, so there are no isomers, see Figure 2; but there is no rotation around a double bond. So, *Z*- and *E*-isomers are separate compounds and are not easily converted from one to the other.

Hint

You will also see the terms *cis* and *trans* used to describe the positions of groups attached to a double bond.

E-Z is from the German *Entgegen* (opposite – *trans*) and *Zusammen* (together – *cis*).

Optical isomerism

Optical isomers occur when there are four different substituents attached to one carbon atom. This results in two isomers that are mirror images of one another, but are not identical. For example bromochlorofluoromethane exists as two mirror image forms:

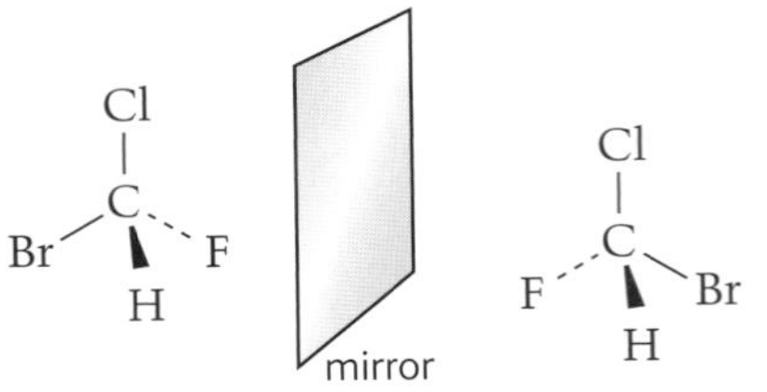

Cl | C (Br, F, H) — mirror — Cl | C (F, Br, H)

Hint

It really helps to use models to understand optical isomerism. Even matchsticks and Plasticine will do.

The ball and stick models of bromochlorofluoromethane in Figure 3 may help you to see that these are not identical.

Imagine rotating one of the molecules about the C—Cl bond (pointing upwards) until the two bromine atoms (in red) are in the same position.

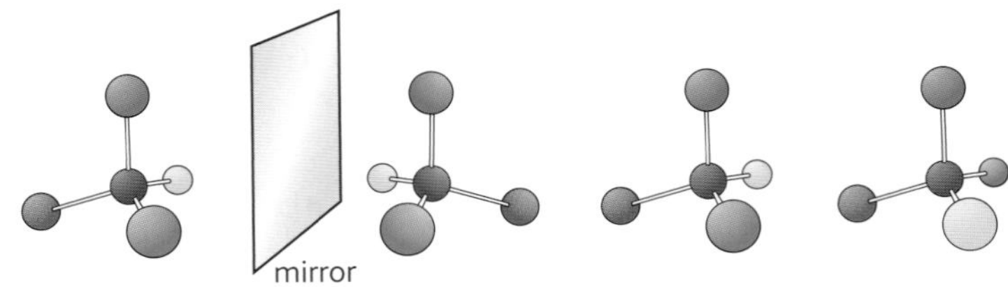

Figure 3 *Bromochlorofluoromethane has a pair of mirror isomers which are not identical*

AQA Examiner's tip

Drawn structures of optical isomers should show a tetrahedral arrangement of groups around a central carbon atom.

The positions of the hydrogen (blue) and fluorine atoms (green) will not match – you cannot superimpose one molecule onto the other.

This is just like a pair of shoes. A left shoe and a right shoe are mirror images, but they are not identical, i.e. they cannot be superimposed – try it.

Pairs of molecules like this are called **optical isomers** because they differ in the way they rotate the plane of polarisation of polarised light: either clockwise (a (+)-isomer) or anticlockwise(a (–)-isomer) (see section 'Optical activity' below).

Chirality

Optical isomers are said to be **chiral** (pronounced 'ky-ral') meaning 'handed' as in left-handed and right-handed, and the two isomers are called a pair of **enantiomers**. The carbon bonded to the four different groups is called the **chiral centre** or the **asymmetric carbon atom,** and is often indicated on formulae by *. You can easily pick out a chiral molecule because it contains at least one carbon atom that has four different groups attached to it.

- All α-amino acids, except aminoethanoic acid (glycine), see Figure 4, the simplest one, have a chiral centre. For example, the chiral centre of α-aminopropanoic acid (2-aminopropanoic acid) is starred:

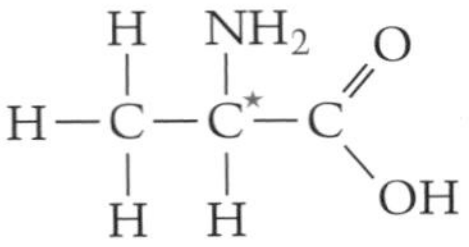

$H_3C{-}C^{*}H(NH_2){-}COOH$ α-aminopropanoic acid

Hint

See page 102 for an explanation of the prefix α- (alpha)

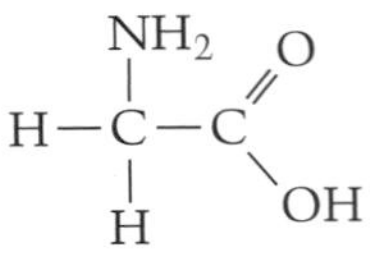

$H{-}CH(NH_2){-}COOH$

glycine

Figure 4 *Aminoethanoic acid (glycine)*

- 2-hydroxypropanoic acid (non-systematic name lactic acid) is also chiral. Although the chiral carbon is bonded to two other carbon atoms, these carbons are part of different groups and you must count the whole group.

H
O
C*
H_3C H CO_2H

2-hydroxypropanoic acid

Optical isomerism happens because the isomers have three-dimensional structures so it can only be shown by three-dimensional representations (or better, by models).

Optical activity

Light consists of vibrating electric and magnetic fields. We can think of it as waves with vibrations occurring in all directions at right angles to the direction of motion of the light wave. If the light passes through a special filter, called a **polaroid** (as in polaroid sunglasses) all the vibrations are cut out except those in one plane, for example the vertical plane (see Figure 5).

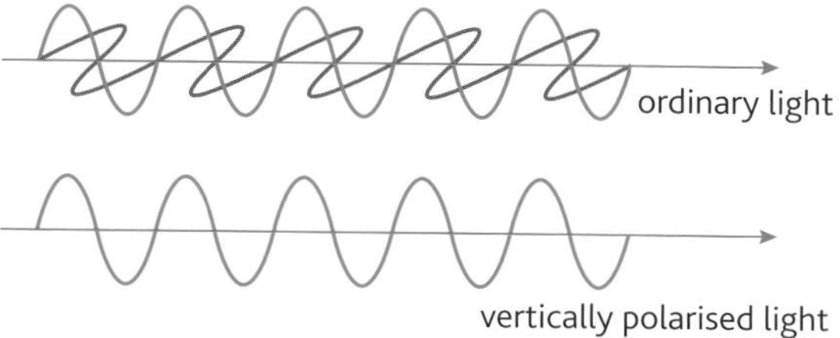

Figure 5

The light is now vertically polarised and it will be affected differently by different optical isomers of the same substance.

Optical rotation can be measured using a **polarimeter** (see Figure 6).

- We pass polarised light through two solutions of the same concentration, each containing a different optical isomer of the same substance.
- One solution will rotate the plane of polarisation through a particular angle, clockwise. We call this the + isomer.
- The other will rotate the plane of polarisation by the same angle, anticlockwise. We call this the – isomer.

(There are several other systems in use for distinguishing pairs of isomers, as well as + and – you may see the following: R and S, D and L, d and l.)

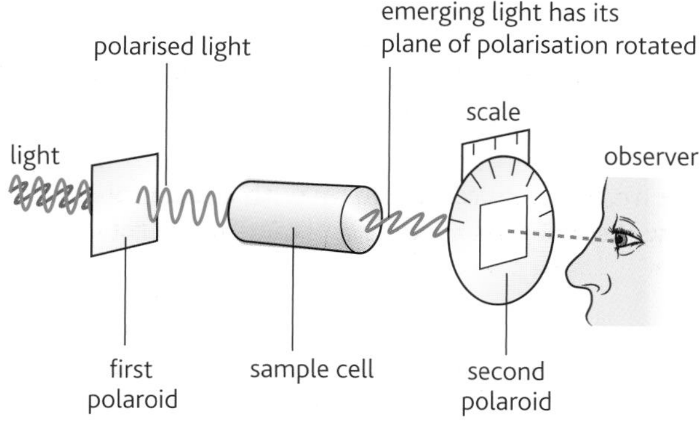

Figure 6

Link

There is more about α-amino acids in Topic 8.1.

Summary questions

1 Which of these molecules can show *E-Z* (*cis-trans*) isomerism?

a $CH_2{=}CH_2$
b $CH_3{-}CH_3$
c $RCH{=}CH_2$
d $RCH{=}CHR$

2 a Give the name of this:

CH_3 H
C=C
H C_2H_5

b What is the name of its geometrical isomer?

3 Which of the following compounds show optical isomerism?

a Cl—C—Br (C also bonded to H and H)

b Cl—C—Br (C also bonded to H and CH_3)

c Cl—C—H (C also bonded to H and H)

d H—C—H (C also bonded to H and H)

4 Mark the chiral centre on this molecule with a *:

CH_3—C—C (C bonded to Cl and H; second C =O and —OH)

4.3 Synthesis of optically active compounds

Learning objectives:

- What is a racemate?
- How is a racemate formed by synthesis?

Specification reference: 3.4.4

A great many of the reactions that are used in organic synthesis to produce optically active compounds actually produce a 50:50 mixture of two optical isomers. This is called a racemic mixture or **racemate** (pronounced 'rass-emm-ate') and is not optically active because the effects of two isomers cancel out.

The synthesis of 2-hydroxypropanoic acid (lactic acid)

H, O, C^*, H_3C, CO_2H, H

2-hydroxypropanoic acid

2-hydroxypropanoic acid (lactic acid) has a chiral centre, marked by * in the structure above. The synthesis below produces a mixture of optical isomers. It can be made in two stages from ethanal.

Stage 1

Hydrogen cyanide is added across the C=O bond to form 2-hydroxypropanenitrile.

This is a nucleophilic addition reaction, see Topic 5.2, in which the nucleophile is the CN^- ion. It takes place as follows:

$:CN^-$; H_3C, $C^{\delta+}=O^{\delta-}$, H $\longrightarrow$ H_3C, CN, C, H, $O:^-$ $\xrightarrow{H^+}$ H_3C, CN, C^*, H, OH

ethanal 2-hydroxypropanenitrile

A mixture of equal amounts of the two enantiomers is formed. This is optically inactive as their effects cancel out.

This reaction has two interesting points:

- The carbon chain length of the product is one greater than that of the starting material. We started with *ethan*al (2 C atoms) and ended with 2-hydroxy*propane*nitrile (3 C atoms). This type of reaction is important in synthesis, whenever a carbon chain needs to be lengthened.
- 2-hydroxypropanenitrile has a chiral centre, the starred carbon, which has four different groups (—CH_3, —H, —OH and —CN). The reaction we used does not favour one of these isomers over the other (i.e. the —CN group could add on with equal probability from above or below the CH_3CHO which is planar) so we get a racemic mixture.

Stage 2

The nitrile group is converted into a carboxylic acid group.

The 2-hydroxypropanenitrile is reacted with water acidified with a dilute solution of hydrochloric acid. This is a hydrolysis reaction:

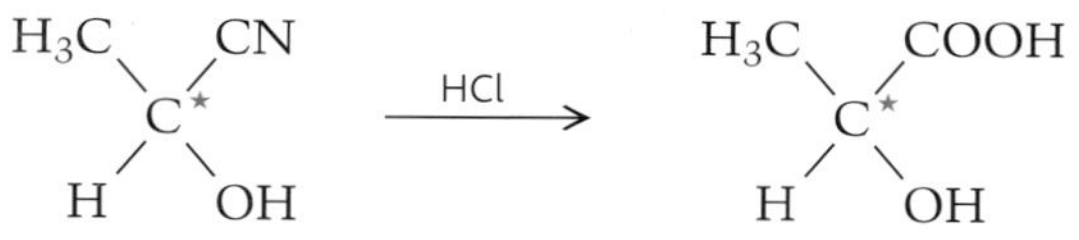

$$CH_3C^*H(CN)(OH) \xrightarrow{HCl} CH_3C^*H(COOH)(OH)$$

2-hydroxypropanoic acid

The balanced equations for the two steps are shown below:

Step 1

$$CH_3CHO + HCN \longrightarrow CH_3CH(CN)(OH)$$

Step 2

$$CH_3CH(CN)(OH) + HCl + 2H_2O \longrightarrow CH_3CH(COOH)(OH) + NH_4Cl$$

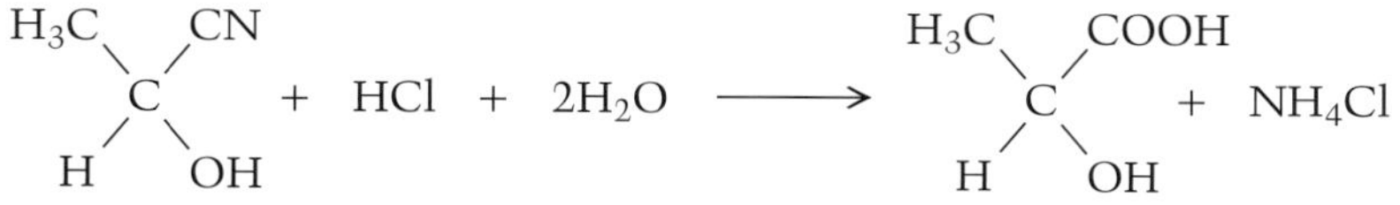

The 2-hydroxypropanoic acid that is produced still has a chiral centre – this has not been affected by the hydrolysis reaction, which only involves the —CN group. So we still have a racemic mixture of two optical isomers, see Figure 1.

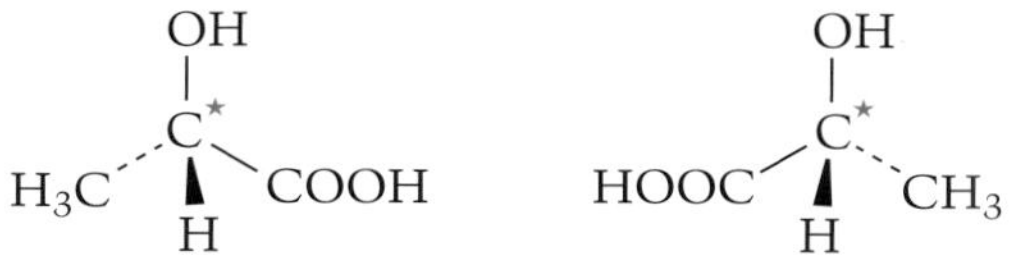

Figure 1 *The optical isomers of 2-hydroxypropanoic acid*

It is often the case that a molecule (with a chiral centre) that is made synthetically, ends up as a mixture of optical isomers. However, the same molecule produced naturally in living systems will often be present as only one optical isomer. Amino acids are a good example of this. All naturally occurring amino acids (except aminoethanoic acid, glycine) are chiral, but in every case only one of the isomers is formed in nature. This is because most naturally occurring molecules are made using enzyme catalysts, which only produce one of the possible optical isomers.

Optical isomers in the drug industry

Some drugs are optically active molecules. For some purposes, a racemic mixture of the two optical isomers will do. For other uses we definitely require one or the other. Many drugs work by a molecule of the active ingredient fitting an area of a cell (called a receptor) like a piece in a jigsaw puzzle. Because receptors have a three-dimensional structure, only one of a pair of optical isomers will fit. In some cases, one optical isomer is an effective drug and the other is inactive. This is a problem – we have three options:

- Separate the two isomers – this may be difficult and expensive as optical isomers have very similar properties.
- Sell the mixture as a drug – this is wasteful because half of it is inactive.

- Design an alternative synthesis of the drug that makes only the required isomer.

The over-the-counter painkiller and anti-inflammatory drug ibuprofen (sold as Nurofen and Cuprofen) is an example. Its structure is:

$$HO-C(=O)-\overset{*}{C}H(CH_3)-C_6H_4-CH_2-CH(CH_3)-CH_3$$

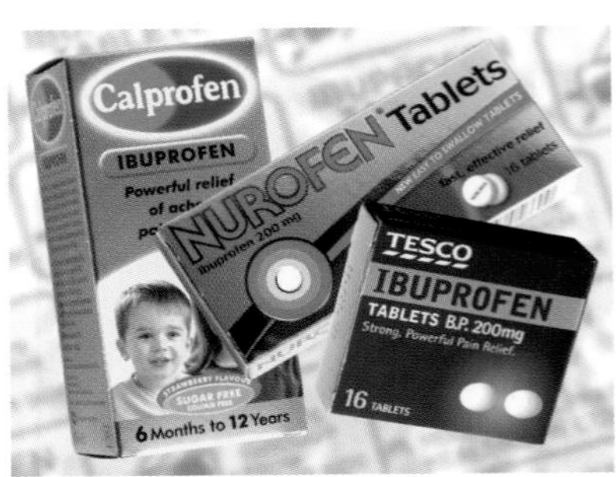

Figure 2 *Nurofen contains ibuprofen, which is a mixture of two optical isomers*

The starred carbon is the chiral centre. At present, most ibruprofen is made and sold as a racemate.

In some cases one of the optical isomers is an effective drug and the other is toxic or has unacceptable side effects. For example, naproxen: one isomer is used to treat arthritic pain, while the other causes liver poisoning. In this case it is vital that only the effective optical isomer is sold.

How science works

The thalidomide tragedy HSW

Around the late 1950s there was a spate of incidents of children born with serious and unusual birth defects – missing, shortened or deformed limbs. There were over 10 000 of these world wide, almost 500 of them in the UK. Eventually it was realised that the common factor was that their mothers had all taken a drug called thalidomide in early pregnancy. The drug had been prescribed to relieve the symptoms of morning sickness. It had been tested on animals and considered safe (although the testing regime was much more relaxed than it would be today) but, crucially, there had been no tests on pregnant animals. In 1961 the drug was withdrawn.

Thalidomide exists as a pair of optical isomers. They differ in how they interact with other chiral molecules, which are common in living things. The isomers are extremely hard to separate and thalidomide was supplied as a racemic mixture produced when the the drug was synthesised. Apparently no one thought to test the two isomers separately.

the chiral carbon atom

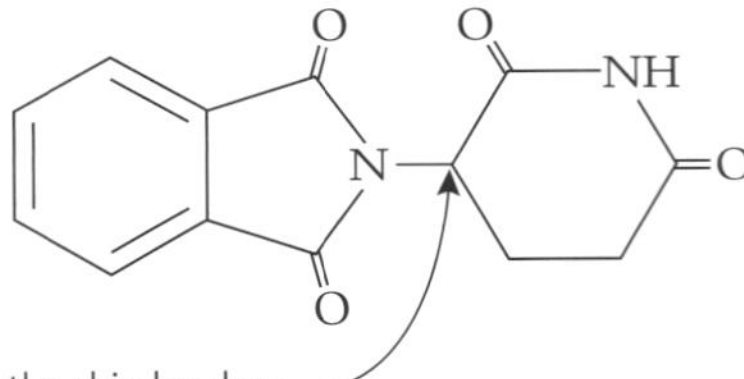

the chiral carbon
remember, there is a hydrogen atom bonded to it which is not drawn in skeletal notation

Figure 3 *One of the enantiomers of thalidomide with the chiral carbon atom marked.*
Key: black = carbon, red = oxygen, pale blue = hydrogen, dark blue = nitrogen

Figure 3 shows one of the two enantiomers of thalidomide with the chiral carbon marked. The other isomer would have the positions of the C—H and the C—N bonds reversed, i.e. the C—H going into the paper and the C—N coming out.

One of the enantiomers, called the *S*-form, is the one that caused the birth defects while the other, the *R*-form, is a safe sedative. It has been suggested that if just the *R*-form had been used, the tragedy would have been averted. However there is evidence that in the human body, *S*-thalidomide is converted into *R*-thalidomide and so even if the pure *R*-form had been produced and taken, patients would have ended up with some of the *S*-form in their bodies.

Postscript

Even after the ban in the early 1960s, pharmacologists continued to work with thalidomide. It appears that so long as it is not given in pregnancy, it is a safe and potentially useful drug and it is now being investigated as a treatment for a number of conditions including leprosy. Chemists have also produced a number of related compounds that are up to 4000 times more effective and have fewer side effects.

Figure 4 *Lactic acid is produced naturally in sour milk. In muscle tissue a build-up of lactic acid causes cramp. The two situations produce different optical isomers*

Appreciate that different optical isomers can have very different drug action.

Summary questions

1 a What would be the product of the reaction of propanal with hydrogen cyanide followed by reaction with dilute hydrochloric acid?

b Does this molecule have a chiral centre? Explain your answer.

2 a What would be the product of the reaction of propanone with hydrogen cyanide followed by reaction with dilute hydrochloric acid?

b Does this molecule have a chiral centre? Explain your answer.

3 Explain why the carbon marked ** in the formula of ibuprofen is *not* a chiral centre.

CH_3 | HO–C(=O)–CH–(benzene ring)–CH_2–**CH(–CH_3)–CH_3

AQA Examination-style questions

1 The amino acid alanine is shown below.

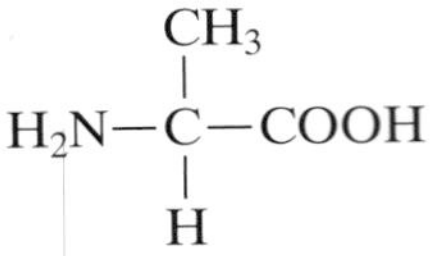

$$H_2N-\underset{\underset{H}{|}}{\overset{\overset{CH_3}{|}}{C}}-COOH$$

Give the systematic name for alanine *(1 mark)*

AQA, 2007

2 Phenylethanone, $C_6H_5COCH_3$, reacts with HCN according to the equation below.

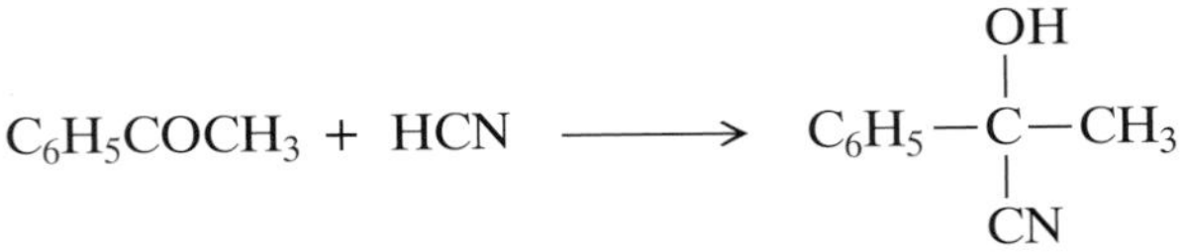

$$C_6H_5COCH_3 + HCN \longrightarrow C_6H_5-\underset{\underset{CN}{|}}{\overset{\overset{OH}{|}}{C}}-CH_3$$

The product formed exists as a racemic mixture. State the meaning of the term racemic mixture and explain why such a mixture is formed in this reaction. *(3 marks)*

AQA, 2007

3 The reaction of but-2-ene with hydrogen chloride forms a racemic mixture of the stereoisomers of 2-chlorobutane.

(a) Name the type of stereoisomerism shown by 2-chlorobutane and give the meaning of the term *racemic mixture*. State how separate samples of the stereoisomers could be distinguished. *(4 marks)*

(b) By considering the shape of the reactive intermediate involved in the mechanism of this reaction, explain how a racemic mixture of the two stereoisomers of 2-chlorobutane is formed. *(3 marks)*

AQA, 2006

4 Consider the reactions shown below.

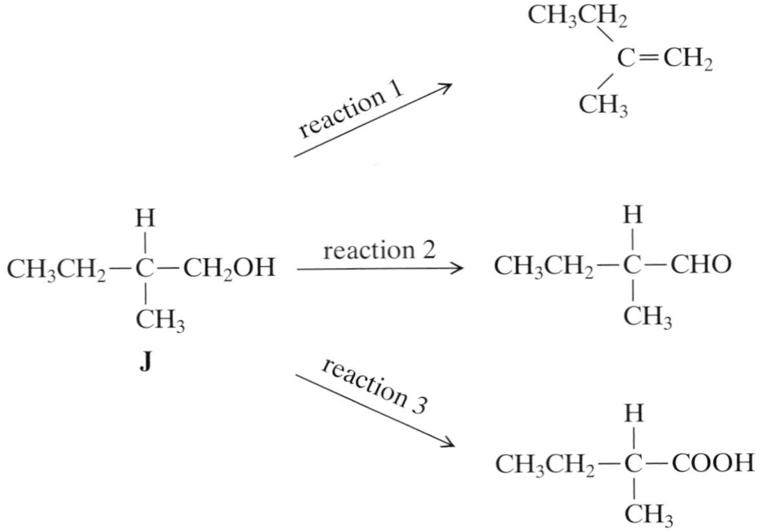

reaction 1: **J** → **K**, $(CH_3CH_2)(CH_3)C{=}CH_2$

reaction 2: **J** → **L**

reaction 3: **J** → **M**

J: $CH_3CH_2-\underset{\underset{CH_3}{|}}{\overset{\overset{H}{|}}{C}}-CH_2OH$

K: $\begin{matrix} CH_3CH_2 \\ \quad\diagdown \\ \qquad C{=}CH_2 \\ \quad\diagup \\ CH_3 \end{matrix}$

L: $CH_3CH_2-\underset{\underset{CH_3}{|}}{\overset{\overset{H}{|}}{C}}-CHO$

M: $CH_3CH_2-\underset{\underset{CH_3}{|}}{\overset{\overset{H}{|}}{C}}-COOH$

(a) Name compound **J**.

(b) Compound **J** exists as a pair of stereoisomers. Name this type of stereoisomerism

(c) Draw the structure of an isomer of **K** which shows stereoisomerism. *(3 marks)*

AQA, 2007

5 State the meaning of the term stereoisomerism *(2 marks)*

Draw the structure of an isomer of C_5H_{10} which shows *E–Z* isomerism and explain how this type of isomerism arises. Name the structure you have drawn. *(3 marks)*

Name the structure below and state the type of isomerism it shows. *(2 marks)*

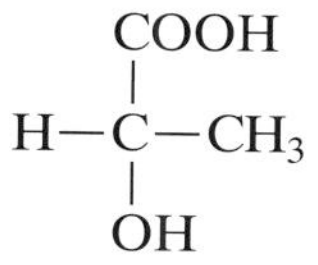

```
       COOH
        |
   H—C—CH3
        |
       OH
```

State how the different isomers of this structure can be distinguished from each other. *(2 marks)*

5 Compounds containing the carbonyl group

5.1 Introduction to carbonyl compounds

Learning objectives:

- What are aldehydes and ketones?
- How are they named?

Specification reference 3.4.5

AQA Examiner's tip

'Alkyl' means based on a saturated hydrocarbon group. 'Aryl' means based on an aromatic system, see Topic 6.1.

Link

You will need to know the oxidation of alcohols studied in *AQA AS Chemistry*, Topic 16.3 and bond polarity studied in *AQA AS Chemistry*, Topic 3.3.

Hint

When an aldehyde group is a substituent on a benzene ring, the suffix -carbaldehyde is used and the carbon is *not* counted as part of the root name.

Hint

You can remind yourself about hydrogen bonding in *AQA AS Chemistry*, Topic 3.6 .

The carbonyl group is shown here: $\rangle C=O$

The group is present in **aldehydes** and **ketones**.

In aldehydes, the carbon bonded to the oxygen (the carbonyl carbon) has at least one hydrogen atom bonded to it, so the general formula of an aldehyde is:

R(H)C=O sometimes written as RCHO.

In ketones, the carbonyl carbon has two organic groups, which we can represent by R and R', so the formula of a ketone is:

R(R')C=O

The R groups in both aldehydes and ketones may be alkyl or aryl.

How to name aldehydes and ketones

Aldehydes are named using the suffix -al. The carbon of the aldehyde functional group is counted as part of the carbon chain of the root. So:

H–C(=O)–H or HCHO is methanal and H–C(H)(H)–C(=O)–H or CH_3CHO is ethanal.

The aldehyde group can *only* occur at the end of a chain, so we do not need a numbering system to show its location.

C_6H_5–C(=O)–H, C_6H_5CHO, is counted as a derivative of benzene (not of methylbenzene) and is called benzenecarbaldehyde. It is often still called by the old name 'benzaldehyde'.

Ketones are named using the suffix -one. In the same way as aldehydes, the carbon atom of the ketone functional group is counted as part of the root. So the simplest ketone:

H–C(H)(H)–C(=O)–C(H)(H)–H, CH_3COCH_3, is called propanone.

No ketone with fewer than three carbon atoms is possible.

We do not need to number the carbon in propanone or in butanone:

```
    H   H   O   H
    |   |   ||  |
H — C — C — C — C — H
    |   |       |
    H   H       H
```

$C_2H_5COCH_3$, because the carbonyl group can only be in one position. With larger numbers of carbon atoms, numbers are needed to locate the carbonyl group on the chain.

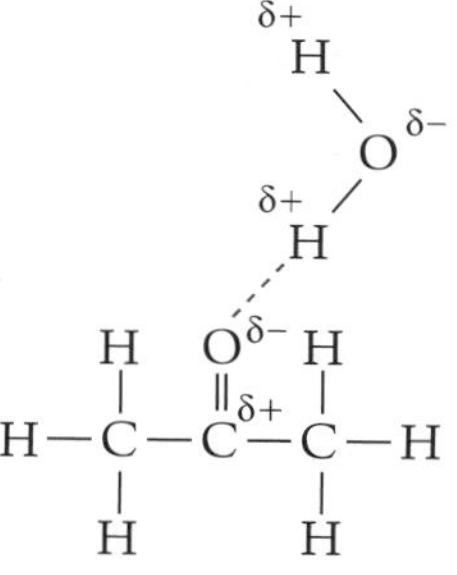

Figure 1 *Hydrogen bonding between propanone and water*

Physical properties of carbonyl compounds

Table 1 *Boiling point data*

Name	Formula	M_r	T_b / K
butane	$CH_3CH_2CH_2CH_3$	60	273
propanone	CH_3COCH_3	58	359
propan-1-ol	$CH_3CH_2CH_2OH$	60	370

The carbonyl group is strongly polar, $C^{\delta+}{=}O^{\delta-}$, so there are dipole–dipole forces between the molecules. These forces mean that boiling points are higher than those of alkanes of comparable relative molecular mass but not as high as those of alcohols, where hydrogen bonding can occur between the molecules, see Table 1.

Solubility in water

Shorter chain aldehydes and ketones mix completely with water because hydrogen bonds form between the oxygen of the carbonyl compound and water, see Figure 1. As the length of the carbon chain increases, carbonyl compounds become less soluble in water.

Methanal, HCHO, is a gas at room temperature. Other short chain aldehydes and ketones are liquids, with characteristic, fairly pleasant smells (propanone is found in many brands of nail varnish remover). Benzenecarbaldehyde smells of almonds and is used to scent soaps and flavour food.

The reactivity of carbonyl compounds

The C=O bond in carbonyl compounds is strong, see Table 2, and you might think that the C=O bond would be the least reactive bond. However, in fact, almost all reactions of carbonyl compounds involve the C=O bond.

This is because the big difference in electronegativity between carbon and oxygen makes the C=O strongly polar: $C^{\delta+}{=}O^{\delta-}$. So, nucleophilic reagents can attack the $C^{\delta+}$. Also, since they contain a double bond, carbonyl compounds are unsaturated and addition reactions are possible.

In fact the most typical reactions of the carbonyl group are nucleophilic additions.

Table 2 *Comparison of bond strengths*

Bond	Mean bond enthalpy/ kJ mol^{-1}
C=O	740
C=C	612
C—O	358
C—C	347

Summary questions

1 Name:

a $CH_3CH_2\overset{O}{\overset{\|}{C}}CH_2CH_3$

b $CH_3CH_2C(=O)H$

2 Explain why:

a No ketone with fewer than three carbons is possible.

b No numbering system is needed in the ketone butanone.

c No numbering is ever needed to locate the position of the C=O group when naming aldehydes.

3 Explain why there are no hydrogen bonds between propanone molecules.

4 Explain why hydrogen bonds can form between propanone and water molecules.

5.2 Reactions of the carbonyl group in aldehydes and ketones

Learning objectives:

- What is the mechanism of nucleophilic addition reactions of carbonyl compounds?
- How do these carbonyl compounds react when oxidised or reduced?

Specification reference: 3.4.5

- Many of the reactions of carbonyl compounds are nucleophilic addition reactions.
- They also undergo redox reactions.

Nucleophilic addition reactions

If we represent the nucleophile as :Nu⁻, the general reaction is:

$$\mathrm{RR'C^{\delta+}{=}O^{\delta-}} \xrightarrow{:\mathrm{Nu}^-} \mathrm{RR'C(Nu)O^-} \xrightarrow{\text{(H}^+\text{ from solvent)}} \mathrm{RR'C(Nu)O{-}H}$$

The addition of hydrogen cyanide is a good example of a nucleophilic addition:

Addition of hydrogen cyanide

Acidified sodium or potassium cyanide is used as a source of cyanide ions. (You will not carry out this reaction in the laboratory because of the toxic nature of the CN^- ion.)

Here the nucleophile is $:CN^-$

With a ketone:

$$\mathrm{RR'C^{\delta+}{=}O^{\delta-}} \xrightarrow{:\mathrm{CN}^-} \mathrm{RR'C(CN)O^-} \xrightarrow{\mathrm{H}^+} \mathrm{RR'C(CN)O{-}H}$$

Or with an aldehyde:

$$\mathrm{RHC^{\delta+}{=}O^{\delta-}} \xrightarrow{:\mathrm{CN}^-} \mathrm{RHC(CN)O^-} \xrightarrow{\mathrm{H}^+} \mathrm{RHC(CN)O{-}H}$$

The overall balanced equation for the reaction with an aldehyde is:

$$\mathrm{RCHO + HCN \longrightarrow R{-}CH(CN){-}OH}$$

This reaction is important in organic synthesis because it increases the length of the carbon chain by one carbon. The products are called hydroxynitriles. (Notice that this is an example where the —OH group is named using the prefix hydroxy- rather than the suffix -ol.)

Note that we have seen in Topic 4.2 that this reaction will produce a racemic mixture of two optical isomers (enantiomers) when carried out with an aldehyde or an unsymmetrical ketone, because the $:CN^-$ ion may attack from above or below the flat C=O group, see Figure 1.

AQA Examiner's tip

Nucleophiles have a lone pair to attack the $C^{\delta+}$. Some nucleophiles are negatively charged, others use the negative end of a dipole to attack $C^{\delta+}$.

AQA Examiner's tip

The –CN group is called 'cyanide' in an inorganic compound and 'nitrile' in an organic compound.

AQA Examiner's tip

In theory we could use hydrogen cyanide as the nucleophile. However this is toxic and, being a gas, it is hard to stop it escaping into the laboratory.

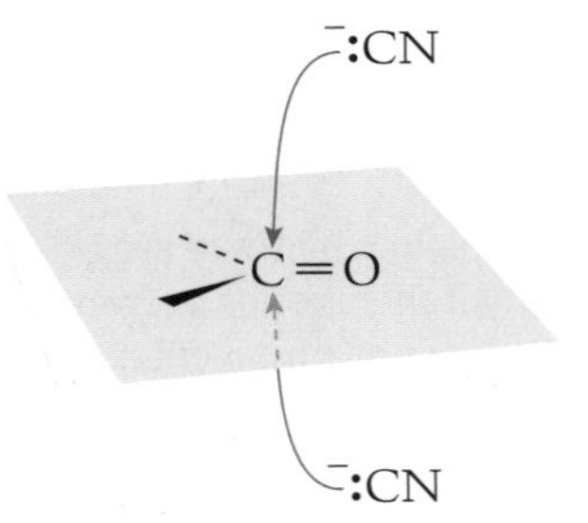

Figure 1 *The :CN⁻ ion may attack from above or below the C=O group*

Redox reactions

Oxidation

Aldehydes can be oxidised to carboxylic acids. Note that we use [O] to represent the oxidising agent.

One oxidising agent commonly used is acidified (with dilute sulfuric acid) potassium dichromate(VI), $K_2Cr_2O_7/H^+$.

Ketones *cannot* be oxidised easily to carboxylic acids because, unlike aldehydes, a C—C bond must be broken. Stronger oxidising agents break the hydrocarbon chain of the ketone molecule resulting in a shorter chain molecule, carbon dioxide and water.

Distinguishing aldehydes from ketones

Weak oxidising agents can oxidise aldehydes but not ketones. This is the basis of two tests to distinguish between them.

1 Fehling's test

Fehling's solution is made from a mixture of two solutions – Fehling's A which contains the Cu^{2+} ion, and is therefore coloured blue, and Fehling's B, which contains an alkali and a complexing agent.

- When an aldehyde is warmed with Fehling's solution, a brick red precipitate of copper(I) oxide is produced as the copper(II) oxidises the aldehyde to a carboxylic acid, and is itself reduced to copper(I).
- Ketones give no reaction to this test.

Figure 2 *When an aldehyde is warmed with Fehling's solution, the blue colour will turn green then a brick-red precipitate forms*

2 The silver mirror test

Tollens' reagent contains the complex ion $[Ag(NH_3)_2]^+$ which is formed when aqueous ammonia is added to an aqueous solution of silver nitrate.

- When an aldehyde is warmed with Tollens' reagent, metallic silver is formed. Aldehydes are oxidised to carboxylic acids by Tollens' reagent. The Ag^+ is reduced to metallic silver. A silver mirror will be formed on the inside of the test tube (which has to be spotlessly clean).

  $RCHO + [O] \longrightarrow RCOOH$ The aldehyde is oxidised.

  $[Ag(NH_3)_2]^+ + e^- \longrightarrow Ag + 2NH_3$ The silver is reduced.
- Ketones give no reaction to this test.

Link

We met with aldehydes and ketones in *AQA AS Chemistry*, Topic 16.3. They are formed from the oxidation of primary and secondary alcohols respectively.

Link

Remember what was covered on the Fehling's test in *AQA AS Chemistry*, Topic 16.3.

Hint

A complexing agent can form co-ordinate (dative bonds) with metal atoms or ions, see *AQA AS Chemistry*, Topic 3.2.

Hint

Benedict's solution is similar to Fehling's solution but is more convenient as it does not have to be prepared by mixing. It also contains Cu^{2+} ions but has a different complexing agent.

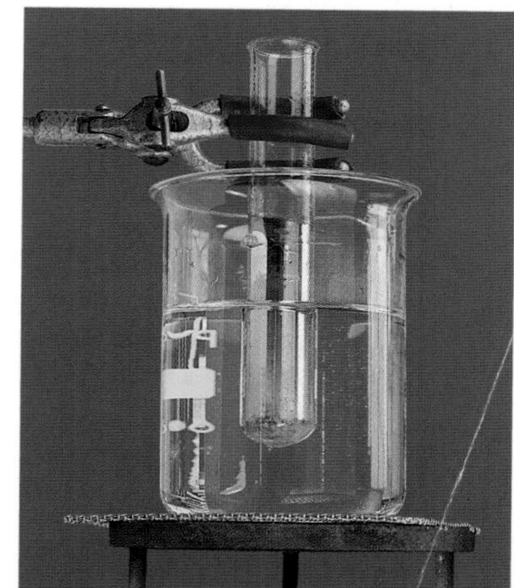

Figure 3 *The reaction of aldehydes with Ag^+ ions was once used as a method of silvering mirrors.*

Reduction

Many reducing agents will reduce both aldehydes and ketones to alcohols. One such reducing agent is sodium tetrahydridoborate(III), $NaBH_4$, in aqueous solution. This generates the nucleophile H^-, the hydride ion.

This reduces $C^{\delta+}=O^{\delta-}$ but not C=C as it is repelled by the high electron density in the C=C bond, but is attracted to the $C^{\delta+}$ of the C=O bond.

Reducing an aldehyde

Aldehydes are reduced to primary alcohols by the following mechanism in which H^- acts as a nucleophile:

:H⁻ attacks $C^{\delta+}$ of R(H)C=O$^{\delta-}$ ⟶ R(H)(H)C–O:⁻ + H^+ ⟶ (H^+ from solvent) R(H)(H)C–OH

primary alcohol

Note that we can use [H] to represent reduction in equations.

$$RHC{=}O + 2[H] \longrightarrow RCH_2OH$$

Reducing a ketone

Ketones are reduced to secondary alcohols in a similar way.

:H⁻ attacks $C^{\delta+}$ of R(R′)C=O$^{\delta-}$ ⟶ R(R′)(H)C–O:⁻ + H^+ ⟶ (H^+ from solvent) R(R′)(H)C–OH

Using [H]:

$$RR'C{=}O + 2[H] \longrightarrow RR'CH(OH)$$

These reactions are nucleophilic addition reactions, (because the H^- ion is a nucleophile).

AQA Examiner's tip

Compounds containing the carbonyl group have a strong absorption in the infra-red spectrum at around 1700 cm^{-1}. This can be used to show the presence of this bond.

Hint

Sodium tetrahydridoborate(III) is sometimes called sodium borohydride.

Summary questions

1 Which of the following is a nucleophile?

H^+, Cl^-, $Cl^•$

2 Sodium tetrahydridoborate(III) generates the nucleophile :H^- and converts aldehydes and ketones to alcohols.

a Would you expect this reagent to reduce >C=C< to –CH–CH– ?

b Explain your answer.

c Predict the product when sodium tetrahydridoborate(III) reacts with:

$H_2C{=}CH{-}CH_2{-}CHO$

3 Hydrogen with a suitable catalyst will add on to C=C bonds as well as reducing the carbonyl group to an alcohol. Predict the product when hydrogen reacts with the compound in question **2c** in the presence of a suitable catalyst.

4 Explain why the reaction of CH_3CHO with HCN forms a racemic mixture, while that with CH_3COCH_3 forms a single compound.

5.3 Carboxylic acids and esters

Learning objectives:

- What are carboxylic acids and esters?
- How are they named?

Specification reference: 3.4.5

Link

You will need to know: the role of an acid in the test for sulfates studied in *AQA AS Chemistry*, Topic 12.1; bond polarity linked to the hydrolysis of esters, oils and fats studied in *AQA AS Chemistry* Topic 3.3; alkane combustion studied in *AQA AS Chemistry*, Topic 6.4 and biodiesel as a fuel (see this book, Topic 5.4) studied in *AS* Topic 6.4.

Carboxylic acids

The carboxylic acid functional group is —C(=O)—O—H, sometimes written as —COOH or as —CO_2H. This group can only be at the end of a carbon chain.

Carboxylic acids have two functional groups that we have seen before: the carbonyl group, >C=O, found in aldehydes and ketones and the hydroxy group, —OH, found in alcohols. Having two groups on the same carbon atom changes the properties of each group. The most obvious difference is that the —OH group in carboxylic acids is much more acidic than the —OH group in alcohols.

The most familiar carboxylic acid is ethanoic acid (acetic acid), which is the acid in vinegar.

How to name carboxylic acids

Carboxylic acids are named using the suffix -oic acid. The carbon atom of the functional group is counted as part of the carbon chain of the root. So:

H—C(=O)—OH, HCOOH, is methanoic acid; H—C(H)(H)—C(=O)—OH, CH_3COOH, is ethanoic acid and so on.

Where there are substituents or side chains on the carbon chain, they are numbered, counting from the carbon of the carboxylic acid as carbon number one. So:

H—C(H)(H)—C(Br)(H)—C(=O)—OH, $CH_3CHBrCOOH$, is 2-bromopropanoic acid;

H—C(H)(H)—C(CH_3)(H)—C(H)(H)—C(=O)—OH, $CH_3CH(CH_3)CH_2COOH$, is 3-methylbutanoic acid.

When the functional group is attached to a benzene ring, the suffix -carboxylic acid is used and the carbon of the functional group is *not* counted as part of the root. So:

C_6H_5—C(=O)—O—H, C_6H_5COOH, is benzenecarboxylic acid (still often called benzoic acid).

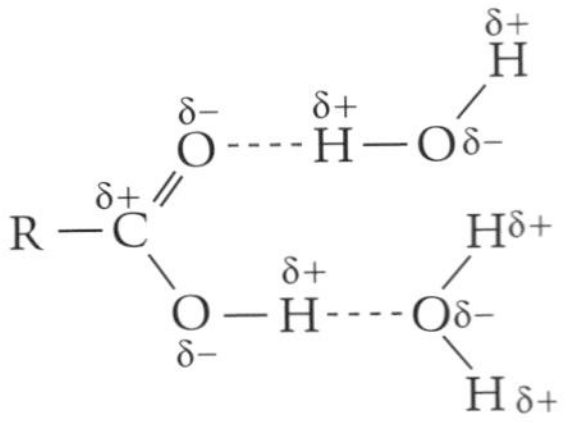

Figure 1 *A molecule of a carboxylic acid forming hydrogen bonds with water*

Physical properties of carboxylic acids

The carboxylic acid group can form hydrogen bonds with water molecules, see Figure 1. For this reason carboxylic acids up to, and including, C_4 (butanoic acid) are completely soluble in water.

The acids also form hydrogen bonds with one another in the solid state. They therefore have much higher melting points than the alkanes of similar relative molecular mass. Ethanoic acid (M_r = 60) melts at 290 K while butane (M_r = 58) melts at 135 K.

One way of identifying a carboxylic acid is to measure its melting point and compare it with tables of known melting points. A Thiele tube may be used, see Figure 2, or the melting point can be found electrically, see Figure 3.

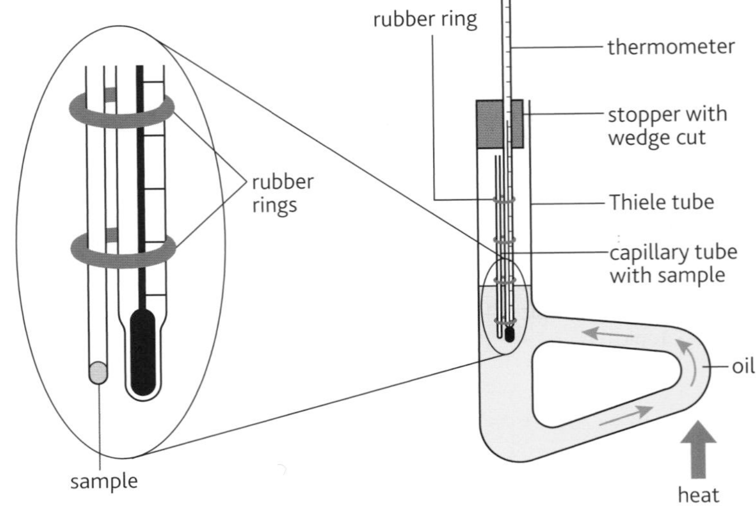

Figure 2 *A Thiele tube may be used to measure a melting point*

Figure 3 *Modern electrical melting point apparatus*

Pure ethanoic acid is sometimes called 'glacial' ethanoic acid because it may freeze on a cold day – its freezing point is 13 °C (260 K). Glacial means 'ice-like'.

The acids have characteristic smells. You will recognise the smell of ethanoic acid as vinegar, while butanoic acid causes the smell of rancid butter.

The non-systematic names of hexanoic and octanoic acids are caproic and capryllic acid respectively, from the same derivation as Capricorn the goat. They are present in goat fat and cause its unpleasant smell.

AQA Examiner's tip

Take care with the names of esters. It is easy to get them the wrong way round. The part of the name relating to the acid comes last. Also, remember that the acid is named from the number of carbon atoms – including the carbon of the functional group.

Esters

Esters are derived from carboxylic acids. The hydrogen (from the OH group of the acid) is replaced by a hydrocarbon group – an alkyl or aryl group (OH is replaced by OR). So the general formula is R—C(=O)—O—R' or RCOOR'.

How to name esters

The names of esters are based on that of the parent acid, for example, all esters from ethanoic acid are called ethanoates. But, the name always begins with the alkyl (or aryl) group that has replaced the hydrogen of the acid, rather than the name of the acid.

For example:

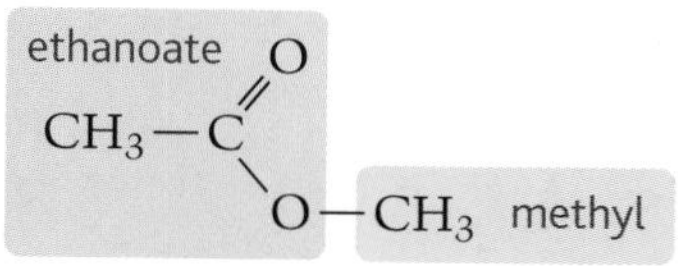

ethanoate $CH_3-C(=O)-O-CH_3$ methyl is called methyl ethanoate.

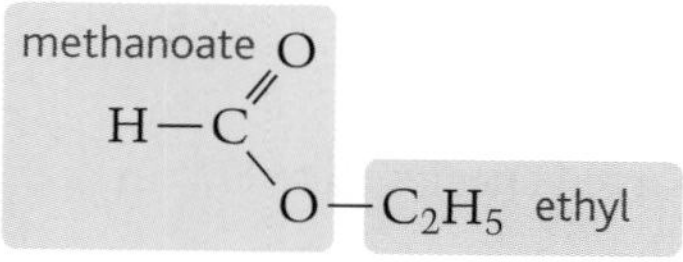

methanoate $H-C(=O)-O-C_2H_5$ ethyl is called ethyl methanoate.

Short chain esters are fairly volatile and have pleasant fruity smells, so that they are often used in flavourings and perfumes. For example 3-methylbutyl ethanoate has the smell of pear drops, octyl ethanoate is orange flavoured, while pentyl pentanoate smells and tastes of apples. They are also used as solvents and plasticisers. Fats and oils are esters with longer carbon chains.

Summary questions

1 Give the name of:

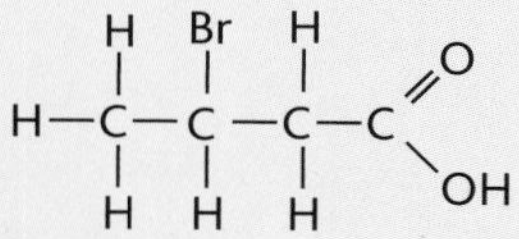

$H-CH_2-CHBr-CH_2-C(=O)OH$ (displayed formula: H–C(H)(H)–C(Br)(H)–C(H)(H)–C(=O)–OH)

2 Write the displayed formula for 3-chloropropanoic acid.

3 Why is it not necessary to call propanoic acid 1-propanoic acid?

4 Give the names of the following esters:

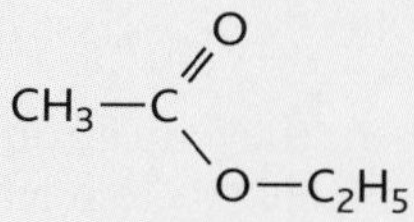

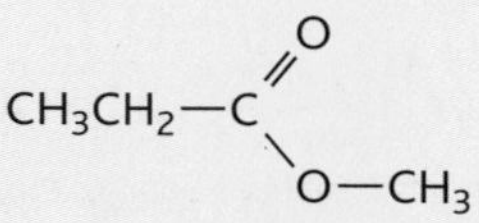

$CH_3-C(=O)-O-C_2H_5$

$CH_3CH_2-C(=O)-O-CH_3$

5.4 Reactions of carboxylic acids and esters

Learning objectives:

- How do carboxylic acids react?
- How are esters formed from carboxylic acids?
- How are esters hydrolysed?
- How are esters used?

Specification reference: 3.4.5

Reactivity of carboxylic acids

The carboxylic acid group is polarised as shown:

$$R-C^{\delta+}(=O^{\delta-})-O^{\delta-}-H^{\delta+}$$

- The $C^{\delta+}$ is open to attack from nucleophiles.
- The $O^{\delta-}$ may be attacked by positively charged species (like H^+, in which case we say it has been protonated).
- The $H^{\delta+}$ may be lost as H^+, in which case the compound is behaving as an acid.

Loss of a proton

If the hydrogen of the —OH group is lost, a negative ion, a carboxylate ion, is left.

$$R-C(=O)-O-H \rightleftharpoons R-C(=O)-O^- + H^+$$

a carboxylate ion

The negative charge is shared over the whole of the carboxylate group.

$$R-C\langle{}^{O}_{O}\rangle^-$$

This **delocalisation** makes the resulting ion more stable.

Carboxylic acids are weak acids, so the equilibrium:

$$R-C(=O)-OH \rightleftharpoons R-C(=O)-O^- + H^+$$

is well over to the left. Even so, they are strong enough to react with sodium hydrogencarbonate, $NaHCO_3$, to release carbon dioxide. This distinguishes them from other organic compounds that contain the –OH group, such as alcohols.

$$CH_3COOH(aq) + NaHCO_3(aq) \longrightarrow CH_3COONa\,(aq) + H_2O(l) + CO_2(g)$$

ethanoic acid — sodium hydrogencarbonate — sodium ethanoate — water — carbon dioxide

Carboxylic acids give CO_2 with $NaHCO_3$(aq) and with solid Na_2CO_3 and solid $NaHCO_3$

Reactions of acids

Carboxylic acids are proton donors and show the typical reactions of acids.

They form ionic salts with the more reactive metals, alkalis, metal oxides or metal carbonates in the usual way. The salts that are formed have the general name carboxylates, and are named from the particular acid. Methanoic acid gives methanoates, ethanoic acid gives ethanoates, propanoic acid gives propanoates, and so on.

For example, ethanoic acid reacts with aqueous sodium hydroxide:

$$\underset{\text{ethanoic acid}}{CH_3COOH(aq)} + \underset{\text{sodium hydroxide}}{NaOH(aq)} \longrightarrow \underset{\text{sodium ethanoate}}{CH_3COONa(aq)} + \underset{\text{water}}{H_2O(l)}$$

Ethanoic acid reacts with aqueous sodium carbonate:

$$\underset{\text{ethanoic acid}}{2CH_3COOH(aq)} + \underset{\text{sodium carbonate}}{Na_2CO_3(aq)} \longrightarrow \underset{\text{sodium ethanoate}}{2CH_3COONa(aq)} + \underset{\text{water}}{H_2O(l)} + \underset{\text{carbon dioxide}}{CO_2(g)}$$

Figure 1 *Carboxylic acids fizz with sodium carbonate*

Esters

Formation of esters

Esters, general formula RCOOR′, are acid derivatives.

Carboxylic acids react with alcohols to form esters. This reaction is speeded up by a strong acid catalyst. This is a reversible reaction and forms an equilibrium mixture of reactants and products. For example:

$$\underset{\text{ethanoic acid}}{CH_3C(=O)OH} + \underset{\text{ethanol}}{C_2H_5OH} \underset{}{\overset{H^+\text{ catalyst}}{\rightleftharpoons}} \underset{\text{ethyl ethanoate}}{CH_3C(=O)O{-}C_2H_5} + \underset{\text{water}}{H_2O}$$

Application

In the laboratory esters are made by warming the appropriate acid and alcohol with concentrated sulfuric acid. The ester will be more volatile than the original alcohol and carboxylic acid and may be distilled off the reaction mixture.

Hydrolysis of esters

The carbonyl carbon atom of an ester has a δ+ charge and is therefore attacked by water acting as a weak nucleophile. This is the reverse of the reaction above. The equation is:

$$\underset{\text{ester}}{R{-}C(=O){-}O{-}R'} + H_2O \overset{H^+\text{ catalyst}}{\rightleftharpoons} \underset{\text{carboxylic acid}}{R{-}C(=O){-}O{-}H} + \underset{\text{alcohol}}{R'{-}O{-}H}$$

The hydrolysis (reaction with water) of esters does not go to completion. It produces an equilibrium mixture containing the ester, water, acid and alcohol. The acid is a catalyst so it affects only the rate at which equilibrium is reached, not the composition of the equilibrium mixture, see *AQA AS Chemistry*, Topic 9.2.

An ester can be hydolysed at room temperature when a strong acid catalyst is used. The balanced equation for the acid catalysed hydrolysis of ethyl ethanoate is:

$$CH_3{-}C(=O){-}O{-}C_2H_5 + H_2O \overset{H^+\text{ catalyst}}{\rightleftharpoons} CH_3{-}C(=O)OH + C_2H_5OH$$

AQA Examiner's tip

When an acid catalyst is used in the hydrolysis of an ester an equilibrium mixture of reactants and products is obtained.

Bases also catalyse hydrolysis of esters. In this case, the salt of the acid is produced rather than the acid itself. This removes the acid from the reaction mixture so an equilibrium is not established and the reaction goes to completion, so that there is more product in the mixture.

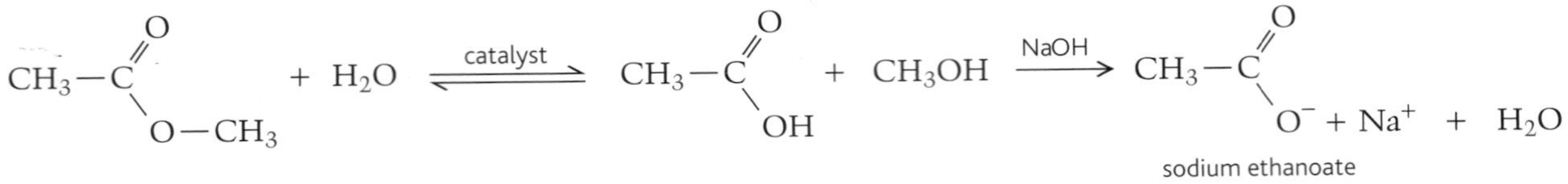

$$CH_3{-}C({=}O){-}O{-}CH_3 + H_2O \xrightleftharpoons{\text{catalyst}} CH_3{-}C({=}O){-}OH + CH_3OH \xrightarrow{\text{NaOH}} CH_3{-}C({=}O){-}O^- + Na^+ + H_2O$$

sodium ethanoate

$$\begin{array}{c} H \\ | \\ H{-}C{-}OH \\ | \\ H{-}C{-}OH \\ | \\ H{-}C{-}OH \\ | \\ H \end{array}$$

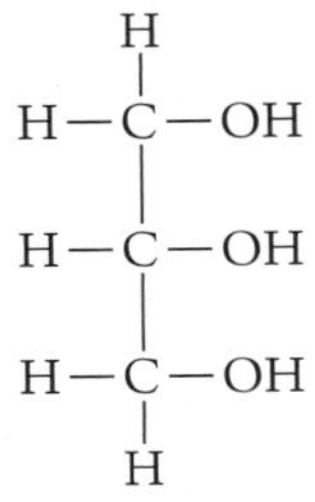

glycerol

glycerol 3 fatty acids

$$\begin{array}{l} \quad\;\; H \qquad\;\; O \\ \quad\;\; | \qquad\;\;\; \| \\ H{-}C{-}O{-}C{-}R \\ \quad\;\; | \qquad\;\; O \\ \quad\;\; | \qquad\;\;\; \| \\ H{-}C{-}O{-}C{-}R' \\ \quad\;\; | \qquad\;\; O \\ \quad\;\; | \qquad\;\;\; \| \\ H{-}C{-}O{-}C{-}R'' \\ \quad\;\; | \\ \quad\;\; H \end{array}$$

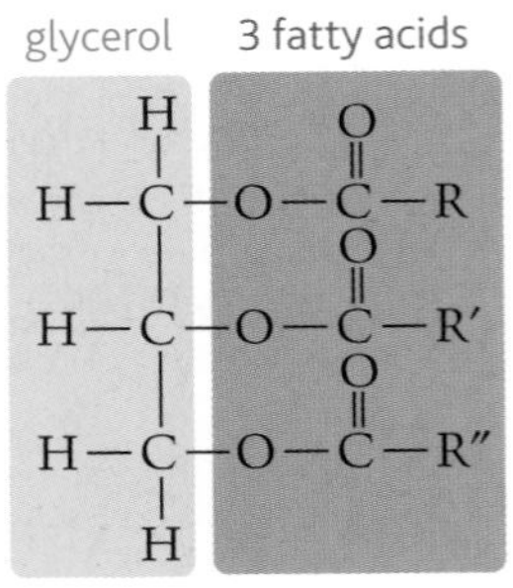

a triglyceride

Figure 4 *Glycerol and a triglyceride*

Uses of esters

Animal and vegetable oils and fats are the esters of the alcohol propane-1,2,3-triol, (non-systematic name 'glycerol'). The only difference between a fat and an oil is that oils are liquid at room temperature, while fats are solid. Oils and fats contain three molecules of long chain (around C_{12}–C_{18}) carboxylic acids called **fatty acids**. Since they are based on glycerol, fats and oils are referred to as **triglycerides**.

Fats and oils can be hydrolysed in acid conditions to give a mixture of glycerol and the component fatty acids.

They can also be hydrolysed by boiling with sodium hydroxide. Both the products are useful: glycerol and a mixture of sodium salts of the three acids which formed part of the ester. These salts are soaps. Soap can be a mixture containing many different salts. The type of soap depends on the fatty acids initially present in the ester.

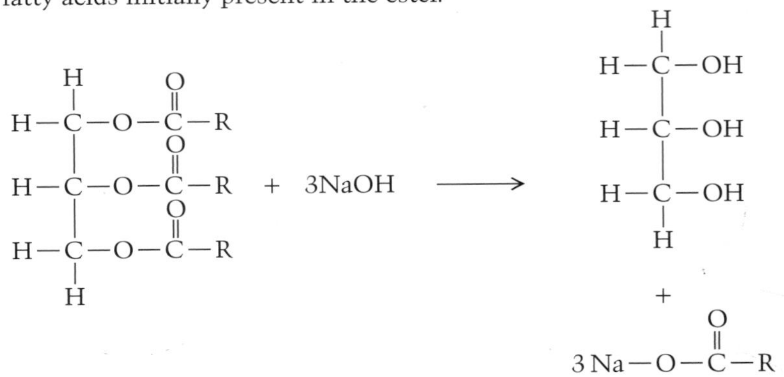

$$\begin{array}{l} \quad\;\; H \qquad\;\; O \\ \quad\;\; | \qquad\;\;\; \| \\ H{-}C{-}O{-}C{-}R \\ \quad\;\; | \qquad\;\; O \\ \quad\;\; | \qquad\;\;\; \| \\ H{-}C{-}O{-}C{-}R \\ \quad\;\; | \qquad\;\; O \\ \quad\;\; | \qquad\;\;\; \| \\ H{-}C{-}O{-}C{-}R \\ \quad\;\; | \\ \quad\;\; H \end{array} + 3NaOH \longrightarrow \begin{array}{c} H \\ | \\ H{-}C{-}OH \\ | \\ H{-}C{-}OH \\ | \\ H{-}C{-}OH \\ | \\ H \end{array} + 3\,Na{-}O{-}\overset{\overset{\displaystyle O}{\|}}{C}{-}R$$

These sodium salts are ionic and dissociate to form Na^+ and $RCOO^-$. $RCOO^-$ has two distinct ends: a long hydrocarbon chain which is non-polar and the COO^- group which is polar and ionic. The hydrocarbon will mix with grease, while the COO^- mixes with water, see Figure 2. So, these 'tadpole' shaped molecules allow grease and water to mix and therefore are used as cleaning agents.

Table 1 *Some common fatty acids*

Name	Formula	Details
stearic acid	$CH_3(CH_2)_{16}CO_2H$	present in most animal fats
palmitic acid	$CH_3(CH_2)_{14}CO_2H$	used in making soaps
oleic acid	$CH_3(CH_2)_7CH{=}CH(CH_2)_7CO_2H$	monounsaturated; it has one double bond, present in most fats and in olive oil
linoleic acid	$CH_3(CH_2)_4(CH{=}CHCH_2)_2(CH_2)_6CO_2H$	polyunsaturated, present in many vegetable oils

Propane-1,2,3-triol (glycerol)

Glycerol has three O—H bonds, so it readily forms hydrogen bonds and is very soluble in water. It is a very important chemical in many industries and has a really wide range of uses.

- It is used extensively in many pharmaceutical and cosmetic preparations. Because it attracts water, it is used to prevent ointments and creams from drying out.
- It is used as a solvent in many medicines, and is present in toothpastes.
- It is used as a solvent in the food industry, for example for food colourings.
- It is used to plasticise various materials like sheets and gaskets, cellophane, special quality papers. Plasticisers are introduced between the molecules of the polymer which makes up the material and by allowing the molecules to slip over each other, the material becomes flexible and smooth. (PVC may contain up to 50% plasticiser, such as esters of hexanedioic acid. Over time, the plasticiser leaks away, leaving the plastic brittle and inflexible.)

How science works

Biodiesel

One possible solution to the reliance on crude oil as a source of fuel for motor vehicles is **biodiesel**. This is a renewable fuel, as it is made from oils derived from crops such as rape seed. Rape seed oil is a triglyceride ester. To make biodiesel the oil is reacted with methanol (with a strong alkali as a catalyst) to form a mixture of methyl esters, which can be used as a fuel in diesel vehicles with little or no modification. This process is being introduced commercially, but the chemistry is relatively simple, so that some people are making their own biodiesel at home starting with used chip-shop oil, for example. Germany has thousands of filling stations supplying biodiesel, and it is cheaper there than ordinary diesel fuel. All fossil diesel fuel sold in France contains between 2% and 5% biodiesel.

$$\begin{array}{l} \text{H}_2\text{C}-\text{O}-\text{CO}-(\text{CH}_2)_{14}\text{CH}_3 \\ \text{HC}-\text{O}-\text{CO}-(\text{CH}_2)_{14}\text{CH}_3 \quad + \quad 3\,\text{CH}_3\text{OH} \\ \text{H}_2\text{C}-\text{O}-\text{CO}-(\text{CH}_2)_{14}\text{CH}_3 \end{array}$$

$$\downarrow$$

$$\begin{array}{l} \text{H}_2\text{C}-\text{OH} \\ \text{HC}-\text{OH} \quad + \quad 3\,\text{CH}_3-\text{O}-\text{CO}-(\text{CH}_2)_{14}\text{CH}_3 \\ \text{H}_2\text{C}-\text{OH} \end{array}$$

biodiesel

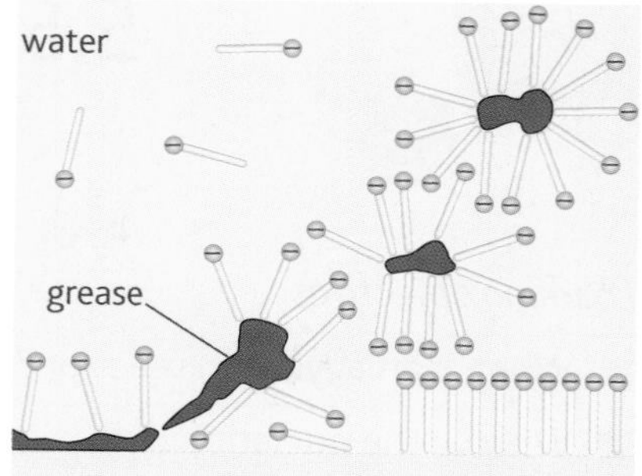

Figure 2 *The action of soap. The hydrocarbon ends of the ions – in yellow, mix with grease and the COO— ends, in blue, lift it into aqueous solution*

How science works

Without plasticiser, PVC is rigid and is used for drain pipes, for example. With plasticiser, it is flexible and can be used as a waterproof fabric in tablecloths and aprons, for example.

Summary questions

1. Carboxylic acids, being acidic, will react with the reactive metals. Give three other reactions that are typical of acids.
2. Name the acid and the alcohol that would react together to give the ester methyl ethanoate.
3. Name the acid and the alcohol that would react together to give the ester ethyl methanoate.
4. Methyl ethanoate and ethyl methanoate are a pair of isomers. Explain what this means.

Figure 3 *A field of rape seed oil, the starting material for biodiesel*

5.5 Acylation

Learning objectives:

- What is an acylation reaction?
- What is the nucleophilic addition–elimination mechanism for acylation reactions?

Specification reference: 3.4.5

The acyl group is:

```
     O
    //
R—C
    \
```

and acylation is the process by which the acyl group is introduced into another molecule.

There is a group of compounds called **acid derivatives**, which all have the acyl group as part of their structure (we met esters in Topic 5.3). Two other important acid derivatives are acid chlorides and acid anhydrides. Acid derivatives are derived from carboxylic acids and have the general formula:

```
     O
    //
R—C
    \
     Z
```

where Z may be a variety of groups, see Table 1.

If R— is CH_3—, the group is called **ethanoyl**.

Table 1 *Some acid derivatives*

—Z	Name of acid derivative	General formula	Example
—OR′	ester	RCOOR′	ethyl ethanoate, $CH_3COOC_2H_5$
—Cl	acid chloride	RCOCl	ethanoyl chloride, CH_3COCl
—OCOR′	acid anhydride	RCOOCOR′	ethanoic anhydride, $CH_3COOCOCH_3$

Link

You will need to know the bond polarity and shapes of molecules studied in *AQA AS Chemistry*, Topics 3.3 and 3.9 and nucleophilic substitution reactions of haloalkanes studied in *AQA AS Chemistry*, Topic 14.2.

The carbonyl group of an acid derivative is polarised as shown:

```
        δ−
       O
  δ+ //
R—C
    \
     Z
```

It is attacked by nucleophiles at the $C^{\delta+}$ and, in the process, the nucleophile replaces Z and thus acquires an acyl group. So, the nucleophile has been acylated.

AQA Examiner's tip

A nucleophile has a lone pair of electrons and attacks positively charged carbon atoms.

The general reaction is:

```
     δ−
     O                                  O
    //                                 //
R—C δ+   +   :Nu⁻   ——→   R—C        +   :Z⁻
    \                                  \
     Z                                  Nu
```

How readily the reaction occurs depends on three factors:

1. The magnitude of the δ+ charge on the carbonyl carbon, which in turn depends on the electron-releasing or attracting power of Z.
2. How easily Z is lost. (Z is called the leaving group.)
3. How good the nucleophile is.

Factors 1 and 2 tend to be linked: groups which strongly attract electrons tend to form stable negative ions, Z^-, and are good leaving groups.

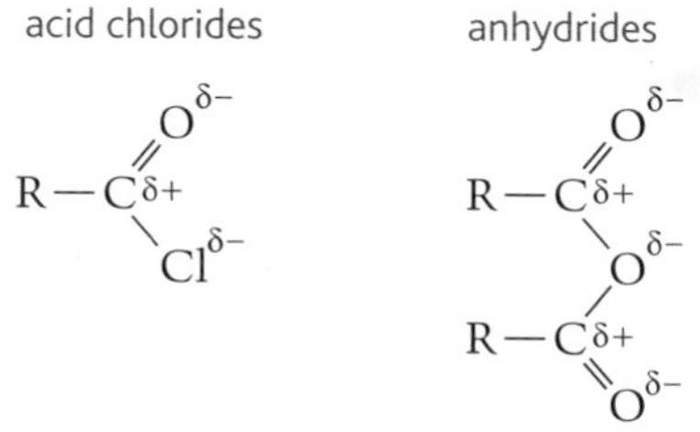

acid chlorides

$R-C^{\delta+}(=O^{\delta-})-Cl^{\delta-}$

anhydrides

$R-C^{\delta+}(=O^{\delta-})-O^{\delta-}-C^{\delta+}(=O^{\delta-})-R$

The Z groups of acyl chlorides and acid anhydrides *withdraw* electrons from the carbonyl carbon. This makes the carbon more positive and makes these compounds reactive. So, acyl chlorides and acid anhydrides are both good acylating agents. Acyl chlorides are somewhat more reactive than acid anhydrides.

Nucleophiles

Nucleophiles must have a lone pair of electrons which they use to attack an electron-deficient carbon, $C^{\delta+}$. The best nucleophiles are the ones that are best at donating their lone pair.

Acyl chlorides and acid anhydrides will both react with all the following nucleophiles, listed in order of reactivity:

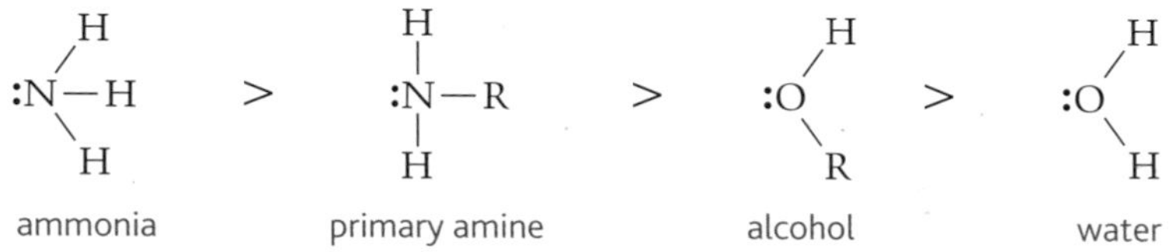

:NH₃	>	:NH₂R	>	:O(H)R	>	:O(H)H
ammonia		primary amine		alcohol		water

The products of the reactions of these nucleophiles with acyl chlorides and acid anhydrides are shown in Table 2. These reactions are called **addition–elimination reactions**. These nucleophiles are all neutral so they must lose a hydrogen ion during the reaction.

One way of looking at these reactions is that a hydrogen atom of the nucleophile ('the active hydrogen') has been replaced by an acyl group.

- If the nucleophile is ammonia the product is an amide.
- If the nucleophile is a primary amine, the product is an N-substituted amide.
- If the nucleophile is the —OH group of an alcohol the product is an ester.
- If the nucleophile is water, the product is a carboxylic acid.

Table 2 *The products of the reactions of acid derivatives with nucleophiles. All reactions take place at room temperature*

← Increasing reactivity (acid derivative)

↑ Increasing reactivity (nucleophile)

nucleophile \ acid derivative	$R-C(=O)-Cl$ acid chloride	$R-C(=O)-O-C(=O)-R$ anhvdride
NH_3 ammonia	$R-C(=O)-NH_2$ amide	$R-C(=O)-NH_2$ amide
$R'-NH_2$ amine	$R-C(=O)-NHR'$ *N*-substituted amide	$R-C(=O)-NHR'$ *N*-substituted amide
$R'-OH$ alcohol	$R-C(=O)-O-R'$ ester	$R-C(=O)-O-R'$ ester
H_2O water	$R-C(=O)-OH$ carboxylic acid	$R-C(=O)-OH$ carboxylic acid

The mechanism of the reactions

The mechanism of these reactions follows the same pattern, shown below, for:

1 Ethanoyl chloride and water (called hydrolysis).

$$CH_3-\overset{\delta+}{C}(=\overset{\delta-}{O})-\overset{\delta-}{Cl} + :OH_2 \longrightarrow CH_3-C(-:O^-)(-Cl)-\overset{+}{O}H_2$$

$$\downarrow$$

$$CH_3-C(=O)-OH + H^+ \longleftarrow CH_3-C(=O)-\overset{+}{O}H_2 + \ddot{C}l^-$$

Examiner's tip

A curly arrow shows movement of a pair of electrons.

2 Ethanoyl chloride and ethanol.

$$CH_3{-}C^{\delta+}(=O^{\delta-})Cl^{\delta-} + H\ddot{O}C_2H_5 \longrightarrow CH_3{-}C(O^-)(Cl){-}\overset{+}{O}(H)C_2H_5$$

$$CH_3{-}C(=O){-}OC_2H_5 + H^+ \longleftarrow CH_3{-}C(=O){-}\overset{+}{O}(H)C_2H_5 + :\ddot{Cl}^-$$

3 Ethanoyl chloride and ammonia. (The H^+ ion that is lost then reacts with a second molecule of ammonia to form NH_4^+.)

$$CH_3{-}C^{\delta+}(=O^{\delta-})Cl^{\delta-} + :NH_3 \longrightarrow CH_3{-}C(O^-)(Cl){-}\overset{+}{N}H_3$$

$$CH_3{-}C(=O)NH_2 + H^+ \longleftarrow CH_3{-}C(=O){-}\overset{+}{N}H_3 + :\ddot{Cl}^-$$

The overall equation may be written:

$$CH_3COCl + 2NH_3 \longrightarrow CH_3CONH_2 + NH_4Cl$$

4 Ethanoyl chloride and methylamine.

$$CH_3{-}C^{\delta+}(=O^{\delta-})Cl^{\delta-} + :N(CH_3)H{-}H \longrightarrow CH_3{-}C(O^-)(Cl){-}\overset{+}{N}(CH_3)H{-}H$$

$$CH_3{-}C(=O){-}N(H){-}CH_3 + H^+ \longleftarrow CH_3{-}C(=O){-}\overset{+}{N}(CH_3)(H){-}H + :\ddot{Cl}^-$$

AQA Examiner's tip

A second NH_3 removes a proton from the intermediate ion to give the final product

Hint

The amine can be regenerated by reaction with sodium hydroxide.

Uses of acylation reactions

Ethanoic anhydride is manufactured on a large scale. Its advantages over ethanoyl chloride as an acylating agent are:

- It is cheaper.
- It is less corrosive.
- It does not react with water as readily.
- It is safer, as the by-product of its reaction is ethanoic acid rather than hydrogen chloride.

One important use is in the production of aspirin, see 'How science works'.

How science works

Aspirin

Aspirin (systematic name 2-ethanoyloxybenzenecarboxylic acid – try asking for that at your local pharmacy!) is probably the most used medicine of all time – it must have been used to treat millions of headaches. We tend to think of it as an over-the-counter remedy for moderate pain, which also reduces fever. However, it has more recently been shown to have many other effects such as reducing the risk of heart attacks and some cancers. It is not without risks itself – it can cause intestinal bleeding, for example, and it has been suggested that if it were to be introduced as a new drug today it would be prescription-only.

Aspirin has a long history. Compounds related to it were originally extracted from willow bark. One old theory held that cures to diseases could be found near the cause, and willow, which grows in damp places, was suggested as a cure for rheumatism, which is made worse by dampness.

In 1890, the German chemist Felix Hofmann produced the ethanoyl (or acyl) derivative of salicylic acid (2-hydroxybenzenecarboxylic acid), from the bark extract, and used it to treat his father's rheumatism. This derivative is what is now used for aspirin.

The reagent used is ethanoyl anhydride:

$$HOC_6H_4COOH + (CH_3CO)_2O \longrightarrow CH_3COOC_6H_4COOH + CH_3COOH$$

Notice that the by-product is ethanoic acid.

1 Work out the atom economy for this reaction (see *AQA AS Chemistry*, Topic 2.6).You will probably need to draw out the displayed formulae first.

2 An alternative acylating agent for this reaction would be ethanoyl chloride.

a Write the equation for the reaction of salicylic acid (2-hydroxybenzenecarboxylic acid) with ethanoyl chloride.

b What is the by-product in this case?

c Work out the atom economy for the reaction.

Summary questions

1 Why is ethanoyl chloride a good acylating agent?

2 Which of the following could be acylated? a NH_4^+ b OH^- c CH_4 ? Explain your answers.

3 Why is acylation called an addition–elimination reaction?

4 Write down the equation for the formation of propanamide from the reaction between ammonia and propanoyl chloride. Give the mechanism for this reaction.

AQA Examination-style questions

1 (a) Write an equation for the formation of methyl propanoate, $CH_3CH_2COOCH_3$, from methanol and propanoic acid. *(1 mark)*

(b) Name and outline a mechanism for the reaction between methanol and propanoyl chloride to form methyl propanoate. *(5 marks)*

(c) Propanoic anhydride could be used instead of propanoyl chloride in the preparation of methyl propanoate from methanol. Draw the structure of propanoic anhydride. *(1 mark)*

(d) (i) Give **one** advantage of the use of propanoyl chloride instead of propanoic acid in the laboratory preparation of methyl propanoate from methanol.

(ii) Give **one** advantage of the use of propanoic anhydride instead of propanoyl chloride in the industrial manufacture of methyl propanoate from methanol. *(2 marks)*

AQA, 2006

2 Consider the sequence of reactions below

$$\underset{\mathbf{P}}{CH_3CH_2CHO} \xrightarrow[\text{HCN}]{\text{Reaction 1}} \underset{\mathbf{Q}}{CH_3CH_2-\overset{\displaystyle H}{\underset{\displaystyle OH}{C}}-CN} \xrightarrow{\text{Reaction 2}} \underset{\mathbf{R}}{CH_3CH_2-\overset{\displaystyle H}{\underset{\displaystyle OH}{C}}-COOH}$$

(a) Name and outline a mechanism for Reaction 1. *(5 marks)*

(b) (i) Name compound **Q**.

(ii) The molecular formula of **Q** is C_4H_7NO. Draw the structure of the isomer of **Q** which shows geometrical isomerism and is formed by the reaction of ammonia with an acyl chloride. *(3 marks)*

(c) Draw the structure of the main organic product formed in each case when **R** reacts separately with the following substances:

(i) methanol in the presence of a few drops of concentrated sulfuric acid;

(ii) acidified potassium dichromate(VI);

(iii) concentrated sulphuric acid in an elimination reaction. *(3 marks)*

AQA, 2006

3 (a) Name and outline a mechanism for the reaction between propanoyl chloride, CH_3CH_2COCl, and methylamine, CH_3NH_2 *(5 marks)*

(b) Draw the structure of the organic product. *(1 mark)*

AQA, 2005

4 A naturally-occurring triester, shown below, was heated under reflux with an excess of aqueous sodium hydroxide and the mixture produced was then distilled. One of the products distilled off and the other was left in the distillation flask.

$$\begin{array}{c} CH_3(CH_2)_{16}COOCH_2 \\ | \\ CH_3(CH_2)_{16}COOCH \\ | \\ CH_3(CH_2)_{16}COOCH_2 \end{array}$$

(a) Draw the structure of the product distilled off and give its name. *(2 marks)*

(b) Give the formula of the product left in the distillation flask and give a use for it. *(2 marks)*

AQA, 2005

6 Aromatic chemistry

6.1 Introduction to arenes

Learning objectives:

- Why is the benzene ring a planar hexagon?
- Why are the carbon–carbon bonds of equal length?

Specification reference: 3.4.6

Arenes are hydrocarbons, based on benzene, C_6H_6, which is the simplest one. Although benzene is an unsaturated molecule, it is very stable. It has a hexagonal (six-sided) ring structure with a special type of bonding. Arenes were first isolated from sweet-smelling oils, such as balsam, and this gave them the name 'aromatic' compounds. Arenes are still called aromatic compounds, but this now refers to their structures rather than their aromas. Benzene and other arenes have characteristic properties.

Benzene is given the special symbol:

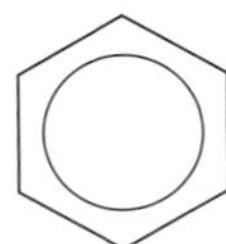

This is a skeletal formula, which does not show the carbon or hydrogen atoms. There is one carbon atom and one hydrogen atom at each 'corner'.

Arenes can have other functional groups (substituents) replacing one or more of the hydrogen atoms in its structure.

Hint

A linear C_6 alkane would have the formula C_6H_{14} – more than twice the number of hydrogens compared with benzene.

Link

You will need to know the covalent bonding studied in *AQA AS Chemistry*, Topic 3.2 and bonding in alkenes studied in Topic 15.1.

Bonding and structure of benzene

The bonding and structure of benzene C_6H_6 was a puzzle for a long time to organic chemists, because:

- In spite of being unsaturated, it does not readily form addition compounds.
- All the carbon atoms were equivalent, which implied that all the carbon–carbon bonds are the same.

How science works 'The most important dream in history?', describes how the puzzle began to be solved.

Benzene consists of a flat, regular hexagon of carbon atoms, each of which is bonded to a single hydrogen atom. The geometry of benzene is shown in Figure 1.

The C—C bond lengths in benzene are intermediate between those expected for a carbon–carbon single bond and a carbon–carbon double bond, see Table 1. So, each bond is intermediate between a single and a double bond.

The symbol (benzene ring symbol) is used to represent this.

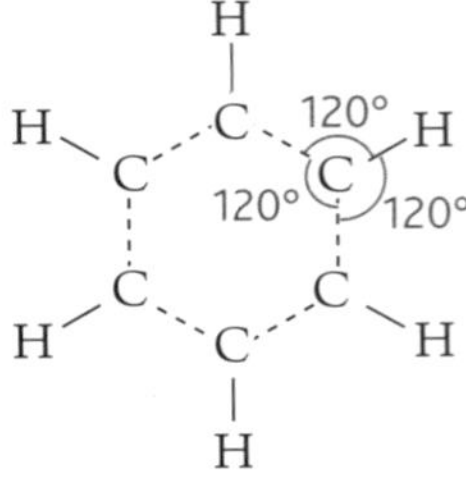

Figure 1 *The geometry of benzene (the dashed lines show the shape and do not represent single bonds)*

We can explain this by using the idea that some of the electrons are delocalised. **Delocalisation** means that electrons are spread over more than two atoms – in this case the six carbon atoms that form the ring.

Each carbon has three covalent bonds: one to a hydrogen atom and the other two to carbon atoms. The fourth electron of each carbon atom is in a p-orbital, and there are six of these. The electrons in the p-orbitals overlap and are **delocalised**. They form a region of electron density above and below the ring, see Figure 2.

Overall, each carbon–carbon bond has a total of three electrons, making it between a single and a double bond. The delocalised system is very important in the chemistry of benzene and its derivatives. It makes benzene unusually stable. This is sometimes called **aromatic stability**.

Table 1 *Carbon–carbon bond lengths*

Bond	Length / nm
C—C	0.154
C┄C (in benzene)	0.140
C=C	0.134
C≡C	0.120

AQA Examiner's tip

Benzene is more stable than the hypothetical molecule cyclohexa-1,3,5-triene because of delocalisation.

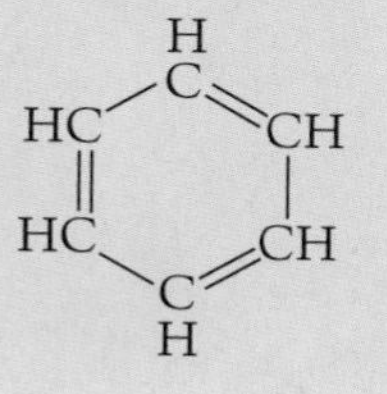

The thermochemical evidence for stability

The enthalpy change for the hydrogenation of cyclohexene is:

cyclohexene + H_2 ⟶ cyclohexane $\Delta H^\ominus = -120\,kJ\,mol^{-1}$

So the hydrogenation of a ring with alternate double bonds would be expected to be three times this:

'Kekulé-type' benzene + $3H_2$ ⟶ cyclohexane $\Delta H^\ominus = -360\,kJ\,mol^{-1}$

The enthalpy change for benzene is in fact:

benzene + $3H_2$ ⟶ cyclohexane $\Delta H^\ominus = -208\,kJ\,mol^{-1}$

If we put these values on an enthalpy diagram, see Figure 3, we can see that benzene is 152 kJ mol^{-1} more stable than the unsaturated ring structure.

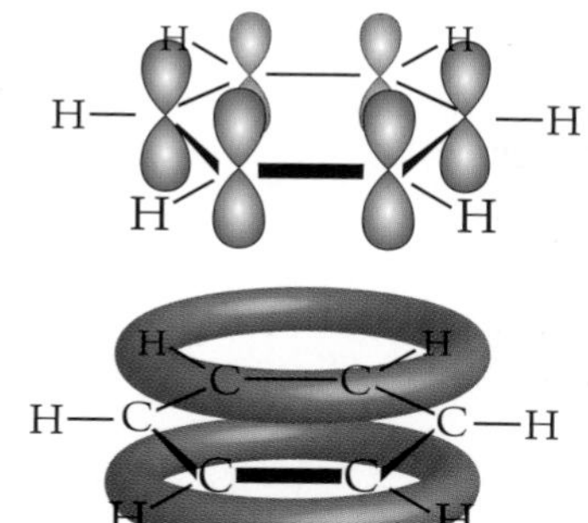

Figure 2 *Delocalisation of p-electrons to form areas of electron density above and below the ring*

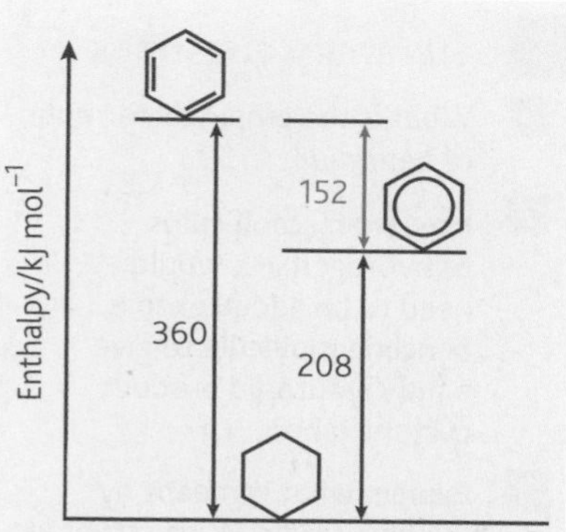

Figure 3

How science works

The most important dream in history?

This is how Friedrich August von Kekulé's insight into a chemical mystery – the structure of benzene – has been described. Benzene, C_6H_6, had been discovered by Michael Faraday but its structure was a puzzle, as the proportion of carbon to hydrogen seemed to be too great for conventional theories. In 1865, the Belgian chemist Friedrich August von Kekulé published a paper in which he suggested that benzene's structure was based on a ring of carbon atoms with alternating double and single bonds.

His idea resulted from a dream of whirling snakes.

'I turned my chair to the fire [after having worked on the problem for some time] and dozed. Again the atoms were gambolling before my eyes. This time the smaller groups kept modestly to the background. My mental eye, rendered more acute by repeated vision of this kind, could now distinguish larger structures, of manifold conformation; long rows, sometimes more closely fitted together; all twining and twisting in snakelike motion. But look! What was that? One of the snakes had seized hold of its own tail, and the form whirled mockingly before my eyes. As if by a flash of lighting I awoke.'

However, even this insight left a number of problems:

- A cyclic triene should show addition reactions, which benzene rarely does.

$$\text{(Kekulé benzene)} + 3Br_2 \longrightarrow \text{(1,2,3,4,5,6-hexabromocyclohexane)}$$

- Kekulé's structure should give rise to two isomeric di-substituted compounds as shown, using skeletal notation:

$$\text{(Kekulé benzene)} + Br_2 \longrightarrow \text{(1,2-dibromobenzene)} + 2\,HBr$$

or

$$\text{(Kekulé benzene)} + Br_2 \longrightarrow \text{(1,2-dibromobenzene)} + 2\,HBr$$

- The hexagon would not be symmetrical: double bonds are shorter than single bonds.

Kekulé himself suggested a solution to the second dilemma by proposing that benzene consisted of structures in rapid equilibrium:

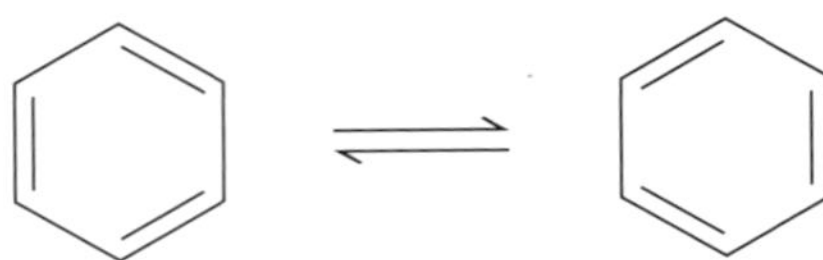

Later this rapid alternation of two structures evolved into the idea of **resonance** between two structures, both of which contribute to the actual structure. The actual structure was thought to be a hybrid (a sort of average) of the two. Such **resonance hybrids** were believed to be more stable than either of the separate structures. Current ideas about the structure of benzene are described in the main text.

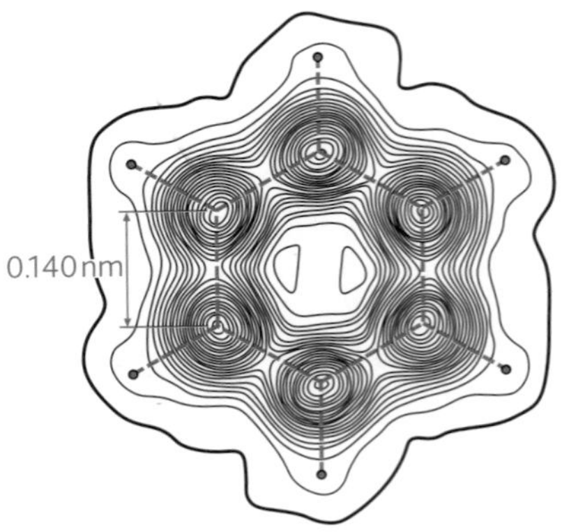

Figure 4 *A technique called X-ray diffraction shows a contour map of the electron density in an individual benzene molecule. This shows that the benzene molecule is a perfect hexagon and each carbon–carbon bond length is 0.140 nm*

Summary questions

1 What is the empirical formula of benzene?

2 How many molecules of hydrogen, H_2, would need to be added onto a benzene molecule to give a fully saturated product cyclohexane?

3 Explain what is meant by 'delocalisation' of electrons in the benzene ring.

6.2 Arenes: physical properties, naming and reactivity

Learning objectives:

- How are substituted arenes named?
- How does the arene ring affect reactivity?

Specification reference: 3.4.6

Physical properties of arenes

Benzene is a colourless liquid at room temperature. It boils at 353 K and freezes at 279 K. Its boiling point is comparable with that of hexane (354 K) but its melting point is much higher than hexane's (178 K). This is because benzene's flat, hexagonal molecules pack together very well in the solid state, Figure 1. They are therefore harder to separate and this must happen for the solid to melt.

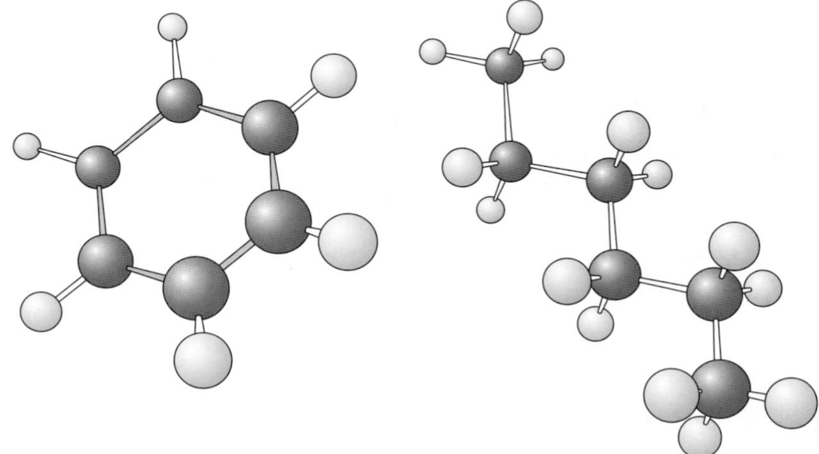

Figure 1 *Benzene molecules (top) can pack together better than hexane molecules, so benzene has a higher melting point than hexane*

Like other hydrocarbons that are non-polar, arenes do not mix with water, but mix with other hydrocarbons and other non-polar solvents.

Hint

Freezing point and melting point are exactly the same temperature.

Hint

Benzene itself is carcinogenic (may cause cancer) so in your practical work in school you are likely to use related compounds that are safer, such as methylbenzene.

Naming aromatic compounds

Substituted arenes are generally named as derivatives of benzene. So benzene forms the root of the name.

CH_3

$C_6H_5CH_3$, is called methylbenzene.

Cl

C_6H_5Cl, is called chlorobenzene and so on.

If there is more than one substituent, we number the ring:

Cl Cl

1,2-dichlorobenzene

Cl Cl

1,4-dichlorobenzene

Examples

You can test yourself by covering the names or the structures

ethylbenzene $C_6H_5C_2H_5$

nitrobenzene $C_6H_5NO_2$

1,2-dimethylbenzene $C_6H_4(CH_3)_2$

Hint

Non-systematic names are still used for many derivatives of benzene. In particular, benzenecarboxylic acid is nearly always called benzoic acid.

AQA Examiner's tip

An electrophile has a positive charge: either as a positive ion or the positive end of a dipole.

Link

You will need to know about enthalpy change studied in *AQA AS Chemistry*, Topic 7.2.

The reactivity of aromatic compounds

Two factors are important to the reactivity of aromatic compounds:

- The ring is an area of high electron density, because of the delocalised bonding, see Topic 6.1, and is therefore attacked by electrophiles.
- The aromatic ring is very stable. It needs energy to be put in to break the ring before the system is destroyed. We call this the 'delocalisation energy'. It means that the ring almost always remains intact in the reactions of arenes.

The above two points mean that most of the reactions of aromatic systems are **electrophilic substitution** reactions.

Summary questions

1 What intermolecular forces act between non-polar molecules?

2 Name:

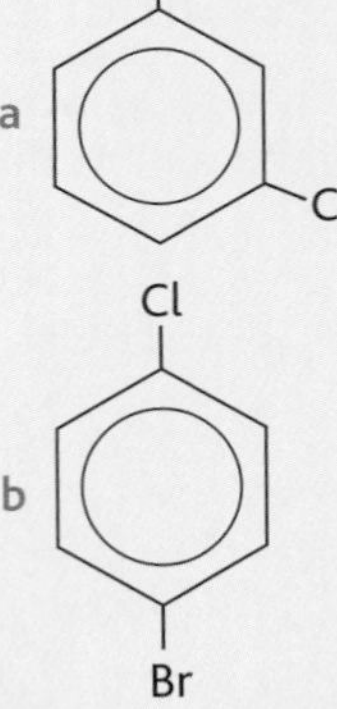

3 Draw the structure of:

a 1,4-dimethylbenzene

b 1,2-dimethylbenzene

4 Which of the following is an electrophile?

R^+ $:NH_3$ NO_2 Cl^-

6.3 Reactions of arenes

Learning objectives:

- Why do arenes react by electrophilic substitution?
- What is the mechanism of nitration?
- What is the mechanism of acylation?

Specification reference: 3.4.6

Figure 1 *Arenes burn with a smoky flame*

Combustion

Arenes burn in air with flames that are noticeably smoky. This is because they have a high carbon : hydrogen ratio. There is usually unburned carbon remaining when they burn in air and this produces soot. A smoky flame suggests an aromatic compound.

Hint

Compare the C : H ratio of benzene, C_6H_6, 1 : 1 to that of cyclohexene, C_6H_{12} (1 : 2).

Electrophilic substitution reactions

Although benzene is unsaturated it does not react like an alkene.

The most typical reaction is an electrophilic substitution that leaves the aromatic system unchanged, rather than addition, which would require the input of the delocalisation energy to destroy the aromatic system.

The mechanism of electrophilic substitutions

The delocalised system of the aromatic ring has a high electron density that attracts electrophiles. At the same time the electrons are attracted towards the electrophile, El^+.

A bond forms between one of the carbon atoms and the electrophile. But, to do this, the carbon must use electrons from the delocalised system. This destroys the aromatic system. To get back the stability of the aromatic system, the carbon loses an H^+ ion. The sum of these reactions is the substitution of H^+ by El^+.

The same overall process occurs in, for example, nitration and Friedel–Crafts acylation reactions.

Link

You will need to know the electrophilic addtion to alkenes studied in *AQA AS Chemistry*, Topic 15.2.

Nitration

Nitration is the substitution of a NO_2 group for one of the hydrogen atoms on an arene ring. The electrophile NO_2^+ is generated in the reaction mixture of concentrated nitric and concentrated sulfuric acids:

$$H_2SO_4 + HNO_3 \longrightarrow H_2NO_3^+ + HSO_4^-$$

H_2SO_4 is a stronger acid than HNO_3 and donates a proton (H^+) to HNO_3, (which is acting as a Brønsted–Lowry base, see Topic 3.1).

$H_2NO_3^+$ then loses a molecule of water to give NO_2^+, which is called the **nitronium ion** or **nitryl cation**.

$$H_2NO_3^+ \rightarrow NO_2^+ + H_2O$$

AQA Examiner's tip

In organic chemistry, 'curly' arrows are used to indicate the movement of pairs of electrons.

AQA Examiner's tip

In the formation of NO_2^+ from HNO_3, nitric acid behaves as a Brønsted–Lowry base when it reacts with H_2SO_4.

NO_2^+ is an electrophile and the following mechanism occurs:

+ $\overset{+}{N}O_2$ ⟶ H NO_2 +

The overall product of the reaction of the nitronium ion, NO_2^+, with benzene is nitrobenzene:

[benzene] + NO_2^+ ⟶ [nitrobenzene] + H^+

nitrobenzene

The balanced equation is:

[benzene] + HNO_3 ⟶ [nitrobenzene] + H_2O

The uses of nitrated arenes

Nitration is an important step in the production of explosives like TNT. Nitration is the first step in making amines (see Topic 7.1), and these in turn are used to make industrial dyes.

How science works

TNT

TNT is is short for trinitrotoluene. It is made by nitrating methylbenzene, common name toluene. TNT is an important high explosive with both military and peaceful applications. It is a solid of low melting point. This property is used both in filling shells, etc., and by bomb disposal teams who can 'steam' TNT out of unexploded bombs.

The explosion of TNT is shown in the following equation:

2 [TNT: ring with CH_3, O_2N, NO_2, NO_2] (s) + $10\frac{1}{2}O_2$(g) ⟶ $14CO_2$(g) + $3N_2$(g) + $5H_2O$(g)

Figure 2 *Filling TNT shells (1940)*

The reaction is strongly exothermic. The rapid formation of a lot of gas as well as heat produces the destructive effect.

Many other compounds with several nitrogen atoms in the molecule are explosive. Another example is 1,3,5-trinitrophenol, which can explode on impact and is therefore useful as a detonator to set off other explosives.

1 What is the systematic name for for TNT? The methyl group is at position 1.

Friedel–Crafts acylation reactions

These reactions use aluminium chloride as a catalyst. The method of doing this was discovered by Charles Friedel and James Crafts.

The mechanism for acylation is a substitution, with RCO substituting for a hydrogen on the aromatic ring.

Acyl chlorides provide the RCO group. They react with $AlCl_3$ to form $AlCl_4^-$ and RCO^+.

$$RCOCl + AlCl_3 \longrightarrow RCO^+ + AlCl_4^-$$

This reaction takes place because the aluminium atom in aluminium chloride has only six electrons in its outer main level and readily accepts a lone pair from the chlorine atom of RCOCl.

RCO^+ is a good electrophile that attacks the benzene ring to form substitution products.

The aluminium chloride is a catalyst – it is reformed by reaction of the $AlCl_4^-$ ion with H^+:

$$AlCl_4^- + H^+ \longrightarrow AlCl_3 + HCl$$

The mechanism for the reaction is:

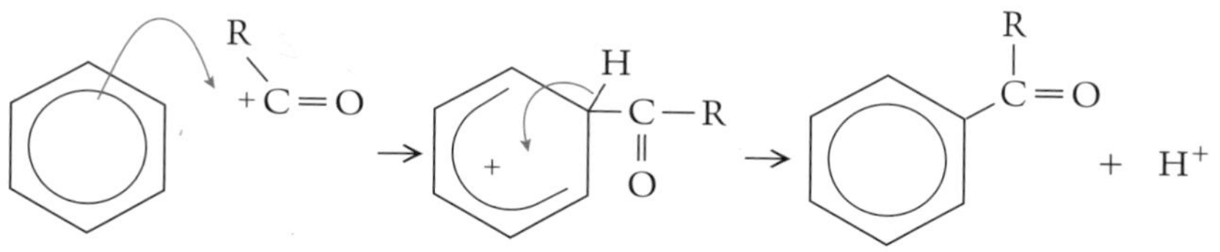

The products are acyl-substituted arenes. The overall reactions are:

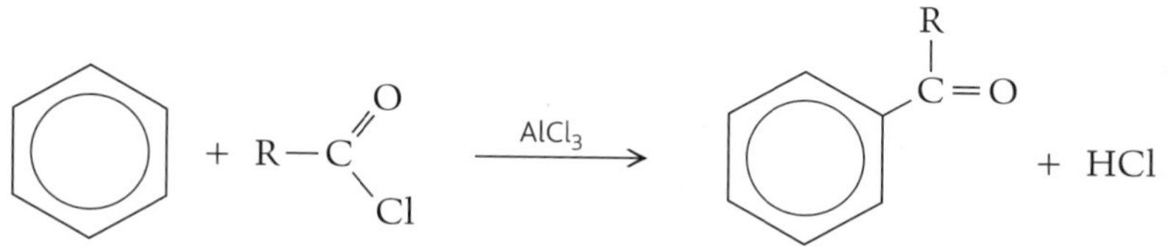

For example, ethanoyl chloride reacts with benzene to form :

CO

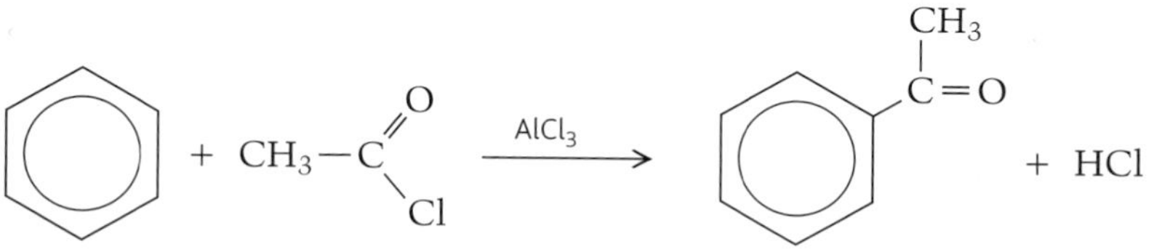

Acylation is a useful step in the synthesis of new substituted aromatic compounds.

Link.

You will need to know the co-ordinate bonding and bond polarity studied in *AQA AS Chemistry*, Topics 3.2 and 3.3 and shapes of molecules studied in *AQA AS Chemistry*, Topic 3.9.

Summary questions

1 Classify **a** nitration **b** Friedel–Crafts reactions as:

A electrophilic substitution

B nucleophilic substitution

C electrophilic addition

D free-radical addition

E free radical substitution

2 Name the two isomers of 1,3-dinitrobenzene.

3 Explain why most of the reactions of benzene are substitutions rather than additions.

4 Write the equation for the reaction between propanoyl chloride with benzene. What species attacks the benzene ring?

AQA Examination-style questions

1 Give reagents and conditions and write equations to show the formation of nitrobenzene from benzene.

Name and outline a mechanism for this reaction of benzene. *(8 marks)*

AQA, 2007

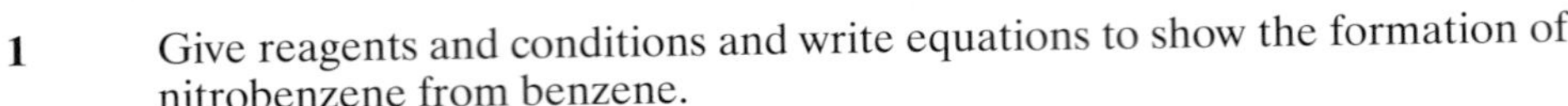

2 A possible synthesis of phenylethene *(styrene)* is outlined below.

$$C_6H_6 \xrightarrow{\text{Reaction 1}} C_6H_5\text{–C(=O)–}CH_3 \xrightarrow{\text{Reaction 2}} C_6H_5\text{–CH(OH)–}CH_3 \xrightarrow{\text{Reaction 3}} C_6H_5\text{–HC=}CH_2$$

In Reaction **1**, ethanoyl chloride and aluminium chloride are used to form a reactive species which then reacts with benzene.

Write an equation to show the formation of the reactive species.

Name and outline the mechanism by which this reactive species reacts with benzene. *(6 marks)*

AQA, 2006

3 An acylium ion has the structure $R\text{—}\overset{+}{C}\text{=O}$ where R is any alkyl group.

In the conversion of benzene into phenylethanone, $C_6H_5COCH_3$, an acylium ion $CH_3\overset{+}{C}O$ reacts with a benzene molecule.

Write an equation to show the formation of this acylium ion from ethanoyl chloride and one other substance.

Name and outline the mechanism of the reaction of this acylium ion with benzene. *(6 marks)*

AQA, 2007

4 An equation for the formation of phenylethanone is shown below. In this reaction a reactive intermediate is formed from ethanoyl chloride. This intermediate then reacts with benzene.

$$C_6H_6 + CH_3COCl \xrightarrow{AlCl_3} C_6H_5\text{–}COCH_3 + HCl$$

(a) Give the formula of the reactive intermediate.

(b) Outline a mechanism for the reaction of this intermediate with benzene to form phenylethanone. *(4 marks)*

5 Propanoyl chloride can be used, together with a catalyst, in the synthesis of 1-phenylpropene from benzene. The first step in the reaction is shown below.

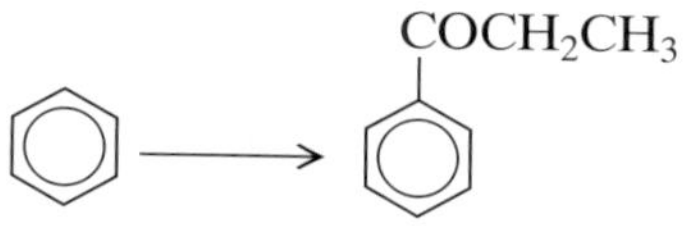

$COCH_2CH_3$

The mechanism of this reaction is an electrophilic substitution. Write an equation to show the formation of the electrophile from propanoyl chloride. Outline the mechanism of the reaction of this electrophile with benzene. *(5 marks)*

AQA, 2004

6 Use the following data to show the stability of benzene relative to the hypothetical cyclohexa-1,2,5-triene.

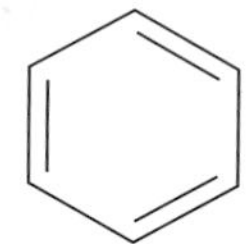

Give a reason for this difference in stability.

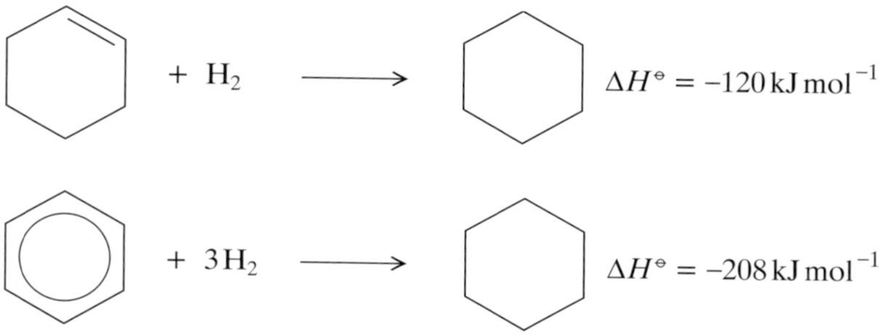

$+ H_2 \longrightarrow$ $\Delta H^\ominus = -120\,\text{kJ mol}^{-1}$

$+ 3H_2 \longrightarrow$ $\Delta H^\ominus = -208\,\text{kJ mol}^{-1}$

(4 marks)

AQA, 2004

7 Amines

7.1 Introduction to amines

Learning objectives:

- What are amines?
- How are they named?
- How do they react?

Specification reference: 3.4.7

This chapter is about a group of compounds called **amines**. Amines can be thought of as derivatives of ammonia in which one or more of the hydrogen atoms in the ammonia molecule have been replaced by alkyl or aryl groups.

$H-\ddot{N}-H$ (with H below N)	$H-\ddot{N}-H$ (with R below N)	$H-\ddot{N}-R'$ (with R below N)	$R''-\ddot{N}-R'$ (with R below N)
ammonia	a primary amine	a secondary amine	a tertiary amine

Amines are very reactive compounds, so they are useful as intermediates in **synthesis** – the making of new molecules.

We use the terms 'primary', 'secondary' and 'tertiary' for amines slightly differently from the way we do with alcohols, see *AQA AS Chemistry*, Topic 16.1. In amines, 1°, 2° and 3° refer to the number of substituents (R-groups) on the *nitrogen* atom. (In alcohols, 1°, 2° and 3° refer to the number of substituents on the *carbon* atom bonded to the —OH group.)

How to name amines

- Primary amines have the general formula RNH_2, where the R can be an alkyl or aryl group. Amines are named using the suffix -amine, for example:

  $CH_3—NH_2$ is methylamine

  $C_2H_5—NH_2$ is ethylamine

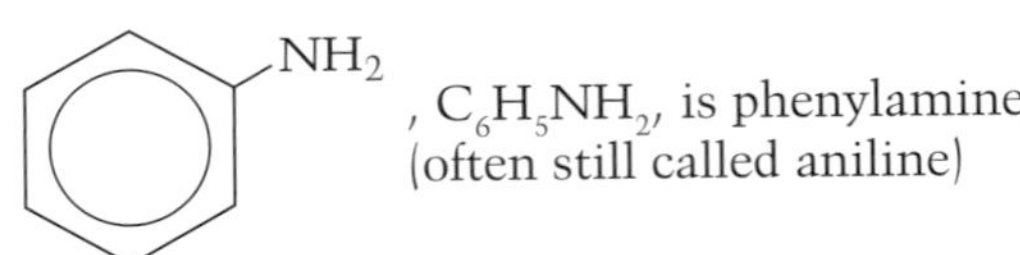

, $C_6H_5NH_2$, is phenylamine, (often still called aniline)

- Secondary amines have the general formula RR′NH, for example:

  $(CH_3)_2N—H$, $(CH_3)_2NH$, is dimethylamine

- Tertiary amines have the general formula RR′R″N, for example:

  $(C_2H_5)_2N—C_2H_5$, $(C_2H_5)_3N$, is triethylamine

Link

An amine is a proton acceptor so it is a Brønsted–Lowry base, see Topic 3.1. An amine is also a Lewis base as it is a lone-pair donor, see Topic 16.1.

Different substituents are written in alphabetical order:

$$\begin{array}{l} CH_3 \\ \quad\backslash \\ \quad N-H, \\ \quad / \\ C_3H_7 \end{array}$$ $CH_3(C_3H_7)NH$, is methylpropylamine

The properties of primary amines

Shape

Ammonia is a pyramidal molecule with bond angles of approximately 107°. (The angles of a perfect tetrahedron are 109.5°.) The difference is caused by the lone pair, which repels more than the bonding pairs of electrons in the N—H bonds. Amines keep this basic shape, see Figure 1.

Boiling points

Amines are polar:

$$R-\underset{H}{\overset{H}{|}}C^{\delta+}-N^{\delta-}\begin{smallmatrix} H^{\delta+} \\ H^{\delta+} \end{smallmatrix}$$

Primary amines can hydrogen bond to one another using their $—NH_2$ groups (in the same way as alcohols with their —OH groups). However, as nitrogen is less electronegative than oxygen (electronegativities: O = 3.5, N = 3.0), the hydrogen bonds are not as strong as those in alcohols. The boiling points of amines are lower than those of comparable alcohols:

methylamine, $M_r = 31$, $CH_3—NH_2$, boiling point = 267 K

methanol, $M_r = 32$, $CH_3—OH$, boiling point = 338 K

Shorter-chain amines such as methylamine and ethylamine are gases at room temperature, and those with slightly longer chains are volatile liquids. They have fishy smells. Rotting fish and rotting animal flesh smell of di- and triamines, produced when proteins decompose.

Solubility

Primary amines with chain lengths up to about C_4 are very soluble both in water and in alcohols because they form hydrogen bonds with these solvents. Most amines are also soluble in less polar solvents. Phenylamine ($C_6H_5NH_2$) is not very soluble in water due to the benzene ring, which cannot form hydrogen bonds.

The reactivity of amines

Amines have a lone pair of electrons and this is important in the way they react. The lone pair may be used to form a bond with:

- an H^+ ion, when we say the amine is acting as a **base**
- an electron-deficient carbon atom, when we say the amine is acting as a **nucleophile**.

Hint

You can remind yourself of the effect of lone pairs on the shapes of molecules in *AQA AS Chemistry*, Topic 3.9.

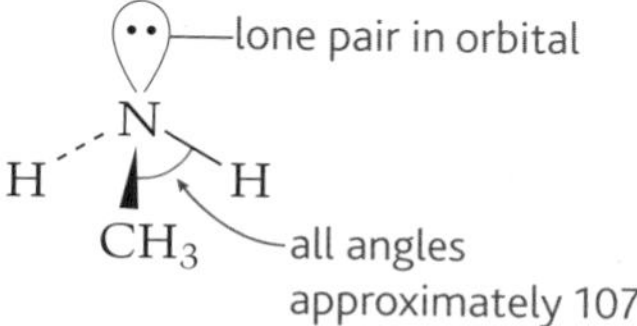

Figure 1 *The shape of the methylamine molecule*

Hint

A lower boiling point means the molecules are easier to separate.

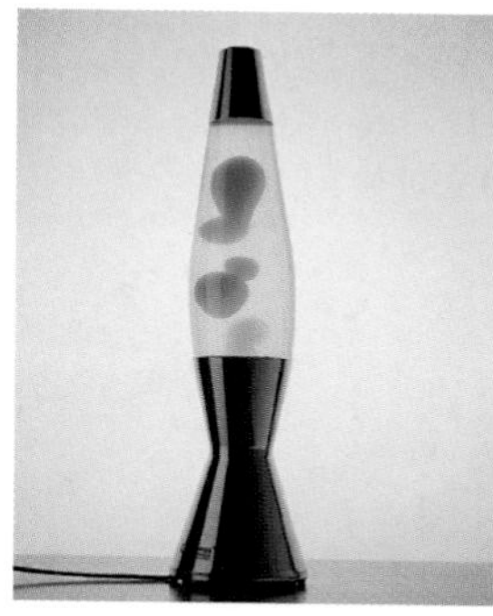

Figure 2 *Phenylamine has almost the same density as water and is not soluble in it. Heat from a bulb at the base of the lava lamp changes the density enough for the phenylamine to float when hot and sink when cool*

Summary questions

1. Classify $C_2H_5—\overset{H}{\overset{|}{N}}—C_3H_7$ as primary, secondary or tertiary.
2. Name the compound in question 1.
3. Write the structural formula of trimethylamine.
4. Predict whether dimethylamine will be a solid, liquid or gas at room temperature.
5. Explain your answer to question 4.

7.2 The base properties of amines

Learning objectives:

- Why do amines behave as Brønsted–Lowry bases?
- Why do the base strengths of amines differ from each other and from ammonia?

Specification reference: 3.4.7

Amines as bases

Amines can accept a proton (an H^+ ion) so they are Brønsted–Lowry bases.

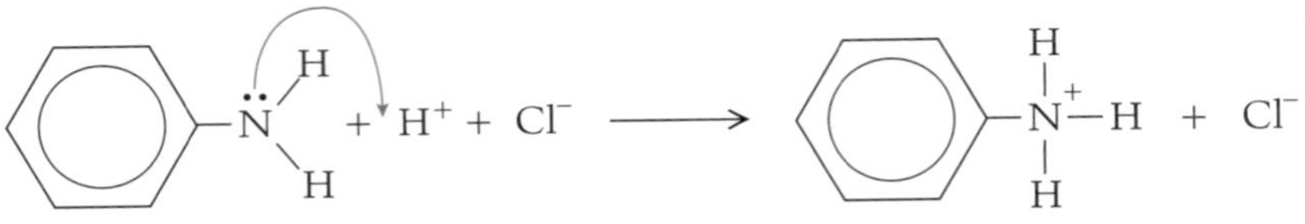

$$C_6H_5\ddot{N}H_2 + H^+ + Cl^- \longrightarrow C_6H_5NH_3^+ + Cl^-$$

phenylamine → phenylammonium chloride (phenylamine hydrochloride) a water-soluble, ionic salt

Reaction as bases

Amines react with acids to form salts. For example, ethylamine, a soluble alkylamine, reacts with dilute hydrochloric acid:

$$C_2H_5\ddot{N}H_2 + H^+ + Cl^- \longrightarrow C_2H_5NH_3^+ + Cl^-$$

ethylamine → ethylammonium chloride (ethylamine hydrochloride)

Hint

The salts of amines are sometimes named as the hydrochloride of the parent amine.

The products are ionic compounds that will crystallise as the water evaporates.

Phenylamine, an arylamine, is relatively insoluble, but it will dissolve in excess hydrochloric acid because it forms the soluble ionic salt.

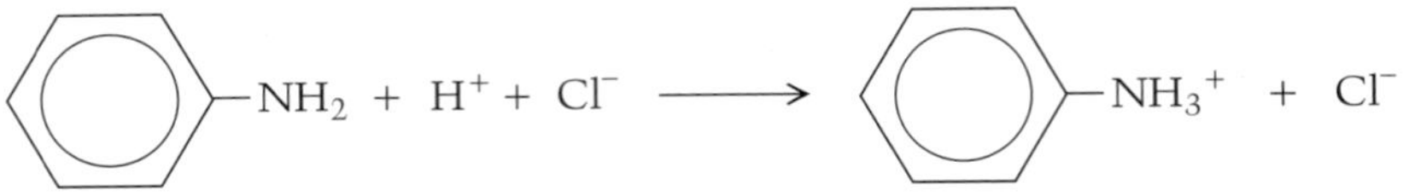

$$C_6H_5NH_2 + H^+ + Cl^- \longrightarrow C_6H_5NH_3^+ + Cl^-$$

phenylamine → phenylammonium chloride (phenylamine hydrochloride) a water-soluble, ionic salt

Hint

The smell of a solution of an amine disappears when an acid in added, due to the formation of the ionic, and therefore involatile, salt.

Then, if a strong base, like sodium hydroxide, is added, it removes the proton from the salt and regenerates the insoluble amine.

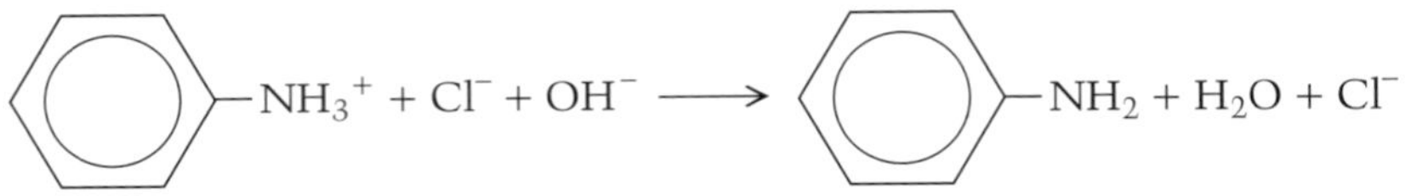

$$C_6H_5NH_3^+ + Cl^- + OH^- \longrightarrow C_6H_5NH_2 + H_2O + Cl^-$$

phenylamine

Comparing base strengths

The strength of a base depends on how readily it will accept a proton, H^+. Both ammonia and amines have a lone pair of electrons that attracts a proton.

Alkyl groups *release* electrons away from the alkyl group and towards the nitrogen atom. This is called **the inductive effect** and is shown by an arrow, as in Figure 1.

The inductive effect of the alkyl group increases the electron density on the nitrogen atom and therefore makes it a better electron pair donor, i.e. more attractive to protons. So, primary alkylamines are stronger bases than ammonia.

Secondary alkylamines have two inductive effects and are therefore stronger bases than primary alkylamines. However, tertiary alkylamines are *not* stronger bases than secondary ones because they are less soluble in water.

Aryl groups *withdraw* electrons from the nitrogen atom because the lone pair of electrons overlaps with the delocalised system on the benzene ring as shown for phenylamine.

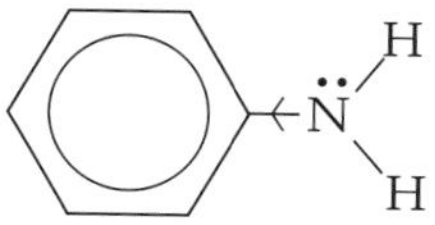

$$C_6H_5 \leftarrow \ddot{N}H_2$$

The nitrogen is a weaker electron pair donor and therefore less attractive to protons, so arylamines are weaker bases than ammonia.

ethylamine > ammonia > phenylamine

strongest ⟶ weakest

Summary questions

1 a Write the equation of dimethylamine reacting with hydrochloric acid.
b Name the product.

2 Phenylamine is not very soluble in water. It forms oily drops that float in the water. Predict what you would see if you:

a Add concentrated hydrochloric acid to a mixture of phenylamine and water.

b Then add sodium hydroxide solution to the resulting solution.

3 Suggest whether dimethylamine will be a weaker or stronger base than ethylamine. Explain your answer.

$$R \rightarrow \ddot{N}H_2$$

Figure 1 *A primary amine. The arrow shows that R releases electrons. This is called the inductive effect*

AQA Examiner's tip

Make sure that you can explain the difference in base strength between ammonia, primary aliphatic and primary aromatic amine.

7.3 Amines as nucleophiles and their synthesis

Learning objectives:

- Why do ammonia and amines act as nucleophiles?
- How do haloalkanes react with ammonia and amines?
- How are amines prepared from nitriles?
- How are aromatic amines synthesised from benzene?

Specification reference: 3.4.7

The lone pair of electrons from an amine will attack positively charged carbon atoms. So, amines, like ammonia, will act as nucleophiles.

Reactions of ammonia with haloalkanes

Primary aliphatic amines are produced when haloalkanes are reacted with ammonia. There is nucleophilic substitution of the halide by NH_2.

$$NH_3 + RX \longrightarrow [RNH_3]^+ X^-$$

$$[RNH_3]^+ X^- + NH_3 \longrightarrow \underset{\text{primary amine}}{RNH_2} + [NH_4]^+ X^-$$

However, the primary amine produced is also a nucleophile and this will react with the haloalkane to produce a secondary amine:

$$RNH_2 + RX \longrightarrow [R_2NH_2]^+ X^-$$

$$[R_2NH_2]^+ X^- + NH_3 \longrightarrow \underset{\text{secondary amine}}{R_2NH} + [NH_4]^+ X^-$$

The secondary amine will react to give a tertiary amine:

$$R_2NH + RX \longrightarrow [R_3NH]^+ X^-$$

$$[R_3NH]^+ X^- + NH_3 \longrightarrow R_3N + [NH_4]^+ X^-$$

and this in turn will react to a produce a quarternary ammonium salt:

$$R_3N + RX \longrightarrow [R_4N]^+ X^-$$

So a mixture of primary, secondary and tertiary amines and a quarternary ammonium salt is produced. This means that this is not a very efficient way of preparing an amine, though the products may be separated by fractional distillation. A large excess of ammonia gives a better yield of primary amine.

The mechanism of the reaction

For all the above reactions the mechanism is essentially the same:

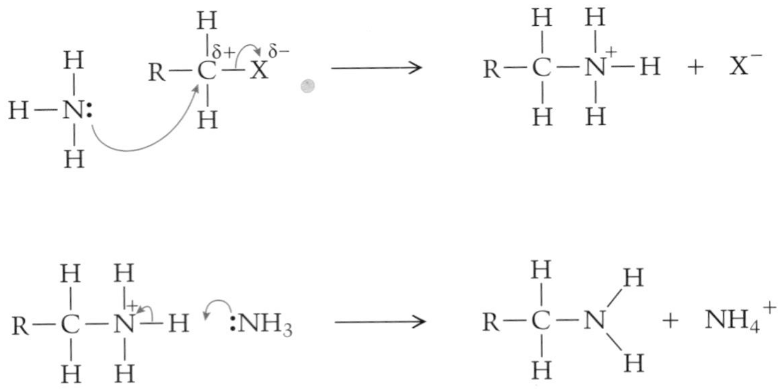

$$H_3N: + R\text{–}CH_2^{\delta+}\text{–}X^{\delta-} \longrightarrow R\text{–}CH_2\text{–}NH_3^+ + X^-$$

$$R\text{–}CH_2\text{–}NH_3^+ + :NH_3 \longrightarrow R\text{–}CH_2\text{–}NH_2 + NH_4^+$$

Link

You will need to know the nucleophilic substitution reactions in haloalkeanes studied in *AQA AS Chemistry*, Topic 14.2, and redox reactions and oxidation states studied in *AQA AS Chemistry*, Topics 10.2 and 10.3.

AQA Examiner's tip

Remember that in these reactions a proton is removed from the initial substitution intermediate so that two moles of ammonia or amine are required for each mole of haloalkane.

Preparation of amines

Primary amines

Reduction of nitriles

Primary aliphatic amines can be prepared from haloalkanes in a two-step process:

Step 1: Haloalkanes react with the cyanide ion in aqueous ethanol. The cyanide ion replaces the halide ion by nucleophilic substitution to form a nitrile:

$$RBr + CN^- \longrightarrow R{-}C{\equiv}N + Br^-$$

Step 2: Nitriles contain the functional group —C≡N. They can be reduced to primary amines by catalytic hydrogenation, for example Ni/H_2:

$$R{-}C{\equiv}N + 2H_2 \longrightarrow R{-}CH_2NH_2$$

This gives a purer product than $RBr + NH_3$ because only the primary amine can be formed.

AQA Examiner's tip

Nitriles cannot be reduced to amines by $NaBH_4$.

Phenylamine

Phenylamine is the simplest arylamine. It is the starting point for making many other chemicals, and is made in industry using benzene produced from crude oil.

Note: This preparation would not be attempted in a school laboratory as benzene is a carcinogen.

Making phenylamine

Phenylamine can be made from benzene.

Step 1: Benzene is reacted with a mixture of concentrated nitric and concentrated sulfuric acid. This produces nitrobenzene:

$$C_6H_6 \text{ (benzene)} + HNO_3 \xrightarrow[H_2SO_4]{conc.} C_6H_5NO_2 \text{ (nitrobenzene)} + H_2O$$

Step 2: Nitrobenzene is reduced to phenylamine, using tin and hydrochloric acid as the reducing agent.

The tin and hydrochloric acid react to form hydrogen, which reduces the nitrobenzene by removing oxygen atoms of the NO_2 group and replacing them with hydrogen atoms.

$$C_6H_5NO_2 + 6[H] \xrightarrow[\text{room temp.}]{Sn/HCl} C_6H_5NH_2 + 2H_2O$$

This could also be written:

$$C_6H_5NO_2 + 6[H] \longrightarrow C_6H_5NH_2 + 2H_2O$$

Since the reaction is carried out in hydrochloric acid, the salt $C_6H_5NH_3^+Cl^-$ is formed and sodium hydroxide is added to liberate the free amine:

$$C_6H_5NH_3^+Cl^- + NaOH \longrightarrow C_6H_5NH_2 + H_2O + NaCl$$

The economic importance of amines

Amines are used in the manufacture of synthetic materials such as nylon and polyurethane, dyes, and drugs.

Quaternary ammonium compounds are used industrially in the manufacture of hair and fabric conditioners. They have a long hydrocarbon chain and a positively charged organic group, so they form cations:

$$\text{(long hydrocarbon chain)}-N^{+}(CH_3)_3 \quad Br^{-}$$

Figure 1 *Hair conditioners*

Both wet fabric and wet hair pick up negative charges on their surfaces. So, the positive charges of the cations attract them to the wet surface and form a coating that prevents the build-up of static electricity. This keeps the surface of the fabric smooth (in fabric conditioner) and prevents 'flyaway' hair (in hair conditioners).

They are called cationic surfactants because in aqueous solution the ions cluster with their charged ends in the water and their hydrocarbon tails on the surface.

How science works

Sulfa drugs

The story of the antibiotic penicillin is well known. It was the result of a chance observation of mould on a discarded Petri dish by Alexander Fleming, and was developed by Howard Flory and Ernst Chain (and a massive industrial effort) into a drug that saved thousands of lives in the Second World War and since. However, it was not the first anti-bacterial drug. Another class of drugs, the sulfanilamides, were already in use before penicillin and may also have had an effect on the course of the war – by saving the life of Prime Minister Winston Churchill.

Towards the end of the nineteenth century, it had been noticed that some dyes used to stain bacteria to make them visible under the microscope could also kill them. Since these dyes were absorbed by the bacteria rather than their surroundings, they might be expected to kill the bacteria but not their host. Eventually the dye Prontosil Rubrum began to be used in medicine to fight bacterial infections.

By the early 1940s it had been established that Prontosil was converted in the body into the compound sulfanilamide which was the active ingredient.

Prontosil Rubrum → sulfanilamide

The drug worked by preventing the bacteria making folic acid, which they need to synthesise DNA and therefore replicate. Bacteria make folic acid from a compound called *para*-aminobenzoic acid (PABA). The sulfanilamide molecule is of a similar shape to PABA and the bacteria try to use it to make folic acid but without success, as it is the wrong molecule. Humans do not need to synthesise folic acid, they get it from their food, and so sulfanilamide kills bacteria but is harmless to humans.

PABA

Since the 1940s over 5000 variations on the sulfanilamide molecule have been synthesised by chemists in an effort to find molecules that are more effective, have fewer side effects are absorbed at a different rate etc. This is one of the main methods used to discover new drugs – to take a molecule with a known beneficial effect and make variations on it in the hope of maintaining or enhancing its activity but reducing any disadvantages that it might have. Nowadays, this process can be speeded up by the technique of combinatorial chemistry – see Topic 8.2.

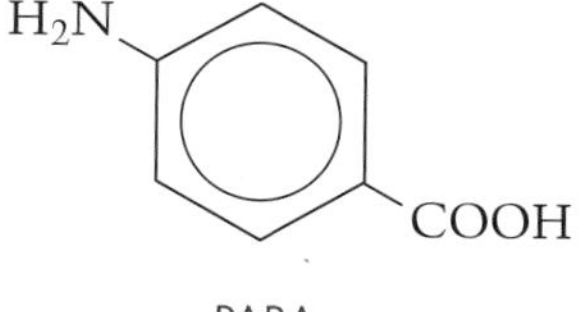

PABA

Although less common than they once were, sulfa drugs are still used today. The one that cured Winston Churchill's pneumonia in 1943 was sulfapyridine, known at the time as M & B 693, after the makers the May & Baker Company. May & Baker is still in business and supplies chemicals for school laboratories as well as making drugs. Look for their labels in your school prep. room.

1 What is the systematic name of PABA?

Summary questions

1 Why is nucleophilic substitution of a halolkane not a good method for preparing a primary amine?

2 a Write the equation for the reaction of chloroethane with an excess of ammonia. Give the reaction mechanism.

b What are the other possible products of this reaction?

8 Amino acids

8.1 Introduction to amino acids

Learning objectives:

- What are amino acids?
- Why do they have both acidic and basic properties?

Specification reference: 3.4.8

$$CH_3-\underset{H}{\overset{NH_2}{C}}-C(=O)OH$$

Figure 1 *α-aminopropanoic acid, also called alanine, written in shorthand as $CH_3CH(NH_2)COOH$*

Hint

Compounds with two functional groups are called **bifunctional compounds**.

Synoptic link

You will need to know the the nature of ionic bonding and states of matter studied in *AQA AS Chemistry*, Topics 3.1 and 3.7.

Amino acids are the building blocks of proteins, which in turn are a vital component of all living systems.

Amino acids have two functional groups: a carboxylic acid and a primary amine. There are 20 important naturally occurring amino acids and they are all α-amino acids (also called 2-amino acids) which means that the amine group is on the carbon next to the $—CO_2H$ group, see Figure 1.

α-amino acids have the general formula:

$$H_2\ddot{N}-\underset{H}{\overset{R}{C}}-C(=O)-O-H$$

Notice that this structure has a carbon bonded to four different groups. The molecule is therefore chiral. Virtually all naturally occurring amino acids exist as the –enantiomer, see Optical activity, Topic 4.2.

Acid and base properties

Amino acids have both an acidic and a basic functional group.

- The carboxylic acid group has a tendency to lose a proton (act as an acid):

$$-C(=O)OH \rightleftharpoons -C(=O)O^- + H^+$$

- The amine group has a tendency to accept a proton (act as a base):

$$H^+ + H-\underset{H}{\ddot{N}}- \rightleftharpoons H-\underset{H}{\overset{H}{N^+}}-$$

Amino acids exist as **zwitterions.** Ions like these have both a permanent positive and negative charge, though the compound is neutral overall.

$$H-\underset{H}{\overset{H}{N^+}}-\underset{H}{\overset{R}{C}}-C(=O)O^-$$

a zwitterion

Because they are ionic, amino acids have high melting points, and dissolve well in water but poorly in non-polar solvents. A typical amino acid is a white solid at room temperature and behaves very much like an ionic salt.

In strongly acidic conditions the lone pair of the $H_2N—$ group accepts a proton to form the positive ion:

$$H-\underset{H}{\overset{H}{N^+}}-\underset{H}{\overset{R}{C}}-C(=O)-O-H$$

- The amino group has gained a hydrogen ion – we say it is **protonated**.

In strongly alkaline solutions, the —O—H group loses a proton to form the negative ion:

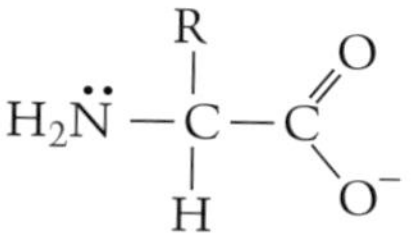

$$H_2\ddot{N}-\underset{H}{\overset{R}{C}}-C\begin{matrix} =O \\ -O^- \end{matrix}$$

- The carboxylic acid group has lost a hydrogen ion – we say it is **deprotonated**.

Table 1 shows some naturally occurring amino acids. Each of these is usually referred to by its non-systematic name (the IUPAC names can be complex) and also by a three-letter abbreviation which is useful when describing the sequences of amino acids in proteins, see Topic 8.2.

Summary questions

1 The systematic name of glycine is 2-aminoethanoic acid. What is the systematic name of alanine (see Table 1)?

2 Explain why alanine is chiral whereas glycine is not.

Table 1 *Twenty naturally occurring amino acids*

Formula	Name and abbreviation	Formula	Name and abbreviation
H_2NCHCO_2H with H on the central C	glycine (Gly)	H_2NCHCO_2H – CHOH – CH_3	threonine (Thr)
H_2NCHCO_2H – CH_3	alanine (Ala)	H_2NCHCO_2H – CH_2SH	cysteine (Cys)
H_2NCHCO_2H – $CHCH_3$ – CH_3	valine (Val)	H_2NCHCO_2H – CH_2 – $CONH_2$	asparagine (Asn)
H_2NCHCO_2H – CH_2 – $CH_3(CH_3)_2$	leucine (Leu)	H_2NCHCO_2H – CH_2 – CH_2CONH_2	glutamine (Gln)
H_2NCHCO_2H – CHC_2H_5 – CH_3	isoleucine (Ile)	H_2NCHCO_2H – CH_2–(benzene ring)–OH	tyrosine (Tyr)
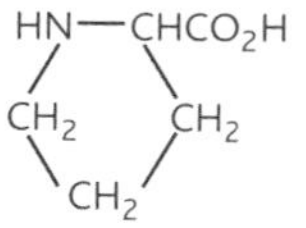 HN—$CHCO_2H$ in a ring with CH_2, CH_2, CH_2	proline (Pro) (Note: Proline is a secondary amine)	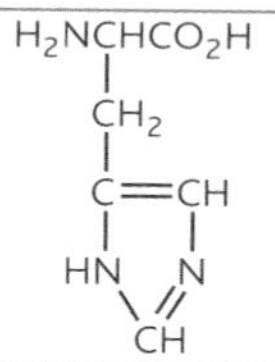 H_2NCHCO_2H – CH_2 – C=CH, HN, N, CH (ring)	histidine (His)
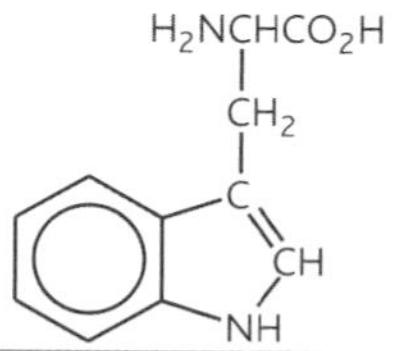 H_2NCHCO_2H – CH_2 – C (ring with CH, NH fused to a benzene ring)	tryptophan (Try)	H_2NCHCO_2H – $(CH_2)_3$ – NH – NH=C—NH_2	arginine (Arg)
H_2NCHCO_2H – CH_2 – CH_2SCH_3	methionine (Met)	H_2NCHCO_2H – $(CH_2)_3$ – CH_2NH_2	lysine (Lys)
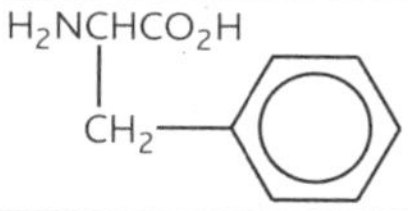 H_2NCHCO_2H – CH_2–(benzene ring)	phenylalanine (Phe)	H_2NCHCO_2H – CH_2CO_2H	aspartic acid (Asp)
H_2NCHCO_2H – CH_2OH	serine (Ser)	H_2NCHCO_2H – CH_2 – CH_2CO_2H	glutamic acid (Glu)

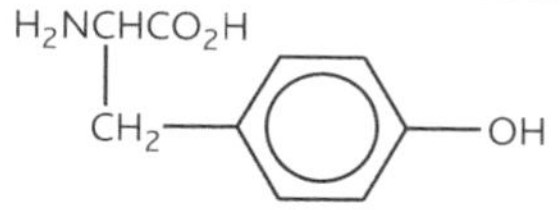

8.2 Peptides, polypeptides and proteins

Learning objectives:

- How do amino acids form proteins?
- How can proteins be broken down?
- Why is hydrogen bonding in proteins important?

Specification reference: 3.4.8

Amino acids link together to form peptides. Molecules containing up to about 50 amino acids are referred to as polypeptides, when there are more than 50 amino acids they are called proteins. Naturally occurring proteins are everywhere – enzymes, wool, hair, muscles are all examples.

Amino acids and the peptide links

An amide has the functional group —$CONH_2$, $-C(=O)NH_2$

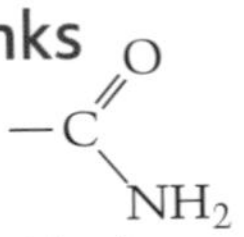

The amine group of one amino acid can react with the carboxylic acid group of another to form an **amide linkage** —CONH—.

This linkage is shown by shading in Figure 1.

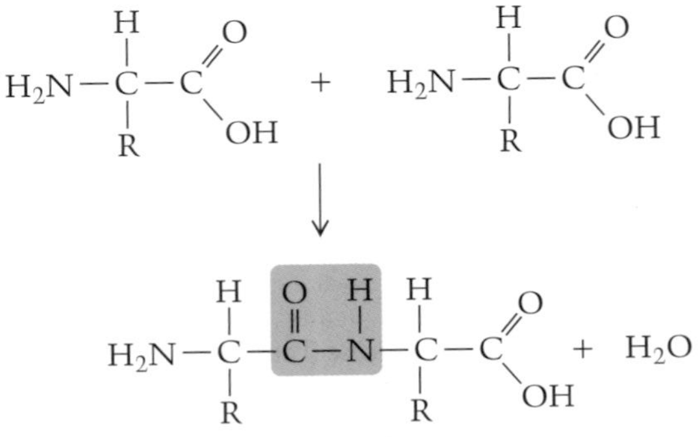

$$H_2N-CH(R)-COOH + H_2N-CH(R)-COOH \rightarrow H_2N-CH(R)-CO-NH-CH(R)-COOH + H_2O$$

a dipeptide

Figure 1 *Formation of a dipeptide*

Compounds formed by the linkage of amino acids are called **peptides**, and the amide linkage is called a peptide linkage in this context. A peptide with two amino acids is called a **dipeptide**. The dipeptide still retains —NH_2 and —CO_2H groups and so can react further to give tri- and tetra- peptides and so on, see Figure 2.

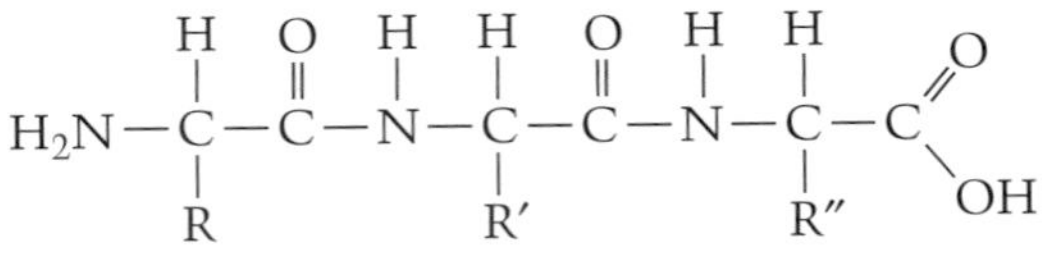

$$H_2N-CH(R)-CO-NH-CH(R')-CO-NH-CH(R'')-COOH$$

Figure 2 *A tripeptide – R, R′ and R″ may be the same or different*

A particular protein will have a fixed sequence of amino acids in its chain. This is called the **primary structure** of the protein. For example, just one short sequence of the protein insulin (the hormone controlling sugar metabolism) runs:

-Ala-Glu-Ala-Leu-Tyr-

(See Table 1 in Topic 8.1.)

Polypeptides and proteins are condensation polymers (see Topic 9.2) because a small molecule, in this case water, is eliminated as each link of the chain forms.

Hydrolysis

When a protein or a peptide is boiled with hydrochloric acid of concentration 6 mol dm^{-3} for about 24 hours it breaks down to a mixture of all the amino acids that made up the original protein or peptide. All the peptide linkages are hydrolysed by the acid, see Figure 3.

$$H_2N-\underset{\displaystyle R}{\overset{\displaystyle H}{C}}-\overset{\displaystyle O}{\overset{\|}{C}}-\overset{\displaystyle H}{N}-\underset{\displaystyle R}{\overset{\displaystyle H}{C}}-C\begin{matrix}\diagup\!\!\!\!/ O\\ \diagdown OH\end{matrix} + H_2O \xrightarrow[\text{catalyst}]{H^+} 2\,H_2N-\underset{\displaystyle R}{\overset{\displaystyle H}{C}}-C\begin{matrix}\diagup\!\!\!\!/ O\\ \diagdown OH\end{matrix}$$

Figure 3 *The hydrolysis of the peptide link*

The mixture of amino acids can be separated and identified using paper chromatography (see Topic 11.7).

Certain enzymes will partially hydrolyse specific proteins. For example, the enzyme trypsin will only break the peptide bonds formed by lysine and arginine. Detective work, based on this and other techniques, enables chemists to find the sequence of amino acids in different proteins.

> **AQA Examiner's tip**
>
> As they can be hydrolysed, proteins are biodegradable.

The structure of proteins

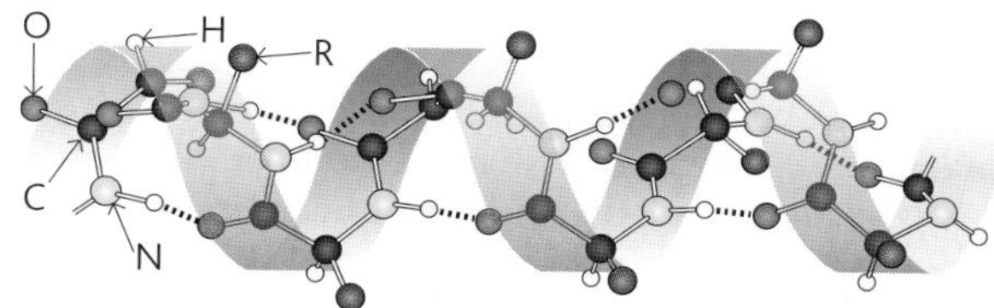

Figure 4 *The helical structure of a protein. Hydrogen bonds are shown as dotted lines.*

> **Link**
>
> You will need to know the bond polarity and forces acting between molecules studied in *AQA AS Chemistry*, Topics 3.3 and 3.5.

Proteins have complex shapes which are held in position by hydrogen bonds. The shapes of proteins are vital to their functions – as enzymes and structural materials in living things, for example. Many proteins are helical (spiral). Hydrogen bonding holds the helix in shape, see Figures 4 and 5.

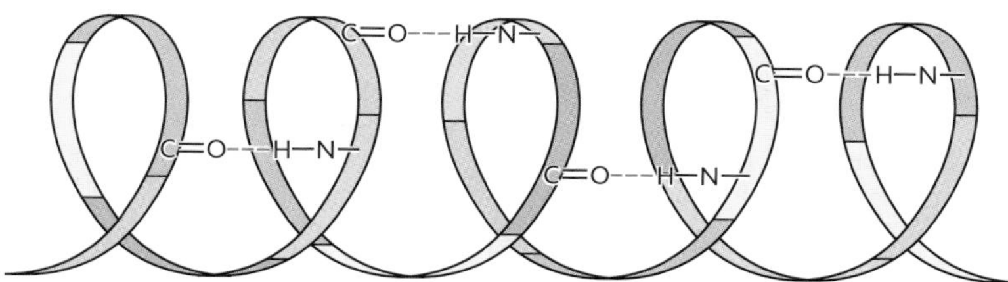

Figure 5 *The helix of a protein is held together by hydrogen bonding. The coloured strips represent amino acids (there are 18 to every 5 turns of the helix)*

Another arrangement of a protein is called **pleating** and the protein ends up as a pleated sheet. The hydrogen bonding is shown in Figure 6.

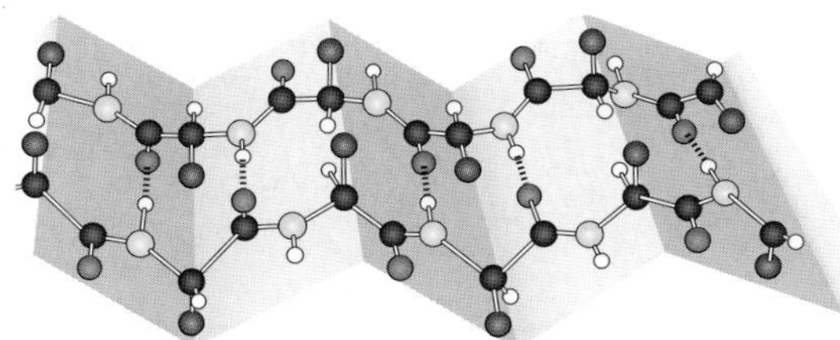

Figure 6 *A pleated sheet protein showing the hydrogen bonds as dotted lines*

The properties of proteins

Chemists have built computer models of the structures of proteins and from these it is possible to see how their structures influence their properties. We will look at just two examples.

Enzymes

Enzymes are immensely efficient protein-based catalysts which occur in living systems. They can accelerate reactions by factors of up to 10^{10}. (This means that a reaction which is complete in *1 second* with the enzyme would take *300 years* without it.)

Enzymes are very specific, usually catalysing just one reaction of one compound called the **substrate** of that enzyme.

Enzymes fit closely to the molecules that are reacting and temporarily hold them in the correct orientation to react. The shape of the enzyme is thus very important. Figure 7 shows a model of the enzyme lysozyme, a naturally occuring antibiotic found in tears. It catalyses the breakdown of polysaccharides, found in the cell walls of bacteria, and this kills the bacteria. The substrate fits into the deep cavity in the enzyme called the **active site** of the enzyme.

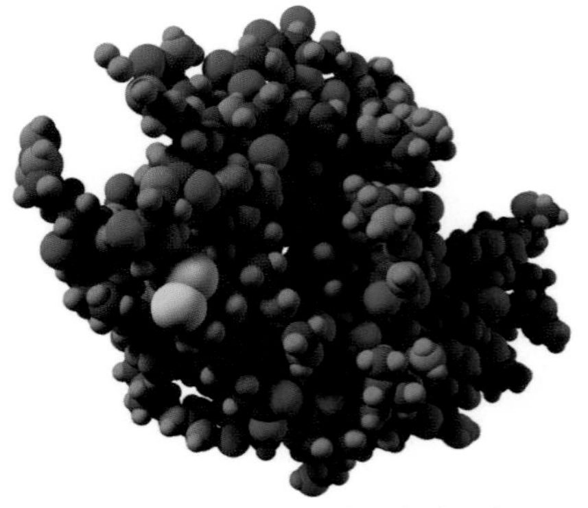

Figure 7 *A lysozyme molecule showing the substrate in yellow (computer graphic)*

Because the catalytic activity of an enzyme is so dependent on its shape, enzymes are very sensitive to changes in temperature and pH. These can disrupt the hydrogen bonds responsible for their shapes. Most enzymes will rapidly denature (change their shape) at temperatures above about 320 K. This is why enzymes have an **optimum temperature** as catalysts. Below the optimum temperature, the reaction is slow for the usual reasons. Above this temperature, the enzyme denatures and loses its catalytic effect.

The stretchiness of wool

Wool is a protein fibre with a helix which is, as usual, held together by hydrogen bonds, Figure 8. When wool is gently stretched, the hydrogen bonds stretch, Figure 9, and the fibre extends. Releasing the tension allows the hydrogen bonds to return to their normal length and the fibre returns to its original shape. However, washing at high temperatures can permanently break the hydrogen bonds and a garment may permanently lose its shape.

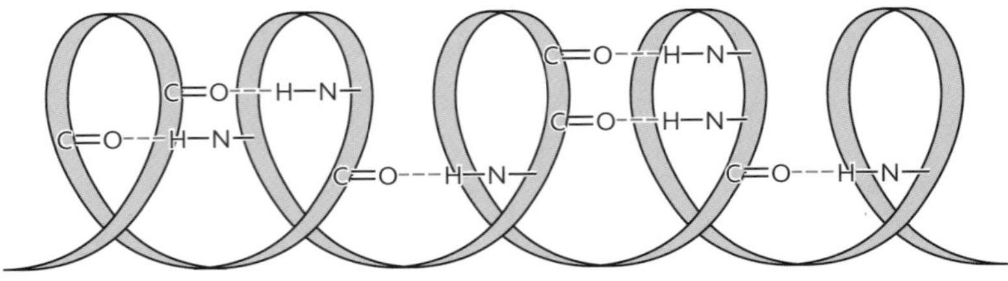

Figure 8 *Hydrogen bonds in wool*

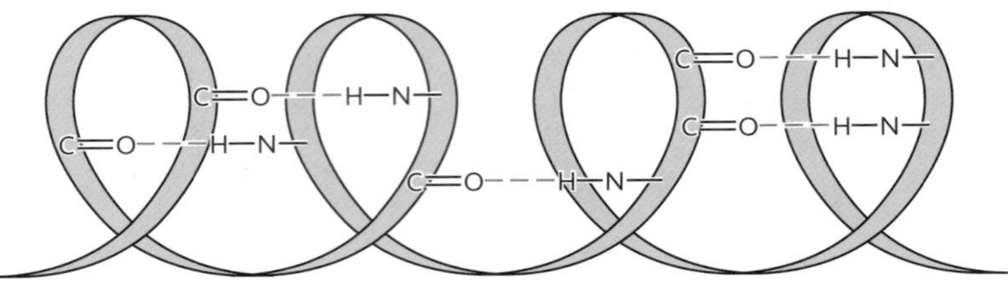

Figure 9 *The wool is gently stretched*

How science works

Combinatorial chemistry

Robots in the lab

Visit a laboratory belonging to a pharmaceutical company which is searching for new drug substances (called 'new chemical entities' or NCEs in the jargon) and you are likely to find robots doing at least some of the work. These are not androids in lab coats, they are essentially motorised syringes under computer control (see Figure 10) but they can take over a lot of routine operations in synthetic organic chemistry.

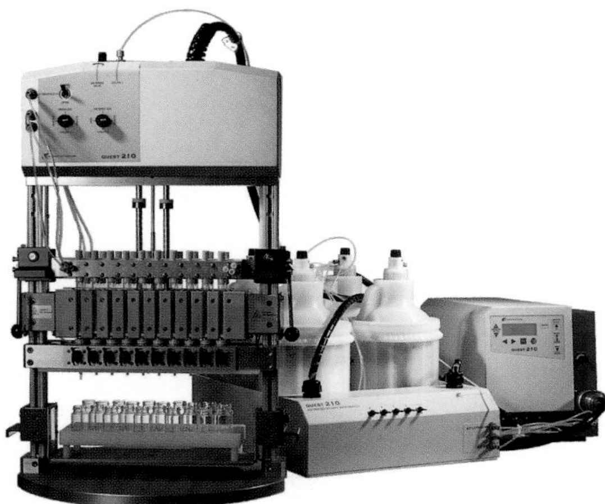

Figure 10 *A combinatorial chemistry 'robot'*

Drug companies deal in 'libraries' of compounds – sets of related compounds, which they then screen for possible activity as drugs. Thanks to recent advances in methods of rapid screening of compounds for activity, there is a demand for more and more compounds to be made. One method of doing this, called combinatorial chemistry, is to make libraries of compound trays often containing 96 sample tubes in an 8 × 12 array., see Figure 11.

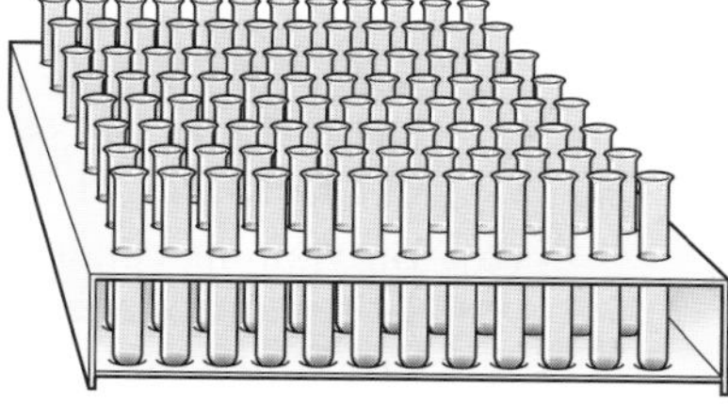

Figure 11 *A library tray*

Using, for example, 8 alcohols and 12 acid chlorides a set (or library) of 96 different esters can be made simply by mixing all possible combinations of alcohol and acid chloride. The robot can be programmed to do this quite simply and the tray of 96 esters can then be used for screening.

It is possible to programme a sequence of chemical operations, not just one. For example, some companies are looking at short chains of amino acids linked in different orders – these are called **oligopeptides** if they have up to 10 amino acids. There are over 10^{13} decapeptides that can be made from the 20 naturally occurring amino acids!

The above technique can be combined with another method called **solid phase chemistry**. Here, one of the starting materials is chemically bonded to plastic beads while a reagent in solution is added to it. The product remains bonded to the bead which makes purification of the product simple – any unwanted solutions can simply be washed away. If required, further reaction steps can be done with the product still bonded to the beads. When required, the product can be released from the bead by reversing the reaction which bonded it in the first place.

Summary questions

1. a What are the functional groups in an amino acid?
   b Which group is acidic and which basic?
2. How many amide (peptide) linkages are there in a tripeptide?

AQA Examination-style questions

1 (a) Name the compound $(CH_3)_2NH$ *(1 mark)*

(b) $(CH_3)_2NH$ can be formed by the reaction of an excess of CH_3NH_2 with CH_3Br. Name and outline a mechanism for this reaction. *(5 marks)*

(c) Name the type of compound produced when a large excess of CH_3Br reacts with CH_3NH_2 Give a use for this type of compound. *(2 marks)*

AQA, 2006

2 Consider the following reaction sequence.

methylbenzene ($C_6H_5CH_3$) —Step 1→ **E** (4-nitromethylbenzene: CH_3 and NO_2 para on benzene ring) —Step 2→ **F** (4-methylphenylamine: CH_3 and NH_2 para on benzene ring)

(a) For Step 2, give a reagent or combination of reagents. Write an equation for this reaction using [H] to represent the reductant. *(2 marks)*

(b) Draw the structure of the species formed by **F** in an excess of hydrochloric acid. *(1 mark)*

(c) Compounds **G** and **H** are both monosubstituted benzenes and both are isomers of **F**. **G** is a primary amine and **H** is a secondary amine. Draw the structures of **G** and **H**. *(2 marks)*

AQA, 2005

3 (a) Name and outline a mechanism for the formation of butylamine, $CH_3CH_2CH_2CH_2NH_2$ by the reaction of ammonia with 1-bromobutane, $CH_3CH_2CH_2CH_2Br$. *(5 marks)*

(b) Butylamine can also be prepared in a two-step synthesis starting from 1-bromopropane, $CH_3CH_2CH_2Br$. Write an equation for each of the two steps in this synthesis. *(3 marks)*

(c) Explain why butylamine is a stronger base than ammonia. *(2 marks)*

(d) Draw the structure of a tertiary amine which is an isomer of butylamine. *(1 mark)*

AQA, 2004

4 Propylamine, $CH_3CH_2CH_2NH_2$ can be formed either by nucleophilic substitution or by reduction.

(a) Draw the structure of a compound which can undergo nucleophilic substitution to form propylamine. *(1 mark)*

(b) Draw the structure of the nitrile which can be reduced to form propylamine. *(1 mark)*

(c) State and explain which of the two routes to propylamine, by nucleophilic substitution or by reduction, gives the less pure product. Draw the structure of a compound formed as an impurity. *(3 marks)*

AQA, 2006

5 (a) The structure of the amino acid *alanine* is shown below.

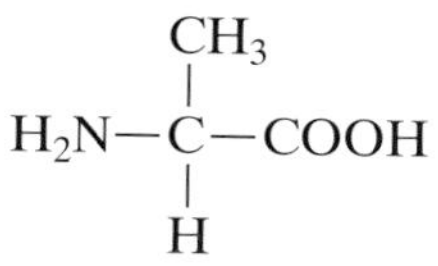

$$\begin{array}{c} CH_3 \\ | \\ H_2N-C-COOH \\ | \\ H \end{array}$$

(i) Draw the structure of the zwitterion formed by *alanine*.

(ii) Draw the structure of the organic product formed in each case from *alanine* when it reacts with:

CH_3OH in the presence of a small amount of concentrated sulfuric acid

Na_2CO_3

CH_3Cl in a 1:1 mole ratio *(4 marks)*

(b) The amino acid *lysine* is shown below.

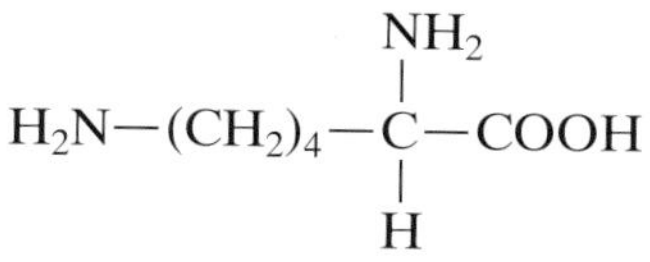

$$\begin{array}{c} NH_2 \\ | \\ H_2N-(CH_2)_4-C-COOH \\ | \\ H \end{array}$$

Draw the structure of the *lysine* species present in a solution at low pH. *(1 mark)*

(c) The amino acid *proline* is shown below.

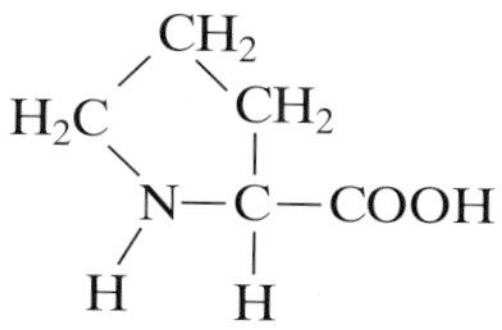

$$\begin{array}{c} CH_2 \\ H_2C \quad\quad CH_2 \\ N-C-COOH \\ H \quad\quad H \end{array}$$

Draw the structure of the dipeptide formed from two *proline* molecules. *(1 mark)*

AQA, 2007

6 The amino acid *alanine* is shown below.

$$\begin{array}{c} CH_3 \\ | \\ H_2N-C-COOH \\ | \\ H \end{array}$$

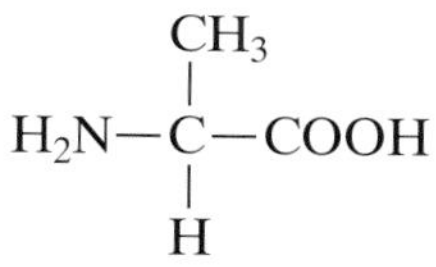

(a) Give the systematic name for alanine. *(1 mark)*

(b) (i) Draw the structure of the dipeptide formed from two alanine molecules, showing clearly the full structure of the peptide link.

(ii) Draw the structure of the organic compound formed by the reaction of alanine with propan-2-ol in the presence of a small amount of the catalyst concentrated sulfuric acid.

(iii) Draw the structure of the *N*–substituted amide formed by the reaction of alanine with ethanoyl chloride. Name the type of mechanism involved. *(4 marks)*

(c) A solution was prepared by reacting alanine with an equal number of moles of hydrochloric acid. This solution was titrated with aqueous sodium hydroxide. The titration curve obtained is shown in the figure below.

(i) Draw the structure of the alanine species present at point **X** on the curve.

(ii) Draw the structure of the alanine species present at point **Y** on the curve. *(2 marks)*

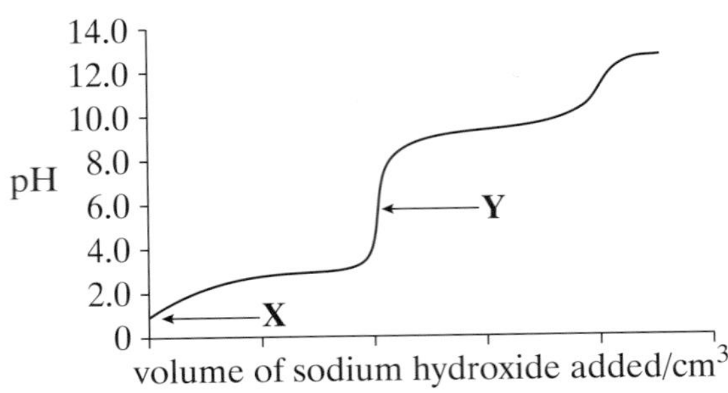

AQA, 2007

7 Draw the structures of the **two** dipeptides which can form when one of the amino acids shown below reacts with the other.

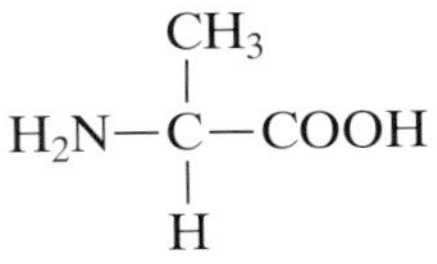

$$\begin{array}{c} CH_3 \\ | \\ H_2N-C-COOH \\ | \\ H \end{array} \qquad \begin{array}{c} CH_2OH \\ | \\ H_2N-C-COOH \\ | \\ H \end{array}$$

structure 1 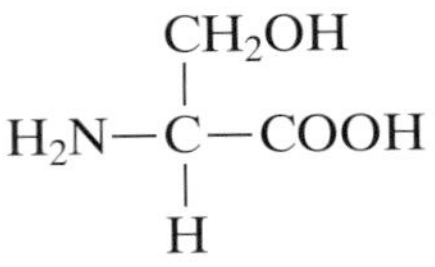 structure 2 *(2 marks)*

AQA, 2006

8 (a) Draw the structure of the species present in solid aminoethanoic acid, H_2NCH_2COOH. *(1 mark)*

(b) Explain why the melting point of aminoethanoic acid is much higher than that of hydroxyethanoic acid, $HOCH_2COOH$. *(2 marks)*

AQA, 2006

9 When the dipeptide shown below is heated under acidic conditions, a single amino acid is produced.

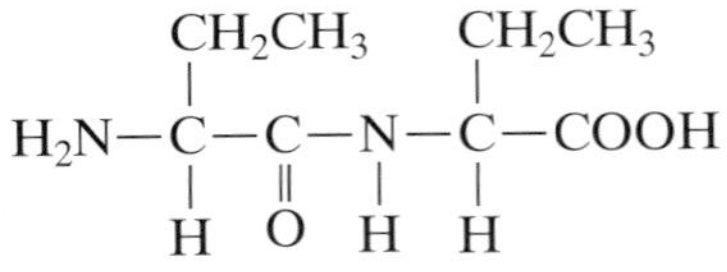

$$\begin{array}{ccccccccc} & & CH_2CH_3 & & & & CH_2CH_3 & & \\ & & | & & & & | & & \\ H_2N & - & C & - & C & - & N & - & C - COOH \\ & & | & & \| & & | & & | \\ & & H & & O & & H & & H \end{array}$$

(a) Name this amino acid. *(1 mark)*

(b) Draw the structure of the amino acid species present in the acidic solution. *(1 mark)*

AQA, 2004

10 Consider the following amino acid

$$\begin{array}{c} \text{H} \\ | \\ \text{H}_2\text{N}-\text{C}-\text{COOH} \\ | \\ \text{CH(CH}_3)_2 \end{array}$$

(a) Draw the structure of the amino acid present in the solution at pH12.

(b) Draw the structure of the dipeptide formed from two molecules of this amino acid.

(c) Protein chains are often arranged in the shape of a helix. Name the type of interaction that is responsible for holding the protein chain in this shape. *(3 marks)*

AQA, 2004

11 The structures of the amino acids alanine and glycine are shown below.

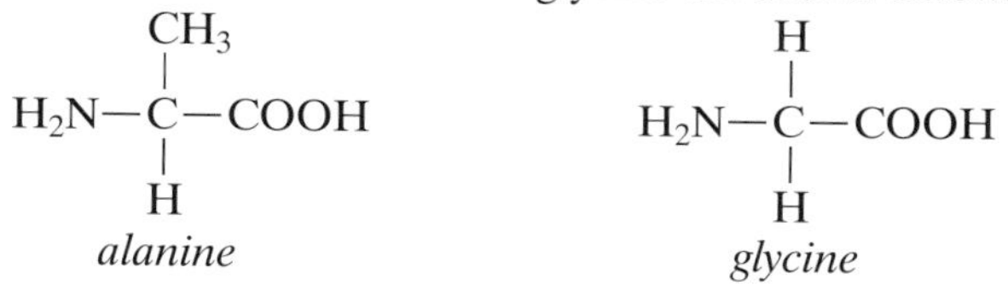

Alanine exists as a pair of stereoisomers.

(a) Explain the meaning of the term stereoisomers.

(b) State how you could distinguish between the stereoisomers. *(4 marks)*

AQA, 2003

9 Polymerisation

9.1 Addition polymers

Learning objectives:

- What is an addition polymer?
- What sort of molecules react to form addition polymers?

Specification reference: 3.4.9

Link

You will need to know the polymerisation of alkenes studied in *AQA AS Chemistry*, Topic 15.3.

Figure 1 *Polymers around us*

AQA Examiner's tip

Addition polymers are named systematically with the prefix 'poly' followed by the name of the monomer in brackets. They are often called poly(alkenes). Non-systematic names are often used for everyday and commercial purposes.

Polymers are very large molecules that are built up from small molecules, called **monomers**. They occur naturally everywhere: starch, proteins, cellulose and DNA are all polymers. The first completely synthetic polymer was Bakelite, which was patented in 1907. Since then, many synthetic polymers have been developed with a range of properties to suit them for very many applications, see Figure 1.

One way of classifying polymers is by the type of reaction by which they are made.

Addition polymers are made from a monomer or monomers with a carbon–carbon double bond. We met addition polymers in *AQA AS Chemistry*, Topic 15.3. Addition polymers are made from monomers based on ethene. The monomer has the general formula:

$$\begin{array}{ccc} H & & H \\ & C{=}C & \\ H & & R \end{array}$$

When the monomers polymerise, the double bond opens and the monomers bond together to form a backbone of carbon atoms as shown:

$$\begin{array}{ccc} H & & H \\ & C{=}C & \\ H & & R \end{array} + \begin{array}{ccc} H & & H \\ & C{=}C & \\ H & & R \end{array} + \begin{array}{ccc} H & & H \\ & C{=}C & \\ H & & R \end{array} \longrightarrow$$

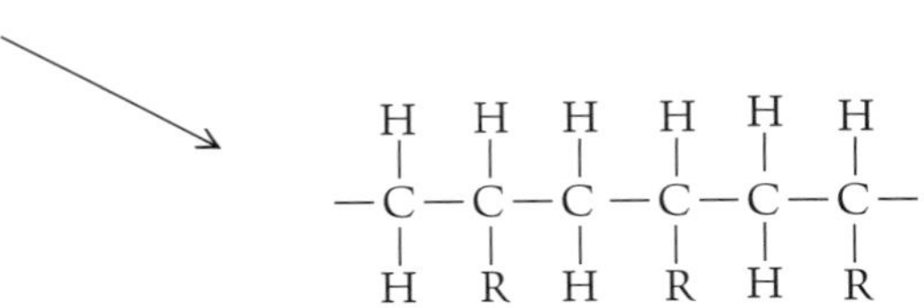

This may also be represented by equations such as:

$$n \begin{array}{cc} H & H \\ | & | \\ C & {=}C \\ | & | \\ H & R \end{array} \longrightarrow \left[\begin{array}{cc} H & H \\ | & | \\ -C & -C- \\ | & | \\ H & R \end{array} \right]_n$$

R may be an alkyl or an aryl group.

For example, phenylethene polymerises to poly(phenylethene):

$$\cdots + H_2C{=}CH(C_6H_5) + H_2C{=}CH(C_6H_5) + H_2C{=}CH(C_6H_5) + \cdots$$

phenylethene

$$\downarrow$$

$$\cdots-CH_2-CH(C_6H_5)-CH_2-CH(C_6H_5)-CH_2-CH(C_6H_5)-\cdots$$

poly(phenylethene)

Figure 2 *Both the model and the packaging are made from polystyrene*

Phenylethene is sometimes called styrene, which is why poly(phenylethene) is usually called polystyrene.

Table 1 gives some examples of addition polymers based on different substituents.

Table 1 *Some addition polymers made from the monomer $H_2C{=}CHR$*

R	Name of polymer	Common or trade name
$-H$	poly(ethene)	polythene (Alkathene)
$-CH_3$	poly(propene)	polypropylene
$-Cl$	poly(chloroethene)	pvc (polyvinyl chloride)
$-C{\equiv}N$	poly(propenenitrile)	acrylic (Acrilan, Courtelle)
$-C_6H_5$	poly(phenylethene)	polystyrene

Table 2 *Addition polymers – each of these polymers is based on ethene but has different properties, depending on the substituent*

Monomer	Polymer
$CH_2{=}CH_2$	$\left[CH_2-CH_2\right]_n$
$CH(CH_3){=}CH_2$	$\left[CH(CH_3)-CH_2\right]_n$
$CH(Cl){=}CH_2$	$\left[CH(Cl)-CH_2\right]_n$
$CH(CN){=}CH_2$	$\left[CH(CN)-CH_2\right]_n$
$CH(C_6H_5){=}CH_2$	$\left[CH(C_6H_5)-CH_2\right]_n$

Identifying the addition polymer formed from the monomer

The best way to think about this is to remember that an addition polymer is formed from monomers with carbon–carbon double bonds.

There is usually only one monomer (though it is possible to have more), and the double bond opens to form a single bond, see Table 2. This will give the repeat unit for the polymer.

Identifying the monomer(s) used to make an addition polymer

An addition polymer must have a backbone of carbon atoms and the monomer must contain at least two carbons, so that there can be a carbon–carbon double bond. So, in the molecule below the monomer is shown in the red brackets:

$$\sim CH_2-\left[CH_2-CH_2\right]-CH_2-CH_2-CH_2\sim \qquad \text{monomer} \quad H_2C{=}CH_2$$

Where some of the carbon atoms have substituents, the monomer must have the substituent, as well as a double bond:

Examiner's tip

Make sure that you understand why polyalkenes are chemically inert.

```
   H  [CH3 H ] CH3 H  CH3
   |  [ |   |]  |   |   |
~~C-[-C - C-]-C - C - C~~
   |  [ |   |]  |   |   |
   H  [ H   H]  H   H   H
```

monomer

```
CH3     H
   \   /
    C=C
   /   \
  H     H
```

Biodegradability

Polyalk*enes*, in spite of their name, have a backbone which is a long chain saturated alk*ane* molecule. Alkanes have strong non-polar C—C and C—H bonds. So, they are very unreactive molecules, which is a useful property in many ways. However, this does mean that they are not attacked by biological agents – like enzymes – and so they are not biodegradable. This is an increasing problem in today's world, where waste disposal is becoming more and more difficult.

Summary questions

1 Which of the following monomers could form an addition polymer?

```
a  H     H        b  F     F
    \   /             \   /
     C=C               C=C
    /   \             /   \
   H     H           F     F

          NH2
           |
c  CH3 — C — COOH    d  H     H
           |              \   /
           H               C=C
                          /   \
                         H     CH3
```

2 a Draw a section of the polymer formed from the monomer

```
H     H
 \   /
  C=C    , showing six carbon atoms.
 /   \
H     Cl
```

b What is the common name of the monomer?

c What is the systematic name of the polymer?

3

```
   F   F   F   F   F   F
   |   |   |   |   |   |
 — C — C — C — C — C — C —
   |   |   |   |   |   |
   F   F   F   F   F   F
```

This is a section of the polymer that non-stick pans are coated with the trade name Teflon.

What is the monomer?

4

```
   Cl  H   Cl  H   Cl  H
   |   |   |   |   |   |
 — C — C — C — C — C — C —
   |   |   |   |   |   |
   H   H   H   H   H   H
```

This is a section of the polymer that drainpipes are made from, trade name polyvinylchloride (PVC)

What is the monomer?

9.2 Condensation polymers

Learning objectives:

- What is a condensation polymer?
- What sorts of molecules react to form condensation polymers?

Specification reference: 3.4.9

Figure 1 *Clothing examples of polyesters and polyamides (nylon)*

A condensation reaction occurs when two molecules react together and a small molecule, often water or hydrogen chloride, is eliminated. For example esters are formed when carboxylic acids and alcohols react together, see Topic 5.3. This is a condensation reaction because water, H_2O is eliminated, H from the alcohol and OH from the carboxylic acid.

$$R{-}C({=}O){-}OH + HO{-}R' \longrightarrow R{-}C({=}O){-}O{-}R' + H_2O$$

carboxylic acid, alcohol → ester, water

Condensation polymers are normally made from two different monomers, each of which has *two* functional groups. Both functional groups can react, so that a long-chain polymer results.

Polyesters, polyamides and polypeptides are all examples of condensation polymers, see Figure 1.

Polyesters

A *poly*ester has the ester linkage —COO— repeated over and over again. To make a polyester we use diols, which have two —OH groups, and dicarboxylic acids, which have two carboxylic acid, —COOH, groups:

$$HO{-}A{-}OH \qquad HO{-}C({=}O){-}B{-}C({=}O){-}OH$$

a diol   a dicarboxylic acid

The functional groups on the ends of each molecule react to form a chain. For example diols and dicarboxylic acids react together to give a polyester by eliminating molecules of water, Figure 2.

$$HO{-}A{-}OH \;\; HO{-}\overset{O}{\overset{\|}{C}}{-}B{-}\overset{O}{\overset{\|}{C}}{-}OH \;\; HO{-}A{-}OH \;\; HO{-}\overset{O}{\overset{\|}{C}}{-}B{-}\overset{O}{\overset{\|}{C}}{-}OH$$

a diol, a dicarboxylic acid; H_2O, H_2O, H_2O eliminated

$$\downarrow$$

$$O{-}A{-}O{-}\overset{O}{\overset{\|}{C}}{-}B{-}\overset{O}{\overset{\|}{C}}{-}O{-}A{-}O{-}\overset{O}{\overset{\|}{C}}{-}B{-}\overset{O}{\overset{\|}{C}}{-}$$

a polyester

Figure 2 *Making a polyester. A and B represent unspecified organic groups, often* $\text{-}(CH_2)_n\text{-}$

The fibre Terylene is a polyester made from benzene-1,4-dicarboxylic acid and ethane-1,2-diol, see Figure 3:

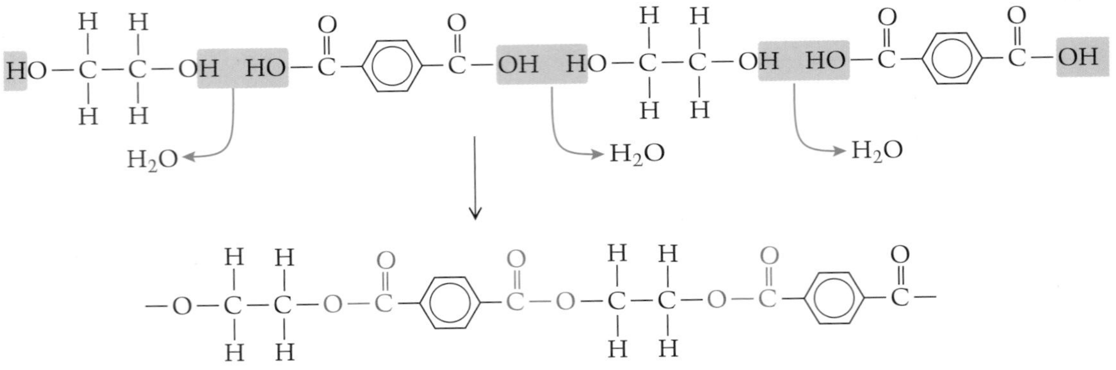

Figure 3 *Terylene is a polyester. The ester links are shown in red. Notice how the C—O is alternately to the left and to the right of the C═O*

AQA Examiner's tip

Make sure that you understand that, unlike polyalkenes, polyester and polyamides can be hydrolysed and are biodegradable.

Polyamides

An amide is formed when a carboxylic acid and an amine react together:

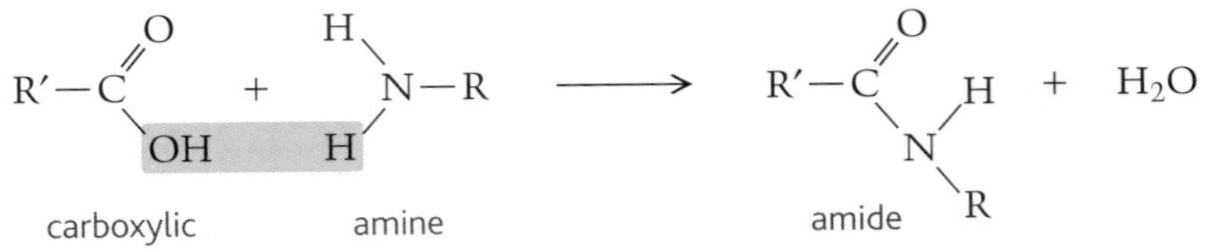

$$R'COOH + HN(H)R \longrightarrow R'CONHR + H_2O$$

carboxylic acid — amine — amide

*Poly*amides have the amide linkage —CONH— repeated over and over again. To make polyamides from two different monomers, a diaminoalkane (which has two amine groups) reacts with a dicarboxylic acid (which has two carboxylic acid groups), see Figure 4.

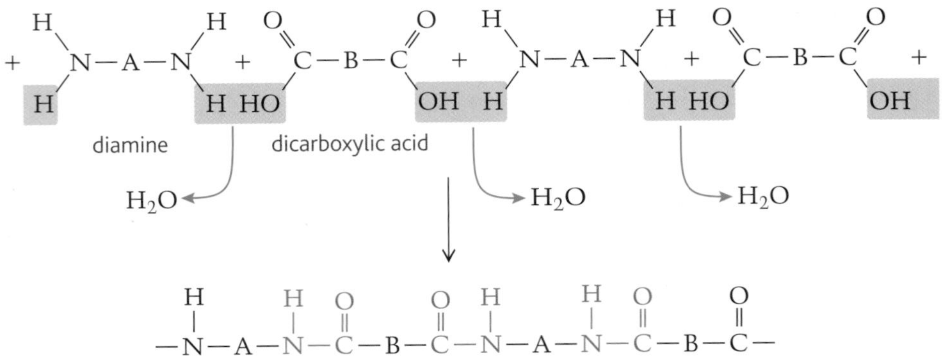

diamine — dicarboxylic acid — a polyamide

Figure 4 *The general equation for making a polyamide, such as Nylon-6,6 or Kevlar. The amide links are in red.*

Both Nylon and Kevlar are condensation polymers.

Nylon

Industrially, Nylon-6,6 is made from 1-6-diaminohexane and hexane-1,6-dicarboxylic acid:

$$H_2N-\overset{H}{\underset{H}{C}}-\overset{H}{\underset{H}{C}}-\overset{H}{\underset{H}{C}}-\overset{H}{\underset{H}{C}}-\overset{H}{\underset{H}{C}}-\overset{H}{\underset{H}{C}}-NH_2$$

1,6-diaminohexane

$$HO-\overset{O}{\overset{\|}{C}}-\overset{H}{\underset{H}{C}}-\overset{H}{\underset{H}{C}}-\overset{H}{\underset{H}{C}}-\overset{H}{\underset{H}{C}}-\overset{O}{\overset{\|}{C}}-OH$$

hexane-1,6-dicarboxylic acid

Figure 5 *When 1-6-diaminohexane and hexane-1,6-dioyldichloride meet, Nylon-6,6 is formed at the interface*

In the laboratory, the reaction goes faster if a diacid chloride is used rather than the dicarboxylic acid and in this case hydrogen chloride is eliminated.

Kevlar

Kevlar is made from benzene-1,4-diamine and benzene-1,4-dicarboxylic acid, see Figure 6.

$$H_2N-C_6H_4-NH_2 \;+\; HO-CO-C_6H_4-CO-OH \;+\; H_2N-C_6H_4-NH_2$$

benzene-1,4-diamine benzene-1,4-dicarboxylic acid

$$\downarrow$$

$$-NH-C_6H_4-NH-CO-C_6H_4-CO-NH-C_6H_4-NH-$$

Kevlar

Figure 6 *Kevlar is a polyamide. Because the amide groups are linking rigid benzene rings, Kevlar has very different properties to Nylon*

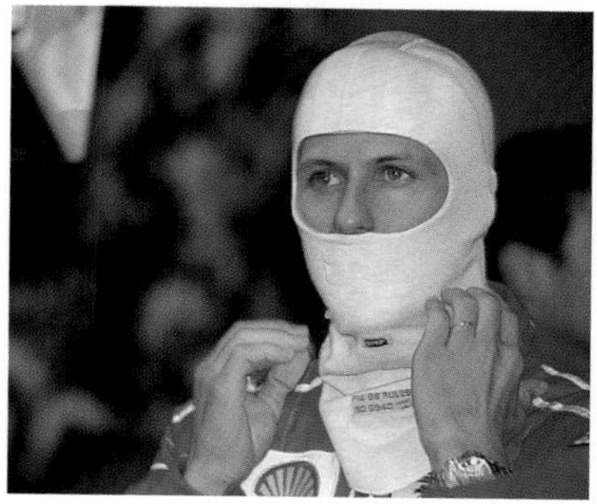

Figure 7 *Racing drivers wear Kevlar clothing because it is fire resistant and abrasion resistant. For example, it is five times stronger than steel, weight for weight. It is used to replace steel in car tyres, for boat sails, for aircraft wings and in all sorts of protective clothing including bullet-proof vests*

Polypeptides and proteins

Polypeptides, are also polyamides. They may be made from a single amino acid monomer, or many different ones.

In a polypeptide, *each* amino acid has both an amine group and a carboxylic acid group. So, the amine group of one amino acid can react with the carboxylic acid group of another. A molecule of water is eliminated and a condensation polymer can begin to form:

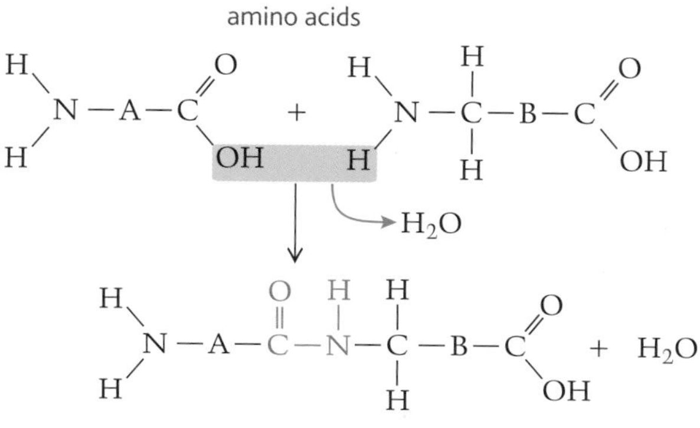

The amide (peptide) linkage is shown in red.

Note

Once a dipeptide is formed, tri-, tetra- and polypeptides can form by further reaction at each end of the molecule.

Notice the difference between a polymer like Nylon-6,6, where there are two monomers, one a diamine, $H_2N—X—NH_2$, and one a dicarboxylic acid, HOOC—Y—COOH, and a polypeptide, where each amino acid monomer has one $—NH_2$ group and one —COOH group, $H_2NCH(R)COOH$. There are 20 naturally occurring varieties of Z, see Topic 8.1.

Idenitfying the repeat unit of a condensation polymer

The repeat unit of a condensation polymer is found by starting at any point in the polymer and stopping when the same pattern of atoms begins again. In the example below the repeat unit is in brackets:

$$\sim\left[\overset{O}{\overset{\|}{C}}-A-\overset{O}{\overset{\|}{C}}-O-B-O\right]\overset{O}{\overset{\|}{C}}-A-\overset{O}{\overset{\|}{C}}\sim$$

AQA Examiner's tip

Check that you can deduce the repeating unit in each type of polymer.

Identifying the monomer(s) of a condensation polymer

The best way to work out the monomer(s) in a condensation polymer is to try and recognise the links formed by familiar functional groups, see Table 1.

AQA Examiner's tip

Make sure that you can deduce the monomers from which a polymer is formed.

Table 1 *Condensation polymers – the repeat unit is inside the bracket*

Monomer 1	Monomer 2	Polymer
$HO-\overset{O}{\overset{\|}{C}}-A-\overset{O}{\overset{\|}{C}}-OH$ dicarboxylic acid	$HO-B-OH$ diol	$\left[\overset{O}{\overset{\|}{C}}-A-\overset{O}{\overset{\|}{C}}-O-B-O\right]_n$
$HO-\overset{O}{\overset{\|}{C}}-A-\overset{O}{\overset{\|}{C}}-OH$ dicarboxylic acid	$H-\overset{H}{\overset{\|}{N}}-B-\overset{H}{\overset{\|}{N}}-H$ diamine	$\left[\overset{O}{\overset{\|}{C}}-A-\overset{O}{\overset{\|}{C}}-\overset{H}{\overset{\|}{N}}-B-\overset{H}{\overset{\|}{N}}\right]_n$
$HO-\overset{O}{\overset{\|}{C}}-\underset{R}{\underset{\|}{C}}-\overset{H}{\overset{\|}{N}}-H$ amino acid		$\left[\overset{O}{\overset{\|}{C}}-\underset{R}{\underset{\|}{\overset{H}{\overset{\|}{C}}}}-\overset{H}{\overset{\|}{N}}\right]_n$

- Start with the repeat unit.
- Break the linkage (at the C—O for a polyester or C—N for a polyamide).
- Add back the components of water for each ester or amide link.

For example:

$$\sim\left[\overset{O}{\overset{\|}{C}}-A-\overset{O}{\overset{\|}{C}}\,\wr\,O-B-O\right]\overset{O}{\overset{\|}{C}}-A-\overset{O}{\overset{\|}{C}}\sim$$

$$\downarrow +H_2O$$

$$HO-\overset{O}{\overset{\|}{C}}-A-\overset{O}{\overset{\|}{C}}-OH \quad \text{and} \quad HO-B-OH$$

monomers

This is exactly the same process that occurs when condensation polymers are hydrolysed.

> **Link**
>
> You will need to know bond polarity studied in *AQA AS Chemistry*, Topic 3.3.

Application

Disposal of polymers

- What are the different ways of disposing of polymers?
- What are the advantages and disadvantages of recycling polymers?

We saw in Topic 9.1 that addition polymers like polyethene and polypropene are not biodegradable because they are basically long-chain alkane molecules. Alkanes are unreactive because they have only strong, non-polar C—H and C—C bonds. There is nothing in the natural environment that will easily break them down and they persist for many years. They are usually disposed of in landfill sites, along with other rubbish, or by incineration. Some may be melted down and remoulded, see *AQA AS Chemistry*, Topic 15.3.

Figure 8 *Undecomposed polythene and polypropylene cause problems for wildlife*

Poly(alkenes) can be burnt to carbon dioxide and water to produce energy, although poisonous carbon monoxide may be released into the atmosphere if combustion is incomplete (when there is a shortage of oxygen).

Burning poly(alkenes) does add to the problem of increasing the level of CO_2 in the atmosphere:

$$\left[CH_2\right]_n + 1\tfrac{1}{2}nO_2 \longrightarrow nCO_2 + nH_2O$$

Other addition polymers, such as polystyrene, may release toxic products on burning. Complete combustion of polystyrene (a hydrocarbon) would produce carbon dioxide and water only. However, under certain conditions the polymer may depolymerise to produce toxic styrene vapour. Incomplete combustion produces carbon monoxide and unburnt carbon particles – black smoke.

Condensation polymers like polyesters and polyamides can be broken down by hydrolysis and are potentially biodegradable by the reverse of the polymerisation reaction by which they were formed.

The reaction below shows the hydrolysis of a polyamide such as nylon. However, this reaction is so slow under everyday conditions that you do not need to worry about your nylon cagoule depolymerising in the rain.

$$\left[\overset{\overset{\displaystyle H}{|}}{N}-R-\overset{\overset{\displaystyle H}{|}}{N}-\overset{\overset{\displaystyle O}{\|}}{C}-R'-\overset{\overset{\displaystyle O}{\|}}{C}\right]_n + nH_2O$$

$$\downarrow$$

$$n\left[\overset{\overset{\displaystyle H}{|}}{N}-R-\overset{\overset{\displaystyle H}{|}}{N}-H \;+\; H-O-\overset{\overset{\displaystyle O}{\|}}{C}-R'-\overset{\overset{\displaystyle O}{\|}}{C}\right]$$

1. If the polymer represents Nylon-6,6, what are R and R′?
2. Write a similar equation for the hydrolysis of a polyester.

Application

Recycling plastics

We are now recycling many of our polyester materials. They are being collected, sorted and then melted and reformed. Fleece garments may well be made from recycled soft drink bottles. With all recycling, the costs and benefits have to be balanced.

Advantages of recycling

- Almost all plastics are derived from crude oil. Recycling saves this expensive and ever diminishing source, as well as the energy used in refining it.
- If plastics are not recycled they mostly end up in landfill sites.

Disadvantages of recycling

The plastics need to be collected, transported and sorted, which uses energy and manpower and is therefore expensive.

How science works

Hermann Staudinger

Hermann Staudinger is rightly considered to be the father of polymer chemistry and he received the 1953 Nobel Prize for chemistry for his discoveries in this field – work which started in the 1920s.

Today, we are comfortable with the idea of giant molecules ('macromolecules') made up of chains of smaller ones. However, in the 1920s this idea was at odds with the established theory, and molecules with relative molecular masses (then called molecular weights) of over 5000 or so, such as rubber, starch, proteins etc., were considered to be made up of small molecules held together by some unknown force. Staudinger was already an established academic chemist (indeed, he had a reaction named after him) and put his reputation on the line by taking up the study of rubber. One distinguished colleague, with ill-disguised contempt, advised him to: 'Drop the idea of large molecules; organic molecules with a molecular weight higher than 5000 do not exist. Purify your rubber, then it will crystallise.'

Staudinger proved that polymers were indeed giant molecules made up of monomers by linking together molecules of methanal (formaldehyde, HCHO) one at a time to make successively bigger molecules, CH_2O, $(CH_2O)_2$, $(CH_2O)_3$ etc. until he produced the high molecular weight substance paraldehyde. He showed that the properties of these molecules gradually changed from those typical of small molecules to those of very large ones. So the very large molecule was simply a chain of small molecules held together by normal covalent bonds – no 'unknown force' was required. A few years later, X-ray diffraction was able to confirm the structures of polymers.

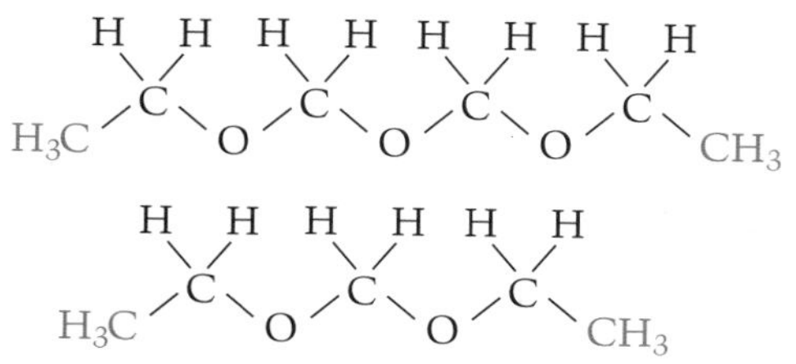

$H_3C-CH_2-O-CH_2-O-CH_2-O-CH_2-CH_3$

$H_3C-CH_2-O-CH_2-O-CH_2-CH_3$

Figure 9 *Two of Staudinger's molecules – the CH_3 groups in red simply 'stop off' the ends of the chains*

Staudinger's work led to modern synthetic polymers such as polythene (poly(ethene)) and nylon (a polyamide) and to an understanding of the structures of natural ones such as proteins, starch and, of course, rubber, which is poly(isoprene). Staudinger actually predicted artificial fibres; nylon was produced by Wallace Carothers in the late 1930s.

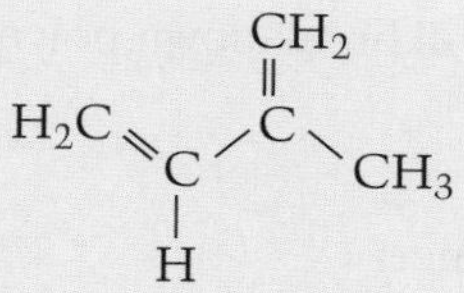

$H_2C=CH-C(=CH_2)-CH_3$

1 This is the structural formula of isoprene, the monomer from which rubber is made. What is its systematic (IUPAC) name?

2 Is isoprene likely to form an addition or a condensation polymer? Explain your answer.

Summary questions

1 There are a number of different types of nylon made from two monomers – a dicarboxylic acid and a diamine.

a The one made from hexane -1,6-dicarboxylic acid and 1,6-diaminohexane is called Nylon-6,6. Suggest where the numbers come from.

b Nylon-6,10 is made from the same dicarboxylic acid as Nylon-6,6. What is the other monomer? Give its name and its formula.

2 Nylons are polyamides. Explain why proteins and peptides are also called polyamides.

3 Terylene is a polyester made from benzene-1,4-dicarboxylic acid and ethane-1,2-diol. Suggest another diol that would react with this acid to make a different polyester.

4 What are the linkages called in the the two polymers below?

a $-A-C(=O)-N(H)-B-N(H)-C(=O)-A-$

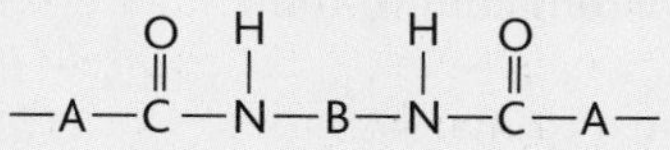

b $-A-C(=O)-O-B-O-C(=O)-A-$

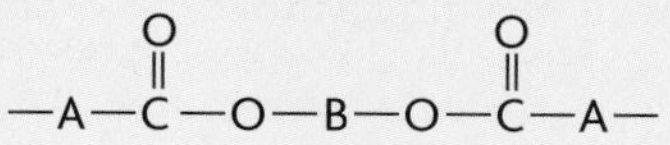

AQA Examination-style questions

1 The repeating units of two polymers, **P** and **Q**, are shown below.

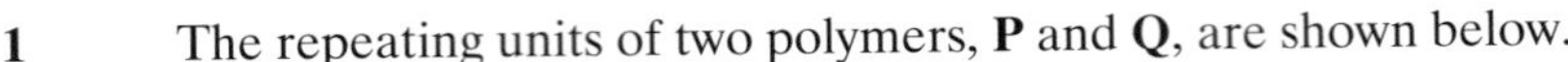

$-C(H)(CH_3)-C(H)(CH_3)-$

P

$-O-C(H)(CH_3)-C(H)(CH_3)-O-C(=O)-C(H)(CH_3)-C(H)(CH_3)-C(=O)-$

Q

(a) Draw the structure of the monomer used to form polymer **P**. Name the type of polymerisation involved. *(2 marks)*

(b) Draw the structures of **two** compounds which react together to form polymer **Q**. Name these **two** compounds and name the type of polymerisation involved. *(5 marks)*

(c) Identify a compound which, in aqueous solution, will break down polymer **Q** but not polymer **P**. *(1 mark)*

AQA, 2006

2 The structure below shows the repeating unit of a polymer.

$-C(=O)-CH_2CH_2-C(=O)-N(H)-CH_2CH_2-N(H)-$

By considering the functional group formed during polymerisation, name this type of polymer and the type of polymerisation involved in its formation. *(2 marks)*

AQA, 2006

3 (a) The compound $H_2C{=}CHCN$ is used in the formation of acrylic polymers.

(i) Draw the repeating unit of the polymer formed from this compound.

(ii) Name the type of polymerisation involved in the formation of this polymer. *(2 marks)*

(b) The repeating unit of a polyester is shown below.

$\left[-CH_2CH_2-O-C(=O)-CH_2CH_2-C(=O)-O-\right]$

(i) Deduce the empirical formula of the repeating unit of this polyester.

(ii) Draw the structure of the acid which could be used in the preparation of this polyester and give the name of this acid.

(iii) Give **one** reason why the polyester is biodegradable. *(4 marks)*

AQA, 2004

4 Consider the hydrocarbon **G**, $(CH_3)_2C{=}CHCH_3$, which can be polymerised.

(a) Name the type of polymerisation involved and draw the repeating unit of the polymer. *(2 marks)*

(b) Draw the structure of an isomer of **G** which shows geometrical isomerism. *(1 mark)*

(c) Draw the structure of an isomer of **G** which does not react with bromine water. *(1 mark)*

AQA, 2004

5 (a) The hydrocarbon **M** has the structure shown below.

$$\begin{array}{l} CH_3CH_2-\underset{\displaystyle CH_3}{\underset{|}{C}}=CH_2 \end{array}$$

(i) Name hydrocarbon **M**.

(ii) Draw the repeating unit of the polymer which can be formed from **M**. State the type of polymerisation occurring in this reaction. *(3 marks)*

(b) Draw the repeating unit of the polymer formed by the reaction between butanedioic acid and hexane-1,6-diamine. State the type of polymerisation occurring in this reaction and give a name for the linkage between the monomer units in this polymer. *(4 marks)*

AQA, 2003

6 (a) Synthetic polyamides are produced by the reaction of dicarboxylic acids with compounds such as $H_2N(CH_2)_6NH_2$

(i) Name the compound $H_2N(CH_2)_6NH_2$

(ii) Give the repeating unit in the polyamide nylon 6,6. *(2 marks)*

(b) Synthetic polyamides have structures similar to those found in proteins.

(i) Draw the structure of 2-aminopropanoic acid.

(ii) Draw the organic product formed by the condensation of two molecules of 2-aminopropanoic acid. *(2 marks)*

AQA, 2002

7 (a) Explain why polyalkenes are chemically inert. *(2 marks)*

(b) Explain why polyesters and polyamides are biodegradeable. *(2 marks)*

(c) Discuss the advantages of recycling polymers. *(2 marks)*

10 Organic synthesis and analysis

10.1 Synthetic routes

Learning objectives:

- How can organic reactions be used to synthesise target molecules?

Specification reference: 3.4.10

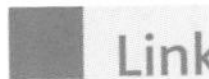

Link

You will need to know all organic chemistry studied at AS.

AQA Examiner's tip

You need to know the reactions of these functional groups:

- alkanes (*AQA AS Chemistry*, Chapter 6)
- alkenes (*AQA AS Chemistry*, Chapter 15)
- haloalkanes (*AQA AS Chemistry*, Chapter 14)
- alcohols (*AQA AS Chemistry*, Chapter 16)
- carbonyl compounds (Chapter 5)
- carboxylic acids and their derivatives (Chapter 5)
- arenes (Chapter 6)
- organic nitrogen compounds (Chapter 7).

AQA Examiner's tip

Be able to compare the yield (see *AQA AS Chemistry*, Topic 2.6) which is a measure of the efficiency of the conversion of a starting material into a product and the atom economy of a process.

This chapter is about working out a series of reactions for making ('synthesising') a given molecule, usually called the **target molecule**. Sometimes (often in exam questions) you will be told the molecule from which you must start; but in industry, the starting material will depend on availability and cost.

Synthesis of a target molecule is a common problem in industries like drug or pesticide manufacture. Suppose a molecule is found to have a particular effect, for example, as an antibiotic. Drug companies may synthesise, on a small scale, a number of compounds of similar structures. These will be screened for possible antibiotic properties. Any promising compounds may then be made in larger quantities for thorough investigation of their effectiveness, side effects and so on, before the final step goes ahead – producing them commercially.

Using the organic reactions we have met in *AQA AS Chemistry* and earlier chapters, we can work out a reaction scheme to convert a starting material into a target molecule.

Working out a scheme

Start by writing down the displayed formula of the starting molecule, A, and the target molecule, X.

Then, one way of working out what route to take is to write down all the compounds which can be made from A and all the ways in which X can be prepared, see Figure 1.

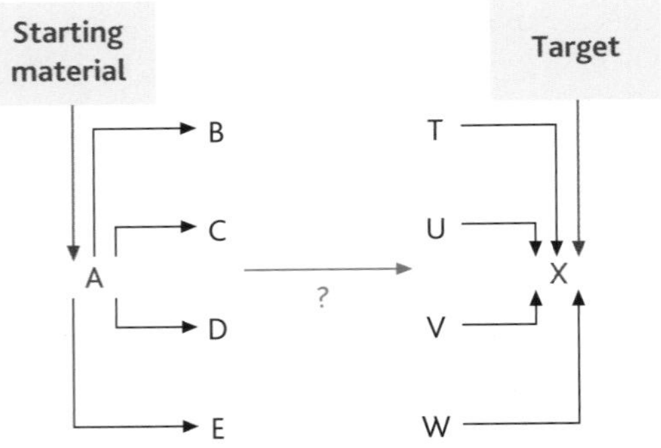

Figure 1 *Devising a synthesis of compound X from compound A*

You may then see how B, C, D or E can be converted, in one or more steps to T, U, V, W. It is important to keep the number of steps as small as possible to maximise the yield of the target.

Sometimes you will be able to see straight away that a particular reaction will be needed. If, for example, the target molecule has one more carbon atom than the starting material, it is probable that the reaction of cyanide ions with a haloalkane will be needed at some stage, as this reaction increases the length of the carbon chain by one, for example:

$$CH_3Br + CN^- \longrightarrow CH_3C{\equiv}N + Br^-$$

bromomethane ethanenitrile

How the functional groups are connected

The inter-relationships between the functional groups you should know are shown in Figure 2. Make sure you can recall the reagents and conditions for each conversion.

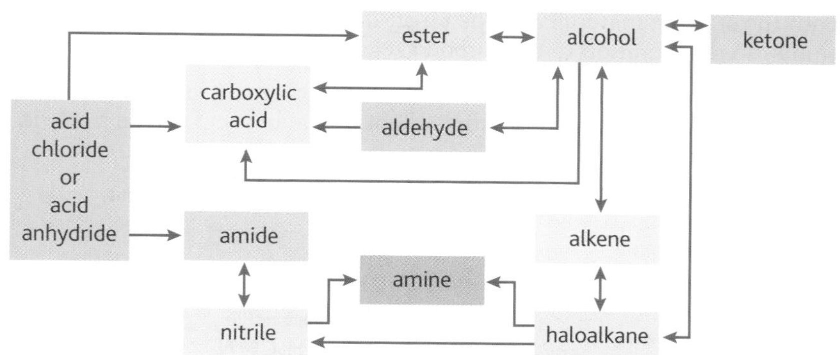

Figure 2 *Inter-relationships between functional groups. You can use this chart to revise your knowledge of organic reactions*

Hint

You need to recall the reactions of all the functional groups you have met, including conditions such as heating, refluxing, use of acidic or alkaline conditions, catalyst.

Reagents used in organic chemistry

Oxidising agents

Potassium dichromate(VI), $K_2Cr_2O_7$ acidified with dilute sulfuric acid will oxidise primary alcohols to aldehydes, and aldehydes to carboxylic acids. Secondary alcohols are oxidised to ketones.

Reducing agents

Different reducing reagents have different capabilities:

- Sodium tetrahydridoborate(III), $NaBH_4$, will reduce C=O but not C=C. It can be used in aqueous solution. This reducing agent will reduce polar unsaturated groups, such as $C^{\delta+}{=}O^{\delta-}$, but not non-polar ones, such as C=C. This is because it generates the nucleophile H^- which attacks $C^{\delta+}$ but is repelled by the electron-rich C=C.
- Hydrogen with a nickel catalyst, H_2/Ni, is used to reduce C=C but not C=O.
- Tin and hydrochloric acid, Sn/H^+, may be used to reduce R—NO_2 to R—NH_2.

Dehydrating agents

- Alcohols can be converted to alkenes by passing their vapours over heated aluminium oxide or by acid-catalysed elimination reactions.

Examples of reaction schemes

1 How can we synthesise propanoic acid starting with1-bromopropane?

$$CH_3CH_2CH_2Br \xrightarrow{?} CH_3CH_2COOH$$

Both the starting material and the target have the same number of carbon atoms, so no alteration to the carbon skeleton is needed.

Now write down all the compounds which can be made in one step from 1-bromopropane and all those from which propanoic acid can be made in one step as shown in Figure 3. You may use Figure 2 to help you.

In this case two of the compounds are the same – the ones in red.

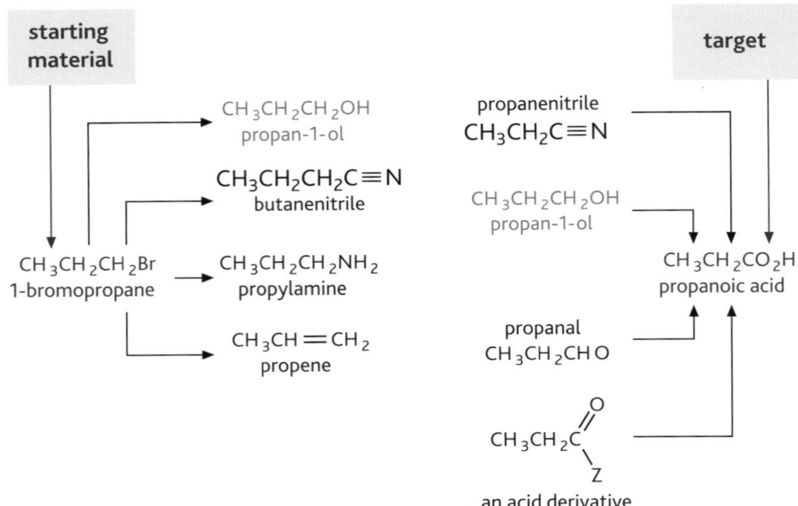

Figure 3 *Devising a synthesis of propanoic acid from 1-bromopropane*

So, 1-bromopropane can be converted into propan-1-ol which can be converted into propanoic acid. So the conversion we require can be done in two steps:

1 $CH_3CH_2CH_2Br \xrightarrow{\text{reflux with NaOH(aq)}} CH_3CH_2CH_2OH$

1-bromopropane → propan-1-ol

2 $CH_3CH_2CH_2OH \xrightarrow{\text{reflux with } K_2Cr_2O_7/H^+} CH_3CH_2CO_2H$

propan-1-ol → propanoic acid

Both these reactions have a good yield.

2 How can we synthesise propylamine starting with ethene?

$$H_2C{=}CH{-}Br \xrightarrow{?} H{-}CH_2{-}CH_2{-}CH_2{-}NH_2$$

Propylamine has one more carbon atom than ethene. This suggests that the formation of a nitrile is involved at some stage.

Write down all the compounds that can be made from ethene and all the compounds from which the propylamine can be made, see Figure 4. Here, no compound, which can be made in one step from the starting material, can be converted into the product, so more than two steps must be required. But we already know that the formation of a nitrile is required. A haloethane can be converted into propanenitrile so the synthesis can be completed in three steps:

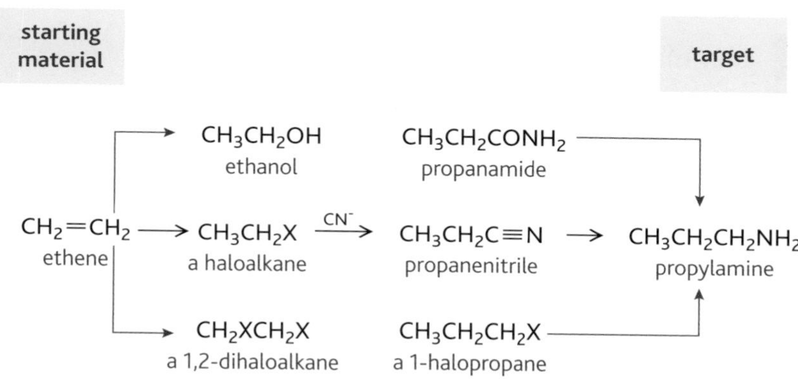

Figure 4 *Devising a synthesis of propylamine from ethene*

1 $CH_2CH_2 \xrightarrow{\text{HBr}} CH_3CH_2Br$
ethene → bromoethane

2 $CH_3CH_2Br \xrightarrow{\text{KCN/dil. }H_2SO_4} CH_3CH_2C{\equiv}N$
bromoethane → propanenitrile

3 $CH_3CH_2C{\equiv}N \xrightarrow{\text{Ni/}H_2} CH_3CH_2CH_2NH_2$
propanenitrile → propylamine

Chloroethane or iodoethane could have been chosen instead of bromoethane.

Aromatic reactions

Figure 5 summarises some of the important reactions of aromatic compounds using benzene as the starting material.

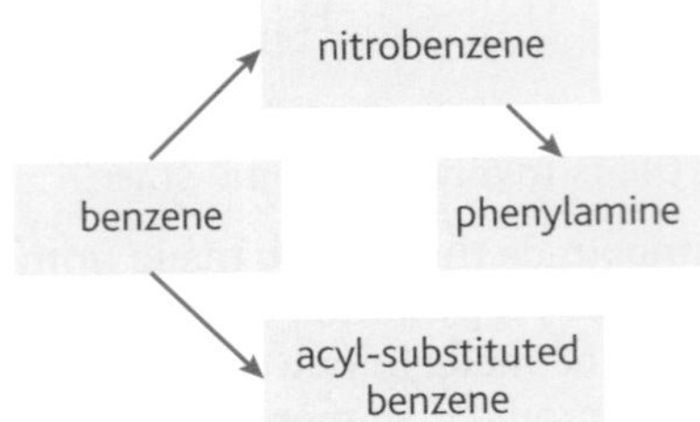

Figure 5 *Some inter-relationships between functional groups in aromatic compounds. Make sure you can recall the reagents and conditions for each conversion*

Summary questions

1 How would you convert, in one step:

a 1-bromobutane to pentanenitrile

b ethanoic acid to methyl ethanoate

c but-1-ene to butan-2-ol

d cyclohexanol to cyclohexene ?

2 How would you convert, in two steps:

a ethene to ethanoic acid

b propanone to 2-bromopropane?

3

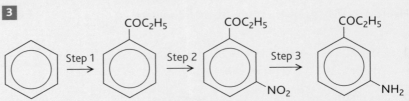

benzene $\xrightarrow{\text{Step 1}}$ $C_6H_5COC_2H_5$ $\xrightarrow{\text{Step 2}}$ COC_2H_5 / NO_2 substituted benzene $\xrightarrow{\text{Step 3}}$ COC_2H_5 / NH_2 substituted benzene

For each step, name the type of reaction taking place and the reagents required.

10.2 Organic analysis

Learning objectives:

- How can organic groups be identified?

Specification reference: 3.4.10

Link

You will need to know all organic chemistry studied in AS modules and this book.

When we are identifying an organic compound we need to know the functional groups present.

Chemical reactions

Some tests are very straightforward:

- Is the compound acidic (suggests carboxylic acid) or basic (suggests an amine)?
- Is the compound solid (suggests long carbon chain or ionic bonding), liquid (suggests medium length carbon chain or polar or hydrogen bonding) or gas (suggests short carbon chain, little or no polarity)?
- Does the compound dissolve in water (suggests polar groups) or not (suggests no polar groups)?
- Does the compound burn with a smoky flame (suggests high C : H ratio, possibly aromatic) or non-smoky flame (suggests low C : H ratio, probably non-aromatic)?

Some specific chemical tests are listed in Table 1.

Table 1 *Chemical tests for functional groups*

Functional group	Test	Result
Alkene —C=C—	Shake with bromine water	Red-brown colour disappears
Haloalkane R—X	1. Add NaOH(aq) and warm 2. Acidify with HNO_3 3. Add $AgNO_3$(aq)	Precipitate of AgX
Alcohol R—OH	Add acidified $K_2Cr_2O_7$	Orange colour turns green with primary or secondary alcohols (also with aldehydes)
Aldehydes R—CHO	Warm with Fehling's solution or warm with Tollens' solution	Blue colour turns to red precipitate Silver mirror forms
Carboxylic acids R—COOH	Add $NaHCO_3$(aq)	CO_2 given off
Acyl chlorides R—COCl	Add $AgNO_3$(aq)	Vigorous reaction. White precipitate of AgCl forms

Summary questions

1. How could you tell if R—X was a chloroalkane, a bromoalkane or an iodoalkane?
2. In the test for a haloalkane:
   a. Explain why it is necessary to acidify with dilute acid before adding silver nitrate.
   b. Why would acidifying with hydrochloric acid not be suitable?
3. A compound decolourises bromine solution and fizzes when sodium hydrogencarbonate solution is added:
   a. What two functional groups does it have?
   b. Its relative molecular mass is 72. What is its structural formula?
   c. Give equations for the two reactions.

AQA Examination-style questions

1 A possible synthesis of phenylethene *(styrene)* is outlined below.

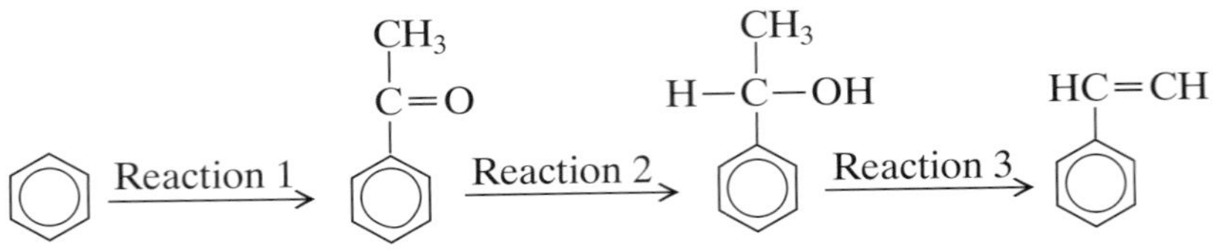

(a) $NaBH_4$ is a possible reagent for Reaction **2**.
Name and outline the mechanism for the reaction with $NaBH_4$ in Reaction **2**.
Name the product of Reaction **2**. *(6 marks)*

(b) Name the type of reaction involved in Reaction **3** and give a reagent for the reaction. *(2 marks)*

AQA, 2006

2 A reaction of benzene is shown below.

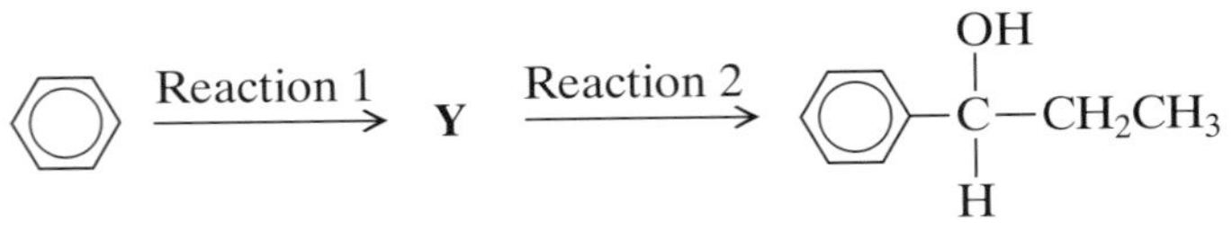

Z

(a) Deduce the structure of **Y** and give the organic reagent needed for Reaction **1**. *(2 marks)*

(b) Give the reagent(s) needed for Reaction **2**. *(1 mark)*

AQA, 2006

3 (a) Describe how propanal, CH_3CH_2CHO, and propanone, CH_3COCH_3, can be distinguished using a chemical test. *(3 marks)*

(b) Compound **Z** can be produced by the reaction of compound **X** with compound **Y** as shown in the synthesis outlined below

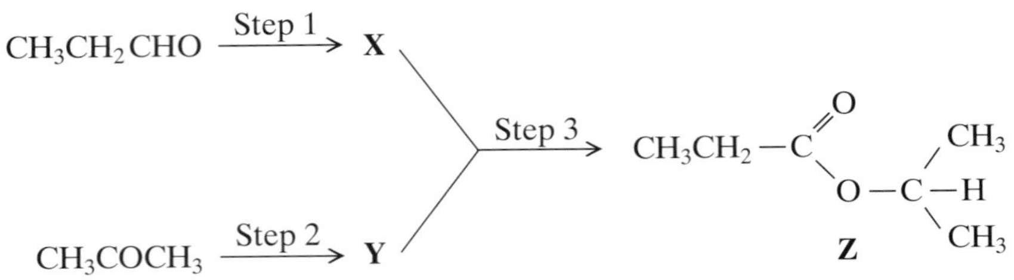

$CH_3CH_2CHO \xrightarrow{\text{Step 1}}$ **X**

$CH_3COCH_3 \xrightarrow{\text{Step 2}}$ **Y**

X + **Y** $\xrightarrow{\text{Step 3}}$ $CH_3CH_2-C(=O)-O-CH(CH_3)_2$ **Z**

Identify compounds **X** and **Y**.
For each of the three steps in the synthesis, name the type of reaction involved and give reagents and conditions. Equations are **not** required. *(8 marks)*

AQA, 2005

4 Draw the structure of the main organic product formed in each case when **R** reacts separately with the following substances:

$$\textbf{R} \text{ is } CH_3CH_2-\underset{\displaystyle OH}{\overset{\displaystyle H}{\underset{|}{\overset{|}{C}}}}-COOH$$

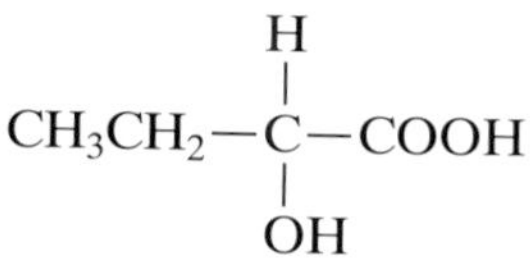

(a) methanol in the presence of a few drops of concentrated sulfuric acid; *(1 mark)*
(b) acidified potassium dichromate(VI); *(1 mark)*
(c) concentrated sulfuric acid in an elimination reaction. *(1 mark)*

AQA, 2006

5 Propanoyl chloride can be used, together with a catalyst, in Step 1 of the synthesis of 1-phenylpropene from benzene as shown below.

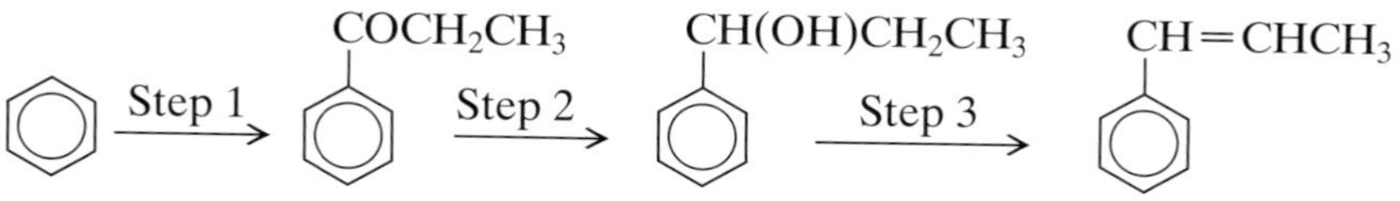

$$C_6H_6 \xrightarrow{\text{Step 1}} C_6H_5COCH_2CH_3 \xrightarrow{\text{Step 2}} \underset{\textbf{Q}}{C_6H_5CH(OH)CH_2CH_3} \xrightarrow{\text{Step 3}} C_6H_5CH{=}CHCH_3$$

(a) $NaBH_4$ can be used in the reaction in Step 2. Name the mechanism involved in this reaction. Molecules of **Q** show optical isomerism but the sample of **Q** formed in Step 2 is optically inactive. State, in terms of their structure, why molecules of **Q** show optical isomerism. Explain, by reference to the mechanism, why the sample of **Q** obtained in Step 2 is not optically active. *(7 marks)*
(b) Identify a suitable reagent for the reaction in Step 3.
Name the type of stereoisomerism shown by the product of this reaction. State what is required in the structure of molecules to allow them to show this type of stereoisomerism. *(4 marks)*

AQA, 2004

11 Structure determination

11.1 Mass spectrometry

Learning objectives:

- How can a mass spectrometer be used to find molecular mass?
- What is fragmentation?
- How can fragmentation be used to help find molecular structure?

Specification reference: 3.4.11

Hint

Remember that cations are positive ions.

We saw in *AQA AS Chemistry*, Topics 1.4 and 17.1, how mass spectrometry is used to measure relative *atomic* masses of isotopes and also relative *molecular* masses. The compound enters the mass spectrometer as a gas or a vapour. It is ionised by high energy electrons fired from an electron gun and the positive ions are accelerated through the instrument as a beam of ionised molecules, which are then deflected by a magnetic field.

The amount of deflection depends on the mass and charge of the ion. The output is then presented as a graph of abundance (vertical axis) against mass/charge ratio, *m/z*, (horizontal axis), but since the charge on the ions is normally 1+, the horizontal axis is effectively relative mass. This graph is called a **mass spectrum**.

Since the majority of ions formed in a mass spectrometer have lost a single electron, they have an unpaired electron and are therefore also free radicals, see *AQA AS Chemistry*, Topic 14.4. They are called radical cations and are written with a dot to show the unpaired electron and a + to show the positive charge, for example, $[C_2H_5OH]^{+\bullet}$.

Measuring relative molecular mass – the molecular ion

Many of the ions will break up (fragment) – some of their bonds break as soon as the ion is formed. However there are normally a few ionised molecules remaining intact to give a peak corresponding to the relative molecular mass, M_r, of the compound. These ionised molecules are called **molecular ions.** The peak furthest to the right of the mass spectrum corresponds to the molecular ion (it has the highest mass). Don't confuse it with the tallest peak in the spectrum, often called the **base peak**.

There may be small peaks of greater mass than the molecular ion in the mass spectrum. These are caused by the presence of isotopes such as ^{13}C in the molecular ion. They are of small abundance – only 1% of carbon is ^{13}C.

Mass spectrometry is the most important technique for measuring M_r.

Figure 1 is the mass spectrum of benzoic acid. The peak furthest to the right is from the molecular ion, and so $M_r = 122$.

Fragmentation

If a molecular ion (a radical cation), breaks up, one fragment will carry a positive charge and the other an unpaired electron. Only the charged fragment will be detected – uncharged fragments will not be deflected.

$$M^{+\bullet} \longrightarrow X^{+} + Y^{\bullet}$$

Although we only need to identify the molecular ion to find the relative molecular mass, the other peaks can give a lot of information about a

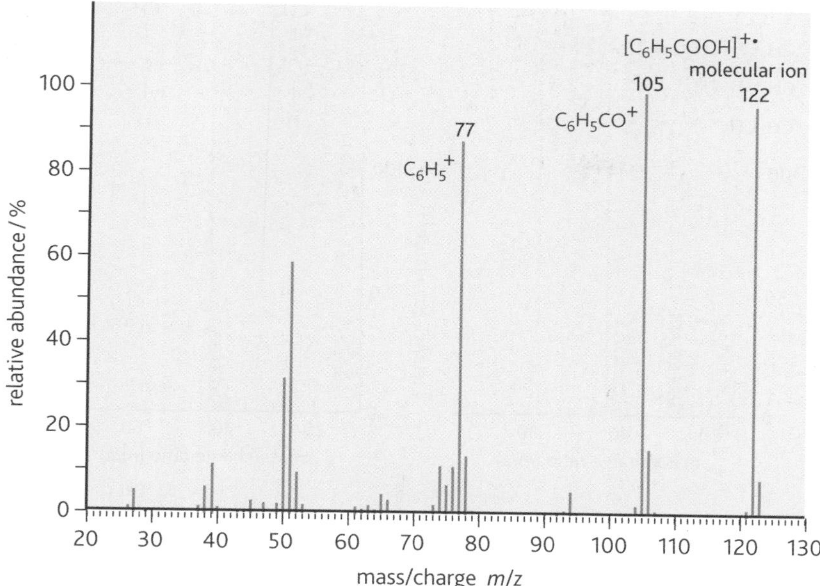

Figure 1 *Mass spectrum of benzoic acid. The large peaks of masses less than 122 are fragments of the original molecule, see below*

compound, because they are the peaks that come from the fragments of the molecule. For example, butane and methylpropane are isomers, and have the same relative molecular mass. So, the mass spectra of the isomers will both give the same value for M_r. However, each spectrum will be different, because the fragments of the two molecules will be different. Look at the two spectra for butane and methylpropane, Figures 2 and 3.

AQA Examiner's tip

Remember that positive ions are detected but uncharged radicals are not.

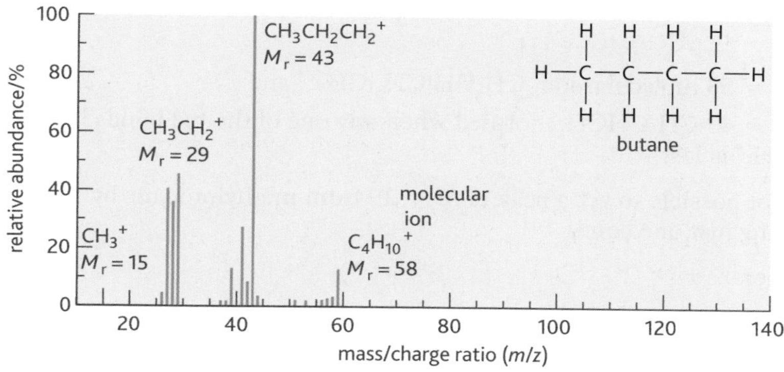

Figure 2 *Mass spectrum of butane*

Butane, $\left[H_3C{-}CH_2{-}CH_2{-}CH_3 \right]^{+\bullet}$ shows the following main peaks:

- M_r = 58 molecular ion, $CH_3CH_2CH_2CH_3^{+\bullet}$ and
- M_r = 43 $CH_3CH_2CH_2^{+}$, formed when the red bond breaks ($CH_3^{\bullet}$ is lost), and
- M_r = 29 $CH_3CH_2^{+}$, formed when the green bond breaks ($C_2H_5^{\bullet}$ is lost).

Any uncharged species are removed by the vacuum pump.

AQA Examiner's tip

The processes by which atoms in an ion rearrange are not required.

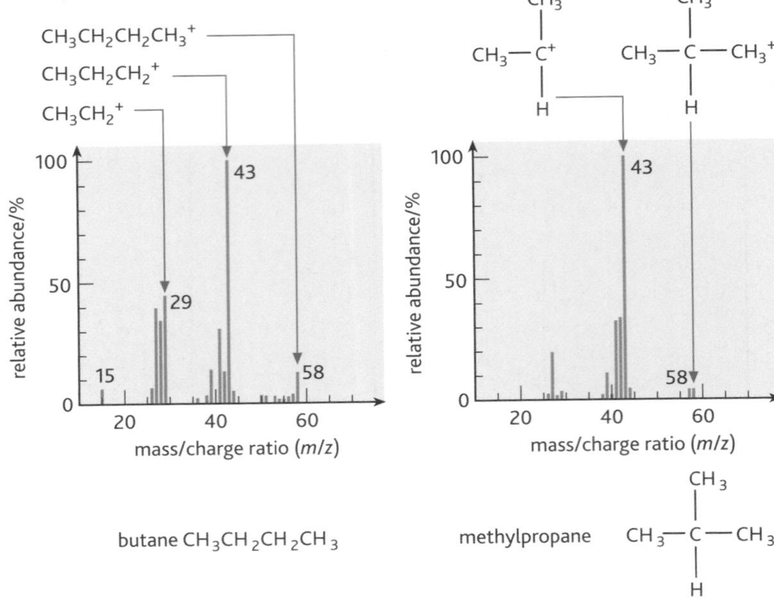

Figure 3 *Mass spectra of butane and methylpropane*

Methylpropane,

```
 [      H   H   H      ]+•
 [      |   |   |      ]
 [  H — C — C — C — H  ]
 [      |   |   |      ]
 [      H   |   H      ]
 [          |          ]
 [      H — C — H      ]
 [          |          ]
            H
```

shows the following main peaks:

- M_r = 58 molecular ion, $CH_3CH(CH_3)CH_3^{+\bullet}$ and
- M_r = 43 $CH_3CHCH_3^+$ formed when any one of the red bonds break ($CH_3^\bullet$ is lost).

It is not possible to get a peak of M_r = 29 from methylpropane by breaking just one bond.

In general:

- Fragmentation is more likely to take place at weaker bonds.
- The more stable the fragment that forms, the greater its abundance in the spectrum.
- The stability of positive ions formed from hydrocarbons (called **carbocations**) is in the order : tertiary > secondary > primary.

Hint

As we have seen, a fragment of mass 43 can also be caused by $CH_3CH_2CH_2^+$.

Fragmentation of carbonyl compounds

A carbonyl compound will typically fragment at the carbonyl group to give an alkyl radical and a stable RCO^+ cation, called an **acylium ion**. This is stable because the RCO^+ ion has a positive charge localised on the carbon atom; the carbonyl group is polarised $C^{\delta+}{=}O^{\delta-}$ because oxygen is more electronegative than carbon:

$$RCOR^{+\bullet} \longrightarrow RCO^+ + R^\bullet$$

An abundant peak at m/z = 43 suggests a CH_3CO group in the parent molecule. This is seen in the mass spectrum of propanone, see Figure 4.

Figure 5 shows the mass spectrum of propanal, CH_3CH_2CHO, which is an isomer of propanone. The peak at $m/z = 58$ is again the molecular ion, while that at $m/z = 29$ represents both $CH_3CH_2^+$ and CHO^+, both of which have the same relative molecular mass. The peaks with one unit of m/z less than these peaks may represent loss of hydrogen atoms from the fragments.

Isotope peaks

Sometimes care is needed in identifying the molecular ion peak. Molecules fly through the mass spectrometer individually, so molecules containing isotopes will produce more than one molecular ion. For example, butane, C_4H_{10}, will give a molecular ion at mass 58 in which all the carbon atoms are carbon-12, and one at 59 in which one of the carbons is carbon-13. Since 1% of carbon atoms are carbon-13, and there are four carbons, this peak will be 4% of the height of the peak at mass 58 – too small to see on our spectrum.

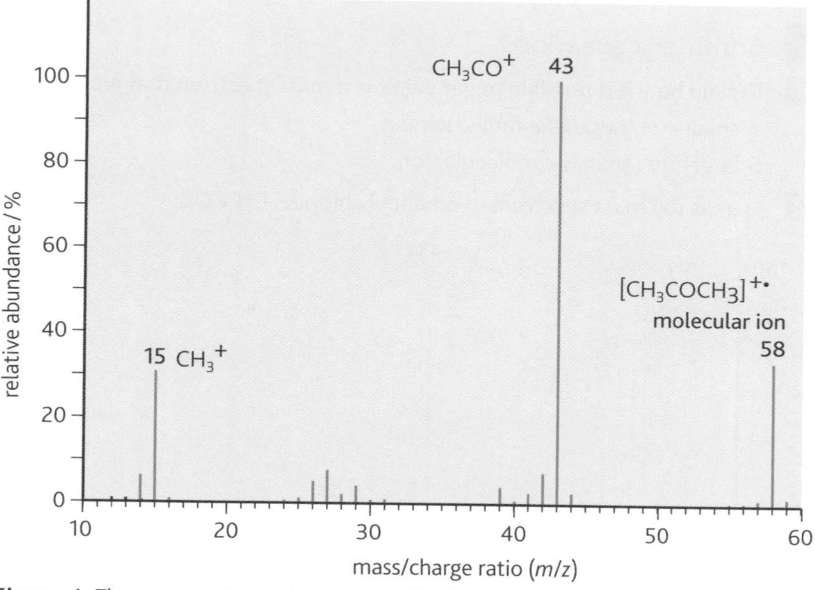

Figure 4 *The mass spectrum of propanone, CH_3COCH_3*

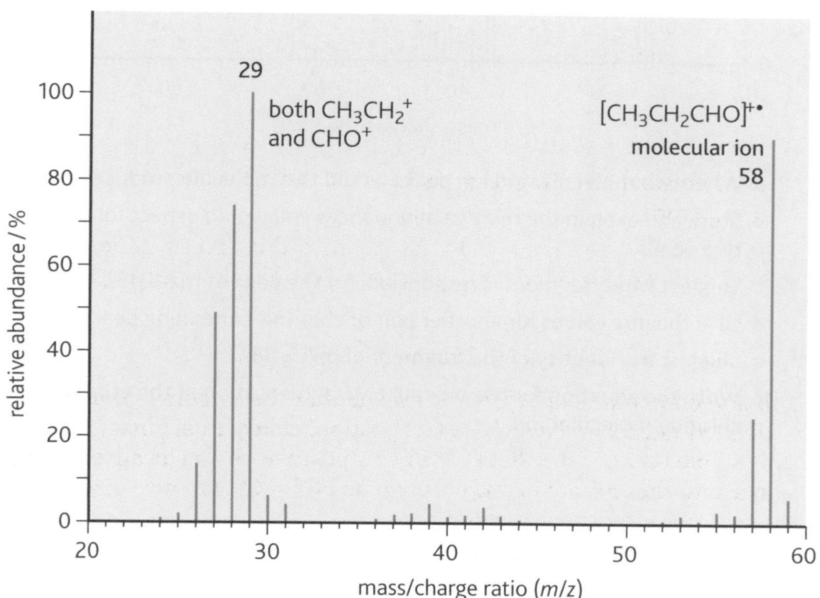

Figure 5 *The mass spectrum of propanal, CH_3CH_2CHO*

AQA Examiner's tip

Acylium ions are stabilised by delocalisation which spreads the positive charge throughout the structure.

The height of this peak, called the $M+1$ peak, tells us the number of carbon atoms in the molecule. For example, a height that is 4% of the main peak means 4 carbons.

Chlorine has two isotopes (^{35}Cl and ^{37}Cl), almost exactly in the abundance ratio 3 : 1. Peaks with intensity ratio 3 : 1 two *m/z* values apart in the spectrum suggest the presence of chlorine.

Bromine has two isotopes (^{79}Br and ^{81}Br), almost exactly in the abundance ratio 1 : 1. Peaks with intensity ratio 1 : 1 two *m/z* values apart in the spectrum suggest the presence of bromine.

Every organic compound has a typical spectrum, which means that an unknown compound can be identified by comparing it with spectra of known compounds.

Summary questions

1 Explain how it is possible to get peaks in a mass spectrum that are:

a smaller *m/z* than the molecular ion

b larger *m/z* than the molecular ion.

2 Here is the mass spectrum of ethanoyl chloride, CH_3COCl:

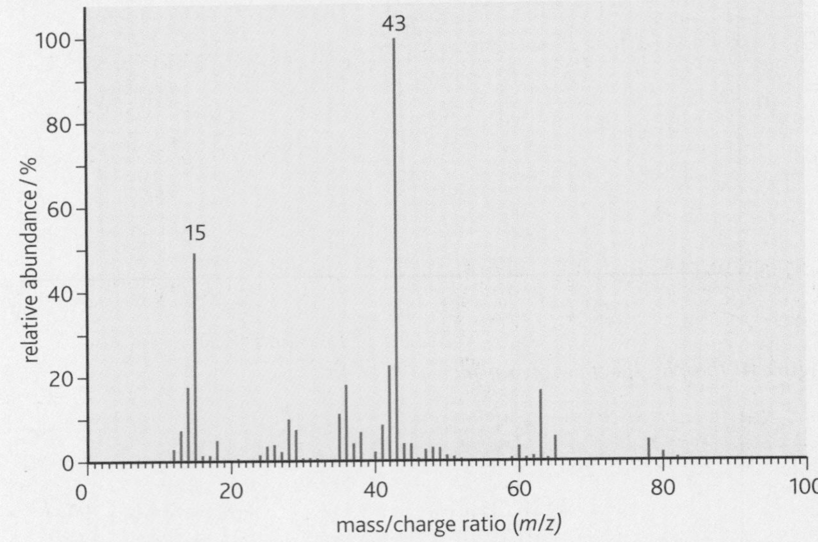

a What two molecular ion ion peaks would this molecule produce?

b State and explain the relative abundances you would expect for these two peaks.

c Suggest what fragment is responsible for the peak at mass 43.

d Give the *m/z* values for another pair of chlorine-containing peaks.

e Suggest the identity of the fragment at $m/z = 15$.

f Write the equation for the most likely fragmentation of the ethanoyl chloride molecular ion.

11.2 Infra-red (IR) spectroscopy

Learning objectives:

- What is the fingerprint region in an infra-red spectrum?
- Which functional groups give characteristic absorption peaks?

Specification reference: 3.4.11

We met with IR spectroscopy in *AQA AS Chemistry*, Topic 17.2. An instrument called an infra-red spectrometer is used to help identify particular groups of atoms. It shines a beam of infra-red radiation through the sample and produces a graph of transmission against wavenumber. The graph is called a **spectrum** and looks like Figure 1. A dip on the spectrum is called a peak.

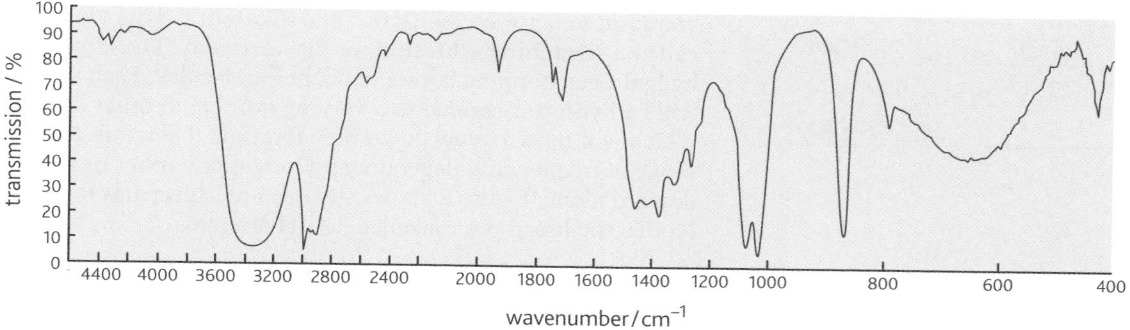

Figure 1 *A typical infra-red spectrum of an organic compound*

AQA Examiner's tip

It is not necessary to learn the wavenumbers of absorptions as data tables are provided in all examinations.

How an infra-red spectrometer works

When we shine a beam of infra–red radiation (heat energy) through a sample, the molecules in the sample absorb energy from the beam and the bonds vibrate more. But, any particular molecule can only absorb radiation that has the same frequency as the natural vibrational frequency of a bond. So, the radiation that emerges from the sample (plotted on a graph as 'transmission') will be missing the frequencies that correspond to the bonds in the sample. We can identify the groups present from these missing frequencies.

The fingerprint region

The area of an IR spectrum below about 1500 cm^{-1} usually has many peaks, caused by the vibrations of the whole molecule. The shape of this region is unique for any particular substance. So, it can be used to identify it by matching its IR spectrum with that of a known sample, just as people can be identified by their fingerprints. It is therefore called the **fingerprint region**. Matching of spectra is done with a computer database.

Identifying groups of atoms

Particular functional groups produce peaks in different areas of the spectrum (see Figure 2) as summarised in Table 1. The frequencies of peaks are called the wavenumbers and are measured in the units, cm^{-1}.

Table 1 *Characteristic infra-red absorptions in organic molecules*

Bond	Wavenumber / cm^{-1}
N—H (amines)	3300–3500
O—H (alcohols)	3230–3550
C—H	2850–3300
O—H (acids)	2500–3000
C≡N	2220–2260
C=O	1680–1750
C=C	1620–1680
C—O	1000–1300
C—C	750–1100

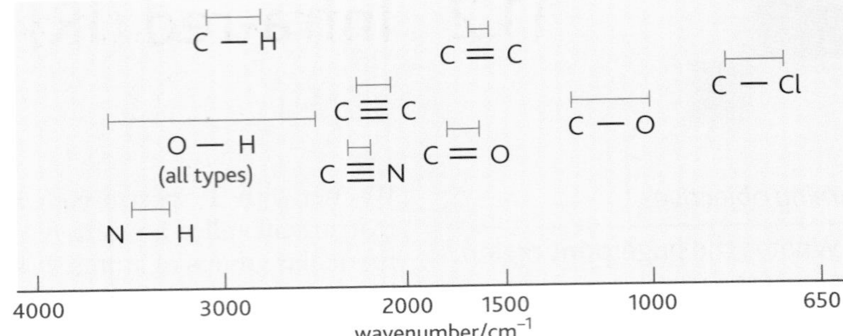

Figure 2 *Infra-red absorptions of some functional groups*

Infra-red spectra of alcohols, R—O—H

The infra-red spectra of alcohols show a peak caused by an O—H vibration at between 3230 cm^{-1} and 3550 cm^{-1}. This vibration is often called a **stretching vibration**, or just a stretch. The large range is caused by hydrogen bonding between alcohol molecules. Each vibrating hydrogen will be hydrogen-bonded to a varying number of other alcohol molecules, which will tend to slow down the vibration. Therefore the O—H has a range of frequencies, depending on how many other molecules are being dragged along. Figure 3 shows the infra-red spectrum for propan-2-ol. Notice the broad peak labelled 'O—H stretch'.

Alcohols also show a narrower peak between 1000 and 1300 cm^{-1} caused by a C—O stretching vibration.

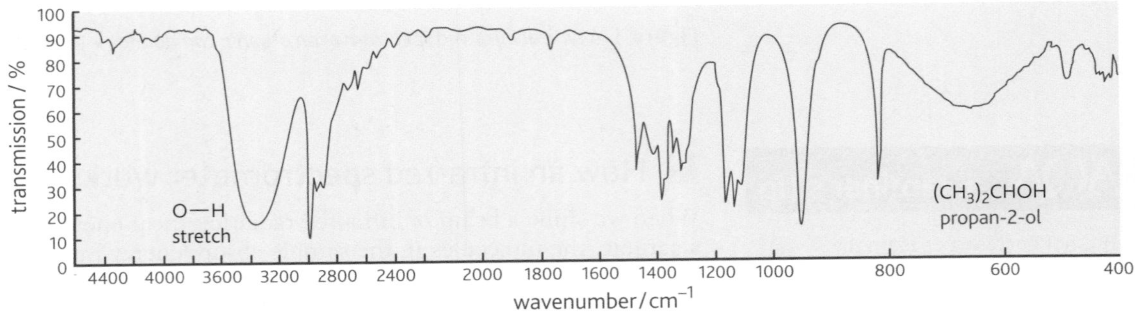

Figure 3 *The infra-red spectrum of propan-2-ol*

Summary questions

1 The vibrations of the atoms in a chemical bond can be thought of as being like the vibration of a ball hanging on a spring. Using this idea, suggest why the vibration frequency of the O—H bond and that of the N—H bond are very similar.

2 This spectrum is of a simple organic compound contaning carbon, hydrogen and oxygen only.

a Could it be an alcohol?

b Explain your answer.

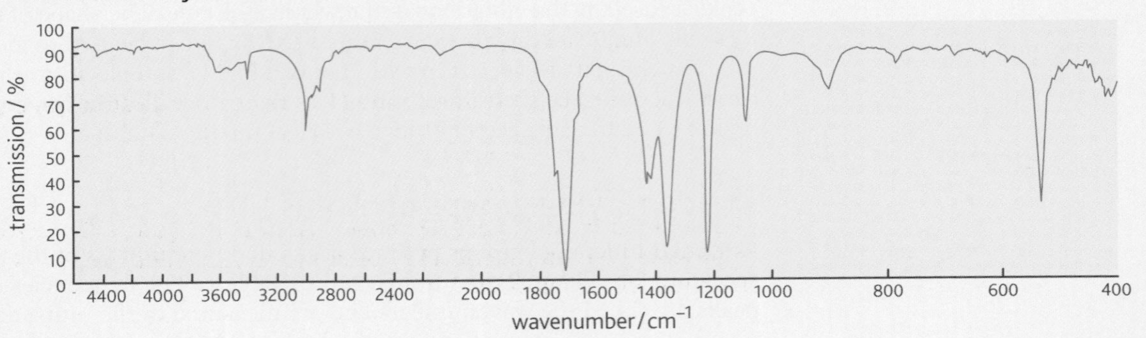

11.3 Infra-red spectra of compounds containing the C=O group

Learning objectives:

- How are the spectra of ketones, aldehydes, carboxylic acids and esters similar and how are they different?

Specification reference: 3.4.11

Compounds containing the functional group C=O are called carbonyl compounds. C=O is found in aldehydes, ketones, carboxylic acids, esters and other compounds as well. It has a stretching frequency of about 1700 cm^{-1}. The actual value varies slightly, depending on the type of compound it is found in, see Table 1.

Table 1 *Position of carbonyl peaks in the IR spectra of different compounds*

Molecule	Wavenumber / cm^{-1}
Ketone (R_2CO)	1725–1700
Aldehyde (RCHO)	1740–1720
Aromatic ketone (R_2CO)	1700–1680
Aromatic aldehyde (RHCO)	1715–1695
Carboxylic acid (RCO_2H)	1725–1700
Ester (RCO_2R)	1750–1730
Amide ($RCONH_2$)	1680–1640
Acid chloride (RCOCl)	1815–1790

Infra-red spectra of ketones and aldehydes

R
C=O
R'
a ketone

R
C=O
H
an aldehyde

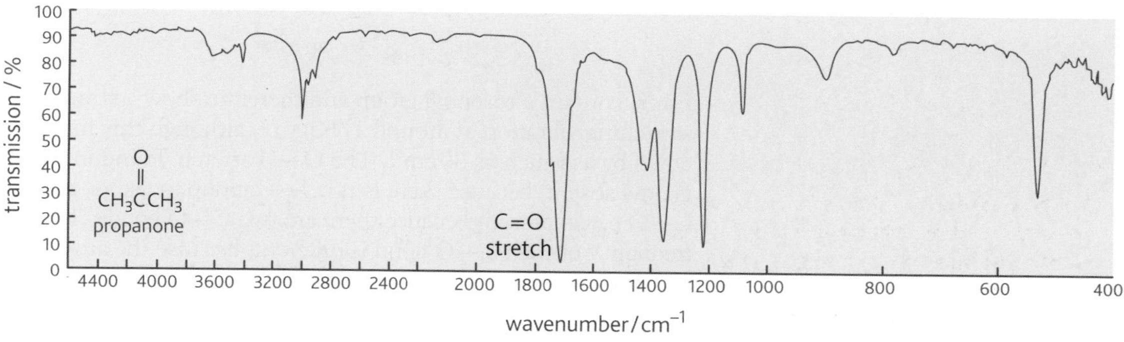

Figure 1 *The infra-red spectrum of propanone*

The peak produced by ketones and aldehydes is usually strong and sharp:

- In aldehydes it is between 1740 and 1720 cm^{-1}.
- In ketones it is between 1725 and 1700 cm^{-1}.

The infra-red spectrum of propanone is shown in Figure 1. The carbonyl group shows a prominent peak at around 1700 cm^{-1} due to a C=O stretching vibration in the ketone.

Infra-red spectra of carboxylic acids

O
H—C
OH

Figure 1 *A carboxylic acid*

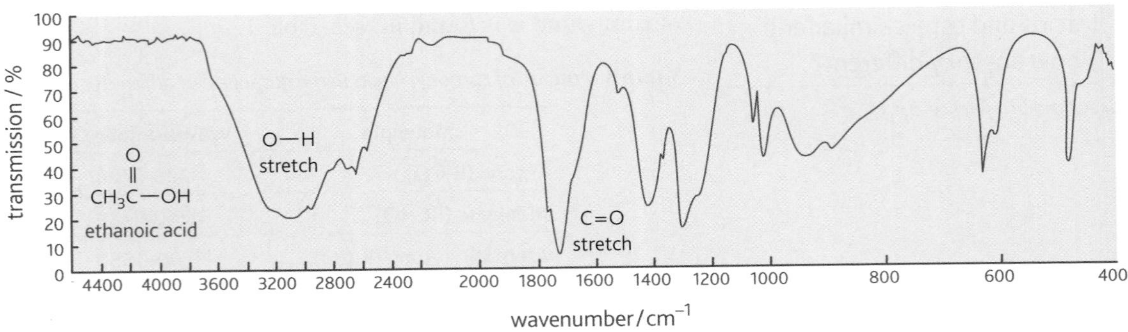

Figure 2 *Infra-red spectrum of ethanoic acid*

Figure 2 shows the infra-red spectrum of ethanoic acid.

There are two important peaks in the spectrum of ethanoic acid. One is at about 3100 cm^{-1} due to an O—H stretch and the other at about 1700 cm^{-1} due to a C=O stretch. We have met both these before, the former in alcohols and the latter in aldehydes and ketones. The O—H peak is broadened due to hydrogen bonding, as in the alcohol spectrum, Topic 11.2.

AQA Examiner's tip

Note that the O—H stretch absorption in alcohols and acids gives rise to very different spectra.

Infra-red spectra of esters

O
‖
R—C—O—R′
an ester

Esters contain a carbonyl group and therefore show a strong C=O stretching vibration at around 1750 cm^{-1}, although this may be shifted up or down by as much as 50 cm^{-1}. The O—H stretch, found in carboxylic acids is now absent, because there is no O—H group in esters, but there are *two* C—O peaks present because there are two C—O bonds. The stretching frequency of each C—O bond is different, because the atoms around them are slightly different. Figure 3 shows the spectrum for ethyl ethanoate.

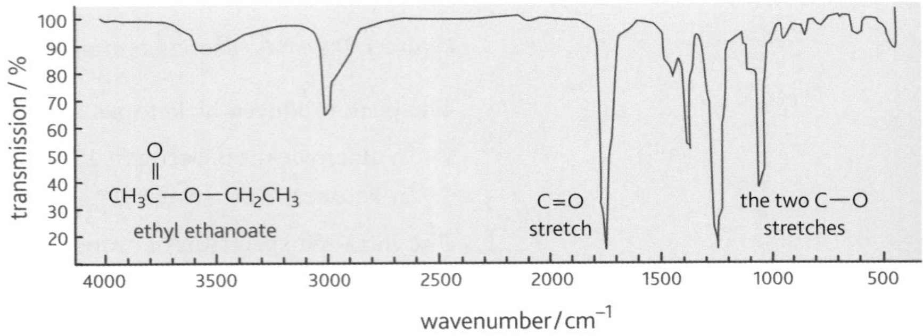

Figure 3 *The infra-red spectrum of ethyl ethanoate*

Identifying impurities

We saw in *AQA AS Chemistry*, Topic 17.2 that infra-red spectra can be used to spot the presence of impurities – a caffeine sample showed that unwanted water was present, when compared to the IR spectrum of a pure sample of caffeine because an O—H stretching peak was seen which cannot appear with pure caffeine.

Summary questions

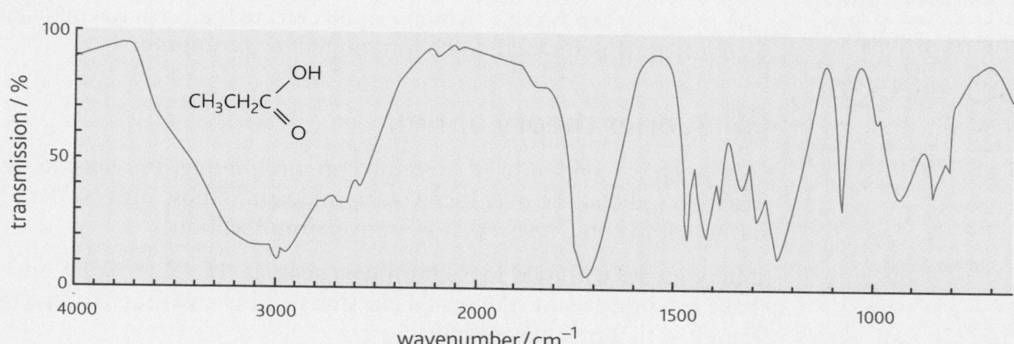

1 The IR spectrum above is of propanoic acid.

a Give the approximate wavenumber of the peak in the spectrum which shows the presence of:

i C=O   ii O—H

b Which of the above peaks would be present in:

i propanal   ii propanone

iii methyl propanoate

iv propan-1-ol   v propan-2-ol?

2 There is an IR peak at about 2800 cm^{-1} caused by a C—H stretching vibration. Explain why this is of little use in helping to identify an organic compound.

3 The peak in the IR spectrum representing the O—H stretch appears quite broad in pure ethanol, but it is sharper in the spectrum of ethanol dissolved in tetrachloromethane. Suggest a reason for this difference.

11.4 Nuclear magnetic resonance (nmr) spectroscopy

Learning objectives:

- What are the principles of nmr?
- What is a ^{13}C nmr spectrum?
- What is the chemical shift?
- What information does a ^{13}C nmr spectrum give?

Specification reference: 3.4.11

Nuclear magnetic resonance spectroscopy (nmr) is used particularly in organic chemistry. It is a powerful technique, because it helps us find the structures of even quite complex molecules.

A magnetic field is applied to a sample, which is surrounded by a source of radio waves and a radio receiver. This generates an energy change in the nuclei in the sample, which can be detected. Electromagnetic energy is emitted, which can then be interpreted by a computer.

A brief theory of nmr

Although you will only be examined on *interpreting* nmr spectra, this background reading may help you to understand how nmr works, although in some respects it is an oversimplification.

Many nuclei with odd mass numbers, such as ^{1}H, ^{13}C, ^{15}N, ^{19}F and ^{31}P have the property of *spin* (as do electrons). This gives them a magnetic field like that of a bar magnet.

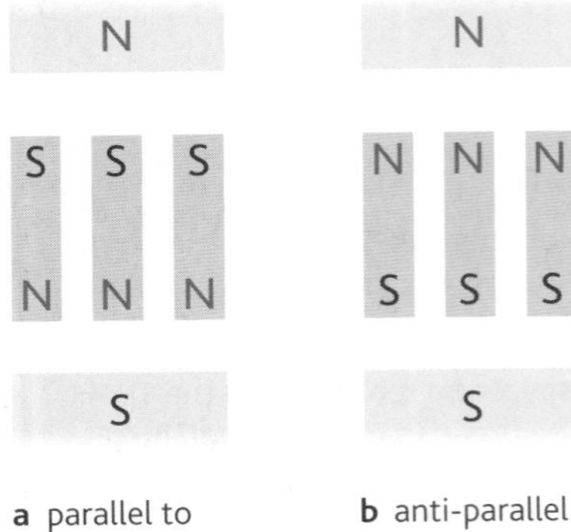

Figure 1 *The two possible orientations of bar magnets in a magnetic field*

If bar magnets are placed in an external magnetic field, they will line up parallel to the field as shown in Figure 1a.

It is also possible that the bar magnets could line up anti-parallel to the field, as in Figure 1b, but this orientation has a higher energy, as the bar magnets have to be forced into position against the repulsion of the external magnetic field. The stronger the external magnetic field and the stronger the bar magnets, the larger the energy gap between the parallel and anti-parallel states.

Something similar applies to nuclei with spin, such as ^{1}H and ^{13}C. There will be some of the nuclei in each energy state but more of them will be in the lower (parallel) one. If electromagnetic energy just equal in energy to the difference between the two positions (ΔE in Figure 2) is supplied, some nuclei will 'flip' between the parallel and anti-parallel positions. This is called **resonance**. The energy required to cause this is in the radio region of the electromagnetic spectrum. It is supplied by a radio frequency source, and the resonances are detected by a radio receiver, see Figure 3. The frequency of the radio waves required to cause 'flipping' for a particular magnetic field is called the **resonant frequency** of that atomic nucleus. A higher frequency corresponds to a larger energy gap between the two states. If the magnetic field is kept constant and the radio frequency gradually increased, different atomic nuclei will come into resonance at different frequencies depending on the strength of their 'atomic magnets'.

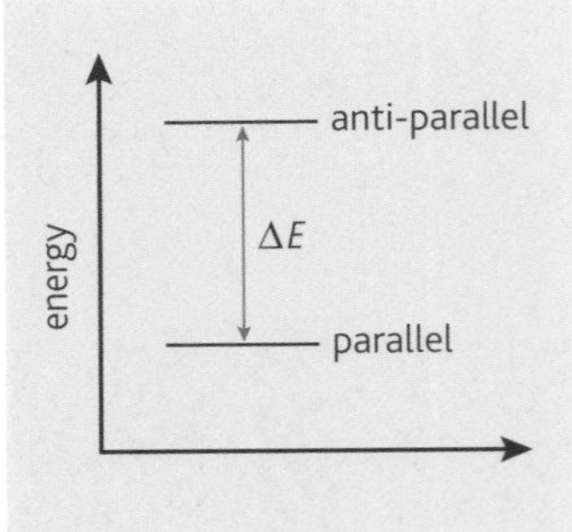

Figure 2 *Energy level diagram of the two orientations of bar magnets in a magnetic field*

In fact, modern instruments use pulses of radio waves of a range of frequencies all at once and analyse the response by a computer technique called 'Fourier transformation', but the principle remains of finding the frequencies at which different nuclei resonate.

Carbon-13 (^{13}C) nmr

Nmr is most often used with organic compounds. Although ^{12}C has no nuclear spin, ^{13}C does have one. While only 1% of carbon atoms are ^{13}C, modern instruments are sensitive enough to obtain a ^{13}C spectrum.

Not all the ^{13}C atoms in a molecule resonate at exactly the same magnetic field strength. Carbon atoms in different functional groups 'feel' the magnetic field differently. This is because all nuclei are **shielded** from the external magnetic field by the electrons that surround them. Nuclei with more electrons around them are better shielded. The greater the electron density around a ^{13}C atom, the smaller the magnetic field felt by the nucleus and the lower the frequency at which it resonates. The nmr instrument produces a graph of energy absorbed (from the radio signal) vertically against a quantity called **chemical shift** (which is related to the resonant frequency) horizontally.

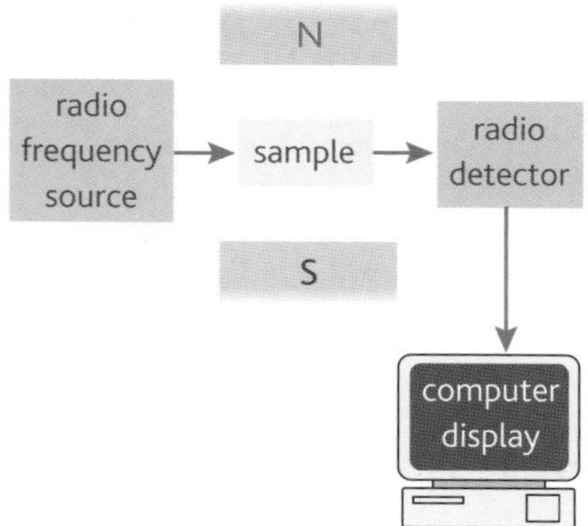

Figure 3 *Schematic diagram of an nmr spectrometer*

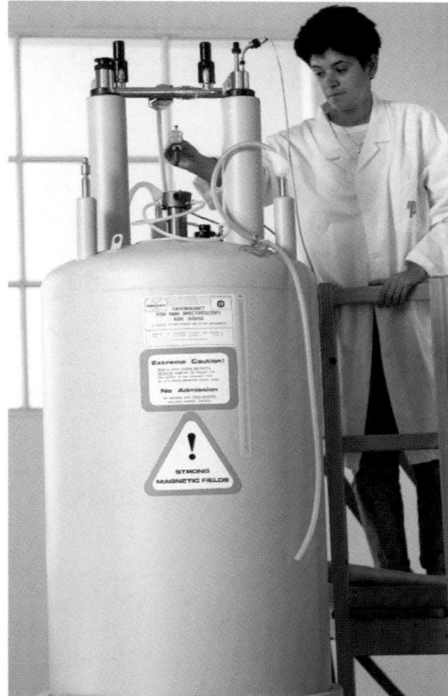

Figure 4 *Modern nmr instruments use electromagnets with superconducting coils to produce the strong magnetic fields required. The large white tank holds a jacket of liquid nitrogen surrounding an inner jacket of liquid helium which cools the magnet coils to 4 K*

The chemical shift

Chemical shift, symbol δ, is measured in units called parts per million (ppm) from a defined zero related to a compound called tetramethylsilane, TMS (see Topic 11.5). δ is related to the difference in frequency between the resonating nucleus and that of TMS. In ^{13}C nmr values of δ range from 0 to around 200 ppm.

The main point about ^{13}C nmr is that carbon atoms in different environments will give different chemical shift values. Figure 5 shows the ^{13}C nmr spectrum of ethanol. It has two peaks, one for each carbon, because the carbon atoms are in different environments – one is further from the oxygen atom than the other. The oxygen atom, being electronegative, draws electrons away from the carbon atom to which it is directly bonded.

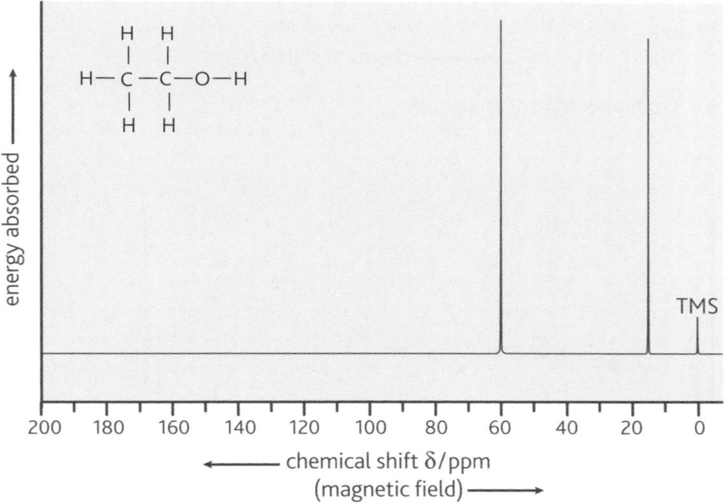

Figure 5 *^{13}C spectrum of ethanol*

Table 1 shows values of ^{13}C chemical shifts for carbon atoms in a variety of environments. The carbon atom at δ = 60 ppm in the ethanol spectrum is the carbon bonded to the oxygen (RCH_2O), while that at δ = 15 ppm is the other carbon (RCH_3) We can explain this because electronegative oxygen atom draws electrons away from the carbon bonded to it. It is 'deshielded' and feels a greater magnetic field and so resonates at a higher frequency and therefore has a *greater* δ value than the other carbon. The other RCH_3, carbon is surrounded by more electrons and therefore shielded and has a smaller δ value.

Hint

On nmr spectra the chemical shift *increases* from right to left.

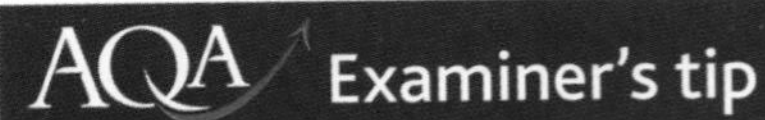

Examiner's tip

Tables of chemical shift data are provided in all examinations.

Table 1 *^{13}C chemical shift values*

Type of carbon	δ / ppm
—C—C—	5–40
R—C—Cl or Br	10–70
R—C(=O)—C—	20–50
R—C—N<	25–60
—C—O— alcohols, ethers or esters	50–90
>C=C<	90–150
R—C≡N	110–125
benzene ring	110–160
R—C(=O)— esters or acids	160–185
R—C(=O)— aldehydes or ketones	190–220

Examiner's tip

The heights of the peaks in ^{13}C nmr spectra are not significant, it is their δ values that are important in interpreting spectra.

More examples of ^{13}C nmr spectra

Figures 6 and 7 show the ^{13}C nmr spectra of the isomers propanone, CH_3COCH_3 and propanal, CH_3CH_2CHO. In propanone, there are just two different environments for the carbon atoms: the two CH_3 groups and the C=O. The spectrum shows two peaks:

- At δ = 205 ppm due to the C=O.
- At δ = 30 ppm due to the CH_3 groups.

Propanal has three different carbon environments:

- The CH_3 group at δ = 5 ppm.
- The CH_2 at δ = 37.
- The CHO group at δ = 205 ppm.

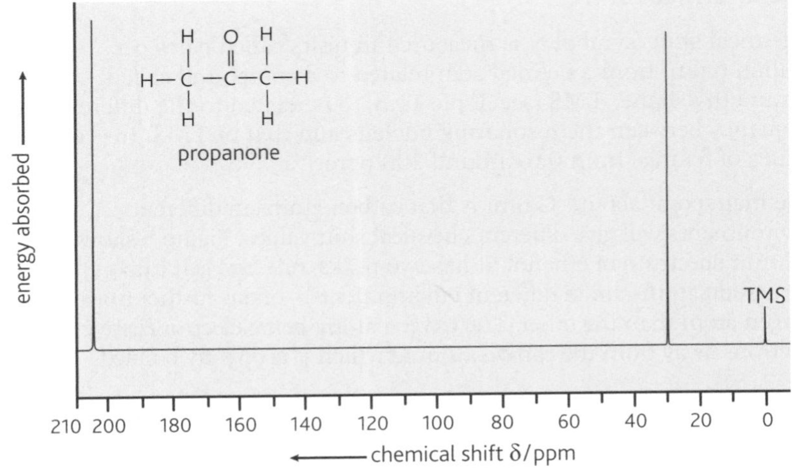

Figure 6 *^{13}C nmr spectrum of propanone*

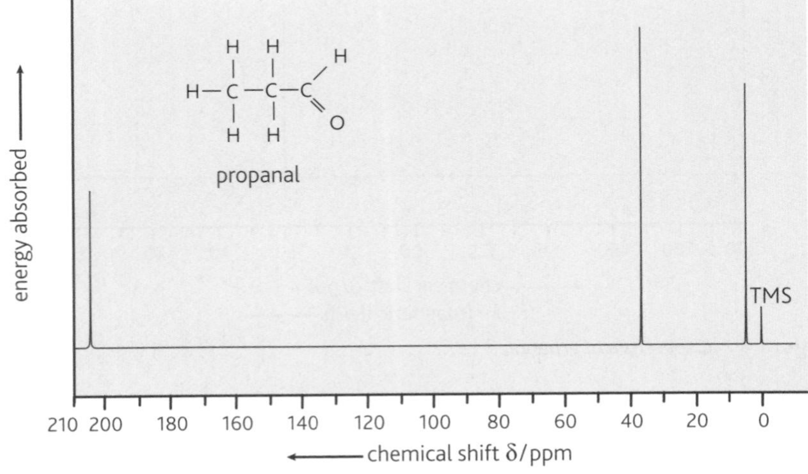

Figure 7 *^{13}C nmr spectrum of propanal*

Summary questions

1 The ^{13}C nmr spectrum of ethanol is discussed above and has two peaks. Methoxymethane is an isomer of ethanol:

```
   H       H
   |       |
H—C—O—C—H
   |       |
   H       H
```

methoxymethane

a How many peaks would you expect to find in its ^{13}C nmr spectrum?

b Explain your answer.

2 The ^{13}C nmr spectra of propan-1-ol and propan-2-ol are given below. State which is which and explain your answer.

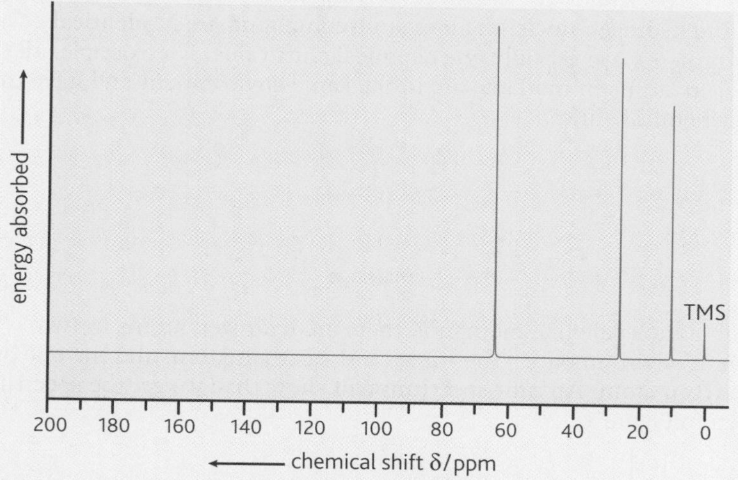

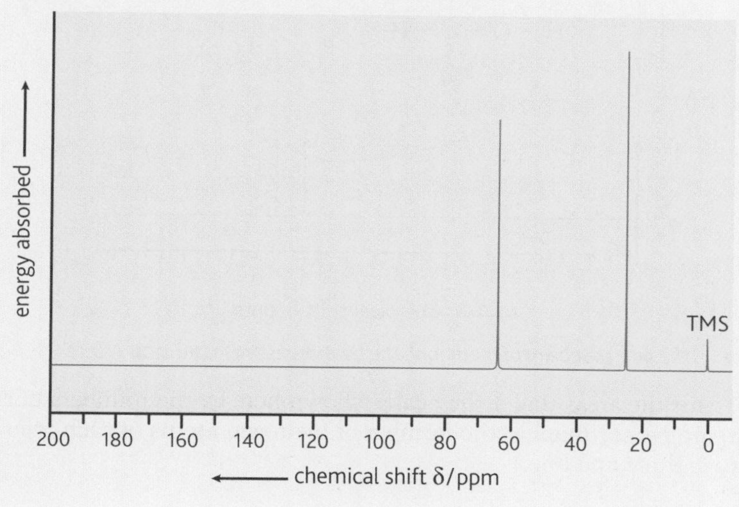

11.5 Proton nmr

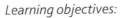

Learning objectives:

- What is a ^{1}H nmr spectrum?
- What information does a ^{1}H nmr spectrum give?
- What does the integration trace show?

Specification reference: 3.4.11

In proton nmr, it is the ^{1}H nucleus that is being examined. Nearly all hydrogen atoms are ^{1}H so it is easier to get an nmr spectrum for ^{1}H than for ^{13}C.

Here it is hydrogen atoms attached to different functional groups that 'feel' the magnetic field differently, because all nuclei are shielded from the external magnetic field by the electrons that surround them. Nuclei with more electrons around them are better shielded. The greater the electron density around a hydrogen atom, the smaller the chemical shift, δ. The values of chemical shift in proton nmr are smaller than those for ^{13}C nmr – most are between 0 and 10 ppm.

If all the hydrogen nuclei in an organic compound are in identical environments, we get only one chemical shift value. For example, all the hydrogen atoms in methane are in the same environment and have the same chemical shift:

```
    H
    |
H — C — H
    |
    H
```

methane

But, in a molecule like methanol, there are hydrogen atoms in two different environments – the three on the carbon atom, and the one on the oxygen atom. An nmr spectrum will show this: we get the spectrum shown in Figure 1.

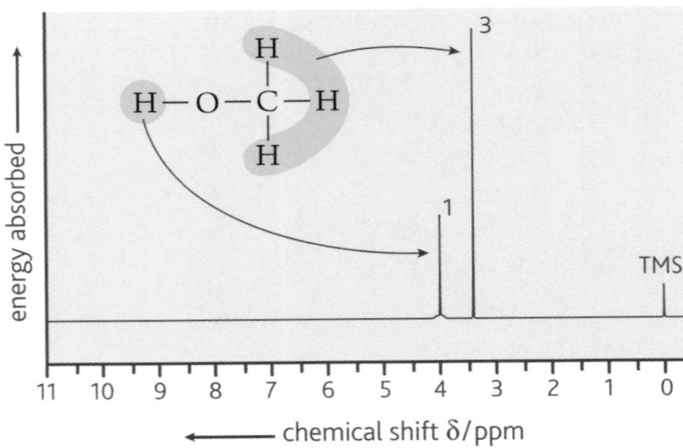

Figure 1 *The nmr spectrum of methanol; the peak areas are in the ratio 1 : 3*

In ^{1}H nmr the areas under the peaks (shown here by the numbers next to them) are proportional to the number of hydrogen atoms of each type – in this case three and one.

The integration trace

In proton n.m.r. spectra, the area of each peak is related to the number of hydrogen atoms producing it. So, in the spectrum of methanol, CH_3OH, the CH_3 peak is three times the area of the OH peak. This can be difficult to evaluate by eye, so the instrument produces a line called the integration trace, shown in red in Figure 2. The relative heights of the steps of this trace give the relative number of each type of hydrogen; 3 : 1 in this case. For simplicity in this book we have in general omitted the integrated trace and given the relative number of hydrogen atoms that each peak represents.

The chemical shift value at which the peak representing each type of proton appears tells us about its environment – the type of functional group of which it is a part.

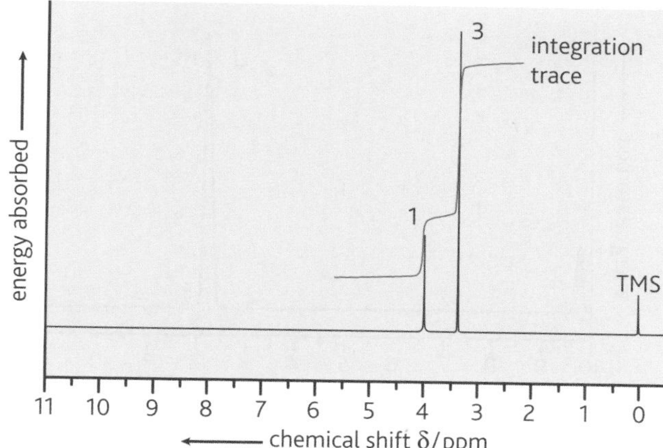

Figure 2 *The nmr spectrum of methanol showing the integration trace in red*

Chemical shift values

Hydrogen atom(s) in any functional group have a particular chemical shift value, see Table 2 on page 250.

Tetramethylsilane

The δ values of chemical shifts are measured by reference to a standard – the chemical shift of the hydrogen atoms in the compound tetramethylsilane ($Si(CH_4)_4$), called TMS, see Figure 3. The chemical shift value of these hydrogen atoms is zero by definition. A little TMS, which is a liquid, may be added to samples before their nmr spectrum are run, and gives a peak at a δ value of exactly zero ppm to calibrate the spectrum, although modern techniques do not require this. All the spectra in this book show a TMS peak at $\delta = 0$.

Other reasons for using TMS are that it is inert, it is non-toxic and it is easy to remove from the sample.

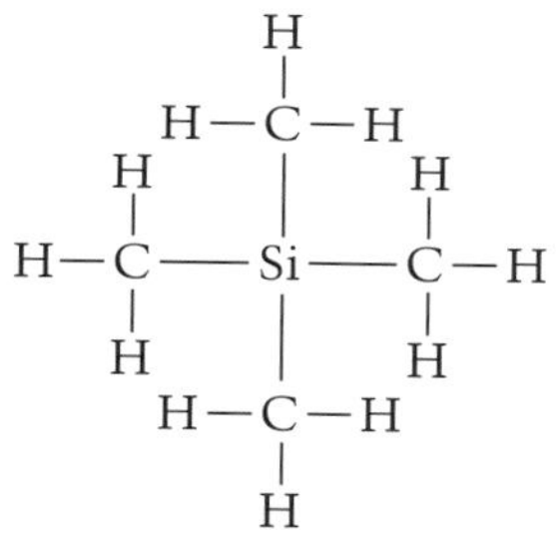

Figure 3 *Tetramethylsilane, TMS – all 12 hydrogen atoms are in exactly the same environment, so they produce a single signal*

Summary questions

1 This question is about the isomers propan-1-ol and propan-2-ol.

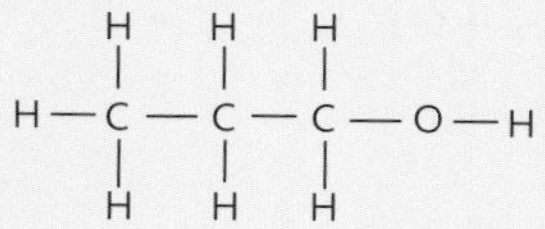

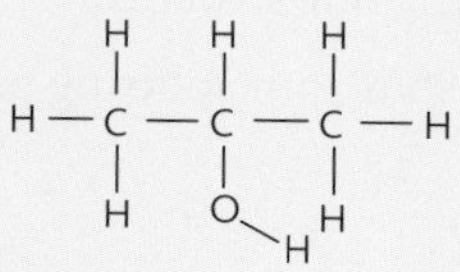

a What is meant by the term 'isomer'?

b Write down the formulae of propan-1-ol and propan-2-ol and mark each of the hydrogen atoms A, B etc. to show which are in different environments.

c How many different environments are there for the hydrogen atoms in:

i propan-1-ol ii propan-2-ol?

d How many hydrogen atoms in each of the different environments, A, B, etc., are there in:

i propan-1-ol ii propan-2-ol?

e Use the data in Table 2 on page 250 to predict the chemical shift for each environment in:

i propan-1-ol ii propan-2-ol?

11.6 Interpreting proton (^1H) nmr spectra

Learning objectives:

- What causes spin-spin coupling?
- What is the $n + 1$ rule?
- How can ^1H nmr spectra be interpreted?

Specification reference: 3.4.11

If we are presented with a spectrum of an organic compound, as in Figure 1, we can find out a lot about its structure.

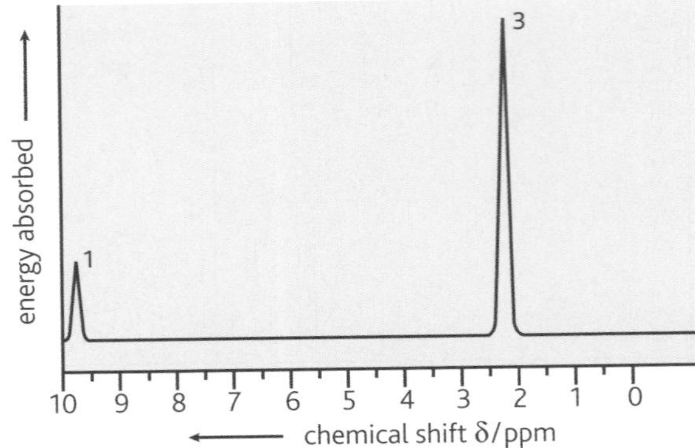

Figure 1 *The nmr spectrum of an organic compound*

The chemical shift values in Table 2 on page 250 tell us that the single hydrogen at chemical shift 9.7 is the hydrogen from a —CHO (aldehyde) group and the three hydrogens at chemical shift 2.2 are those of a —$COCH_3$ group. (This peak could also be caused by—$COCH_2R$, but since there are three hydrogens it must be —$COCH_3$.)

So the compound is likely to be ethanal, CH_3CHO, Figure 2.

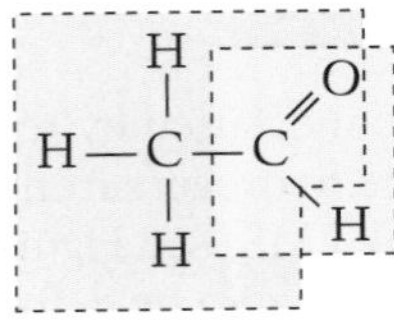

Figure 2 *The two groups that make up ethanal*

AQA Examiner's tip

Spin-spin coupling is not usually seen in ^{13}C nmr spectra due to the low abundance of ^{13}C. This is one reason why ^{13}C spectra are simpler than ^1H spectra.

Spin-spin coupling

If we zoom in on most nmr peaks we see that they are split into particular patterns – this is called spin-spin coupling (also called spin-spin splitting). It happens because the applied magnetic field felt by any hydrogen is affected by the magnetic field of the hydrogen atoms on the neighbouring carbon atoms. This spin-spin splitting gives us information about the neighbouring hydrogen atoms, which can be very helpful when working out structure.

Figure 3 shows the spin-spin splitting patterns.

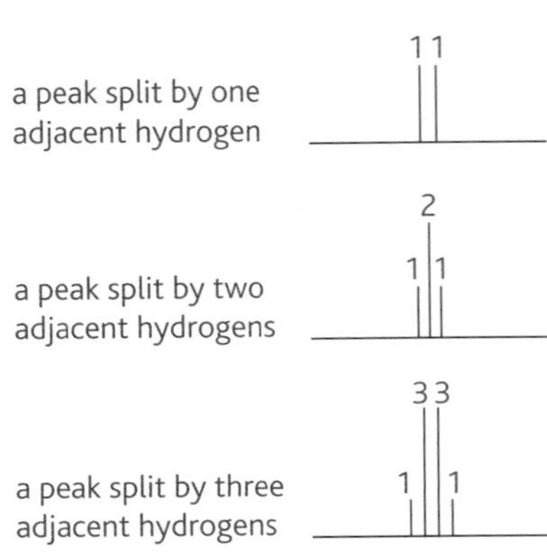

Figure 3 *Nmr splitting patterns*

The $n + 1$ rule

If there is one hydrogen atom on an adjacent carbon, this will split the nmr signal of a particular hydrogen into two peaks each of the same height.

If there are two hydrogen atoms on an adjacent carbon, this will split the nmr signal of a particular hydrogen into three peaks in the height ratio 1 : 2 : 1.

Three adjacent hydrogen atoms will split the nmr signal of a particular hydrogen into four peaks in the height ratio 1 : 3 : 3 : 1.

This is called the $n + 1$ rule:

n hydrogens on an adjacent carbon atom will split a peak into $n + 1$ smaller peaks.

Some examples of interpreting ¹H nmr spectra

Ethanal

If we zoom in on the peaks in the spectrum of ethanal shown in Figure 1, we see spin-spin splitting, see Figure 4.

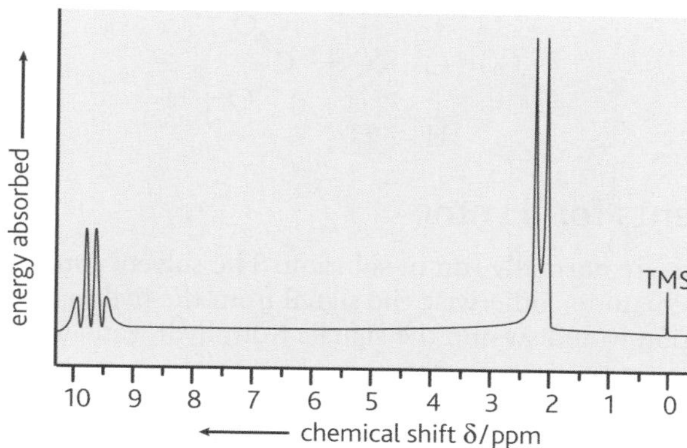

Figure 4 *The nmr spectrum of ethanal, CH_3CHO*

As we have seen above, there are two types of hydrogen environments:

- There is a single peak of chemical shift 9.7. This is the hydrogen of a —CHO group. This peak is split into 4 (height ratios 1: 3 : 3 : 1) by the three hydrogens of the adjacent —CH_3 group.
- The peak with chemical shift 2.2 is caused by three hydrogens of a —CH_3 group. This peak is split into two (height ratios 1 : 1) by the one hydrogen of the adjacent —CHO group.

Propanoic acid

Figure 5 shows the nmr spectrum of propanoic acid.

It is useful to make a table of the peaks by reference to Table 2 on page 250.

From the chemical shift value alone, the peak at 2.4 could be caused by either of the groups shown. However the fact that there are just two hydrogens means that it must correspond to —COC**H_2**R.

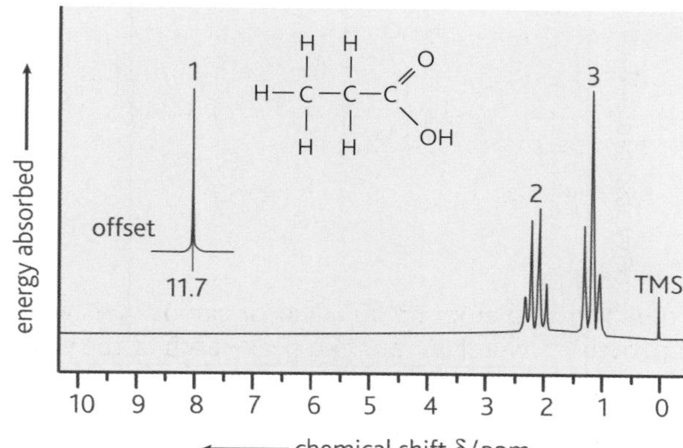

Figure 5 *The nmr spectrum of propanoic acid, CH_3CH_2COOH*

Table 1

Chemical shift, δ	Type of hydrogen	Number of hydrogens
11.7	—COOH	1
2.4	—$COCH_2R$ or —$COCH_3$	2
1.1	RCH_3	3

AQA Examiner's tip

Spin-spin coupling is not seen when equivalent hydrogens are on adjacent carbon atoms, e.g. $HOCH_2CH_2OH$ has only two single peaks in its nmr spectrum.

Looking at the spin-spin splitting:

- The peak at 11.7 is not split. This is because the adjacent carbon has no hydrogens bonded to it, —COOH.
- The peak at 2.4 is split into four. This indicates that the adjacent carbon has three hydrogens bonded to it. So, the R in —$COC\mathbf{H}_2R$ must be —CH_3.
- The peak at 1.1 is split into three. This indicates that the adjacent carbon has two hydrogens bonded to it. So, the R in RCH_3 must be —CH_2.

So, if we put these groups together we make propanoic acid:

Solvents for ^1H nmr

Nmr spectra are normally run in solution. The solvent must not contain any hydrogen atoms, otherwise the signal from the hydrogen atoms in the solution would swamp the signals from hydrogen atoms in the sample, because there are vastly more of them.

One solvent commonly used is tetrachloromethane, CCl_4, which has no hydrogen atoms. Other solvents contain deuterium, which is an isotope of hydrogen and has the symbol D. Deuterium does not produce an nmr signal in the same range as hydrogen, though it has the same chemical properties. Some examples of deuterium-based solvents are deuterotrichloromethane, $CDCl_3$, deuterium oxide, D_2O, and perdeuterobenzene, C_6D_6.

More examples of interpreting and predicting nmr spectra

Propanone

The nmr spectrum of propanone is shown in Figure 6.

The nmr spectrum of propanone has just one peak. This means that all the hydrogen atoms in the molecule are in identical environments. The chemical shift value of 2.1 indicates that this corresponds to —$COCH_3$ or —$COCH_2R$.

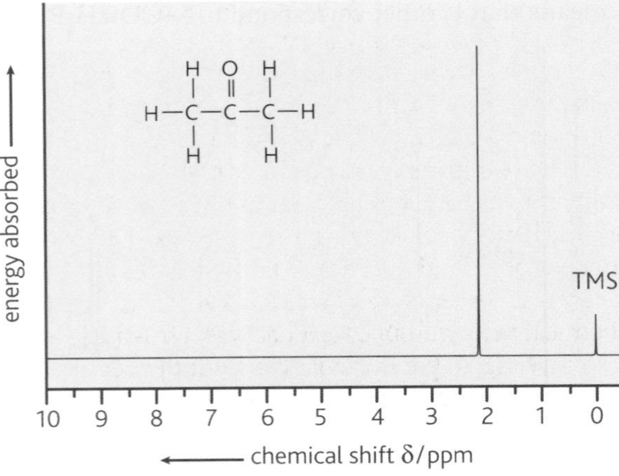

Figure 6 *The nmr spectrum of propanone*

AQA Examiner's tip

There are six hydrogen atoms in a molecule of propanone, all of which are in an identical environment. However, we cannot tell the number from the spectrum because the peak areas in nmr spectra are only relative. This means that we can tell that in methanol, for example, that the area under the —CH_3 peak is three time that of the —OH peak but not the absolute number of each type of hydrogen (the absolute numbers could be 2 and 6, for example).

Predicting nmr spectra

Chemists making new compounds may predict the spectrum of a compound they are making and compare their prediction with that of the compound they actually produce, to check that their reaction has gone as intended.

Ethyl ethanoate

There are three sets of hydrogen atoms in different environments. The values of chemical shift are predicted using Table 2 on page 250.

We can predict the spectrum shown in Figure 7, by dividing up the molecule as shown:

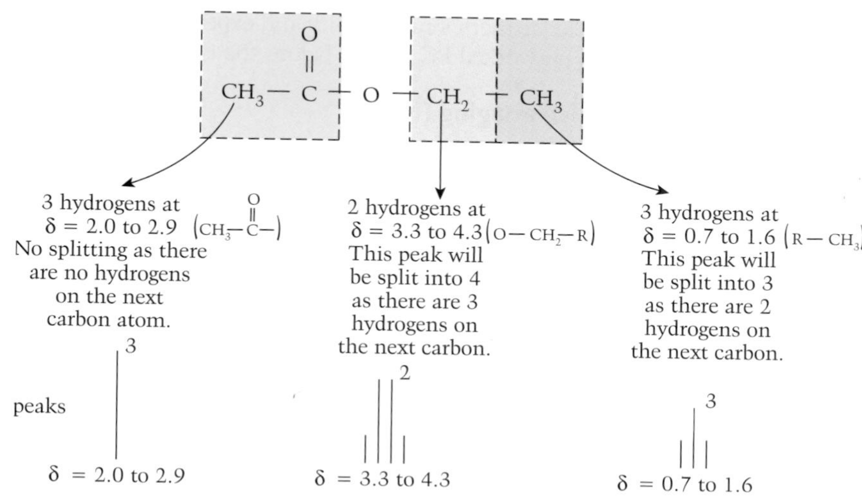

3 hydrogens at δ = 2.0 to 2.9 (CH₃–C(=O)–)
No splitting as there are no hydrogens on the next carbon atom.
2 hydrogens at δ = 3.3 to 4.3 (O–CH₂–R)
This peak will be split into 4 as there are 3 hydrogens on the next carbon.
3 hydrogens at δ = 0.7 to 1.6 (R–CH₃)
This peak will be split into 3 as there are 2 hydrogens on the next carbon.
peaks
δ = 2.0 to 2.9
δ = 3.3 to 4.3
δ = 0.7 to 1.6

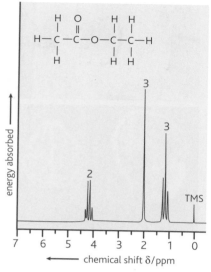

Figure 7 *The nmr spectrum of ethyl ethanoate*

How science works

The birth of nmr

Nmr (nuclear magnetic resonance) is probably the most important analytical technique used by organic chemists today. Indeed, one Nobel Prize-winning chemist has been quoted as saying 'when the nmr goes down, the organic chemists go home'.

The chemical usefulness of the technique was discovered almost by accident, however. The effect began to be investigated by physicists just before and after the Second World War, and it appears that the researchers were helped in building their apparatus by the availability of cheap electronic components from surplus wartime radar equipment. The aim of the experiment was to measure the magnetic properties of atomic nuclei (their magnetic moments to be precise). They succeeded in their measurements, but were frustrated to find that the same atomic nucleus in different chemicals gave different results. For example, the two nitrogen atoms in ammonium nitrate, NH_4NO_3, gave different values. They realised that this was because the nitrogen nuclei were being shielded from the magnetic field by the electrons that surrounded them, and that as the two nitrogen atoms were in different chemical environments they were shielded to different extents. Then the 'chemical penny dropped'! What was a frustration to the physicists trying to investigate the nucleus was a gift to chemists whose prime interest was what was happening to the electrons! Nmr could tell chemists about the degree to which electrons were surrounding atoms, so it could distinguish between the hydrogen atoms in the CH_3, CH_2 and OH groups in ethanol, CH_3CH_2OH, for example.

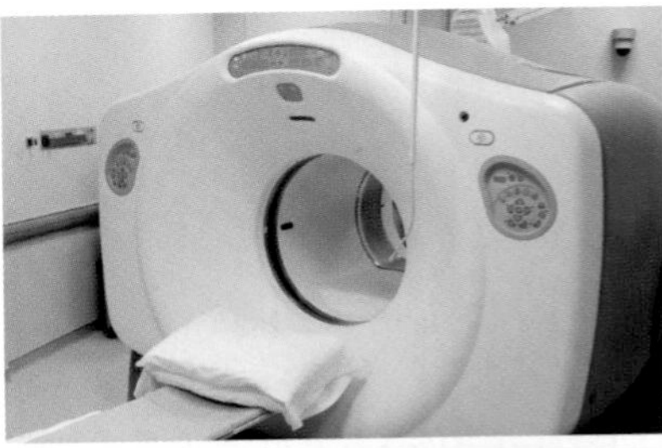

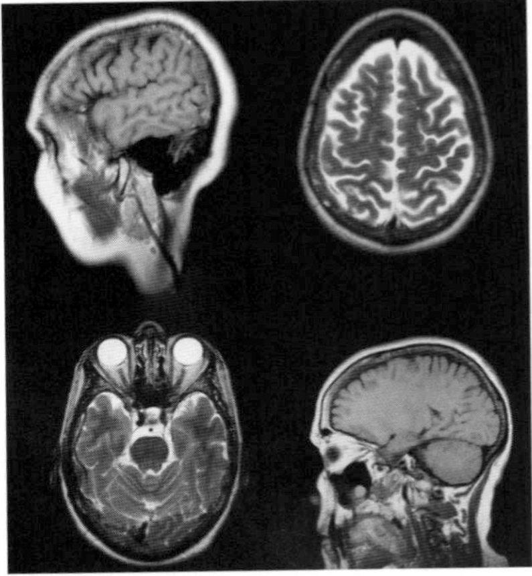

Figure 9 *MRI scanner and a scan obtained by using this technique*

Manipulating the data

Nmr is a technique that generates a lot of information and it has benefited enormously from the development of computers to process and present the data that it generates. Back in the early days of the 1950s and early 1960s, the data was produced from the instrument on paper tape and had to be manually transferred to punched cards which had to be *posted* to a computer centre to be put onto magnetic tape and processed. (In those days, a powerful computer might be the size of a house – no PC in every home and lab then.) The results would be posted back to the researchers, maybe a week later, provided that no one dropped the cards or tore the paper tape. Later, instruments used mechanical chart recorders. Nowadays, a researcher will drop off a compound at her department's nmr facility and expect to have the spectrum up on her networked PC almost before she is back at her lab.

Magnetic resonance imaging (MRI)

Nmr can be used to investigate the human body – this was first realised by Felix Bloch, who found he got a strong signal by placing his finger in an nmr spectrometer. This signal was coming from protons in the water molecules that make up a large proportion of the human body. Water in different parts of the body (normal cells and cancer cells, for example) gives slightly different nmr signals.

MRI scanning of parts of the body, to help diagnose medical conditions, is now routine. The patient passes through a scanner where the magnetic field varies across the body. This, along with sophisticated computer processing of the nmr signal allows a three-dimensional image of the body to be built up. The technique is harmless as, unlike X-rays, neither the radio waves nor the magnetic field can damage cells. However, the name 'magnetic resonance imaging' is used rather than 'nuclear magnetic resonance' because of the association of the word 'nuclear' with radioactivity in the mind of the public.

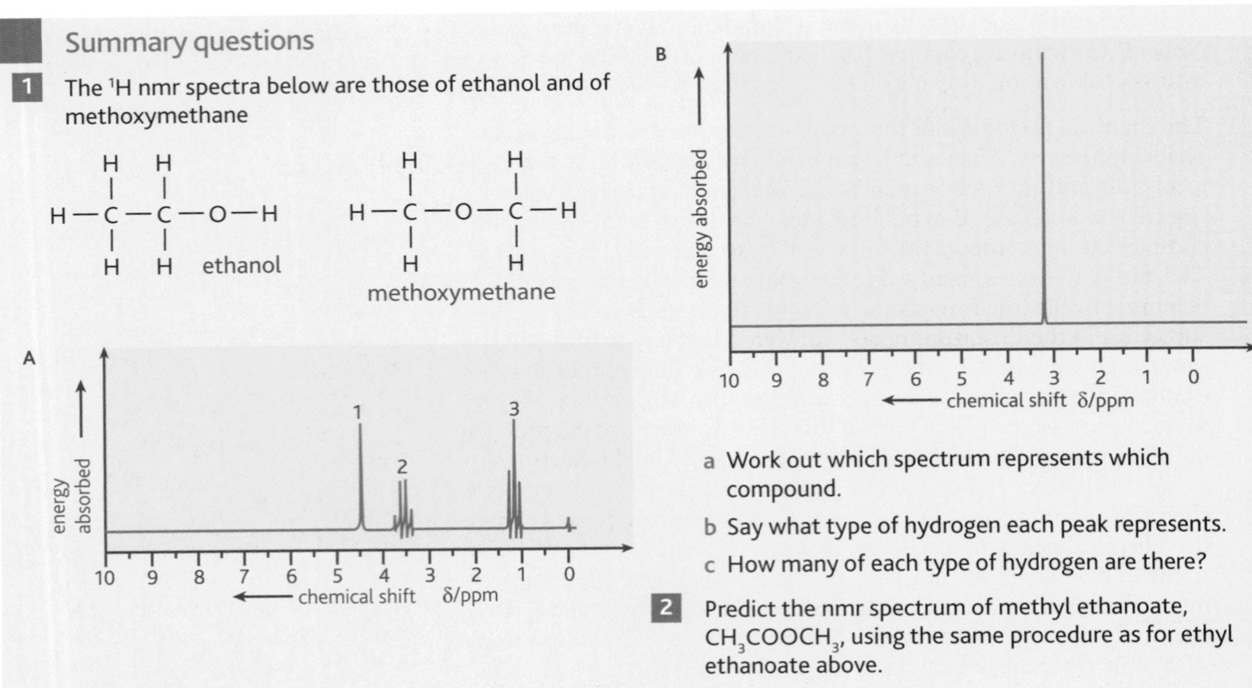

Summary questions

1 The ^1H nmr spectra below are those of ethanol and of methoxymethane

a Work out which spectrum represents which compound.

b Say what type of hydrogen each peak represents.

c How many of each type of hydrogen are there?

2 Predict the nmr spectrum of methyl ethanoate, CH_3COOCH_3, using the same procedure as for ethyl ethanoate above.

11.7 Chromatography

Learning objectives:

- Why can similar substances be separated using chromatography?
- What is column chromatography?
- What is gas–liquid chromatography?

Specification reference: 3.4.11

Figure 1 *The cellulose of the paper holds many trapped water molecules (the stationary phase). Here, ethanol is the mobile phase, or eluent*

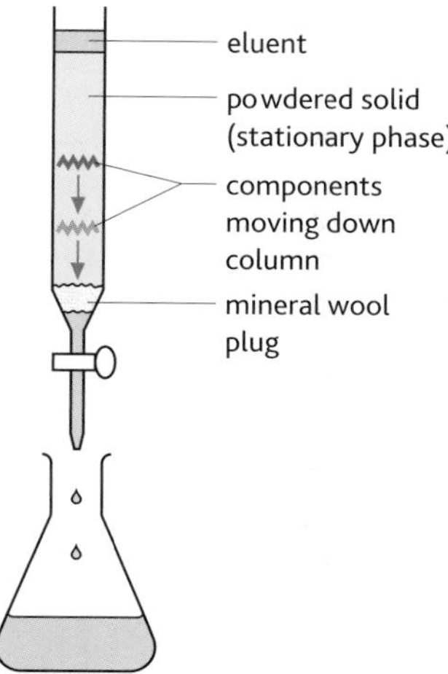

Figure 2 *Column chromatography*

You will probably be familiar with paper chromatography, which is often used to separate the dyes in, for example, felt-tip pens.

Chromatography describes a whole family of separation techniques. They all depend on the principle that a mixture can be separated if it is dissolved in a solvent and then the resulting solution (now called the mobile phase) moves over a solid (the stationary phase).

- The **mobile phase** carries the soluble components of the mixture with it. The more soluble the component in the mobile phase, the faster it moves. The solvent in the mobile phase is often called the eluent (in column chromatography).
- The **stationary phase** will hold back the components in the mixture that are attracted to it. The more affinity a component has for the stationary phase the slower it moves with the solvent.

So, if suitable mobile and stationary phases are chosen, a mixture of similar substances can be separated completely, because every component of the mixture has a unique balance between its affinity for the stationary and for the mobile phase. In fact, chromatography is often the only way that very similar components of a mixture can be separated.

Column chromatography

Column chromatography uses a powder, such as silica, aluminium oxide or a resin, as the stationary phase. This is packed into a narrow tube – the column – and a solvent (the eluent) is added at the top, see Figure 2. As the eluent runs down the column, the components of the mixture move at a different rate and can be collected separately in a flask at the bottom. More than one eluent may be used to get a better separation. This method has the advantage that fairly large amounts can be separated and collected. For example, a mixture of amino acids can be separated into its pure components by this method.

Gas–liquid chromatography, GC

This technique is one of the most important modern analytical techniques. The basic apparatus is shown in Figure 3.

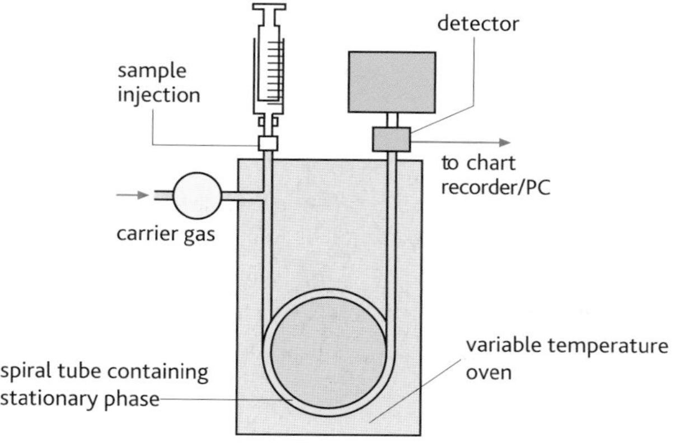

Figure 3 *Gas–liquid chromatography, GC*

AQA Examiner's tip

Separation depends on the balance between solubility in the moving phase and retention in the stationary phase.

The stationary phase is a powder, coated with oil. It is either packed into or coated onto the inside of a long capillary tube, up to 100 m long and less than ½ mm in diameter. The mobile phase is usually an unreactive gas, such as nitrogen or helium. After injection, the sample is carried along by the gas and the mixture separates as some of the components move along with the gas and some are retained by the oil, each to a different degree. This means that the components leave the column at different times after injection – they have different **retention times**.

Various types of detectors are used, including ones that measure the thermal conductivity of the emerging gas. The results may be presented on a graph, see Figure 4. The area under each peak is proportional to the amount of that component.

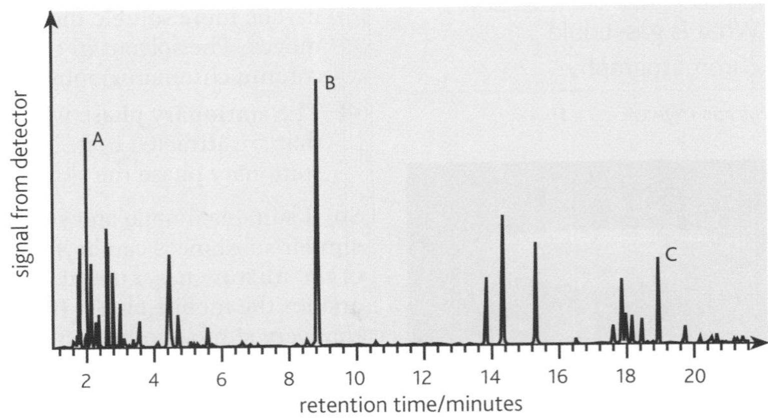

Figure 4 *Typical GC trace; each peak represents a different component*

In some instruments the components are fed directly into a mass spectrometer, IR or nmr spectrometer for identification. Today the whole process is automated and computer controlled.

As an analytical method for separating mixtures, GC is extremely sensitive. It can separate minute traces of substances in foodstuffs, and even link crude oil pollution found on beaches with its tanker of origin by comparing oil samples. Perhaps its best-known use is for testing athletes' blood or urine for drug taking.

The identification of a component is done by matching its retention time with that of a known substance under the same conditions. This is then confirmed by comparing the mass spectra of the two substances.

Figure 5 *Operator at GC apparatus*

Summary questions

1. What is the difference between column chromatography and gas–liquid chromatography?
2. Why is GC so important in forensic detective work? Give a possible example not in the text.
3. From the GC in Figure 4 above, identify from A, B and C:
   a the most abundant component in the mixture
   b the one with the greatest affinity for the solid phase
   c the one with the greatest affinity for the gas phase
   d the one with the greatest retention time.

AQA Examination-style questions

1 (a) The infra-red spectrum of compound **A**, $C_3H_6O_2$, is shown below.

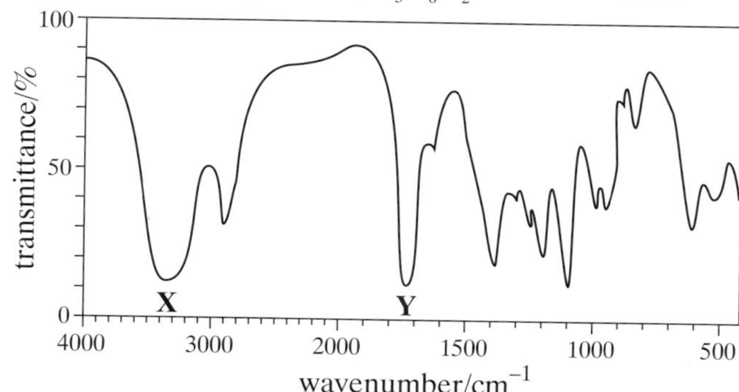

Identify the functional groups which cause the absorptions labelled **X** and **Y**.

Using this information draw the structures of the three possible structural isomers for **A**.

Label as **A** the structure which represents a pair of optical isomers. *(6 marks)*

(b) Draw the structures of the three **branched-chain** alkenes with molecular formula C_5H_{10}

Draw the structures of the three dibromoalkanes, $C_5H_{10}Br_2$, formed when these three alkenes react with bromine.

One of these dibromoalkanes has only three peaks in its proton nmr spectrum. Deduce the integration ratio and the splitting patterns of these three peaks. *(10 marks)*

AQA, 2006

2 (a) The reaction of but-1-ene with chlorine produces 1,2-dichlorobutane, $C_4H_8Cl_2$

(i) Given that chlorine exists as a mixture of two isotopes, ^{35}Cl and ^{37}Cl, predict the number of molecular ion peaks and their *m*/*z* values in the mass spectrum of $C_4H_8Cl_2$

(ii) The mass spectrum of 1,2-dichlorobutane contains peaks at *m*/*z* = 77 and 79. Draw the structure of the fragment ion which produces the peak at *m*/*z* = 77 and write an equation showing its formation from the molecular ion. *(6 marks)*

(b) The reaction of but-2-ene with hydrogen chloride forms a racemic mixture of the stereoisomers of 2-chlorobutane.

(i) Name the type of stereoisomerism shown by 2-chlorobutane and give the meaning of the term *racemic mixture*. State how separate samples of the stereoisomers could be distinguished.

(ii) By considering the shape of the reactive intermediate involved in the mechanism of this reaction, explain how a racemic mixture of the two stereoisomers of 2-chlorobutane is formed. *(7 marks)*

(c) The reaction of but-2-ene with chlorine produces 2,3-dichlorobutane, $C_4H_8Cl_2$

(i) State the number of peaks, their integration ratio and any splitting of peaks in the proton nmr spectrum of 2,3-dichlorobutane.

(ii) Compound **S**, an isomer of $C_4H_8Cl_2$, produces a proton nmr spectrum which consists only of a singlet, a triplet and a quartet with an integration ratio of 3 : 3 : 2 respectively.

Compound **T**, also an isomer of $C_4H_8Cl_2$, produces a proton nmr spectrum which consists only of two singlets with an integration ratio of 3 : 1.

Draw the structures of **S** and of **T**. *(6 marks)*

AQA, 2006

3 This question concerns four isomers, **W**, **X**, **Y** and **Z**, with the molecular formula $C_5H_{10}O_2$

(a) The proton nmr spectrum of **W** shows 4 peaks.
The table below gives the chemical shifts, δ values, for each of these peaks, together with their splitting patterns and integration values.

δ/ppm	2.18	2.59	3.33	3.64
Splitting pattern	singlet	triplet	singlet	triplet
Integration value	3	2	3	2

State what can be deduced about the structure of **W** from the presence of the following in its nmr spectrum.

(i) The singlet peak at $\delta = 2.18$

(ii) The singlet peak at $\delta = 3.33$

(iii) Two triplet peaks.

(iv) Hence, deduce the structure of **W**. *(4 marks)*

(b) The infra-red spectrum of **X** is shown below.

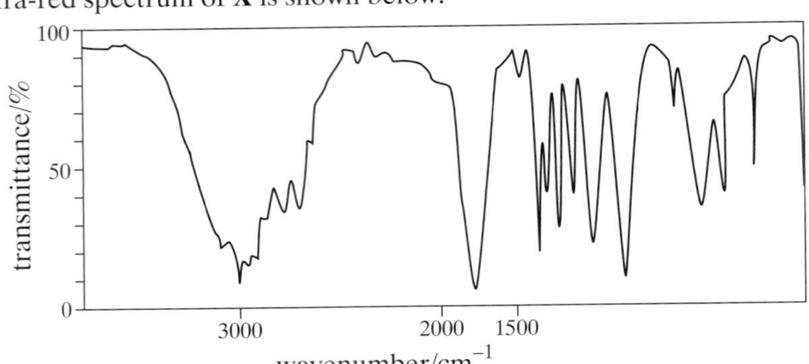

(i) What can be deduced from the broad absorption centred on $3000\,cm^{-1}$ in the infra-red spectrum of **X**?

(ii) Given that the proton nmr spectrum of **X** contains only two peaks with the integration ratio 9:1, deduce the structure of **X**. *(2 marks)*

AQA, 2005

4 Each of the parts (a) to (c) below concerns a different pair of isomers.
Draw one possible structure for each of the species **C**, **D**, **E**, **F**, **I** and **J**, using Table 2 on page 262 where appropriate.

(a) Compounds **C** and **D** have the molecular formula $C_2H_4O_2$
Each has an absorption in its infra-red spectrum at about $1700\,cm^{-1}$ but only **D** has a broad absorption at $3350\,cm^{-1}$ *(2 marks)*

(b) Compounds **E** and **F** are esters with the molecular formula $C_5H_{10}O_2$
The proton nmr spectrum of **E** consists of two singlets only whereas that of **F** consists of two quartets and two triplets. *(2 marks)*

(c) Compounds **I** and **J** have the molecular formula C_6H_{12}
Each has an absorption in its infra-red spectrum at about $1650\,cm^{-1}$ and neither shows geometrical isomerism. The proton nmr spectrum of **I** consists of a singlet only whereas that of **J** consists of a singlet, a triplet and a quartet. *(2 marks)*

AQA, 2005

5 Ester **X**, $CH_3CH_2COOCH_3$, can be produced by the reaction between propanoyl chloride and methanol.

(a) Name **X**. *(1 mark)*

(b) The proton nmr spectrum of **X** is shown below together with that of an isomeric ester, **Y**. Deduce which of Spectrum 1 and Spectrum 2 is that obtained from **X**. Use the data on page 250 and the integration data on the spectra to help you to explain your deduction. Suggest a structure for **Y**.

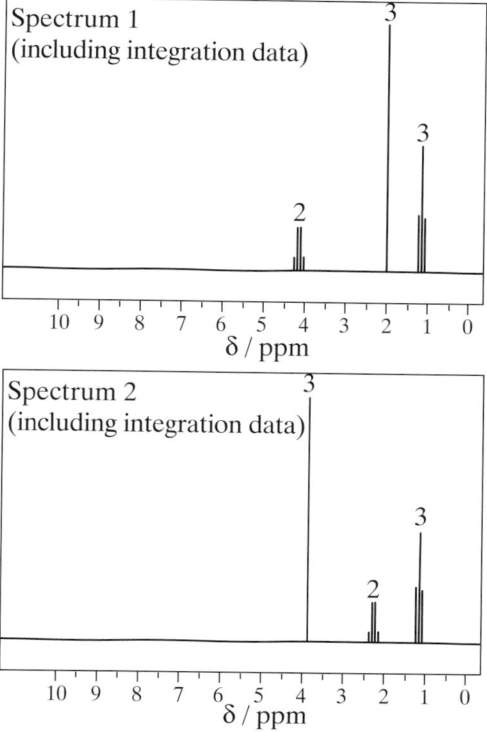

(4 marks)

AQA, 2005

6 Compound **Q** has the molecular formula C_4H_7ClO and does not produce misty fumes when added to water.

(a) The infra-red spectrum of **Q** contains a major absorption at 1724 cm^{-1}. Identify the bond responsible for this absorption. *(1 mark)*

(b) The mass spectrum of **Q** contains two molecular ion peaks at m/z = 106 and m/z = 108. It also has a major peak at m/z = 43.

(i) Suggest why there are two molecular ion peaks.

(ii) A fragment ion produced from **Q** has m/z = 43 and contains atoms of **three** different elements. Identify this fragment ion and write an equation showing its formation from the molecular ion of **Q**. *(3 marks)*

(c) The proton nmr spectrum of **Q** was recorded.

(i) Suggest a suitable solvent for use in recording this spectrum of **Q**.

(ii) Give the formula of the standard reference compound used in recording proton nmr spectra. *(2 marks)*

(d) The proton nmr spectrum of **Q** shows three peaks. Complete the table below to show the number of adjacent, non-equivalent protons responsible for the splitting pattern.

	Peak 1	**Peak 2**	**Peak 3**
Integration value	3	3	1
Splitting pattern	doublet	singlet	quartet
Number of adjacent, non-equivalent protons	1		

(1 mark)

(e) Using the information in parts (a), (b) and (d), deduce the structure of compound **Q**. *(1 mark)*

AQA, 2004

Examination-style questions

Unit 4 questions: Kinetics, equilibria and organic chemistry

1 (a) The table shows the results of three experiments to investigate the rate of reaction between compounds A and B. All three experiments were carried out at the same temperature.

	Experiment 1	Experiment 2	Experiment 3
Initial concentration of A/mol dm^{-3}	3.90×10^{-2}	7.80×10^{-2}	7.80×10^{-2}
Initial concentration of B/mol dm^{-3}	9.60×10^{-2}	2.40×10^{-2}	1.20×10^{-2}
Initial rate/mol dm^{-3} s^{-1}	5.00×10^{-5}	5.00×10^{-5}	2.50×10^{-5}

Use the data in the table to deduce the order of reaction with respect to A and the order of reaction with respect to B. *(2 marks)*

(b) The reaction between compounds **C** and **D** at given temperature is first order with respect to **C** and second order with respect to **D**.

(i) Write a rate equation for this reaction.

(ii) When the initial concentration of **C** is 2.50×10^{-2} mol dm^{-3}, the initial rate of reaction is 1.45×10^{-4} mol dm^{-3} s^{-1}. When the initial concentration of **C** is 2.50×10^{-2} mol dm^{-3} and the initial concentration of **D** is 6.65×10^{-3} mol dm^{-3} the initial rate of reaction is 1.45×10^{-4} mol dm^{-3} s^{-1}. Calculate the value of the rate constant at this temperature and deduce its units. *(4 marks)*

AQA, 2008

2

$$\underset{\mathbf{E}}{C_4H_8} \xrightarrow[\text{HBr}]{\text{Reaction 1}} \underset{\mathbf{F}}{\overset{a}{CH_3}-\underset{Br}{\overset{H}{C}}-CH_2-\overset{b}{CH_3}} \xrightarrow[\text{NH}_3]{\text{Reaction 2}} \underset{\mathbf{G}}{CH_3-\underset{NH_2}{\overset{H}{C}}-CH_2-CH_3}$$

(a) (i) Name the mechanism for Reaction 1.

(ii) Compound **F** is the **only** product formed in Reaction 1. Deduce the structure of compound **E**. *(2 marks)*

(b) Name and outline a mechanism for Reaction 2. *(5 marks)*

(c) Compound **G** is a primary amine with molecular formula $C_4H_{11}N$

In reaction 2, the percentage conversion of **F** into **G** is 53.4%.

(i) Calculate the mass of **G** formed in Reaction 2 from 10.0 g of **F**.

(ii) Suggest a reason, other than experimental technique, for the relatively low percentage conversion of **F** into **G** in Reaction 2. *(4 marks)*

(d) Predict the total number of peaks in the proton nmr spectrum of **F**. State the splitting pattern of the peak for the protons labelled *a* and the splitting pattern of the peak for the protons labelled *b*. *(3 marks)*

(e) Draw the structure of the following isomers of **G**.

(i) The isomer which is a primary amine and has two peaks in its proton nmr spectrum.

(ii) The isomer which is a secondary amine and has four peaks in its proton nmr spectrum.

(iii) The isomer which is a tertiary amine. *(3 marks)*

AQA, 2008

3 (a) Each part below concerns a different pair of isomers.
Draw one possible structure for each of the compounds **A** to **J**.
Use Table 2 on page 250 where appropriate.

(i) Compounds **A** and **B** have the molecular formula C_6H_{12}
Both have only one peak in their proton nmr spectra.
A has an absorption at 1650 cm^{-1} in its infra-red spectrum but **B** does not.

(ii) Compounds **C** and **D** have the molecular formula $C_5H_{10}O$ and both have only two peaks in their proton nmr spectra.
C forms a silver mirror with Tollens' reagent but **D** does not.

(iii) Compounds **E** and **F** have the molecular formula $C_3H_6O_2$ and both have only a quartet, a triplet and a singlet peak in their proton nmr spectra.
E gives an effervescence with aqueous sodium hydrogencarbonate but **F** does not.

(iv) Compounds **G** and **H** have the molecular formula C_6H_{12}
G shows geometrical isomerism but not optical isomerism.
H shows optical isomerism but not geometrical isomerism.

(v) Compounds **I** and **J** have the molecular formula $C_5H_{12}O$
I cannot be oxidised by acidified potassium dichromate(VI) but can be dehydrated to form an alkene.
J can be oxidised by acidified potassium dichromate(VI) but cannot be dehydrated to form an alkene. *(10 marks)*

(b) Consider the compound below.

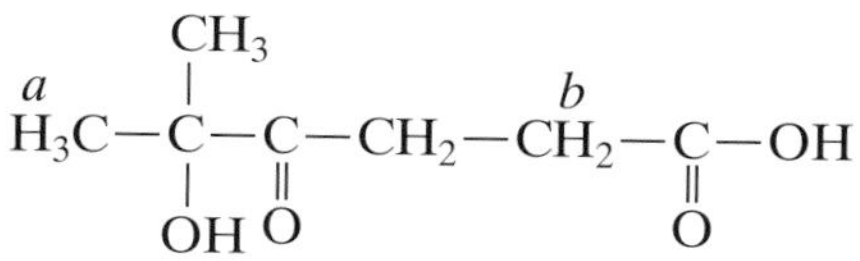

$$\overset{a}{H_3C}-\underset{OH}{\overset{CH_3}{\overset{|}{\underset{|}{C}}}}-\underset{\underset{O}{\|}}{C}-CH_2-\overset{b}{CH_2}-\underset{\underset{O}{\|}}{C}-OH$$

(i) Predict the number of peaks in its proton nmr spectrum.
(ii) The protons labelled *a* and *b* each produce a peak in the proton nmr spectrum.
Name the splitting pattern for each of these peaks. *(3 marks)*

AQA, 2008

4 (a) Amide **R**, $CH_3CH_2CONHCH_3$, can be formed by the reaction of CH_3CH_2COCl with CH_3NH_2

(i) Name amide **R**. Name and outline a mechanism for the reaction of CH_3CH_2COCl with CH_3NH_2 to form **R**.
(ii) **R** can also be formed by the reaction of an acid anhydride with CH_3NH_2
Draw the structure of this acid anhydride.
(iii) In the mass spectrometer, fragmentation of the molecular ion of $CH_3CH_2CONHCH_3$ produces a peak with $m/z = 57$. Write an equation for this fragmentation. *(10 marks)*

(b) Consider the following reaction sequence.

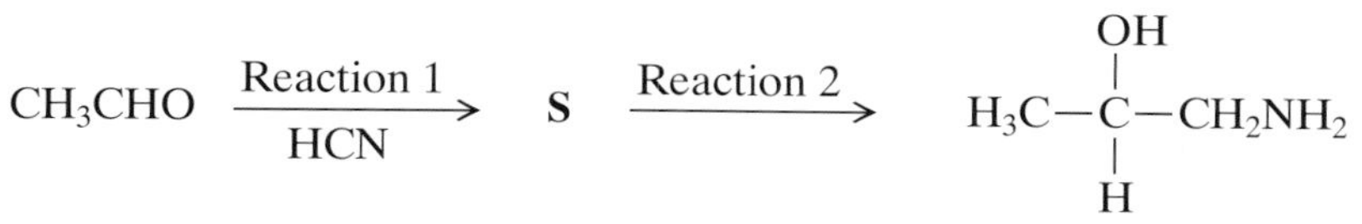

$$CH_3CHO \xrightarrow[\text{HCN}]{\text{Reaction 1}} \mathbf{S} \xrightarrow{\text{Reaction 2}} H_3C-\underset{H}{\overset{OH}{\overset{|}{\underset{|}{C}}}}-CH_2NH_2$$

Name the mechanism for Reaction 1 and deduce the structure of compound **S**.
Give the reagents and name the type of reaction occurring in Reaction 2. *(4 marks)*

AQA, 2007

5 In this question, give all pH and pK_a values to 2 decimal places.

(a) Hydrochloric acid is described as a strong Brønsted–Lowry acid.

(i) State what is meant by the term *Brønsted–Lowry acid*.

(ii) State why hydrochloric acid is described as *strong*. *(2 marks)*

(b) A sample of hydrochloric acid contains 7.05×10^{-3} mol of hydrogen chloride in $50\,cm^3$ of solution.

(i) Calculate the concentration, in mol dm^{-3}, of this hydrochloric acid.

(ii) Write an expression for the term *pH*.

(iii) Calculate the pH of this hydrochloric acid.

(iv) When water is added to this $50\,cm^3$ sample of acid the pH increases. Calculate the total volume of the solution when the pH becomes exactly 1.00 *(6 marks)*

(c) The value of the acid dissociation constant, K_a, for the weak acid HX is 6.10×10^{-5} mol dm^{-3} at 25 °C.

(i) Write an expression for the acid dissociation constant, K_a, for the acid HX.

(ii) Calculate the pH of a 0.255 mol dm^{-3} solution of HX at 25 °C. *(4 marks)*

(d) A given volume of a buffer solution contains 6.85×10^{-3} mol of the weak acid HY and 2.98×10^{-3} mol of the salt NaY. The pH of the buffer solution is 3.78

(i) Calculate the value of pK_a for the acid HY at this temperature.

(ii) State and explain the effect on the pH of the buffer solution when a small amount of hydrochloric acid is added. *(7 marks)*

AQA, 2007

6 Compounds **J**, **K**, **L** and **M** are structural isomers of $C_4H_{10}O_2$

Some of these isomers are ethers. Ethers contain the C–O–C linkage.

Isomers **J**, **K**, **L** and **M** can be distinguished using proton nmr spectroscopy and infra-red spectroscopy.

(a) The substance TMS is used as a standard in recording proton nmr spectra. Draw the structure of TMS and give two reasons why it is used as a standard. *(3 marks)*

(b) State the number of peaks in the proton nmr spectrum of isomer **J**, $CH_3OCH_2CH_2OCH_3$ *(1 mark)*

(c) (i) Isomer **K**, shown below, has five peaks in its proton nmr spectrum. Predict the splitting pattern of the peaks due to the protons labelled *a* and *b*.

a *b*

$CH_3CH_2OCH_2CH_2OH$

(ii) Identify the wavenumber of an absorption which would be present in the infrared spectrum of **K** but which would not be present in the infra-red spectrum of **J**. *(3 marks)*

(d) Isomer **L**, $HOCH_2CH_2CH_2CH_2OH$, can be used to form polyesters.

(i) Give the name of **L**.

(ii) Isomer **L** reacts with pentanedioic acid to form a polyester. Name the type of polymerisation involved and draw the repeating unit of the polyester formed. *(4 marks)*

(e) The proton nmr spectrum of isomer **M** is shown below. The measured integration trace gives the ratio 0.4 to 2.4 to 1.2 for the peaks at δ4.6, 3.3 and 1.3, respectively.

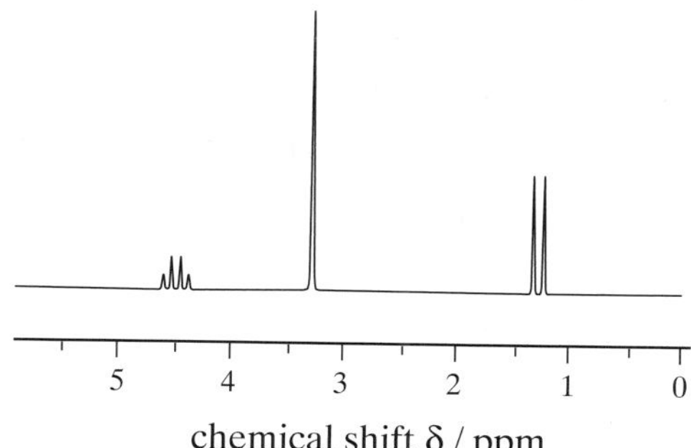

(i) State what you can deduce from the integration value for the peak at δ3.3

(ii) Use Table 2 on page 250 to help you identify the type of proton leading to the peak at δ3.3

(iii) Draw the part of the structure which can be deduced from the splitting of the peaks at δ1.3 and δ4.6 and from their integration values.

(iv) Hence, deduce the structure of **M**. *(4 marks)*

AQA, 2007

7 (a) Describe, by giving reagents and stating observations, how you could distinguish between the compounds in the following pairs using simple test-tube reactions.

(i)

$CH_3-C(=O)-O-H$ **P** and $CH_3-O-C(=O)-O-H$ **Q**

(ii)

CH_3CH_2COCl **R** and CH_3CH_2Cl **S**

(6 marks)

(b) (i) Give the reagents needed for the reduction of nitrobenzene to form phenylamine. Write an equation for the reaction. Use [H] to represent the reductant.

(ii) Name the type of mechanism for the reaction between phenylamine and bromomethane. Draw the structure of the product of the reaction of phenylamine with a large excess of bromomethane. *(5 marks)*

AQA, 2007

UNIT 5

Energetics, redox and inorganic chemistry

Chapters in this unit

This unit returns to physical chemistry and inorganic chemistry extending some of the themes covered in *AQA AS Chemistry*.

Thermodynamics builds from the ideas in *AQA AS Chemistry* about energetics and introduces the ideas of entropy – how disorder drives reactions – and free energy, a way of predicting whether a reaction is able to happen at a given temperature.

Periodicity: The chemical properties of the Period 3 elements and their compounds are studied to establish patterns and trends in chemical behaviour across the period.

In **Redox equilibria**, redox reactions are compared and half equations are assigned electrode potentials, which can be used to predict the direction of redox reactions.

The transition metals have unique electron structures, which gives their compounds characteristic properties. These include colour, complex ion formation, and their use as catalysts and in medicine.

Reactions of inorganic compounds in aqueous solution: Many metal ions in solution are surrounded by water molecules and form metal-aqua ions. This chapter looks at the hydrolysis and substitution reactions of these ions.

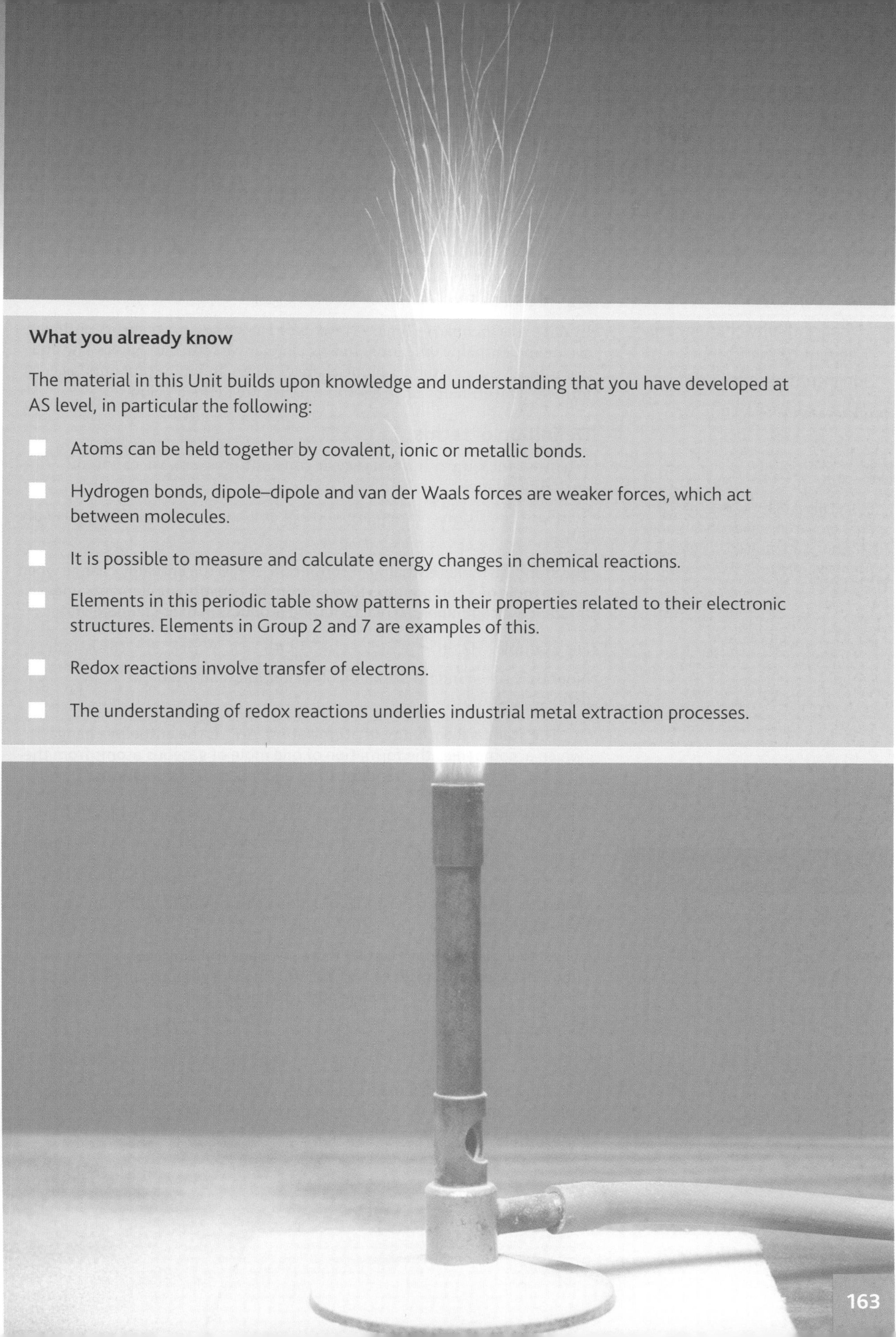

What you already know

The material in this Unit builds upon knowledge and understanding that you have developed at AS level, in particular the following:

- Atoms can be held together by covalent, ionic or metallic bonds.
- Hydrogen bonds, dipole–dipole and van der Waals forces are weaker forces, which act between molecules.
- It is possible to measure and calculate energy changes in chemical reactions.
- Elements in this periodic table show patterns in their properties related to their electronic structures. Elements in Group 2 and 7 are examples of this.
- Redox reactions involve transfer of electrons.
- The understanding of redox reactions underlies industrial metal extraction processes.

12 Thermodynamics

12.1 Enthalpy change

Learning objectives:

- What enthalpy changes are relevant to the formation of ionic compounds?

Specification reference: 3.5.1

Link

You will need to know the energetics, states of matter; ionic bonding and change of state studied in *AQA AS Chemistry*, Topics 3.1, 3.7 and 7.3.

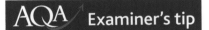

AQA Examiner's tip

Make sure that you know these definitions.

Hess's law

In *AQA AS Chemistry*, Topic 7.4 we used Hess's law to construct enthalpy cycles and enthalpy diagrams. In this chapter we return to Hess's law and use it to investigate the enthalpy changes when an ionic compound is formed. The enthalpy changes you will use are defined below.

Definition of terms

When we measure a heat change at constant pressure, we call it an **enthalpy change**.

Standard conditions chosen are 100 kPa and a stated temperature, usually 298 K.

The standard molar enthalpy of formation, $\Delta H^{\ominus}_f$ is the enthalpy change when one mole of a compound is formed from its constituent elements under standard conditions, all reactants and products in their standard states.

For example: $H_2(g) + \frac{1}{2}O_2(g) \longrightarrow H_2O(l)$ $\quad \Delta H^{\ominus}_f = -286\,kJ\,mol^{-1}$

Note that the standard enthalpy of formation of an element is, by definition, zero.

The standard enthalpy of atomisation, $\Delta H^{\ominus}_{at}$ is the enthalpy change which accompanies the formation of one mole of gaseous atoms from the element in its standard state under standard conditions.

For example: $Mg(s) \longrightarrow Mg(g)$ $\quad \Delta H^{\ominus}_{at} = +147.7\,kJ\,mol^{-1}$

$\frac{1}{2}Br_2(l) \longrightarrow Br(g)$ $\quad \Delta H^{\ominus}_{at} = +111.9\,kJ\,mol^{-1}$

$\frac{1}{2}Cl_2(g) \longrightarrow Cl(g)$ $\quad \Delta H^{\ominus}_{at} = +121.7\,kJ\,mol^{-1}$

Note that this is given per mole of chlorine or bromine *atoms* and not per mole of chlorine or bromine molecules.

First ionisation energy (first IE) is the standard enthalpy change when one mole of gaseous atoms is converted into a mole of gaseous ions each with a single positive charge.

For example: $Na(g) \longrightarrow Na^+(g) + e^-$ $\quad \Delta H^{\ominus}_i = +\ 496\,kJ\,mol^{-1}$

or first IE $= +496\,kJ\,mol^{-1}$

Note that the **second ionisation energy** (second IE) refers to the loss of a mole of electrons from a mole of singly positively charged ions.

For example: $Na^+(g) \longrightarrow Na^{2+}(g) + e^-$ $\quad \Delta H^{\ominus}_i = +\ 4563\,kJ\,mol^{-1}$

or second IE $= +\ 4563\,kJ\,mol^{-1}$

The first electron affinity (EA), $\Delta H^{\ominus}_{ea}$, is the standard enthalpy change when a mole of gaseous atoms is converted to a mole of gaseous ions, each with a single negative charge.

For example: $O(g) + e^- \longrightarrow O^-(g)$ $\Delta H^{\ominus}_{ea} = -141.1\,kJ\,mol^{-1}$

or first EA $= -141.1\,kJ\,mol^{-1}$

Note that this refers to single atoms, not to oxygen molecules O_2.

The second electron affinity (EA), $\Delta H^{\ominus}_{ea}$, is the enthalpy change when a mole of electrons is added to a mole of gaseous ions each with a single negative charge to form ions each with two negative charges.

For example: $O^-(g) + e^- \longrightarrow O^{2-}(g)$ $\Delta H^{\ominus}_{ea} = +798\,kJ\,mol^{-1}$

or second EA $= +798\,kJ\,mol^{-1}$

Lattice formation enthalpy, $\Delta H^{\ominus}_{L}$, is the standard enthalpy change when one mole of solid ionic compound is formed from its gaseous ions.

For example: $Na^+(g) + Cl^-(g) \longrightarrow NaCl(s)$ $\Delta H^{\ominus}_{L} = -788\,kJ\,mol^{-1}$

Note that when a lattice forms, energy is given out so $\Delta H^{\ominus}$ is always negative for this process.

The opposite process, when one mole of ionic compound separates into its gaseous ions, is called the **enthalpy of lattice dissociation**. It has the same numerical value as the lattice enthalpy, but $\Delta H^{\ominus}$ is always positive for this process.

Enthalpy of hydration, $\Delta H^{\ominus}_{hyd}$, is the standard enthalpy change when water molecules surround one mole of gaseous ions.

For example: $Na^+ + aq \longrightarrow Na^+(aq)$ $\Delta H^{\ominus}_{hyd} = -406\,kJ\,mol^{-1}$

or $Cl^- + aq \longrightarrow Cl^-(aq)$ $\Delta H^{\ominus}_{hyd} = -363\,kJ\,mol^{-1}$

Enthalpy of solution, $\Delta H^{\ominus}_{sol}$, is the standard enthalpy change when one mole of solute dissolves completely in sufficient solvent to form a solution in which the molecules or ions are far enough apart not to interact with each other.

For example: $NaCl(s) + aq \longrightarrow Na^+(aq) + Cl^-(aq)$ $\Delta H^{\ominus}_{sol} = +19\,kJ\,mol^{-1}$

Mean bond enthalpy is the enthalpy change when one mole of gaseous molecules each breaks a covalent bond to form two free radicals, averaged over a range of compounds.

For example: $CH_4(g) \longrightarrow C\,(g) + 4H(g)$ $\Delta H^{\ominus}_{diss} = +1664\,kJ\,mol^{-1}$

So the mean (or average) C—H bond energy in methane is: $\dfrac{1664}{4}$

$= +416\,kJ\,mol^{-1}$

It is important to have an equation to refer to for enthalpy changes.

Ionic bonding

In a simple model of ionic bonding, electrons are transferred from metal atoms to non-metal atoms. Positively charged metal ions and negatively charged non-metal ions are formed that all have a stable outer shell of electrons. These ions arrange themselves into a lattice so that ions of opposite charge are next to one another, see Figure 1.

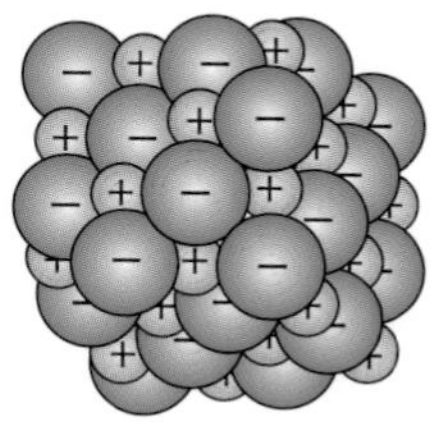

Figure 1 *Part of an ionic lattice*

Hint

Do not confuse ionisation energy that refers to electron *loss* with electron affinity, which refers to electron *gain*.

Enthalpy changes on forming ionic compounds

If a cleaned piece of solid sodium is placed in a gas jar containing chlorine gas, an exothermic reaction takes place, forming solid sodium chloride:

$$Na(s) + \tfrac{1}{2}Cl_2(g) \longrightarrow NaCl(s) \qquad \Delta H^{\ominus}_{f} = -411\,kJ\,mol^{-1}$$

We can think of it as taking place in several steps:

- The reaction involves solid sodium, not gaseous, and chlorine *molecules*, not separate atoms, so we must start with the enthalpy changes for atomisation:

  $$Na(s) \longrightarrow Na(g) \qquad \Delta H^{\ominus}_{at} = +108\,kJ\,mol^{-1}$$
  $$\tfrac{1}{2}Cl_2(g) \longrightarrow Cl(g) \qquad \Delta H^{\ominus}_{at} = +122\,kJ\,mol^{-1}$$

  Notice that energy has to be *put in* to 'pull apart' the atoms ($\Delta H^{\ominus}_{at}$ is positive in both cases).

- The gaseous sodium atoms must give up an electron to form gaseous Na^+ ions:

  $$Na(g) \longrightarrow Na^+(g) + e^-$$

  The enthalpy change for this process is the enthalpy change of first ionisation (ionisation energy, first IE) of sodium and is + 496 kJ mol^{-1}.

- The chlorine atoms must gain an electron to form gaseous Cl^- ions:

  $$Cl(g) + e^- \longrightarrow Cl^-(g)$$

  The enthalpy change for this process of electron *gain* is the first electron affinity, first EA. The first electron affinity for the chlorine atom is –349 kJ mol^{-1}, i.e. energy is given out when this process occurs.

There is a further energy change. At room temperature sodium chloride exists as a solid lattice of alternating positive and negative ions, and not as separate gaseous ions. If positively charged ions come together with negatively charged ions, they form a solid lattice and energy is given out due to the attraction between the oppositely charged ions. This is called the lattice formation enthalpy, $\Delta H^{\ominus}_{L}$, and it refers to the process:

$$Na^+(g) + Cl^-(g) \longrightarrow NaCl(s) \qquad \Delta H^{\ominus}_{L} = -788\,kJ\,mol^{-1}$$

The five processes that lead to the formation of NaCl(s) from its elements.

- Atomisation of Na:
  $$Na(s) \longrightarrow Na(g) \qquad \Delta H^{\ominus}_{at} = +108\,kJ\,mol^{-1}$$
- Atomisation of chlorine:
  $$\tfrac{1}{2}Cl(g) \longrightarrow Cl(g) \qquad \Delta H^{\ominus}_{at} = +122\,kJ\,mol^{-1}$$
- Ionisation (e$^-$ loss) of Na:
  $$Na(g) \longrightarrow Na^+(g) + e^- \qquad \text{first IE} = +496\,kJ\,mol^{-1}$$
- Electron affinity of Cl:
  $$Cl(g) + e^- \longrightarrow Cl^-(g) \qquad \text{first EA} = -349\,kJ\,mol^{-1}$$
- Formation of lattice:
  $$Na^+(g) + Cl^-(g) \longrightarrow NaCl(s) \qquad \Delta H^{\ominus}_{L} = -788\,kJ\,mol^{-1}$$

Hess's law tells us that the total energy (or enthalpy) change for a chemical reaction is the same *whatever route is taken*, provided that the initial and final conditions are the same. It does not matter whether the reaction actually takes place *via* these steps or not.

So the sum of the first five energy changes is equal to the enthalpy change of formation of sodium chloride. We can calculate any one of the quantities, provided all the others are known. We do this in the next topic by using a thermochemical cycle, called a Born–Haber cycle (the same Haber as in the Haber process).

Summary questions

1. a What is the value of ΔH for this process?
   $Na\,Cl(s) \longrightarrow Na^+(g) + Cl^-(g)$
   b Explain your answer.
   c What is the term that describes this process?

2. Explain why:
   a Loss of an electron from a sodium atom (ionisation) is an endothermic process.
   b Gain of an electron by a chlorine atom is an exothermic process.

3. a Magnesium forms Mg^{2+} ions. Write the equation to represent:
   i the first
   ii the second
   ionisation of magnesium.
   b In terms of the enthalpies for the two processes in part a, what is the enthalpy change when a $Mg^{2+}(g)$ ion is formed from a Mg(g) atom?

12.2 Born–Haber cycles

Learning objectives:

- How is a Born–Haber cycle constructed for a simple ionic compound?
- How can Born–Haber cycles be used to predict enthalpies of formation of theoretical compounds?

Specification reference: 3.5.1

A **Born–Haber cycle** is a thermochemical cycle that includes all the enthalpy changes involved in the formation of an ionic compound. We construct it by starting with the elements in their standard states. All elements in their standard states have zero enthalpy by definition.

The Born–Haber cycle for sodium chloride

There are six steps in the Born–Haber cycle for the formation of sodium chloride, see Topic 12.1. Here we will use the cycle to calculate the lattice enthalpy. The other five steps are shown in Figure 1. (Remember that if we know any five, we can calculate the other). Figure 1 shows you how each step is added to the one before, starting from the elements in their standard state. Positive (endothermic changes) are shown upwards, and negative exothermic changes downwards.

$$Na(s) \longrightarrow Na(g) \qquad \Delta H^{\ominus}_{at} = +108\,kJ\,mol^{-1}$$

$$\tfrac{1}{2}Cl_2(g) \longrightarrow Cl(g) \qquad \Delta H^{\ominus}_{at} = +122\,kJ\,mol^{-1}$$

$$Na(g) \longrightarrow Na^+(g) + e^- \qquad \text{first IE} = +496\,kJ\,mol^{-1}$$

$$Cl(g) + e^- \longrightarrow Cl^-(g) \qquad \text{first EA} = -349\,kJ\,mol^{-1}$$

$$Na(s) + \tfrac{1}{2}Cl_2(g) \longrightarrow NaCl(s) \qquad \Delta H^{\ominus}_{f} = -411\,kJ\,mol^{-1}$$

When drawing Born–Haber cycles:

- Make up a rough scale, e.g. 1 line of lined paper to100 kJ mol^{-1}.
- Plan out roughly first to avoid going off the top or bottom of the paper. (The zero line representing elements in their standard state will need to be in the middle of the paper.)
- Remember to put in the sign of each enthalpy change and an arrow to show its direction. Positive enthalpy changes go up, negative enthalpy changes go down.

Using a Born–Haber cycle we can see why the formation of an ionic compound from its elements is an exothermic process. This is mainly due to the large amount of energy given out when the lattice forms.

AQA Examiner's tip

Most errors in Born–Haber cycle calculations result either from lack of knowledge of the enthalpy change definitions, or from their incorrect application.

1 Elements in their standard states. This is the energy zero of the diagram.

2 Add in the atomisation of sodium. This is positive, so it is drawn 'uphill'.

3 Add in the atomisation of chlorine. This too is positive, so draw 'uphill'.

4 Add in the ionisation of sodium, also positive and so drawn 'uphill'.

5 Add in the electron affinity of chlorine. This is a negative energy change and so it is drawn 'downhill'.

6 Add in the enthalpy of formation of sodium chloride, also negative and drawn 'downhill'.

7 The final unknown quantity is the lattice formation enthalpy of sodium chloride. The size of this is 788 kj mol^{-1} from the diagram. Lattice energy is the change from separate ions to solid lattice and we must therefre go 'downhill', so LE($Na^+ + Cl^-$)(s) = – 788 kJ mol^{-1}.

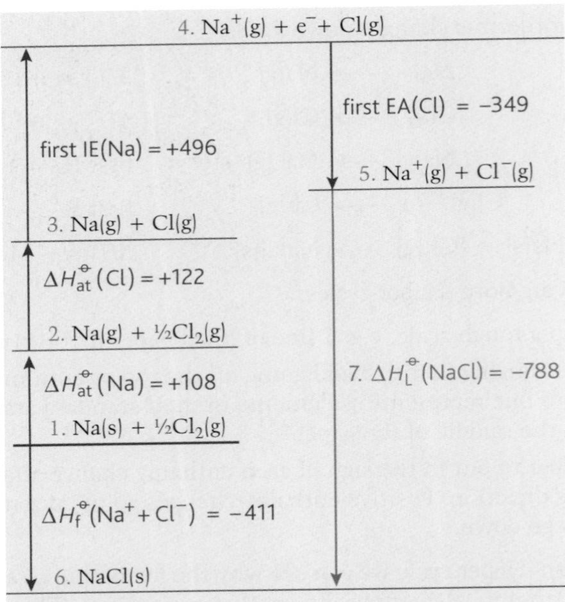

Figure 1 *Stages in the construction of the Born–Haber cycle for sodium chloride, NaCl to find the lattice enthalpy of NaCl. All enthalpies are in kJ mol^{-1}.*

The Born–Haber cycle for magnesium chloride

Figure 2 shows the complete Born–Haber cycle for the formation of magnesium chloride, $MgCl_2$, from its elements, together with notes on how it is constructed.

Since *two* chlorines are involved all the quantities related to Cl are doubled, i.e. 2 × $\Delta H^\ominus_{at}$, 2 × first electron affinity (*not* first + second electron affinities).

Also notice that the ionisation of magnesium, Mg ⟶ Mg^{2+} is the first ionisation enthalpy *plus* the second ionisation enthalpy. The second ionisation enthalpy is larger because it is more difficult to lose an electron from a positively charged ion than from a neutral atom.

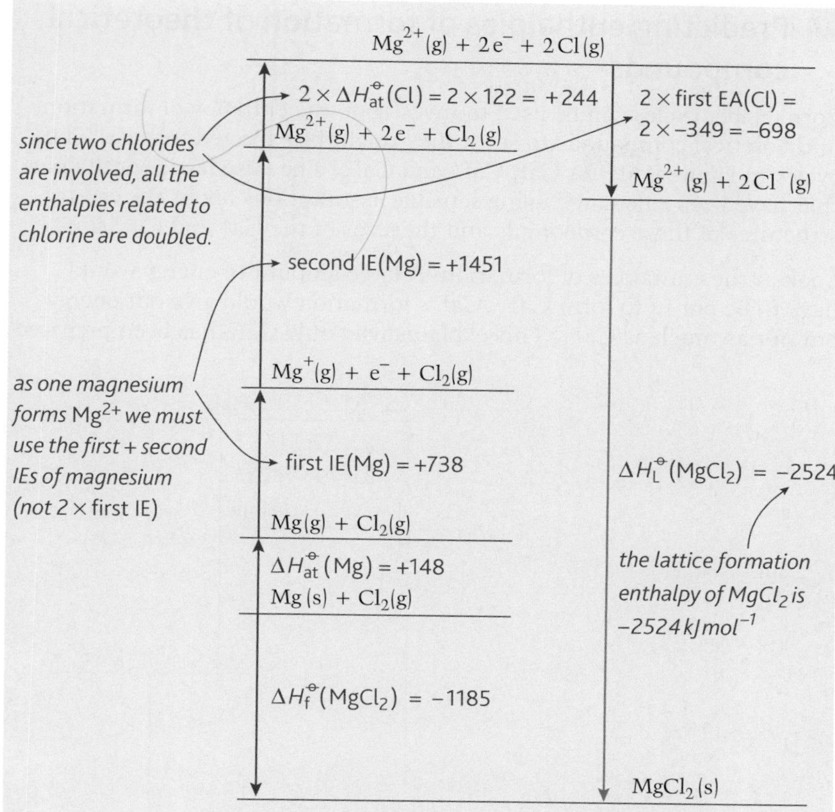

Figure 2 *The Born–Haber cycle for magnesium chloride, $MgCl_2$. All enthalpies are in $kJ\,mol^{-1}$*

Hint

First electron affinities of *all* elements are negative because the added electron is attracted by the nuclear charge. Second (and subsequent) electron affinities are *always* positive because a negatively charged electron is being added to an already negatively charged ion.

Trends in lattice enthalpies

The lattice formation enthalpies of some simple ionic compounds of formula $M^+ X^-$ are given in Table 1.

Table 1 *Some values of lattice formation enthalpies for compounds M^+X^-*

		Larger negative ions (anions) →			
		F^-	Cl^-	Br^-	I^-
Larger positive ions (cations) ↓	Li^+	−1031	−848	−803	−759
	Na^+	−918	−788	−742	−705
	K^+	−817	−711	−679	−651
	Rb^+	−783	−685	−656	−628
	Cs^+	−747	−661	−635	−613

Notice the trend that larger ions lead to smaller lattice enthalpies. This is because the opposite charges do not approach each other as closely when the ions are larger.

Table 2 shows lattice enthalpies for some compounds $M^{2+}X^{2-}$.

Note the same trend related to size of ions as before in Table 1.

Comparing Table 1 with Table 2 shows that for ions of approximately similar size (i.e. formed from elements in the same group of the periodic table, such as Na^+ and Mg^{2+} or F^- and O^{2-}) the lattice enthalpy increases with the size of the charge. This is because ions with double the charge give out roughly twice as much energy when they come together.

Table 2 *Some values of lattice formation enthalpies for compounds $M^{2+}X^{2-}$*

		Larger anions →	
		O^{2-}	S^{2-}
Larger cations ↓	Be^{2+}	−4443	−3832
	Mg^{2+}	−3791	−3299
	Ca^{2+}	−3401	−3013
	Sr^{2+}	−3223	−2848
	Ba^{2+}	−3054	−2725

Predicting enthalpies of formation of theoretical compounds

Born–Haber cycles can be used to investigate the enthalpy of formation of theoretical compounds to see if they might be expected to exist. The cycles in Figure 3 are for CaF, CaF_2 and CaF_3. They use lattice enthalpies that have been calculated using sensible assumptions about the crystal structures of these compounds and the sizes of the Ca^+ and Ca^{3+} ions.

Look at the enthalpies of formation. A large amount of energy would have to be put in to form CaF_3. CaF's formation would give out energy but not as much as CaF_2. This explains why only CaF_2 has been prepared

AQA Examiner's tip

The stated enthalpy change indicated by the arrow must correspond to the stated change in the species

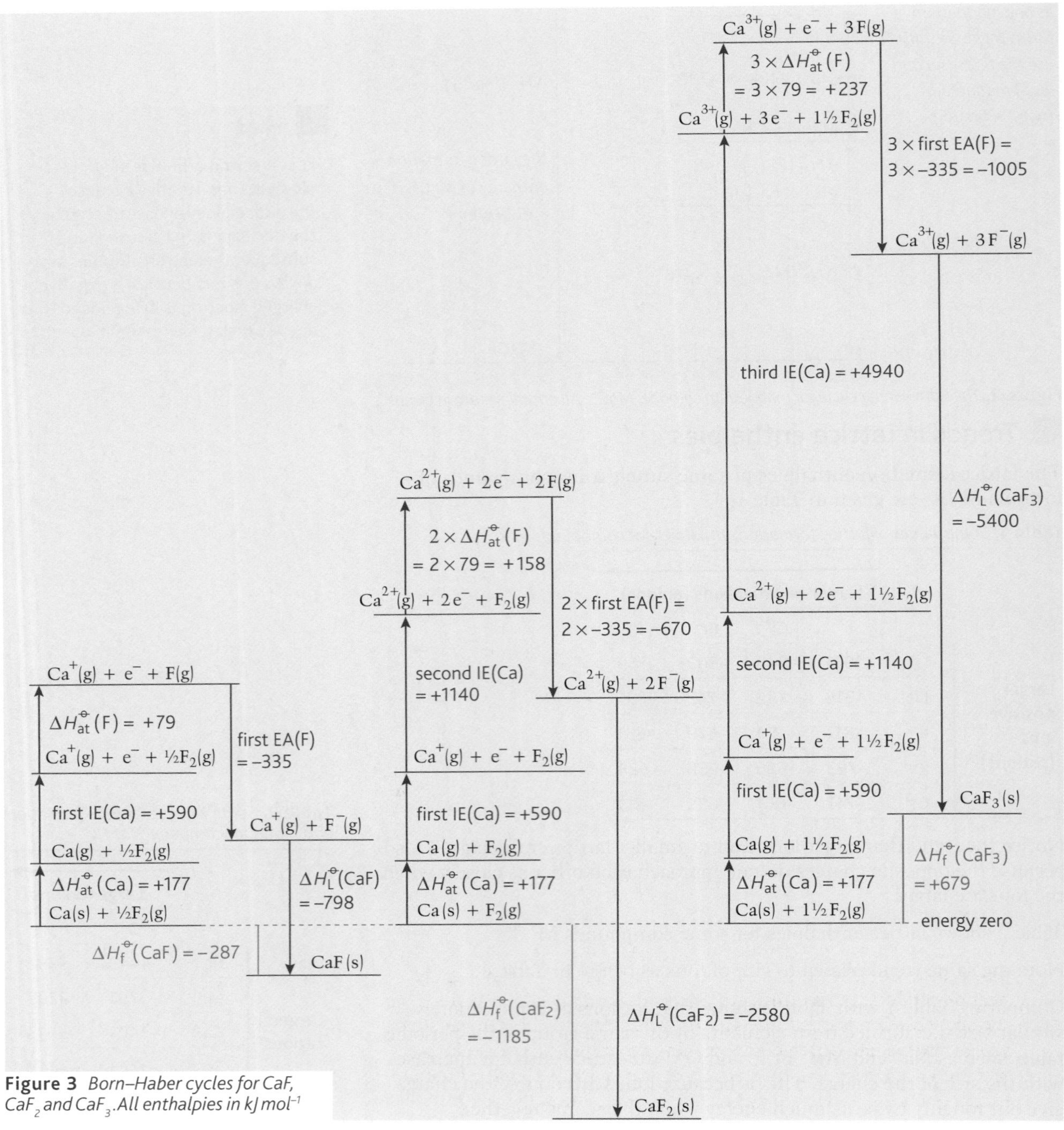

Figure 3 *Born–Haber cycles for CaF, CaF_2 and CaF_3. All enthalpies in kJ mol^{-1}*

as a stable compound. CaF has indeed been made but readily turns into CaF_2 + Ca. We say it is unstable with respect to CaF_2 + Ca.

We can see from the relative enthalpy levels of CaF and CaF_2 on Figure 3 that CaF_2 is 1185 − 287 = 898 kJ mol⁻¹ below CaF.

We can draw a thermochemical cycle to calculate ΔH for the reaction:

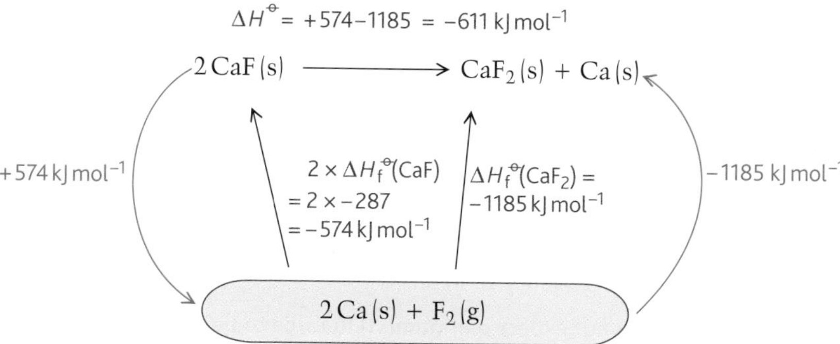

How science works

The first noble gas compound

The noble gases are often called the inert gases and, until 1962, they seemed to be just that – inert. There were no known compounds of them at all. This was explained on the basis of their stable electron arrangements. It had been predicted that there might be compounds of krypton and xenon with fluorine, but no one took much notice. However, in 1962 British chemist Neil Bartlett created a chemical sensation when he announced that he had prepared the first noble gas compound, xenon hexafluoroplatinate(V). Although the name may seem exotic, Bartlett predicted that the compound had a good chance of existing by using a very simple piece of chemical theory.

He had previously found that the powerful oxidising agent platinum(VI) fluoride gas, PtF_6, would oxidise oxygen molecules to form the compound dioxygenyl hexfluoroplatinate(V), $O_2^+PtF_6^-$, in which the oxidising agent has removed an electron from an oxygen molecule.

He then realised that the first ionisation energy of xenon (the energy required to remove an electron from an atom of it) was a little less than that of the oxygen molecule, so that if platinum(VI) fluoride could remove an electron from oxygen, it should also be able to remove one from xenon. The values are:

$Xe(g) \longrightarrow Xe^+(g) + e^-$ $\quad \Delta H = +1170\,\text{kJ mol}^{-1}$ (first IE of xenon)

$O_2(g) \longrightarrow O_2^+(g) + e^-$ $\quad \Delta H = +1183\,\text{kJ mol}^{-1}$ (first IE of an oxygen molecule)

Note that this is not the same as the first ionisation energy of an oxygen *atom*.

The experiment itself was surprisingly simple, as soon as the two gases came into contact, the compound was formed immediately – no heat or catalyst was required. In Bartlett's own words: 'When I broke the seal between the red PtF_6 gas and the colourless xenon gas, there was an immediate interaction, causing an orange-yellow solid to precipitate. At once I tried to find someone with whom to share the exciting finding, but it appeared that everyone had left for dinner!'

This was one of those moments when all the textbooks had to be re-written.

The reaction can be represented:

$$Xe(g) + PtF_6(g) \longrightarrow Xe^+PtF_6^-(s)$$

although more recently it has been realised that the formula of the product may be a little more complex than this.

There are now over 100 noble gas compounds known, although most are highly unstable.

1 Write an equation to represent the first ionisation energy of an oxygen atom.

2 If we assume that noble gas compounds are formed with positive noble gas ions, suggest why compounds of xenon and krypton were predicted rather than ones of helium or neon.

3 Why might you not expect platinum(VI) fluoride to be a gas?

4 Explain the oxidation states of the elements in $Xe^+PtF_6^-$.

Summary questions

1 a Draw a Born–Haber cycle to find the lattice formation enthalpy for sodium fluoride, NaF. The values for the relevant enthalpy terms are given below.

b What is the lattice formation enthalpy of NaF, given these values?

$Na(s) \longrightarrow Na(g)$ $\Delta H^\ominus_{at} = +108\ kJ\ mol^{-1}$

$\frac{1}{2}F_2(g) \longrightarrow F(g)$ $\Delta H^\ominus_{at} = +79\ kJ\ mol^{-1}$

$Na(g) \longrightarrow Na^+(g) + e^-$ first IE = $+496\ kJ\ mol^{-1}$

$F(g) + e^- \longrightarrow F^-(g)$ first EA = $-328\ kJ\ mol^{-1}$

$Na(s) + \frac{1}{2}F_2(g) \longrightarrow NaF(s)$ $\Delta H^\ominus_f = -574\ kJ\ mol^{-1}$

12.3 More enthalpy changes

Learning objectives:

- How is the enthalpy change of solution found?
- What evidence can theoretical calculations for lattice enthalpies provide about bonding?

Specification reference: 3.5.1

Finding the enthalpy of solution

Ionic solids can only dissolve well in polar solvents. In order to dissolve an ionic compound the lattice must be broken up. This requires an input of energy – the lattice enthalpy. The separate ions are then solvated by the solvent molecules, usually water. These cluster round the ions so that the positive ions are surrounded by the negative ends of the dipole of the solvent molecules and the negative ions are surrounded by the positive ends of the dipoles of the solvent molecules. This is called **hydration** when the solvent is water, see Figure 1.

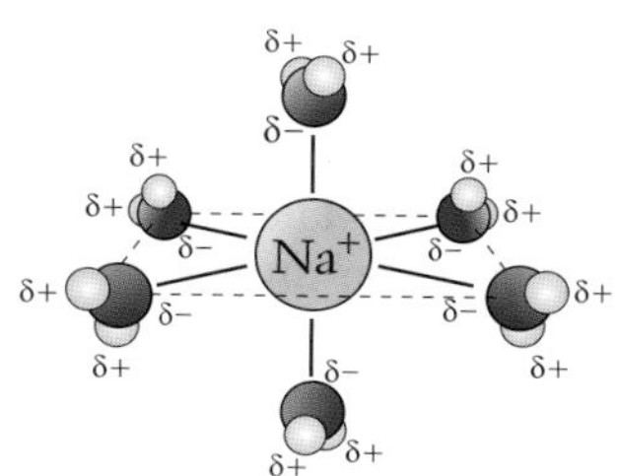

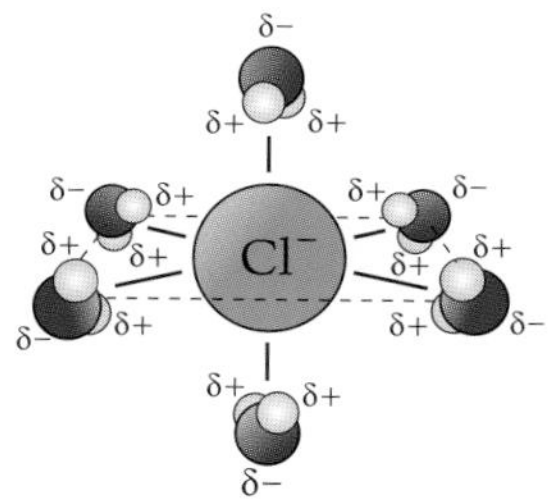

Figure 1 *The hydration of sodium and chloride ions by water molecules*

The enthalpy change of hydration shows the same trends as lattice enthalpy: it is more negative for more highly charged ions and less negative for bigger ions.

We can think of dissolving an ionic compound in water as the sum of three processes:

1. Breaking the ionic lattice to give separate gaseous ions – the lattice dissociation enthalpy has to be put in.
2. Hydrating the positive ions (cations) – the enthalpy of hydration is given out.
3. Hydrating the negative ions (anions) – the enthalpy of hydration is given out.

For ionic compounds the enthalpy change of hydration has rather a small value and may be positive or negative. For example the enthalpy of hydration, $\Delta H^{\ominus}_{hyd}$, for sodium chloride is given by the equation:

$$NaCl(s) + aq \longrightarrow Na^+(aq) + Cl^-(aq)$$

It may be calculated via a thermochemical cycle as shown below.

These are the steps that are needed:

4. $NaCl(s) \longrightarrow Na^+(g) + Cl^-(g)$ $\qquad \Delta H^{\ominus}_{L} = +788\,kJ\,mol^{-1}$
   This is the enthalpy change for lattice dissociation.
5. $Na^+(g) + aq + Cl^-(g) \longrightarrow Na^+(aq) + Cl^-(g)$ $\qquad \Delta H^{\ominus}_{hyd} = -406\,kJ\,mol^{-1}$
   This is the enthalpy change for the hydration of the sodium ion.
6. $Na^+(aq) + Cl^-(g) + aq \longrightarrow Na^+(aq) + Cl^-(aq)$ $\qquad \Delta H^{\ominus}_{hyd} = -363\,kJ\,mol^{-1}$
   This is the enthalpy change for the hydration of the chloride ion.
7. So $\Delta H^{\ominus}_{hyd}(NaCl) = \Delta H^{\ominus}_{L}(NaCl) + \Delta H^{\ominus}_{hyd}(Na^+) + \Delta H^{\ominus}_{hyd}(Cl^-)$
   $\qquad +780 \qquad -406 \qquad -363 \quad = +19\,kJ\,mol^{-1}$

The process of dissolving can also be represented on an enthalpy diagram as shown in Figure 2 or calculated directly as above. Either method is equally acceptable.

Figure 2 *Thermochemical cycle for the enthalpy of hydration of sodium chloride*

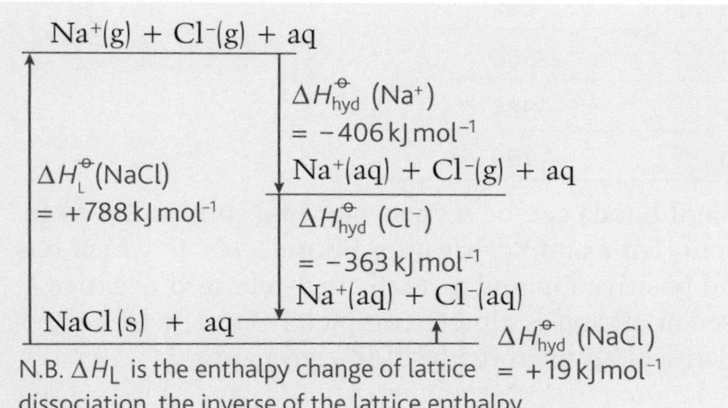

N.B. ΔH_L is the enthalpy change of lattice dissociation, the inverse of the lattice enthalpy

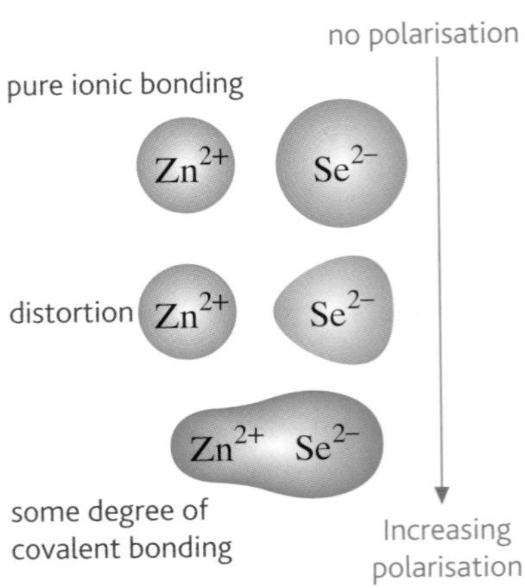

Figure 3 *Polarisation in zinc selenide*

Lattice enthalpies and bonding

It is possible to work out a theoretical value for the lattice formation enthalpy of an ionic compound if we know the charge on the ions, their distance apart and the geometry of their structure.

For many ionic compounds, the lattice formation enthalpy determined from experimental values via a Born–Haber cycle agrees very well with that calculated theoretically, and this confirms that we have the correct model of ionic bonding in that compound. However, there are some compounds when there is a large discrepancy between the two values for lattice formation enthalpy because the bond in question has some covalent character.

For example, zinc selenide, ZnSe, has an experimental lattice formation enthalpy of $-3611\,\text{kJ}\,\text{mol}^{-1}$. The theoretical value, based on the model of complete ionisation (Zn^{2+} + Se^{2-}) is $-3305\,\text{kJ}\,\text{mol}^{-1}$, some 10% lower. The greater experimental value implies some extra bonding is present.

This can be explained as follows. The ion Zn^{2+} is relatively small and has a high positive charge, while Se^{2-} is relatively large and has a high negative charge. The small Zn^{2+} can approach closely to the electron clouds of the Se^{2-} and distort them by attracting them towards it. The Se^{2-} is fairly easy to distort, because its large size means the electrons are far from the nucleus and its double charge means there is plenty of negative charge to distort. This distortion means there are more electrons than expected concentrated *between* the Zn and Se nuclei, and represents a degree of electron sharing or covalency which accounts for the lattice enthalpy discrepancy. The Se^{2-} ion is said to be **polarised**. This is shown in Figure 3.

The factors which increase polarisation are:

- positive ion (cation): small size, high charge
- negative ion (anion): large size, high charge.

Table 1 shows some values of experimentally determined lattice enthalpies, compared with those calculated assuming pure ionic bonding. Notice that the biggest discrepancy (the most extra 'covalent-type' bonding) is cadmium iodide. The cadmium ion is small and doubly charged, while the iodide ion is large and easily polarised.

Table 1 *Some values of experimental and calculated lattice enthalpies*

Compound	Experimental value of LE / $\text{kJ}\,\text{mol}^{-1}$	Calculated value of LE assuming ionic bonding / $\text{kJ}\,\text{mol}^{-1}$
LiF	–1031	–1021
NaCl	–780	–777
KBr	–679	–667
CaF_2	–2611	–2586
CdI_2	–2435	–1986
AgCl	–890	–769

So all ionic and covalent bonds can be seen as part of a continuum from ionic to purely covalent. For example, caesium fluoride, Cs^+F^- which has a large, singly charged positive ion and a small singly charged negative ion, is hardly polarised at all and is almost completely ionic, whereas a bond between two identical atoms *must* be 100% covalent.

AQA Examiner's tip

Make sure that you know why lattice enthalpies obtained by calculation and from a Born–Haber cycle can differ.

Summary questions

1 Draw a diagram to calculate the enthalpy of hydration of potassium bromide using the experimental value of lattice enthalpy in Table 1. For K^+, $\Delta H^{\ominus}_{hyd} = -322\,\text{kJ}\,\text{mol}^{-1}$ For Br^-, $\Delta H^{\ominus}_{hyd} = -335\,\text{kJ}\,\text{mol}^{-1}$. Why is the value relatively small?

2 Explain why compounds of beryllium and aluminium are nearly all significantly covalent. Would you expect the calculated value of lattice enthalpy to be greater or smaller than the experimental value? Explain your answer.

12.4 Calculating enthalpy changes using mean bond enthalpies

Learning objectives:

- What is meant by a 'mean bond enthalpy'?
- How can mean bond enthalpies be use to calculate an enthalpy change?

Specification reference: 3.5.1

AQA Examiner's tip

Mean bond enthalpy is the energy (enthalpy) that must be put in to break a particular bond, e.g. O—H. It is the average for the bond in question taken over a range of compounds containing that bond.

Table 1

Bond	Bond enthalpy / $kJ\,mol^{-1}$
C—H	413
C—C	347
Cl—Cl	243
C—Cl	346
Cl—H	432
Br—Br	193
Br—H	366
C—Br	290
O—H	464
C—O	358
C—I	228
C—F	467
C=C	612
I—I	151

Hint

An accurate value of $\Delta H^{\ominus}_{reaction}$ can be calculated if the values of enthalpies of formation or combustion are known.

Lattice enthalpy, see Topic 12.2, is a measure of strength of *ionic* bonding – the more negative the lattice formation enthalpy the more energy is required to break the structure apart, so the stronger the ionic bonding. Bond enthalpies give a measure of the strength of *covalent* bonding.

The standard enthalpy of bond dissociation is the enthalpy change when a mole of gaseous molecules each breaks a covalent bond to form two free radicals.

Bond enthalpies refer to a specific bond in a molecule and have slightly different values depending on the environment of the bond. For example, the C—F bond enthalpy is 452 $kJ\,mol^{-1}$ in CH_3F, but 485 $kJ\,mol^{-1}$ in CF_4.

As we saw in *AQA AS Chemistry*, Topic 7.7, when these values are averaged over several compounds we have the mean bond dissociation enthalpy. Table 1 gives some values for these.

Although they are only approximate, mean (or average) bond enthalpies (often called just 'bond energies') are extremely useful.

1 Comparing the strengths of bonds

This may help us to see which bond in a molecule is most likely to break.

For example in bromoethane,

```
    H   H
    |   |
H — C — C — Br
    |   |
    H   H
```

the mean bond energies are:

C—H	413 $kJ\,mol^{-1}$
C—C	437 $kJ\,mol^{-1}$
C—Br	290 $kJ\,mol^{-1}$

So we might predict that the C—Br bond is most likely to break, and this is in fact the case in most of the reactions of bromoethane.

We might also compare similar compounds such as CH_3CH_2F, CH_3CH_2Cl, CH_3CH_2Br and CH_3CH_2I. The relevant bond energies are:

C—F	467 $kJ\,mol^{-1}$
C—Cl	346 $kJ\,mol^{-1}$
C—Br	290 $kJ\,mol^{-1}$
C—I	228 $kJ\,mol^{-1}$

This suggests that in reactions where the C—X bond breaks, C_2H_5I might react more readily than C_2H_5F. (This is in fact the case, but care is needed because there may be other factors involved.)

2 In Hess's law cycles

These can be used to calculate approximate enthalpies changes for reactions where this cannot be measured experimentally, or when enthalpies of formation or combustion are not available. They can therefore be used to help predict whether a compound can be prepared.

Hess's law (see *AQA AS Chemistry*, Topic 7.4) states that the enthalpy change of a reaction is the same, whatever route is taken from reactants to products. So a reaction could be carried out (in principle) by breaking all the bonds in the reactant(s) to form separate gaseous atoms and then re-assembling these ions into the products. We can work out the approximate enthalpy changes for these two processes easily using mean bond enthalpies. We simply add up the mean bond enthalpies of every bond in the reactant(s). This is the energy that has to be put in to convert the reactants into separate atoms. We then add up all the bond enthalpies of the product(s). This is the energy given out when the atoms form the products. The difference is the enthalpy change of the reaction. If more energy is given out than was put in, the reaction is exothermic and the sign of ΔH is negative. If more energy is taken in than was given out, the reaction is endothermic and the sign of $\Delta H^{\ominus}$is positive.

For example, to find $\Delta H^{\ominus}_{reaction}$ for:

$$CH_2{=}CH_2(g) + H_2O(l) \longrightarrow CH_3CH_2OH(l)$$

First draw out the displayed formulae of reactants and products:

AQA Examiner's tip

Remember that bond breaking is an endothermic process and that bond making is an exothermic process.

```
H       H                              H   H
 \     /                               |   |
  C = C    +   H—O—H   ——————>     H — C — C — O — H
 /     \                               |   |
H       H                              H   H
```

To convert the reactants into separate atoms, we must break:

4 × C—H = 4 × 413	= 1652 kJ mol^{-1}
1 × C=C	= 612 kJ mol^{-1}
2 × O—H = 2 × 464	= 928 kJ mol^{-1}
Total energy put in:	**= 3192 kJ mol^{-1}**

To convert the atoms into the products, we must make:

5 × C—H = 5 × 413	= 2065 kJ mol^{-1}
1 × C—C	= 347 kJ mol^{-1}
1 × C—O	= 358 kJ mol^{-1}
1 × O—H	= 464 kJ mol^{-1}
Total energy given out:	**= 3234 kJ mol^{-1}**

The difference is 42 kJ mol^{-1} and more energy is given out than was put in, so ΔH is negative.

This can be displayed as a cycle, see Figure 1, or an enthalpy level diagram, Figure 2.

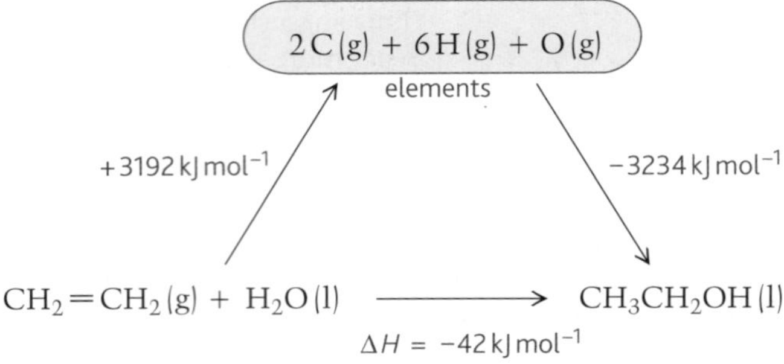

Figure 1 *Thermochemical cycle for* $CH_2{=}CH_2(g) + H_2O(l) \longrightarrow CH_3CH_2OH(l)$

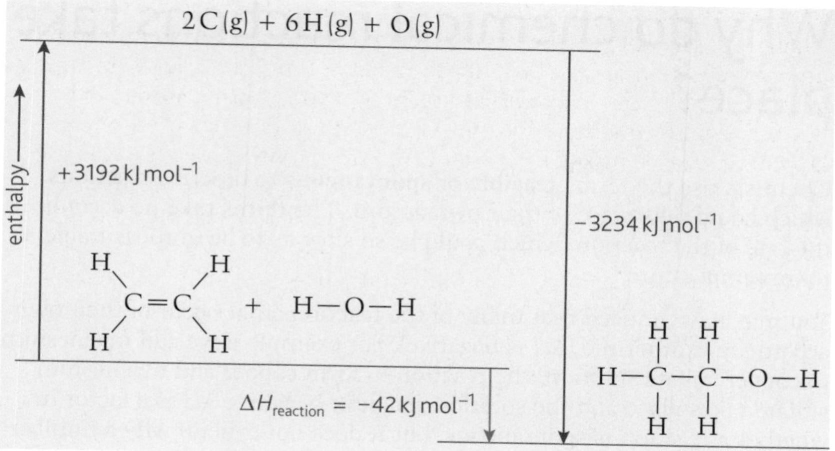

Figure 2 *Enthalpy level diagram for $CH_2{=}CH_2(g) + H_2O(l) \longrightarrow CH_3CH_2OH(l)$*

This is an approximate value because we have used mean bond enthalpies. Values calculated with this method will normally be within about 10% of the true value (calculated using enthalpies of formation or combustion.)

However, there is often a short cut with bond energy calculations. Look again at the displayed formulae:

```
H       H                                H   H
 \     /                                 |   |
  C = C     +   H—O—H    ——————>    H—C—C—O—H
 /     \                                 |   |
H       H                                H   H
```

Only the bonds in red need to actually break and only those in green need to actually be made. This simplifies the calculation:

Bonds to be broken:

1 × C=C	= 612 kJ mol⁻¹
1 × O—H	= 464 kJ mol⁻¹
Total energy put in:	**= 1076 kJ mol⁻¹**

To convert the atoms into the products, we must make:

1 × C—H	= 413 kJ mol⁻¹
1 × C—C	= 347 kJ mol⁻¹
1 × C—O	= 358 kJ mol⁻¹
Total energy given out:	**= 1118 kJ mol⁻¹**

$\Delta H = -42\,\text{kJ mol}^{-1}$, as before.

The method can also be represented on a thermochemical cycle or an enthalpy level diagram. Check that you get the same answer using these methods.

Bond enthalpy calculations are quick and easy and, although approximate, will give an indication of the sign and magnitude of ΔH which may indicate whether the reaction is likely to take place or not. Exothermic reactions tend to take place while endothermic ones do not, although this is not the whole story as we shall see in the next chapter.

AQA Examiner's tip

Mean bond enthalpies can be used to calculate approximate enthalpy changes for reactions when direct measurement is a problem.

Link

There are several examples of this type of calculation in *AQA AS Chemistry*, Topic 7.7.

Summary questions

1. Use the bond enthalpies in Table 1 to work out approximate values of ΔH for the following reactions:

   a $CH_2{=}CH_2 + I_2 \longrightarrow CH_2ICH_2I$

   b $CH_3CH_3 + Cl_2 \longrightarrow CH_3CH_2Cl + HCl$

   It would be useful to do each calculation i) in full (breaking and making all the bonds), ii) by the shorthand method (considering only the bonds that actually need to break and make), and iii) by a thermochemical cycle, to satisfy yourself that each method gives the same answer.

12.5 Why do chemical reactions take place?

Learning objectives:

- What is entropy?
- Why do endothermic reactions occur?
- How and why does a temperature change affect feasibility?

Specification reference: 3.5.1

Hint

This reaction takes place on your tongue when you eat sherbet – you can feel your tongue getting cold!

AQA Examiner's tip

In chemistry the words 'spontaneous' and 'feasible' mean exactly the same thing - that a reaction has a tendency to happen.

Chemists use the terms **feasible** or **spontaneous** to describe reactions which could take place of their own accord. The terms take no account of the rate of the reaction, which could be so slow as to be unmeasurable at room temperature.

You may have noticed that many of the reactions that occur of their own accord are exothermic (ΔH is negative). For example if we add magnesium to copper sulfate solution, the reaction to form copper and magnesium sulfate takes place and the solution gets hot. Negative ΔH is a factor in whether a reaction is spontaneous, but it does not explain why a number of endothermic reactions are spontaneous.

For example, both the following reactions, which occur spontaneously, are endothermic (ΔH is positive):

$$C_6H_8O_7(aq) + 3NaHCO_3(aq) \longrightarrow Na_3C_6H_5O_7(aq) + 3H_2O(l) + 3CO_2(g)$$

citric acid; sodium hydrogencarbonate; sodium citrate; water; carbon dioxide

$$NH_4NO_3(s) + (aq) \longrightarrow NH_4NO_3(aq)$$

ammonium nitrate; aqueous ammonium nitrate

Randomness or entropy

Many processes which take place spontaneously involve mixing or spreading out, for example liquids evaporating, solids dissolving to form solutions, gases mixing.

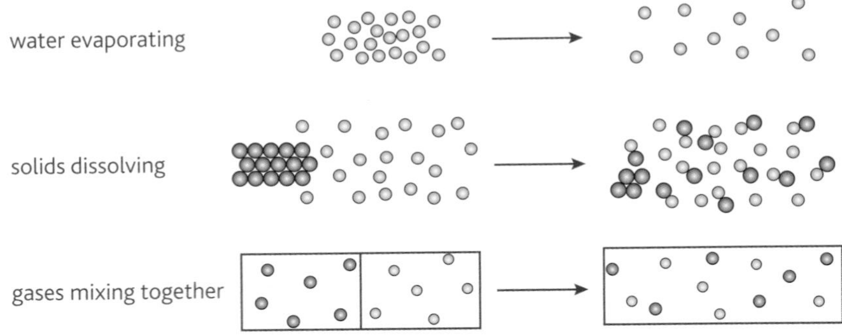

Figure 1 *Spontaneous processes*

This is the clue to the second factor which drives chemical processes – a tendency towards randomising or disordering. Gases are more random than liquids, which are more random than solids, because of the arrangement of their particles.

So, endothermic reactions may be spontaneous if they involve 'spreading out', randomising or disordering. This is true of the two reactions above – the arrangement of the particles in the products is more random than in the reactants.

The randomness of a system, expressed mathematically, is called the **entropy** of the system and is given the symbol ***S***. A reaction like the two above, in which the products are more disordered than the reactants, will have positive values for the entropy change ΔS.

Entropies have been determined for a vast range of substances and can be looked up in tables and databases. They are usually quoted for standard conditions: 298 K and 100 kPa pressure. Table 1 gives some examples.

Table 1 *Some values of entropy*

Substance	State at standard conditions	Entropy, S / $J K^{-1} mol^{-1}$
carbon (diamond)	solid	2.4
carbon (graphite)	solid	5.7
copper	solid	33
iron	solid	27
ammonium chloride	solid	95
calcium carbonate	solid	93
calcium oxide	solid	40
iron(III) oxide	solid	88
water (ice)	solid	48
water	liquid	70
mercury	liquid	76
water (steam)	gas	189
hydrogen chloride	gas	187
ammonia	gas	192
carbon dioxide	gas	214

Notice how, in general, gases have larger values than liquids, which have larger values than solids.

Take care: The units of entropy are $J K^{-1} mol^{-1}$, not $kJ K^{-1} mol^{-1}$. This can cause confusion.

Note the entropy increase when water turns to steam. Entropies increase with temperature, largely because at higher temperatures particles spread out and randomness increases.

AQA Examiner's tip

Unlike enthalpies, the entropies of elements in their standard states are *not* zero. All entropies are positive numbers, but it is possible to have a negative entropy *change* for a reaction.

Calculating entropy changes

The entropy change for a reaction can be calculated by adding all the entropies of the products and subtracting the sum of the entropies of the reactants. For example:

$$CaCO_3(s) \longrightarrow CaO(s) + CO_2(g)$$

Using the values from the table:

$$\text{Entropy of products} = 40 + 214 = 254\,J K^{-1} mol^{-1}$$

$$\text{Entropy of reactant} = 93\,J K^{-1} mol^{-1}$$

$$\Delta S = 254 - 93 = +161\,J K^{-1} mol^{-1}$$

This is a large positive value; a gas is formed from a solid.

The Gibbs free energy change, ΔG

We have seen above that a combination of *two* factors govern the feasibility of a chemical reaction:

- the **enthalpy change**
- the **entropy change.**

These two factors are combined in a quantity called the **Gibbs free energy, *G***. If the change in G, ΔG, for a reaction is negative, then this reaction is feasible; if ΔG is positive, the reaction is not feasible.

ΔG combines the entropy change (ΔH) and entropy change (ΔS) factors as follows:

$$\Delta G = \Delta H - T\Delta S$$

ΔG depends on temperature, because of the term $T\Delta S$. This means that some reactions may be feasible at one temperature and not at another.

So an endothermic reaction can become feasible when temperature is increased if there is a large enough positive entropy change. (Notice that a *positive* entropy change will make ΔG more *negative* because of the negative sign in the $T\Delta S$ term.)

How science works

The Gibbs free energy is named after the American chemist Josiah Willard Gibbs. He was quite versatile: as well as his chemistry research he taught Latin at Yale University and invented a railway braking system!

Here are some examples of how this works.

Take the reaction:

$$CaCO_3(s) \longrightarrow CaO(s) + CO_2(g) \qquad \Delta H = +178\,kJ\,mol^{-1}$$

We have seen above that $\Delta S = +161\,J\,K^{-1}\,mol^{-1} = 0.161\,kJ\,K^{-1}\,mol^{-1}$ (remember to convert the entropy units by dividing by 1000 because enthalpy is measured in *kilojoules* per mole and entropy in *joules* per kelvin per mole).

So at room temperature (298 K):

$$\Delta G = \Delta H - T\Delta S$$

$$\Delta G = 178 - (298 \times 0.161) = +130\,kJ\,mol^{-1}$$

This positive value means that the reaction is not feasible at room temperature. The reverse reaction will have $\Delta G = -130\,kJ\,mol^{-1}$ and will be feasible:

$$CaO(s) + CO_2(g) \longrightarrow CaCO_3(s)$$

This is the reaction that occurs in desiccators to absorb carbon dioxide.

However, if we do the calculation for a temperature of 1500 K, we get a different result:

At 1500 K:

$\Delta G = \Delta H - T\Delta S$

$\Delta G = -178 - (1500 \times 0.161)$

$\Delta G = -178 - 242$

$\Delta G = -64\,kJ\,mol^{-1}$

ΔG is negative and the reaction *is* feasible at this temperature. This is the reaction that occurs in a lime kiln to make lime (calcium oxide) from limestone (calcium carbonate).

What happens when $\Delta G = 0$?

There is a temperature at which $\Delta G = 0$ for this reaction. This is the point at which the reaction is just feasible. We can calculate this temperature:

$$\Delta G = \Delta H - T\Delta S$$

$$0 = \Delta H - T\Delta S$$

$$\Delta H = T\Delta S \text{ where } \Delta H = +178\,\text{kJ mol}^{-1} \text{ and } \Delta S = 0.161\,\text{kJ K}^{-1}$$

$$\text{So } T = \frac{178}{0.161} = 1105.6\,\text{K}$$

In fact the reaction does not suddenly flip from feasible to non-feasible. In a closed system an equilibrium exists around this temperature in which both products and reactants are present.

Calculating an entropy change

We can use the temperature at which $\Delta G = 0$ to calculate an entropy change. For example a solid at its melting point is equally likely to exist as a solid or a liquid – an equilibrium exists between solid and liquid. So ΔG for the melting process must be zero and:

$$0 = \Delta H - T\Delta S$$

For example, the melting point for water is 273 K and the enthalpy change for melting is $6.0\,\text{kJ mol}^{-1}$. Putting these values into the equation:

$$0 = 6.0 - 273 \times \Delta S$$

$$\Delta S = \frac{6.0}{273} = 0.022\,\text{kJ K}^{-1}\,\text{mol}^{-1} = +\ 22\,\text{J K}^{-1}\,\text{mol}^{-1}$$

This is the entropy change that occurs when ice changes to water. It is positive, which we would expect as the moleculaes in water are more disordered than those in ice.

Extracting metals

A good way of extracting metals from their oxide ores is to heat them with carbon, which removes the oxygen as carbon dioxide and leaves the metal. This has the advantage that carbon (in the form of coke) is cheap. The gaseous carbon dioxide simply diffuses away, so there is no problem separating it from the metal (although it does contribute to global warming as it is a greenhouse gas). We can use ΔG to investigate under what conditions the reaction might be feasible for different metals.

One of the most important metals is iron and its ore is largely iron(III) oxide, Fe_2O_3. We can calculate $\Delta G^{\ominus}$ from a thermochemical cycle.

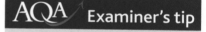

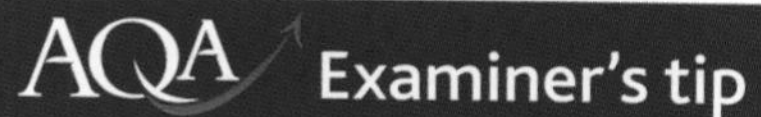

Check that you know the principles of metal extraction.

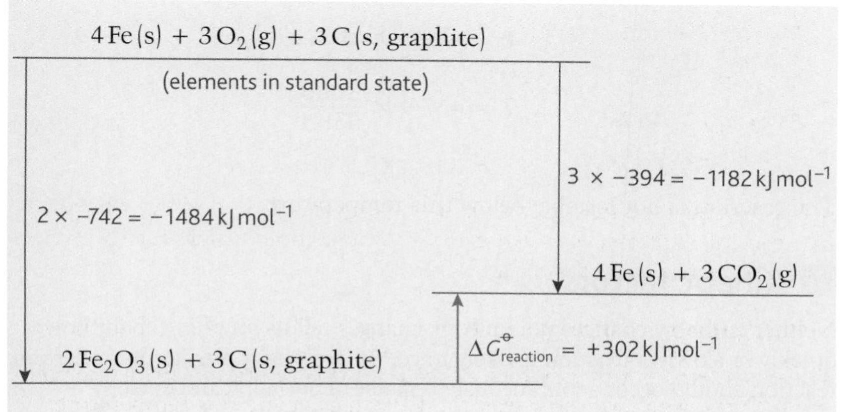

Figure 2 *Free energy diagram for the reduction of iron(III) oxide by graphite*

$2Fe_2O_3(s) + 3C(s, \text{graphite}) \longrightarrow 4Fe(s) + 3CO_2(g) \quad \Delta G^{\ominus} = +302\,kJ\,mol^{-1}$

so this reaction is not feasible under standard conditions (298 K).

Will the reaction take place at a higher temperature?

We can work out the temperature at which the reaction just becomes feasible (this is when $\Delta G = 0$) using:

$$\Delta G = \Delta H - T\Delta S$$

Calculating ΔH

ΔH for the reaction can be calculated from the following thermochemical cycle, see *AQA AS Chemistry*, Topic 7.6.

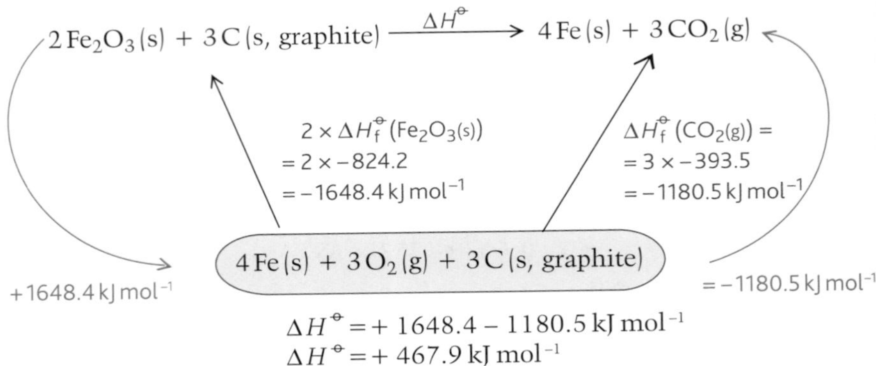

$\Delta H^{\ominus} = +\,1648.4 - 1180.5\,kJ\,mol^{-1}$

$\Delta H^{\ominus} = +\,467.9\,kJ\,mol^{-1}$

Calculating ΔS

We can calculate the entropy change of the reaction by finding the difference between the sum of the entropies of all the products and the sum of the entropies of all the reactants:

	$2Fe_2O_3(s) + 3C(s, \text{graphite})$	$\longrightarrow$	$4Fe(s) + 3CO_2(g)$
S/ J K^{-1} mol^{-1}:	$(2 \times 87.4) + (3 \times 5.7)$		$(4 \times 27.3) + (3 \times 213.6)$
	191.9		750.0

$$\Delta S = +558.1\,J\,K^{-1}\,mol^{-1}$$

Notice that this is large and positive, as we would expect from a reaction in which two solids produce a gas.

Putting these values into $\Delta G = \Delta H - T\Delta S$

$$0 = +467.9 - T \times \frac{558.1}{1000}$$

$$T = 467.9 \times \frac{1000}{558.1}$$

$$= 838.4\,K$$

The reaction is not feasible below this temperature.

Hint

In fact, in the blast furnace a higher temperature is used, above the melting point of iron (1808 K), so that the iron is formed as a liquid. Also, the carbon is not pure graphite, but coke.

Kinetic factors

Neither enthalpy changes nor entropy changes tell us *anything* about how quickly or slowly a reaction is likely to go. So, we might predict that a certain reaction should occur spontaneously because of enthalpy and entropy changes, but the reaction might take place so slowly that for practical purposes it does not occur at all. In other words there is a large activation energy barrier for the reaction (see *AQA AS Chemistry*, Topic 8.1).

Carbon gives an interesting example :

$$C(s, graphite) + O_2(g) \longrightarrow CO_2(g) \qquad \Delta H^\ominus = -393.5\,kJ\,mol^{-1}$$

The reaction is exothermic and entropy increases as we go from an ordered solid to a disordered gas, so we would expect the reaction to 'go' on both counts. We can calculate the actual values of ΔS and hence find ΔG.

Calculating ΔS

ΔS for the reaction is the sum of the entropies of the product minus the sum of the entropies of the reactants.

$$C(s, graphite) + O_2(g) \longrightarrow CO_2(g) \qquad \Delta H^\ominus = -394\,kJ\,mol^{-1}$$

S/ $J\,K^{-1}\,mol^{-1}$: 5.7 205.0 213.6

So $\Delta S_{reaction} = 213.6 - (5.7 + 205.0)$

$\Delta S_{reaction} = +2.9\,J\,K^{-1}\,mol^{-1}$, positive as we predicted.

Calculating ΔG

$$\Delta G = \Delta H - T\Delta S$$

So under standard condition (approximately room temperature and pressure):

$$\Delta G = -394 - \left(298 \times \frac{2.9}{1000}\right)$$

Remember to divide the entropy value by 1000 to convert from $J\,K^{-1}\,mol^{-1}$ to $kJ\,K^{-1}\,mol^{-1}$.

$$\Delta G = -394 - 0.86$$

$\Delta G = -394.86\,kJ\,mol^{-1}$, negative so the reaction is feasible.

However, experience with graphite (the 'lead' in pencils) tells us that the reaction does not take place at room temperature – although it will take place at higher temperatures. At room temperature, the reaction is so slow that in practice it doesn't take place at all.

Since the branch of chemistry dealing with enthalpy and entropy changes is called **thermodynamics**, and that dealing with rates is called **kinetics**, graphite is said to be thermodynamically unstable but kinetically stable.

AQA Examiner's tip

Entropies of elements in their standard states are *not* zero.

Substance	$S^\ominus / J\,K^{-1}\,mol^{-1}$
$Mg(s)$	32.7
$MgO(s)$	26.9
$MgCO_3(s)$	65.7
$Zn(s)$	41.6
$ZnO(s)$	43.6
$Pb(NO_3)_2(s)$	213.0
$PbO(s)$	68.7
$NO_2(g)$	240.0
$O_2(g)$	205
$CO_2(g)$	213.6
$H_2O(l)$	69.7
$H_2O(g)$	188.7

Summary questions

1 a Without doing a calculation, predict whether the entropy change for the following reactions will be significantly positive, significantly negative or approximately zero and explain your reasoning.

i $Mg(s) + ZnO(s) \longrightarrow MgO(s) + Zn(s)$

ii $2Pb(NO_3)_2(s) \longrightarrow 2PbO(s) + 4NO_2(g) + O_2(g)$

iii $MgO(s) + CO_2(g) \longrightarrow MgCO_3(s)$

iv $H_2O(l) \longrightarrow H_2O(g)$

b Calculate $\Delta S^\ominus$ for each reaction using data in the table in the margin above. Comment on your answers.

2 For the reaction:

$MgO(s) \longrightarrow Mg(s) + \frac{1}{2}O_2(g)$

$\Delta H^\ominus = +602\,kJ\,mol^{-1}$

$\Delta S^\ominus = +109\,J\,K^{-1}\,mol^{-1}$

a Using the equation $\Delta G = \Delta H - T\Delta S$, calculate ΔG at:

i 1000 K

ii 6000 K

iii At which temperature is the reaction feasible?

b Calculate the temperature when $\Delta G = 0$.

3 Calculate the entropy change for:

$NH_3(g) + HCl(g) \longrightarrow NH_4Cl(s)$

ammonia, hydrogen chloride, ammonium chloride

The entropy values are:

$S^\ominus$ NH_3 $192\,J\,K^{-1}\,mol^{-1}$

$S^\ominus$ HCl $187\,J\,K^{-1}\,mol^{-1}$

$S^\ominus$ NH_4Cl $95\,J\,K^{-1}\,mol^{-1}$

AQA Examination-style questions

1 A Born–Haber cycle for the formation of calcium sulfide is shown below. The cycle includes enthalpy changes for all Steps except Step **F**. (The cycle is not drawn to scale.)

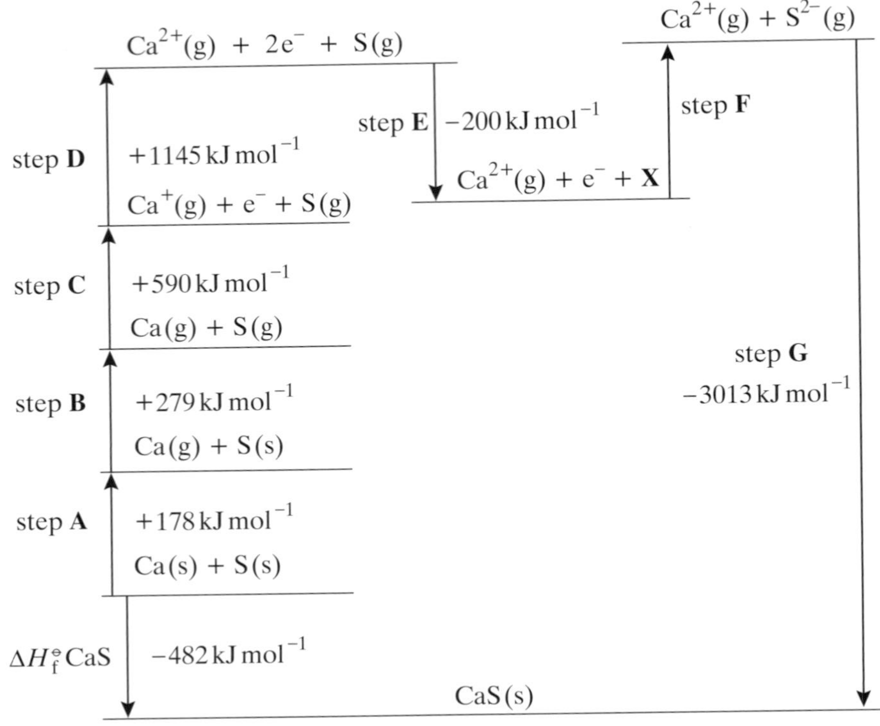

(a) Give the full electronic arrangement of the ion S^{2-} *(1 mark)*

(b) Identify the species **X** formed in Step **E**. *(1 mark)*

(c) Suggest why Step **F** is an endothermic process. *(2 marks)*

(d) Name the enthalpy change for each of the following steps.

 (i) Step **B**

 (ii) Step **D**

 (iii) Step **F** *(3 marks)*

(e) Explain why the enthalpy change for Step **D** is larger than that for Step **C**. *(2 marks)*

(f) Use the data shown in the cycle to calculate a value for the enthalpy change for Step **F**. *(2 marks)*

AQA, 2005

2 The sketch graph below shows how the entropy of a sample of water varies with temperature.

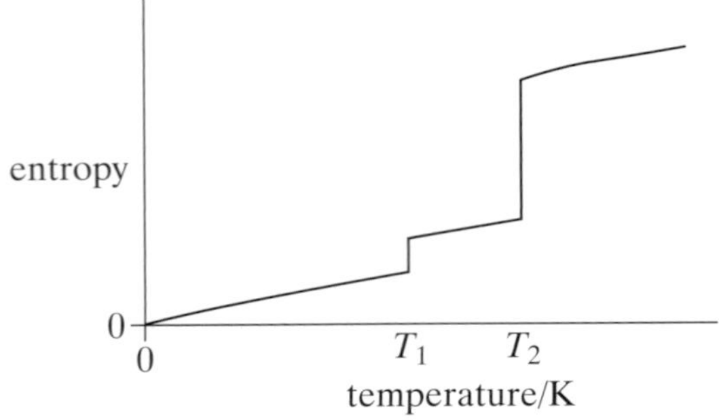

(a) Suggest why the entropy of water is zero at 0 K. *(1 mark)*

(b) What change of state occurs at temperature T_1? *(1 mark)*

(c) Explain why the entropy change, ΔS, at temperature T_2 is much larger than that at temperature T_1. *(2 marks)*

(d) It requires 3.49 kJ of heat energy to convert 1.53 g of liquid water into steam at 373 K and 100 kPa.

(i) Use these data to calculate the enthalpy change, ΔH, when 1.00 mol of liquid water forms 1.00 mol of steam at 373 K and 100 kPa.

(ii) Write an expression showing the relationship between free-energy change, ΔG, enthalpy change, ΔH, and entropy change, ΔS.

(iii) For the conversion of liquid water into steam at 373 K and 100 kPa, $\Delta G = 0\,\text{kJ mol}^{-1}$

Calculate the value of ΔS for the conversion of one mole of water into steam under these conditions. State the units.

(If you have been unable to complete part (d)(i) you should assume that $\Delta H = 45.0\,\text{kJ mol}^{-1}$. This is not the correct answer.) *(6 marks)*

AQA, 2006

3 (a) (i) Draw a fully-labelled Born–Haber cycle for the formation of solid barium chloride, $BaCl_2$, from its elements. Include state symbols for all species involved.

(ii) Use your Born–Haber cycle and the standard enthalpy data given below to calculate a value for the electron affinity of chlorine.

Enthalpy of atomisation of barium	$+180\,\text{kJ mol}^{-1}$
Enthalpy of atomisation of chlorine	$+122\,\text{kJ mol}^{-1}$
Enthalpy of formation of barium chloride	$-859\,\text{kJ mol}^{-1}$
First ionisation enthalpy of barium	$+503\,\text{kJ mol}^{-1}$
Second ionisation enthalpy of barium	$+965\,\text{kJ mol}^{-1}$
Lattice formation enthalpy of barium chloride	$-2056\,\text{kJ mol}^{-1}$

(9 marks)

(b) Use data from part (a)(ii) and the entropy data given below to calculate the lowest temperature at which the following reaction becomes feasible.

$$BaCl_2(s) \longrightarrow Ba(s) + Cl_2(g)$$

	$BaCl_2(s)$	Ba(s)	$Cl_2(g)$
$S^\ominus$/ J K^{-1} mol^{-1}	124	63	223

(4 marks)

AQA, 2003

4 Use the data in the table below to answer the questions which follow.

Substance	$Fe_2O_3(s)$	Fe(s)	C(s)	CO(g)	$CO_2(g)$
$\Delta H_f^\ominus$ / kJ mol^{-1}	–824.2	0	0	–110.5	–393.5
$S^\ominus$ / J K^{-1} mol^{-1}	87.4	27.3	5.7	197.6	213.6

(a) The following equation shows one of the reactions which can occur in the extraction of iron.

$$Fe_2O_3(s) + 3CO(g) \longrightarrow 2Fe(s) + 3CO_2(g)$$

(i) Calculate the standard enthalpy change and the standard entropy change for this reaction.

(ii) Explain why this reaction is feasible at all temperatures. *(9 marks)*

(b) The reaction shown by the following equation can also occur in the extraction of iron.

$$Fe_2O_3(s) + 3C(s) \longrightarrow 2Fe(s) + 3CO(g) \qquad \Delta H^\ominus = +492.7\,\text{kJ mol}^{-1}$$

The standard entropy change, $\Delta S^\ominus$, for this reaction is $+542.6\,\text{J K}^{-1}\,\text{mol}^{-1}$

Use this information to calculate the temperature at which this reaction becomes feasible. *(3 marks)*

(c) Calculate the temperature at which the standard free-energy change, $\Delta G^\ominus$ has the same value for the reactions in parts (a) and (b). *(3 marks)*

AQA, 2003

13 Periodicity

13.1 Reactions of Period 3 elements

Learning objectives:

- How, and under what conditions, do sodium and magnesium react with water?
- How do the elements from sodium to sulfur react with oxygen?

Specification reference: 3.5.2

Link

You will need to know AS Periodicity, AS Group 2 chemistry studied in *AQA AS Chemistry*, Topics 4.2, 4.3, 12.1 and the whole of *AQA AS Chemistry*, Chapter 3; and be able to balance equations when reactants and products are specified as studied in *AQA AS Chemistry*, Topic 2.5.

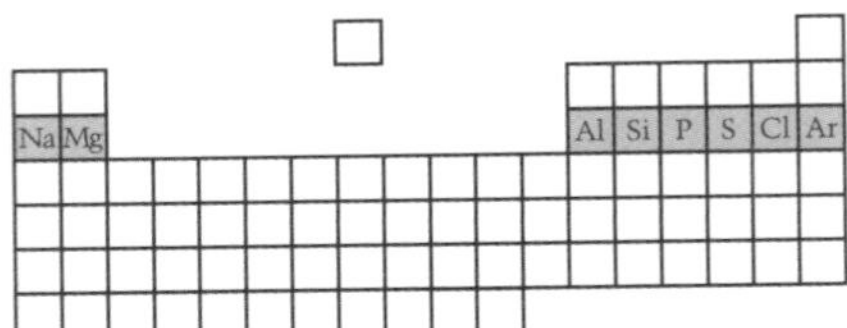

As we move across a period in the periodic table from left to right, there are a number of trends in the properties of the elements. In *AQA AS Chemistry*, Topics 4.2 and 4.3 we looked at the physical properties of the elements from sodium to argon in Period 3. Here we will examine some of the chemical reactions of these elements.

The elements

As we saw in *AQA AS Chemistry*, Topic 4.2 the most obvious physical trend in the elements is from metals on the left to non-metals on the right.

- Sodium, magnesium and aluminium are metallic – they are shiny (when freshly exposed to air), conduct electricity, and react with dilute acids to give hydrogen and salts.
- Silicon is a semi-metal (or metalloid) – it conducts electricity to some extent, a property that is useful in making semiconductor devices.
- Phosphorus, sulfur and chlorine are typical non-metals – in particular, they do not conduct electricity and have low melting and boiling points.
- Argon is a noble gas. It is chemically unreactive and exists as separate atoms.

The redox reactions of the elements

The reactions of the elements in Period 3 are all redox reactions, since every element starts with an oxidation state of zero, and, after it has reacted, ends up with a positive or a negative oxidation state.

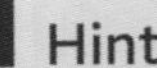

Hint

Oxidation states may also be called **oxidation numbers**. The two terms mean exactly the same thing.

Reactions with water

Sodium and magnesium are the only metal elements in Period 3 that react with cold water. (Chlorine is the only non-metal that reacts with water.)

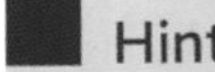

Hint

We saw in *AQA AS Chemistry*, Topic 11.4 that chlorine reacts with water in a reversible reaction to form chloric(I) acid and hydrochloric acid (HCl).

Sodium

The reaction of sodium with water is vigorous – the sodium floats on the surface of the water and fizzes rapidly, melting because of the heat given out by the reaction. A strongly alkaline solution of sodium hydroxide is formed (pH 13–14). The oxidation state changes are shown as small numbers above the following symbol equations:

$$\overset{0}{2Na(s)} + 2\overset{+1\,-2}{H_2O(l)} \longrightarrow 2\overset{+1\,-2+1}{NaOH(aq)} + \overset{0}{H_2}(g)$$

Magnesium

The reaction of magnesium is very slow at room temperature, only a few bubbles of hydrogen are formed after some days. The resulting solution is less alkaline than in the case of sodium because magnesium hydroxide is only sparingly soluble (pH around 10).

$$\overset{0}{Mg(s)} + 2\overset{+1\,-2}{H_2O(l)} \longrightarrow \overset{+2\,-2+1}{Mg(OH)_2(aq)} + \overset{0}{H_2}(g)$$

The reaction is much faster with heated magnesium and steam and gives magnesium oxide and hydrogen.

$$\overset{0}{Mg(s)} + \overset{+1\,-2}{H_2O(l)} \longrightarrow \overset{+2\,-2}{MgO(s)} + \overset{0}{H_2}(g)$$

All these reactions are redox ones, in which the oxidation state of the metal increases and that of some of the hydrogen atoms decreases.

Figure 1 *Magnesium burning in oxygen*

Reaction with oxygen

All the elements in Period 3 (except for argon) are relatively reactive. Their oxides can all be prepared by direct reaction of the element with oxygen. The reactions are exothermic.

Sodium burns brightly in air (with a characteristic yellow flame) to form white sodium oxide:

$$\overset{0}{2Na(s)} + \tfrac{1}{2}\overset{0}{O_2(g)} \longrightarrow \overset{+1\,-2}{Na_2O(s)}$$

Hint

The sodium oxide formed may have a yellowish appearance due to the production of some sodium peroxide, Na_2O_2.

Magnesium

A strip of magnesium ribbon burns in air with a bright white flame. The white powder that is produced is magnesium oxide. If burning magnesium is lowered into a gas jar of oxygen the flame is even more intense, see Figure 1.

magnesium + oxygen ⟶ magnesium oxide

$$\overset{0}{2Mg(s)} + \overset{0}{O_2(g)} \longrightarrow \overset{+2-2}{2MgO(s)}$$

The oxidation states show how magnesium has been oxidised (its oxidation state has increased) and oxygen has been reduced (its oxidation number has decreased).

Aluminium

When aluminium powder is heated and then lowered into a gas jar of oxygen, it burns brightly to give aluminium oxide – a white powder, see Figure 2.

aluminium + oxygen ⟶ aluminium oxide

$$\overset{0}{4Al(s)} + \overset{0}{3O_2(g)} \longrightarrow \overset{+3\,-2}{2Al_2O_3(s)}$$

Aluminium is a reactive metal, but it is always coated with a strongly bonded surface layer of oxide – this protects it from further reaction. So, aluminium appears to be an unreactive metal and is used for many

Figure 2 *Aluminium burning in oxygen. Powdered aluminium is being sprinkled into the flame*

Hint

Note that the sum of the oxidation states in Al_2O_3 is zero (as it is in all compounds): (2 × 3) + (3 × −2) = 0

everyday purposes – saucepans, garage doors, window frames etc. Even if the surface is scratched, the exposed aluminium reacts rapidly with the air and seals off the surface.

Silicon

Silicon will also form the oxide if it is heated strongly in oxygen:

$$\overset{0}{Si}(s) + \overset{0}{O_2}(g) \longrightarrow \overset{+4\,-2}{SiO_2}(s)$$

Phosphorus

Red phosphorus must be heated before it will react with oxygen. White phosphorus spontaneously ignites in air and the white smoke of phosphorus pentoxide is given off. Red and white phosphorus are **allotropes** of phosphorus – the same element with the atoms arranged differently.

$$4\overset{0}{P}(s) + 5\overset{0}{O_2}(g) \longrightarrow \overset{+5\,-2}{P_4O_{10}}(s)$$

If the supply of oxygen is limited, phosphorus trioxide, P_2O_3, is also formed.

Figure 3 *Sulfur burning in oxygen*

Sulfur

When sulfur powder is heated and lowered into a gas jar of oxygen, it burns with a blue flame to form the colourless gas sulfur dioxide (and a little sulfur trioxide also forms), see Figure 3.

$$\text{sulfur} + \text{oxygen} \longrightarrow \text{sulfur dioxide}$$

$$\overset{0}{S}(s) + \overset{0}{O_2}(g) \longrightarrow \overset{+4\,-2}{SO_2}\ (g)$$

In all these redox reactions, the oxidation state of the Period 3 element increases and that of the oxygen decreases (from 0 to −2 in each case). The oxidation state changes are shown as small numbers above the symbol equations above. Notice how the oxidation number of the Period 3 element in the oxide increases as we move from left to right across the period.

Hint

The empirical formula of phosphorus pentoxide is P_2O_5. In the gas phase it forms molecules of P_4O_{10} and is sometimes referred to as phosphorus(V) oxide.

$$P_4 + 5O_2 \longrightarrow P_4O_{10}$$

Phosphorus trioxide is also called phosphorus(III) oxide.

Summary questions

1. Metals are shiny, conduct electricity and if they are reactive, react with acids to give hydrogen. Give three more properties not mentioned in the text.
2. Non-metals do not conduct electricity. Give two more properties typical of non-metals.
3. a What is the oxidation state of sodium in all its compounds?
   b What is the oxidation state of oxygen in sodium peroxide, Na_2O_2? What is unusual about this?
   c Show that the sum of the oxidation states in magnesium hydroxide is zero.
4. What is the oxidation state of sulfur in sulfur trioxide?

13.2 The oxides of elements in Period 3

Learning objectives:

- How are the physical properties of the oxides explained in terms of their structure and bonding?
- How do the oxides react with water?
- How can the structure of the oxides explain the trend in their reactions in water?

Specification reference: 3.5.2

As we move across Period 3 from left to right there are some important trends in the physical properties of the Period 3 *compounds*. These trends are a result of the change from metal elements on the left of the periodic table to non-metal elements on the right. The oxides are representative of these trends.

The metal oxides

Sodium, magnesium and aluminium oxides are examples of compounds formed by a metal combined to a non-metal. They form giant ionic lattices where the bonding extends throughout the compound. This results in high melting points.

The bonding in aluminium oxide is ionic but has some covalent character. This is because aluminium forms a very small ion with a large positive charge and the so can approach closely to the O^{2-} and distort its electron cloud. So, the bond also has some added covalent character, see Figure 1. We met with this idea in Topic 12.3, when we saw that the bonding in zinc selenide was not purely ionic, but had some degree of covalent character.

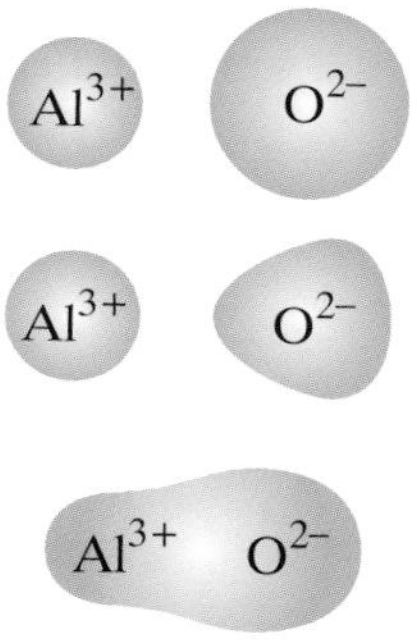

pure ionic bonding Al^{3+} O^{2-}

distortion Al^{3+} O^{2-}

some degree of covalent bonding Al^{3+} O^{2-}

Figure 1 *The covalent character of the bonding in aluminium oxide*

It is possible to predict the ionic character of a bond by considering the difference in electronegativities between the two atoms. The bigger the difference, the greater the ionic character of the bond. Caesium oxide, Cs_2O, is about 80% ionic. The electronegativities are Cs = 0.7, O = 3.5. A bond between two identical atoms such as that in O_2 *must* be 100% covalent.

The non-metal oxides

Silicon oxide has a giant covalent (macromolecular) structure. Again the bonding extends throughout the giant structure, but this time it is covalent, see Figure 2. Again we have a compound with high melting point because many strong covalent bonds must be broken to melt it.

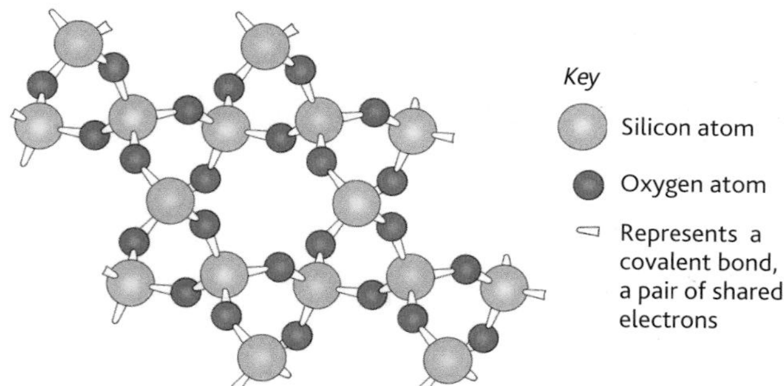

Figure 2 *Silicon dioxide is a macromolecule*

Phosphorus and sulfur oxides exist as separate covalently bonded molecules. The phosphorus oxides are solids. The intermolecular forces are weak van der Waals and dipole–dipole forces, see *AQA AS Chemistry*, Topic 3.5. Their melting points are relatively low. Sulfur dioxide and sulfur trioxide are gases at 298 K.

The trends in the physical properties of the oxides are summarised in Table 1.

Table 1 *The trends in the physical properties of some of the oxides in Period 3*

	Na_2O	MgO	Al_2O_3	SiO_2	P_4O_{10}	SO_3	SO_2
T_m/K	1548	3125	2345	1883	573	290	200
bonding	ionic	ionic	ionic/covalent	covalent	covalent	covalent	covalent
structure	giant ionic	giant ionic	giant ionic	giant covalent (macromolecular)	molecular	molecular	molecular

AQA Examiner's tip

Make sure that you understand the link between physical properties and bonding.

Note the trend in melting points: $P_4O_{10} > SO_3 > SO_2$

This is related to the increase in intermolecular forces between the larger molecules.

Reaction of oxides with water

Basic oxides

Sodium and magnesium oxides are both bases.

Sodium oxide reacts with water to give sodium hydroxide solution – a strongly alkaline solution:

$$Na_2O(s) + H_2O(l) \longrightarrow 2Na^+(aq) + 2OH^-(aq) \qquad \text{pH of solution} \sim 14$$

Magnesium oxide reacts with water to give magnesium hydroxide, which is sparingly soluble in water and produces a somewhat alkaline solution:

$$MgO(s) + H_2O(l) \longrightarrow Mg(OH)_2(s) \rightleftharpoons Mg^{2+}(aq) + 2OH^-(aq)$$

pH of solution ~ 9

Hint

Silicon dioxide is the main constituent of sand which does not dissolve in water!

Insoluble oxides

Aluminium oxide is insoluble in water.

Silicon dioxide is insoluble in water.

Acidic oxides

Non-metals on the right of the periodic table typically form acidic oxides. For example:

Phosphorus pentoxide reacts quite violently with water to produce an acidic solution of phosphoric(V) acid. This ionises, so the solution is acidic, see Topic 3.1:

$$P_4O_{10}(s) + 6H_2O(l) \longrightarrow 4H_3PO_4(aq)$$

$H_3PO_4(aq)$ ionises in stages, the first being:

$$H_3PO_4(aq) \rightleftharpoons H^+(aq) + H_2PO_4^-(aq)$$

Sulfur dioxide is fairly soluble in water and reacts with it to give an acidic solution of sulfuric(IV) acid (sulfurous acid). This partially dissociates producing H^+ ions, which cause the acidity of the solution:

$$SO_2(g) + H_2O(l) \longrightarrow H_2SO_3(aq)$$

$$H_2SO_3(aq) \rightleftharpoons H^+(aq) + HSO_3^-(aq)$$

Sulfur trioxide reacts violently with water to produce sulfuric acid (sulfuric(VI) acid):

$$SO_3(g) + H_2O(l) \longrightarrow H_2SO_4(aq) \longrightarrow H^+(aq) + HSO_4^-(aq)$$

The overall pattern is that metal oxides (on the left of the period) form alkaline solutions in water and non-metal oxides (on the right of the period) form acidic ones, while those in the middle do not react.

Table 2 summarises these reactions.

Table 2 *The oxides in water*

Oxide	Bonding	Ions present after reaction with water	Acidity/alkalinity	Approx. pH (Actual values depend on concentration)
Na_2O	ionic	$Na^+(aq)$, $OH^-(aq)$	strongly alkaline	13–14
MgO	ionic	$Mg^{2+}(aq)$, $OH^-(aq)$	somewhat alkaline	10
Al_2O_3	covalent/ionic	insoluble, no reaction	—	7
SiO_2	covalent	insoluble, no reaction	—	7
P_4O_{10}	covalent	$H^+(aq) + H_2PO_4^-(aq)$	strong acid	0–1
SO_2	covalent	$H^+(aq) + HSO_3^-(aq)$	weak acid	2–3
SO_3	covalent	$H^+(aq) + HSO_4^-(aq)$	strong acid	0–1

The behaviour of the oxides with water can be understood if we look at their bonding and structure – see Table 1.

- Sodium and magnesium oxides, to the left of the periodic table, are composed of ions.
- Sodium oxide contains the oxide ion, O^{2-}, which is a very strong base (it strongly attracts protons) and so readily reacts with water to produce hydroxide ions – a strongly alkaline solution.
- Magnesium oxide also contains oxide ions. However, its reaction with water produces a less alkaline solution than sodium oxide because it is less soluble than sodium oxide.
- Aluminium oxide is ionic but the bonding is too strong to be separated, partly because of the additional covalent bonding it has.
- Silicon dioxide is a giant macromolecule and water will not affect this type of structure.
- Phosphorus oxides and sulfur oxides are covalent molecules and react with water to form acid solutions.

The general trend is alkalis ⟶ acids as we go across the period.

Summary questions

1 a Write down an equation for the reaction of sodium oxide with water.

b i State the oxidation number of sodium before and after the reaction.

ii Has the sodium been oxidised, reduced or neither?

2 a What ion is responsible for the alkalinity of the solutions formed when sodium oxide and magnesium oxide react with water?

b What range of pH values represents an alkaline solution?

3 Phosphorus forms another oxide P_4O_6.

a Would you expect it to react with water to form a neutral, acidic or alkaline solution?

b Explain your answer.

c Write an equation for its reaction with water.

13.3 Oxides of the elements of Period 3 and their reactions with acids and bases

Learning objectives:

- How do the oxides of the elements in Period 3 react with acids?
- How do the oxides of the elements in Period 3 react with bases?
- What are the equations for these reactions?

Specification reference: 3.5.2

As we saw in Topic 13.2, the general trend is alkalis $\longrightarrow$ acids as we go across the period. So, we could predict that the alkaline oxides will react with acids and the acidic oxides will react with bases.

Sodium and magnesium oxides

Sodium oxide and magnesium oxide react with acids to give salt and water only.

For example:

Sodium oxide reacts with sulfuric acid to give sodium sulfate:

$$Na_2O(s) + H_2SO_4(aq) \longrightarrow Na_2SO_4(aq) + H_2O(l)$$

Magnesium oxide reacts with hydrochloric acid to give magnesium chloride:

$$MgO(s) + 2HCl(aq) \longrightarrow MgCl_2(aq) + H_2O(l)$$

Aluminium oxide

Aluminium oxide reacts *both* with acids and alkalis. It is called an **amphoteric** oxide.

For example, with hydrochloric acid, aluminium chloride is formed:

$$Al_2O_3(s) + 6HCl(aq) \longrightarrow 2AlCl_3(aq) + 3H_2O(l)$$

With hot, concentrated sodium hydroxide, sodium aluminate is formed:

$$Al_2O_3(s) + 2NaOH(aq) + 3H_2O(l) \longrightarrow 2NaAl(OH)_4(aq)$$

Silicon dioxide

Silicon dioxide will react as a weak acid with strong bases, for example with hot concentrated sodium hydroxide a colourless solution of sodium silicate is formed:

$$SiO_2(s) + 2NaOH(aq) \longrightarrow Na_2SiO_3(aq) + H_2O(l)$$

Phosphorus pentoxide, P_4O_{10}

The reaction of phosphorus pentoxide with an alkali is really the reaction of phosphoric(v) acid, because this is formed when phosphorus pentoxide reacts with water. Phosphoric acid has three —OH groups, and each of these has an acidic hydrogen atom. So, it will react with sodium hydroxide in three stages, as each hydrogen in turn reacts with a hydroxide ion and is replaced by a sodium ion:

$$H_3PO_4(aq) + NaOH(aq) \longrightarrow NaH_2PO_4(aq) + H_2O(l)$$

$$NaH_2PO_4(aq) + NaOH(aq) \longrightarrow Na_2HPO_4(aq) + H_2O(l)$$

$$Na_2HPO_4(aq) + NaOH(aq) \longrightarrow Na_3PO_4(aq) + H_2O(l)$$

AQA Examiner's tip

Make sure that you know the products of these reactions and that you can write equations for the reactions occurring.

How science works

In the production of iron, at the high temperatures inside the blast furnace, calcium oxide reacts with silicon dioxide (sand) to produce a liquid slag, calcium silicate. This is also an example of the acidic silicon dioxide reacting with a base:

$$SiO_2(s) + CaO(l) \longrightarrow CaSiO_3(l)$$

Overall:

$$3NaOH(aq) + H_3PO_4(aq) \longrightarrow Na_3PO_4(aq) + 3H_2O(l)$$

Sulfur dioxide

If we add sodium hydroxide to an aqueous solution of sulfur dioxide, we first form sodium hydrogensulfate(IV):

$$SO_2(aq) + NaOH(aq) \longrightarrow NaHSO_3(aq)$$

Followed by sodium sulfate(IV):

$$NaHSO_3(aq) + NaOH(aq) \longrightarrow Na_2SO_3(aq) + H_2O(l)$$

Summary questions

1 Write balanced symbol equations for the reactions of:

a sodium oxide with hydrochloric acid

b magnesium oxide with sulfuric acid

c aluminium oxide with nitric acid.

2 $SiO_2(s) + 2NaOH(aq) \longrightarrow Na_2SiO_3(aq) + H_2O(l)$

a Copy the equation above and write the oxidation numbers above each atom.

b Is the reaction a redox reaction?

c Explain your answer to b.

3 Write a balanced symbol for the reaction of phosphorus pentoxide with water.

How science works

Sulfur dioxide reacts with the base calcium oxide to form calcium sulfite (calcium sulfate(IV)). This is the first step of one of the methods of removing sulfur dioxide from flue gases in power stations:

$$CaO(s) + SO_2(g) \longrightarrow CaSO_3(s)$$

The calcium sulfite is further converted to calcium sulfate, $CaSO_4$ and sold as gypsum for plastering.

AQA Examination-style questions

1 (a) Suggest why the melting point of magnesium oxide is much higher than the melting point of magnesium chloride. *(2 marks)*

(b) Magnesium oxide and sulfur dioxide are added separately to water. In each case describe what happens. Write equations for any reactions which occur and state the approximate pH of any solution formed. *(6 marks)*

(c) Write equations for two reactions which together show the amphoteric character of aluminium hydroxide. *(4 marks)*

AQA, 2006

2 State what is observed when separate samples of sodium oxide and phosphorus(V) oxide are added to water. Write equations for the reactions which occur and, in each case, state the approximate pH of the solution formed. *(6 marks)*

AQA, 2005

3 In the questions below, each of the three elements **X**, **Y** and **Z** is one of the Period 3 elements Na, Mg, Al, Si or P.

(a) The oxide of element **X** has a high melting point. The oxide reacts readily with water to form a solution with a high pH.

(i) Deduce the type of bonding present in the oxide of element **X**.

(ii) Identify element **X**.

(iii) Write an equation for the reaction between water and the oxide of element **X**. *(3 marks)*

(b) Element **Y** has an oxide which react vigorously with water to form a solution containing strong acid.

(i) Deduce the type of bonding present in the oxide of element **Y**.

(ii) Identify element **Y**.

(iii) Identify an acid which is formed when the oxide of element **Y** reacts with water. *(3 marks)*

(c) The oxide of element **Z** is a crystalline solid with a very high melting point. This oxide is classified as an acidic oxide but it is not soluble in water.

(i) Deduce the type of crystal shown by the oxide of element **Z**.

(ii) Identify element **Z**.

(iii) Write an equation for a reaction which illustrates the acidic nature of the oxide of element **Z**. *(4 marks)*

AQA, 2004

4 Consider the following oxides.

Na_2O, MgO, Al_2O_3, SiO_2, P_4O_{10}, SO_3

(a) Identify one of the oxides from the above which

(i) can form a solution with a pH less than 3

(ii) can form a solution with a pH greater than 12 *(2 marks)*

(b) Write an equation for the reaction between

(i) MgO and HNO_3

(ii) SiO_2 and $NaOH$

(iii) Na_2O and H_3PO_4 *(3 marks)*

(c) Explain, in terms of their type of structure and bonding, why P_4O_{10} can be vaporised by gentle heat but SiO_2 cannot. *(4 marks)*

AQA, 2003

5 Write equations for the reactions which occur when the following compounds are added separately to water. In each case, predict the approximate pH of the solution formed when one mole of each compound is added to 1 dm^3 of water.

Sodium oxide

Sulfur dioxide

(4 marks)

AQA, 2003

6 (a) **P** and **Q** are oxides of Period 3 elements.

Oxide **P** is a solid with a high melting point. It does not conduct electricity when solid but does conduct when molten or when dissolved in water. Oxide **P** reacts with water forming a solution with a high pH.

Oxide **Q** is a colourless gas at room temperature. It dissolves in water to give a solution with a low pH.

(i) Identify **P**. State the type of bonding present in **P** and explain its electrical conductivity. Write an equation for the reaction of **P** with water.

(ii) Identify **Q**. State the type of bonding present in **Q** and explain why it is a gas at room temperature. Write an equation for the reaction of **Q** with water. *(9 marks)*

(b) **R** is a hydroxide of a Period 3 element. It is insoluble in water but dissolves in both aqueous sodium hydroxide and aqueous sulfuric acid.

(i) Give the name used to describe this behaviour of the hydroxide.

(ii) Write equations for the reactions occurring.

(iii) Suggest why **R** is insoluble in water.

(6 marks)

AQA, 2002

14 Redox equilibria

14.1 Redox equations

Learning objectives:

- What do the terms 'oxidation', 'reduction', 'oxidising agent' and 'reducing agent' mean in terms of electron transfer?
- How are redox equations balanced using oxidation numbers?
- How are half equations used to deduce overall equations for redox reactions?

Specification reference: 3.5.3

Synoptic link

You will need to know redox reactions (studied in *AQA AS Chemistry*, Topic 10.3). You will also need to know the oxidising reactions of halogens, the reducing ability of halide ions and the reactions of NaX with sulfuric acid, and the reactions of chlorine with water and sodium hydroxide (studied in *AQA AS Chemistry*, Topics 11.2 and 11.3), and understand that extraction of metals involves reduction (see *AQA AS Chemistry*, Topic 13.1).

You will remember from, *AQA AS Chemistry*, Chapter 10 that redox (reduction–oxidation) reactions are ones in which electrons are transferred from one species (atom, molecule or ion) to another. The phrase 'OIL RIG will help you remember that **O**xidation **I**s **L**oss (of electrons) and **R**eduction **I**s **G**ain (of electrons).

A **reducing agent** is a species that gives away electrons and an **oxidising agent** one that accepts them.

Oxidation states

Oxidation states, sometimes called **oxidation numbers,** are a simple way of keeping track of redox reactions, so that it is easy to see which species has been oxidised and which reduced. They help in balancing equations for redox reactions. The oxidation state of an element in a compound is effectively the number of electrons it has lost or gained when forming bonds. The rules for finding oxidation states are given in *AQA AS Chemistry*, Topic 10.2 and are repeated here.

Rules for finding oxidation states

The following rules will allow you to work out oxidation states.

1 Uncombined elements have oxidation state = 0.

2 Some elements always have the same oxidation state in all their compounds. Others usually have the same oxidation state. Table 1 gives the oxidation states of these elements.

Table 1 *The usual oxidation states of some elements*

Element	Oxidation state in compound	Example
hydrogen, H	+1 (except in metal hydrides, e.g. NaH, where it is –1)	HCl
Group 1	Always +1	NaCl
Group 2	Always +2	$CaCl_2$
aluminium, Al	Always +3	$AlCl_3$
oxygen , O	–2 (except in peroxides where it is –1, and compounds with F such as OF_2, where it is +2)	Na_2O
fluorine, F	Always –1	NaF
chlorine, Cl	–1 (except in compounds with F and O, where it has positive values.)	NaCl

3 The sum of all the oxidation states in a compound = 0, since all compounds are neutral.

4 The sum of the oxidation states of a complex ion, such as NH_4^+ or SO_4^{2-}, equals the charge on the ion.

Here are some more examples.

Simple compounds

Example: Aluminium oxide, Al_2O_3

Oxygen is always –2 and there are three of these making –6. As this is a neutral compound, the sum of the oxidation states must be zero. So the two Al atoms must contribute +6, that is +3 each.

O –2; Al +3

Complex ions

These are ions which have two or more atoms bonded covalently, but where the whole group of atoms has a charge.

Example 1

What is the oxidation state of the N atom in the ammonium ion, NH_4^+, in, for example, ammonium chloride, NH_4Cl ($NH_4^+Cl^-$)? The ammonium ion has a single positive charge.

Hydrogen is + 1 and there are four of them, giving +4.

The sum of the oxidation numbers = charge on the ion which is +1.

So the oxidation number of the nitrogen atom must be –3.

H +1; N –3

Example 2

What is the oxidation number of the Cr atom in the ion $Cr_2O_7^{2-}$?

O is –2, so the oxygens contribute $7 \times -2 = -14$

The charge on the ion is –2.

So the two chromiums must contribute a total of +12, i.e. +6 each.

So the oxidation number of Cr is +6.

Notice that this could not possibly correspond to a real ionic charge of Cr^{6+}. The bonding within the complex ion is largely covalent.

Balancing redox equations

If we know the starting materials and the products of a redox reaction, we can work out a balanced symbol equation for the reaction from the relevant half equations.

In order to do this, we use the following steps:

Step 1: Write the half equations. (You may need to work these out if complex ions and other species such as H^+ are involved.)

Step 2: We need to make sure that the number of electrons in each half equation is the same so that the electrons cancel out, by multiplying one or both equations to make the number of electrons the same in each case.

Step 3: We then add the half equations. The electrons cancel and we have a balanced equation. We may be able to cancel other species that appear on both sides – often H^+ or H_2O.

AQA Examiner's tip

Make sure that you know the rules for assigning oxidation states and are able to apply them.

Hint

Practice is the key to working with oxidation states.

Example 1

Chlorine will oxidise iron(II) to iron (III) and is itself reduced to chloride ions.

Step 1: The relevant half equations are:

A $Cl_2(g) + 2e^- \longrightarrow 2Cl^-(aq)$ The chlorine has been reduced.

B $Fe^{2+}(aq) \longrightarrow Fe^{3+}(aq) + e^-$ The iron has been oxidised.

Step 2: A involves two electrons and B one. So, we must multiply (both sides) of B by two:

$$2Fe^{2+}(aq) \longrightarrow 2Fe^{3+}(aq) + 2e^-$$

Step 3: Add A and B and cancel the electrons.

$$Cl_2(g) + 2e^- \longrightarrow 2Cl^-(aq)$$

$$2Fe^{2+}(aq) \longrightarrow 2Fe^{3+}(aq) + 2e^-$$

$$Cl_2(g) + \cancel{2e^-} + 2Fe^{2+}(aq) \longrightarrow 2Cl^-(aq) + 2Fe^{3+}(aq) + \cancel{2e^-}$$

So the balanced equation is:

$$Cl_2(g) + 2Fe^{2+}(aq) \longrightarrow 2Cl^-(aq) + 2Fe^{3+}(aq)$$

Example 2

In acid solution, dichromate(VI) ions ($Cr_2O_7^{2-}$) will oxidise sulfate(IV) ions (SO_3^{2-}) to sulfate(VI) (SO_4^{2-}) ions and are themselves reduced to Cr^{3+}.

In this case each half equation needs to be worked out carefully.

Step 1: Work out the half equations:

$Cr_2O_7^{2-}(aq) \longrightarrow Cr^{3+}(aq)$ The chromium has been reduced.

- First balance the Cr: $Cr_2O_7^{2-}(aq) \longrightarrow 2Cr^{3+}(aq)$
- Use up oxygen by forming water with H^+ ions in the acid solution: $Cr_2O_7^{2}(aq)^- + 14H^+(aq) \longrightarrow 2Cr^{3+}(aq) + 7H_2O(l)$
- Now balance for charge with electrons, which gives: **A** $Cr_2O_7^{2-}(aq) + 14H^+(aq) + 6e^- \longrightarrow 2Cr^{3+}(aq) + 7H_2O(aq)$

And $SO_3^{2-} \longrightarrow SO_4^{2-}$ The sulfur has been oxidised.

- Add water to balance the oxygen – this produces H^+ ions on the right-hand side.
- Now balance for charge with electrons: **B** $SO_3^{2-}(aq) + H_2O(l) \longrightarrow SO_4^{2-}(aq) + 2H^+(aq) + 2e^-$

Step 2: A involves six electrons and **B** two, so we must multiply **B** by three:

$$3SO_3^{2-}(aq) + 3H_2O(l) \longrightarrow 3SO_4^{2-}(aq) + 6H^+(aq) + 6e^-$$

Step 3: Add **A** and **B** and cancel the electrons and any species that appear on both sides of the equation (H^+ and H_2O in this case):

$$Cr_2O_7^{2-}(aq) + 14H^+(aq) + 6e^- \longrightarrow 2Cr^{3+}(aq) + 7H_2O(aq)$$

$$3SO_3^{2-}(aq) + 3H_2O(l) \longrightarrow 3SO_4^{2-}(aq) + 6H^+(aq) + 6e^-$$

$$Cr_2O_7^{2-}(aq) + 14H^+(aq) + 3SO_3^{2-}(aq) + 3H_2O(l) + \cancel{6e^-} \longrightarrow 2Cr^{3+}(aq) + 7H_2O(aq) + 3SO_4^{2-}(aq) + 6H^+(aq) + \cancel{6e^-}$$

So the balanced equation is:

$$Cr_2O_7^{2-}(aq) + 8H^+(aq) + 3SO_3^{2-}(aq) \longrightarrow 2Cr^{3+}(aq) + 3SO_4^{2-} + 4H_2O(aq)$$

Whenever you believe you have balanced an equation, check that:

1 The chemical balance is right, i.e. that there are the same number of atoms of all elements left and right of the arrow.

2 That the charges balance, i.e. that the total charge of all the ions on the left is equal to that on the right.

If either of these does not balance, you have made a mistake and will need to check back.

There are more examples of this in the next topic, where we use $E^\ominus$ values to predict the direction of the half reactions.

Check that you can deduce equations for the reduction of sulfuric acid by bromide and iodide ions.

Summary questions

1 Give the oxidation states of the transition metal atom in the following species:

a VO_3^-
b CrO_4^{2-}
c $CuSO_4$
d $Fe(OH)_3$
e $Fe(OH)_2$

2 Zinc can reduce dichromate(VI) ions in acid solution to chromium(III) ions.

The relevant half equations are:

$$Cr_2O_7^{2-}(aq) + 14H^+(aq) + 6e^- \longrightarrow 2Cr^{3+}(aq) + 7H_2O(aq)$$

and

$$Zn^{2+}(aq) + 2e^- \longrightarrow Zn(s)$$

Construct a balanced symbol equation for the reaction.

14.2 Electrode potentials and the electrochemical series

Learning objectives:

- How are half equations written for the reactions at an electrode?
- What is a standard electrode potential?
- How are standard electrode potentials measured?
- What is the conventional representation of a cell?

Specification reference: 3.5.3

If we place two different metals in a salt solution and connect them together as in Figure 1, an electric current flows so that electrons pass from the more reactive metal to the less reactive. This is the basis of batteries that power everything from MP3 players to milk floats.

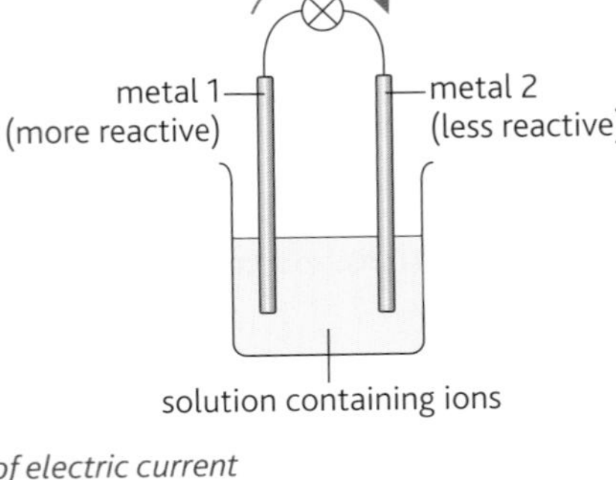

Figure 1 *Flow of electric current*

This topic and the following two look at how electricity is produced by electrochemical cells and how we can use this to explain and predict redox reactions (which are all about electron transfer).

Half cells

If we dip a rod of metal, into a solution of its own ions, an equilibrium is set up.

For example, dipping zinc into zinc sulfate solution sets up the following equilibrium:

$$Zn(s) + (aq) \rightleftharpoons Zn^{2+}(aq) + 2e^-$$

The equilibrium will be far to the left. The zinc acquires a negative charge. We say the zinc gains a negative electrical potential. This arrangement is called an **electrode**, see Figure 2.

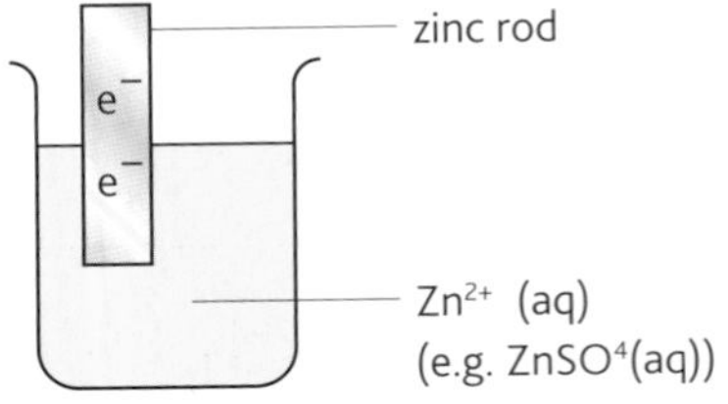

Figure 2 *A zinc electrode*

If we could measure this potential, it would tell us how readily electrons are released by the metal – that is, how good a reducing agent the metal is. (Remember that reducing agents release electrons.)

However we cannot measure electrical potential directly, only potential *difference* (often called voltage). What we *can* do is to connect together two different electrodes and measure the **potential difference** between them with a voltmeter, as shown in Figure 3 for copper and zinc electrodes.

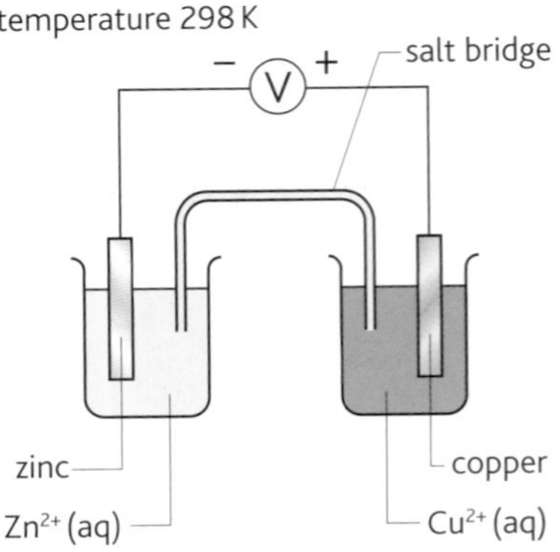

Figure 3 *Two electrodes connected together with a voltmeter to measure the potential difference*

The electrical circuit is completed by a **salt bridge,** the simplest form of which is a piece of filter paper soaked in a solution of a salt (usually saturated potassium nitrate). (This is used, rather than a piece of wire, to avoid further metal/ion potentials in the circuit.)

If we connect the two electrodes shown to the voltmeter, we get a potential difference (voltage) of 1.10 V (if the solutions are 1.00 mol dm^{-3} and the temperature 298 K). The voltmeter shows us that the zinc electrode is the more negative.

The fact that the zinc electrode is negative tells us that zinc loses its electrons more readily than does copper – it is a better reducing agent. If the voltmeter were removed and electrons allowed to flow, they would do so from zinc to copper. The following changes would take place:

1 Zinc would dissolve to form $Zn^{2+}(aq)$, increasing the concentration of $Zn^{2+}(aq)$.

2 The electrons would flow through the wire to the copper rod where they would combine with $Cu^{2+}(aq)$ ions (from the copper sulfate solution) so depositing fresh copper on the rod and decreasing the concentration of $Cu^{2+}(aq)$.

That is, the following two **half reactions** would take place:

$$Zn(s) \longrightarrow Zn^{2+}(aq) + 2e^-$$

and

$$Cu^{2+}(aq) + 2e^- \longrightarrow Cu(s)$$

adding:

$$Zn(s) + Cu^{2+}(aq) + \cancel{2e^-} \longrightarrow Zn^{2+}(aq) + Cu(s) + \cancel{2e^-}$$

When we add the two half reactions, the electrons cancel out and we get the overall reaction:

$$Zn(s) + Cu^{2+}(aq) \longrightarrow Zn^{2+}(aq) + Cu(s)$$

This is the reaction we get on putting zinc directly into a solution of copper ions. It is a redox reaction with zinc being oxidised and copper ions reduced. If the two half cells are connected they generate electricity. This forms an electrical cell called the Daniell cell see Figure 4.

The hydrogen electrode

If we want to compare the tendency of different metals to release electrons, we must have a standard electrode to which any other half cell can be connected for comparison. The half cell chosen is called the standard hydrogen electrode, see Figure 5.

We bubble hydrogen gas into a solution of $H^+(aq)$ ions. Since hydrogen doesn't conduct, we make electrical contact via a piece of unreactive platinum metal (coated with finely divided platinum to increase the surface area and allow any reaction to proceed rapidly). The electrode is used under standard conditions of $[H^+(aq)] = 1.00\,mol\,dm^{-3}$, pressure 100 kPa and temperature 298 K.

The potential of the standard hydrogen electrode is *defined* as zero, so if it is connected to another electrode (see Figure 6), the measured voltage, called the electromotive force (emf, E), is the electrode potential of that cell. If the second cell is at standard conditions ([metal ions] = $1.00\,mol\,dm^{-3}$, temperature = 298 K), then the emf is given the symbol $E^\ominus$, pronounced 'E standard'. Electrodes with negative values of $E^\ominus$ are better at releasing electrons (better reducing agents) than hydrogen.

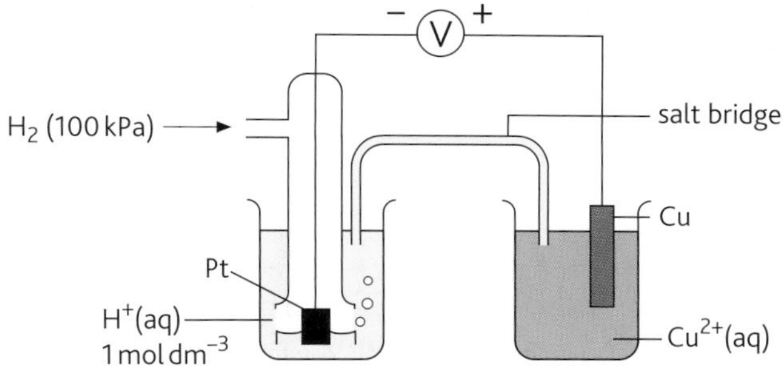

Figure 6 *Measuring E$^\ominus$ for a copper electrode*

Hint

A perfect voltmeter does not allow any current to flow – it merely measures the electrical 'push' or pressure which tends to make current flow.

AQA Examiner's tip

The salt chosen for the salt bridge must not react with either of the solutions in the half cells.

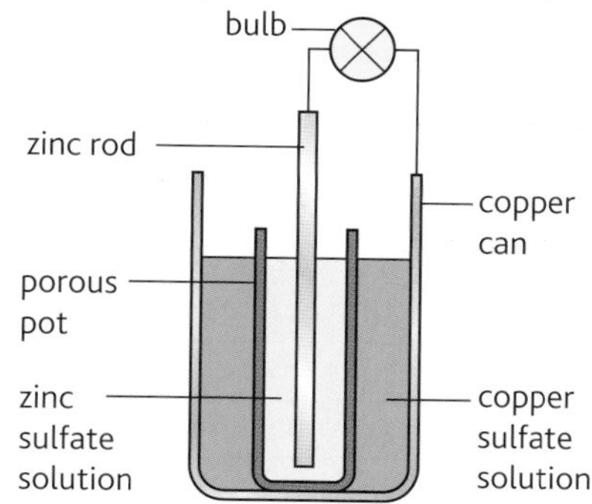

Figure 4 *A Daniell cell lighting a bulb. The porous pot acts like a salt bridge*

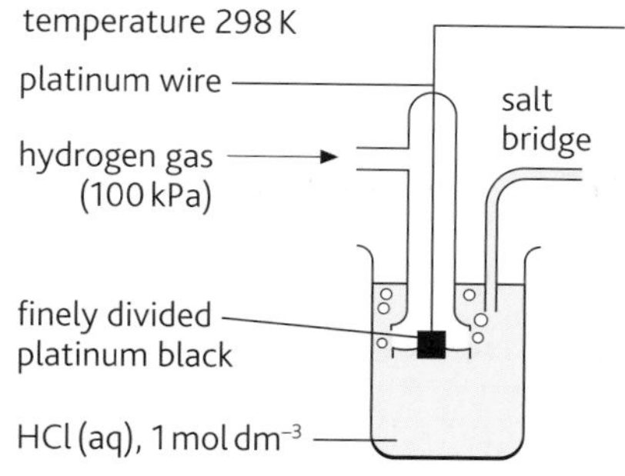

Figure 5 *The standard hydrogen electrode*

Oxidation occurs at the negative electrode; reduction occurs at the positive electrode.

Changing the conditions, such as the concentration of ions or temperature, of an electrode will change its electrical potential.

The electrochemical series

A list of some $E^\ominus$ values for metal/metal ion standard electrodes is given in Table 1.

The equilibria are written with the electrons on the left of the arrow, i.e. as a reduction. These are called **electrode potentials**, sometimes known as **reduction potentials.** (Remember RIG – 'Reduction is gain'.)

Arranged in this order *with the most negative values at the top* this list is called the **electrochemical series.** Notice that the number of electrons involved has no effect on the value of $E^\ominus$.

Table 1 *Some $E^\ominus$ values. Good reducing agents appear top right, e.g. Li(s), good oxidising agents appear bottom left, e.g $Ag^+(aq)$*

Half reaction	$E^\ominus$/V
$Li^+(aq) + e^- \longrightarrow Li(s)$	−3.03
$Ca^{2+}(aq) + 2e^- \longrightarrow Ca(s)$	−2.87
$Al^{3+}(aq) + 3e^- \longrightarrow Al(s)$	−1.66
$Zn^{2+}(aq) + 2e^- \longrightarrow Zn(s)$	−0.76
$Pb^{2+}(aq) + 2e^- \longrightarrow Pb(s)$	−0.13
$2H^+(aq) + 2e^- \longrightarrow H_2(g)$	0.00
$Cu^{2+}(aq) + 2e^- \longrightarrow Cu(s)$	+0.34
$Ag^+(aq) + e^- \longrightarrow Ag(s)$	+0.80

The voltage obtained by connecting two standard electrodes together is found by the difference between the two $E^\ominus$ values. So connecting a $Al^{3+}(aq)/Al(s)$ standard electrode to a $Cu^{2+}(aq)/Cu(s)$ standard electrode would give a voltage of 2.00 V, see Figure 7.

If we connect an $Al^{3+}(aq)/Al(s)$ standard electrode to a $Cu^{2+}(aq)/Cu(s)$ standard electrode, the emf will be 2.00 V and the $Al^{3+}(aq)/ Al(s)$ electrode will be negative.

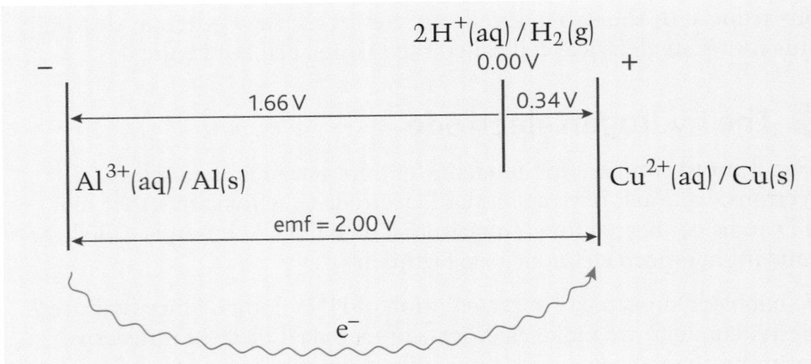

Figure 7 *Calculating the value of the voltage when two electrodes are connected*

Hint

Worked example:

What is $E^\ominus$ for this half reaction?
$2Li^+(aq) + 2e^- \longrightarrow 2Li(s)$

Answer:

-3.03 V, as the number of electrons makes no difference to electrical potential.

If we connect an $Al^{3+}(aq)/Al(s)$ standard electrode to a $Pb^{2+}(aq)/Pb(s)$ standard electrode the emf will be 1.53 V and the $Al^{3+}(aq)/Al(s)$ electrode will be the negative electrode of the cell, see Figure 8.

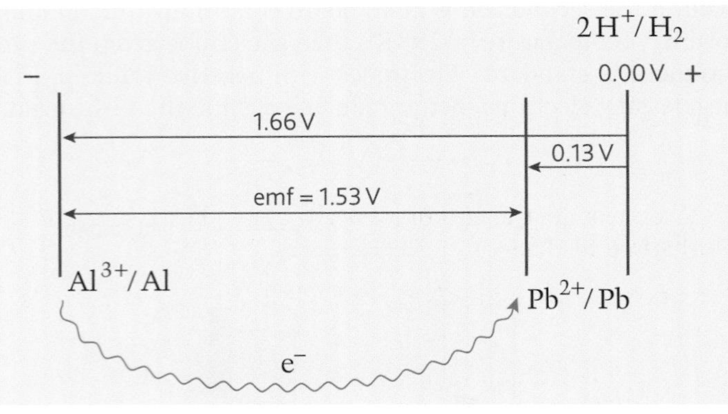

Figure 8 *Calculating the value of the emf for an Al^{3+}/Al electrode connected to a Pb^{2+}/Pb electrode*

It is well worth sketching diagrams like the ones shown in Figures 7 and 8. It will prevent you getting muddled with signs. Remember that more negative values are drawn to the left on the diagrams.

For example, if we connect an Al^{3+}(aq)/Al(s) standard electrode to a Zn^{2+}(aq)/Zn(s) standard electrode, see Figure 9, the voltmeter will,read 0.90 V and the Al^{3+}(aq)/Al(s) electrode will be negative.

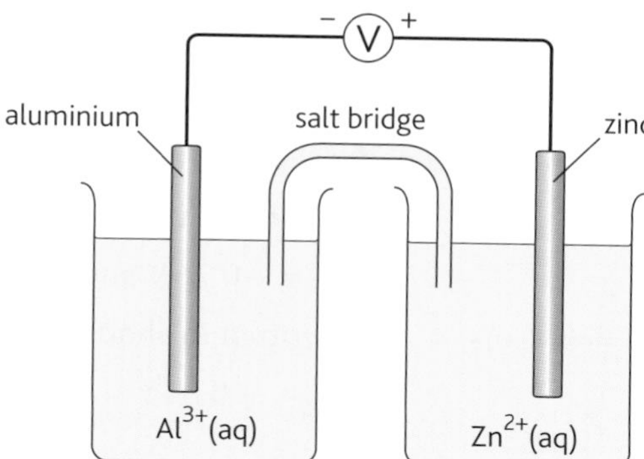

Figure 9 *Connecting a pair of electrodes*

Cell representation

There is shorthand for writing down the cell formed by connecting two electrodes. The conventions are those recommended by IUPAC (International Union of Pure and Applied Chemistry). The usual apparatus diagram is shown in Figure 9 and the cell diagram is written using the following conventions:

- A vertical solid line indicates a **phase boundary,** e.g. between a solid and a solution.
- A double vertical line shows a **salt bridge.**
- When giving the value of the emf, $E^\ominus$, we state the polarity (i.e. whether it is positive or negative) of the right-hand electrode, as the cell representation is written. In the case of the aluminium and copper cells in Figure 7 the copper half cell is positive (it is connected to the positive terminal of the voltmeter) and, if allowed to flow, electrons would go from aluminium to copper.

$Al(s)|Al^{3+}(aq)||Cu^{2+}(aq)|Cu(s)$ $\quad E^\ominus_{cell} = +2.00\,V$

We could equally well have written the cell:

$Cu(s)|Cu^{2+}(aq)||Al^{3+}(aq)|Al(s)$ $\quad E^\ominus_{cell} = -2.00\,V$

This still tells us that electrons flow from aluminium to copper as we always give the polarity of the right-hand electrode.

So emf = $E^\ominus(R) - E^\ominus(L)$

where $E^\ominus(R)$ represents the emf of the right hand electrode and $E^\ominus(L)$ that of the left hand electrode.

The cell representation for a silver electrode connected to a Pb^{2+}(aq)/Pb(s) half cell would be:

$Ag(s)|Ag^{+}(aq)||Pb^{2+}(aq)|Pb(s)$ $\quad E^\ominus_{cell} = -0.93\,V$

Summary questions

1 a Represent the following on a conventional cell diagram:

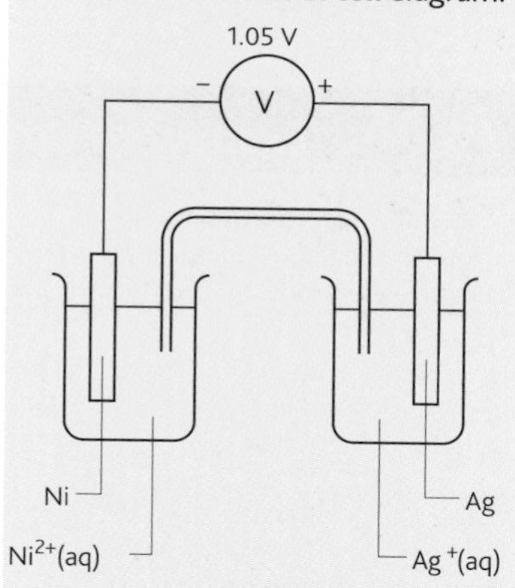

b If the voltmeter was replaced by a wire, in which direction would the electrons flow? Write equations for the reactions occurring in each beaker and write an equation for the overall cell reaction.

2 Calculate $E^\ominus_{cell}$ for:

a $Zn(s)|Zn^{2+}(aq) || Pb^{2+}(aq)|Pb(s)$

b $Pb(s)|Pb^{2+}(aq) || Zn^{2+}(aq) Zn(s)$

14.3 Predicting the direction of redox reactions

Learning objectives:

- How can standard electrode potentials be used to predict the direction of a redox reaction?

Specification reference: 3.5.3

It is possible to use standard electrode potentials to decide on the feasibility of a reaction. When we connect a pair of electrodes, the electrons will flow from the more negative to the more positive and not in the opposite direction. So, the signs of the electrodes tell us the direction of a redox reaction.

Think again of the following electrodes, Figure 1:

$Zn^{2+}(aq) + 2e^- \rightleftharpoons Zn(s)$ (written in short as $Zn^{2+}(aq)/Zn(s)$) $E^\ominus = -0.76\,V$ and

$Cu^{2+}(aq) + 2e^- \rightleftharpoons Cu(s)$ (written in short as $Cu^{2+}(aq)/Cu(s)$) $E^\ominus = +0.34\,V$

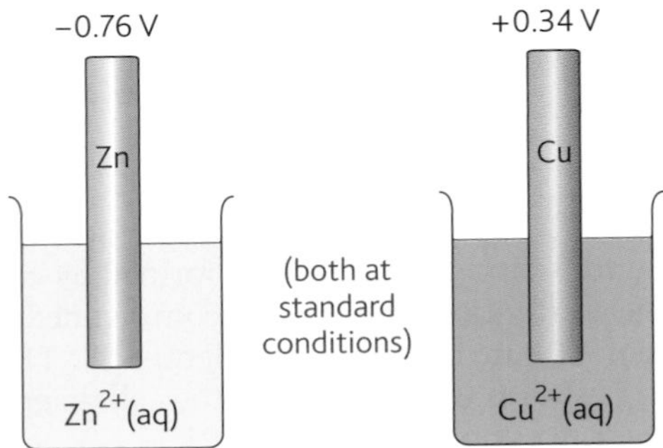

Figure 1 *The two standard electrodes. Their potentials are measured with respect to a standard hydrogen electrode*

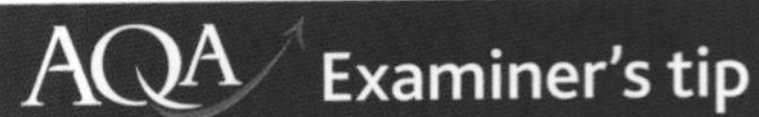

AQA Examiner's tip

Electrons flow spontaneously from the negative electrode to the positive electrode.

Figure 2 shows these two electrodes connected together. Electrons will tend to flow from zinc (the more negative) to copper (the more positive).

So, we know which way the two half reactions must go. We can use a diagram to represent the cell and if we then include $E^\ominus$ values for the two electrodes, we can find the emf for the cell. Figure 3 is the diagram for the zinc/copper cell. You can see how it is related to the apparatus.

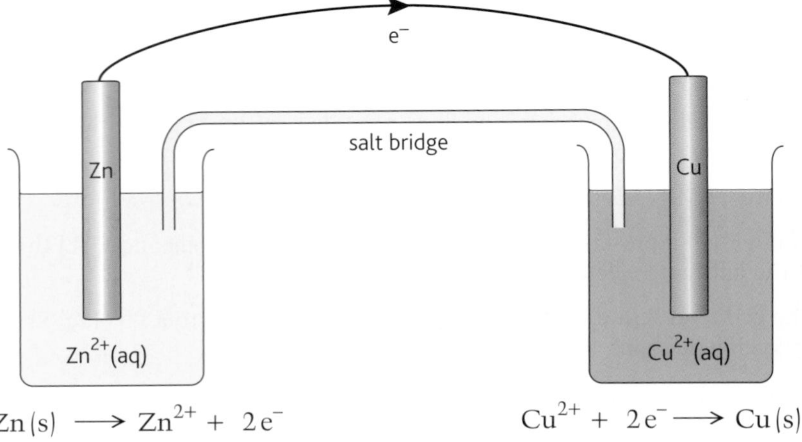

$Zn(s) \longrightarrow Zn^{2+} + 2e^-$ $Cu^{2+} + 2e^- \longrightarrow Cu(s)$

Figure 2 *Connecting $Zn^{2+}(aq)/Zn(s)$ and $Cu^{2+}(aq)/Cu(s)$ electrodes*

So the two equations are:

$$Zn(s) \longrightarrow Zn^{2+}(aq) + 2e^-$$

and

$$Cu^{2+}(aq) + 2e^- \longrightarrow Cu(s)$$

The overall effect is:

$$Zn(s) \longrightarrow Zn^{2+}(aq) + 2e^-$$

adding $Cu^{2+}(aq) + 2e^- \longrightarrow Cu(s)$

$$Cu^{2+}(aq) + Zn(s) + \cancel{2e^-} \longrightarrow Cu(s) + Zn^{2+}(aq) + \cancel{2e^-}$$

So this reaction is feasible and is the reaction that actually happens, either by connecting the two electrodes or more directly by adding Zn to $Cu^{2+}(aq)$ ions in a test tube. The reverse reaction:

$$Cu(s) + Zn^{2+}(aq) \longrightarrow Zn(s) + Cu^{2+}(aq)$$

is *not* feasible and does not occur.

We can go through this process whenever we wish to predict the outcome of a redox reaction.

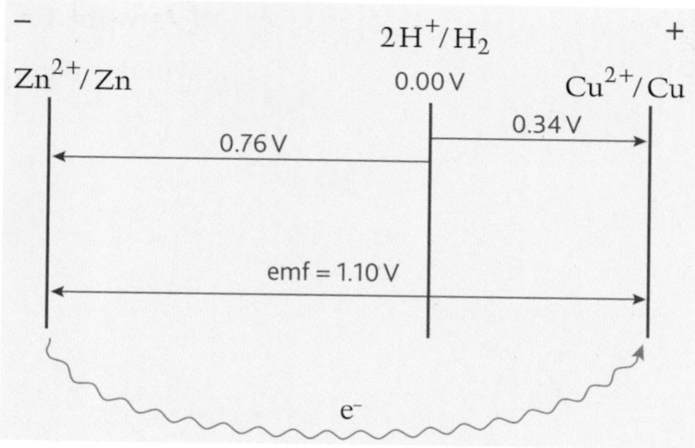

Figure 3 *Predicting the direction of electron flow when a Zn^{2+}/Zn electrode is connected to a Cu^{2+}/Cu electrode*

Further examples of predicting the direction of redox reactions

We can extend the electrochemical series to systems other than simple metal / metal ion ones, see Table 1.

Table 1 *$E^\ominus$ values for more reduction half equations*

Reduction half equation	$E^\ominus$/ V
$Li^+(aq) + e^- \longrightarrow Li(s)$	–3.03
$Ca^{2+}(aq) + 2e^- \longrightarrow Ca(s)$	–2.87
$Al^{3+}(aq) + 3e^- \longrightarrow Al(s)$	–1.66
$Zn^{2+}(aq) + 2e^- \longrightarrow Zn(s)$	–0.76
$Cr^{3+}(aq) + e^- \longrightarrow Cr^{2+}(aq)$	–0.41
$Pb^{2+}(aq) + 2e^- \longrightarrow Pb(s)$	–0.13
$2H^+(aq) + 2e^- \longrightarrow H_2(g)$	0.00
$Cu^{2+}(aq) + e^- \longrightarrow Cu^+(aq)$	+0.15
$Cu^{2+}(aq) + 2e^- \longrightarrow Cu(s)$	+0.34
$I_2(aq) + 2e^- \longrightarrow 2I^-(aq)$	+0.54
$Fe^{3+}(aq) + e^- \longrightarrow Fe^{2+}(aq)$	+0.77
$Ag^+(aq) + e^- \longrightarrow Ag(s)$	+0.79
$Br_2(aq) + 2e^- \longrightarrow 2Br^-(aq)$	+1.07
$Cl_2(aq) + 2e^- \longrightarrow 2Cl^-(aq)$	+1.36
$MnO_4^- + 8H^+(aq) + 5e^- \longrightarrow Mn^{2+}(aq) + 4H_2O(l)$	+1.51
$Ce^{4+}(aq) + e^- \longrightarrow Ce^{3+}(aq)$	+1.70

Example 1

Will the following reaction occur or not?

$$Fe^{3+}(aq) + Cl^{-}(aq) \longrightarrow Fe^{2+}(aq) + \frac{1}{2}Cl_2(aq)$$

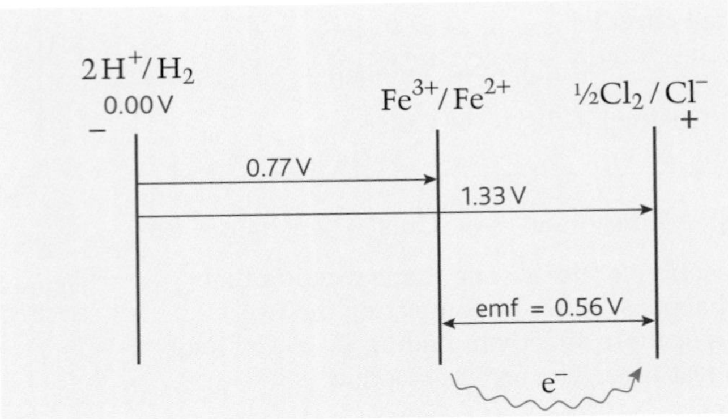

Figure 4 *Working out the emf for: $Fe^{3+}(aq) + Cl^{-}(aq) \longrightarrow Fe^{2+}(aq) + \frac{1}{2}Cl_2(aq)$*

Figure 4 shows that the emf is 0.56 V with iron the more negative. So, electrons will flow from the Fe^{3+}/Fe^{2+} standard electrode to the $\frac{1}{2}$ Cl_2/Cl^- standard electrode.

This means that:

$$Fe^{2+} \longrightarrow Fe^{3+} + e^-$$

$$\frac{1}{2}Cl_2 + e^- \longrightarrow Cl^-$$

$$Fe^{2+} + \frac{1}{2}Cl_2 + \cancel{e^-} \longrightarrow Fe^{3+} + Cl^- + \cancel{e^-}$$

Will occur rather than the reverse reaction above, so

$$Fe^{3+}(aq) + Cl^{-}(aq) \longrightarrow Fe^{2+}(aq) + \frac{1}{2}Cl_2(aq)$$

is *not* feasible. So, chlorine will oxidise iron(II) ions to iron(III) ions.

Example 2

Will the following reaction occur or not?

$$Fe^{3+}(aq) + I^{-}(aq) \longrightarrow Fe^{2+}(aq) + \frac{1}{2}I_2(aq)$$

Figure 5 shows that the emf is 0.23 V with iodine the more negative. So, electrons will flow from the $\frac{1}{2}I_2/I^-$ electrode to the Fe^{3+}/Fe^{2+} electrode.

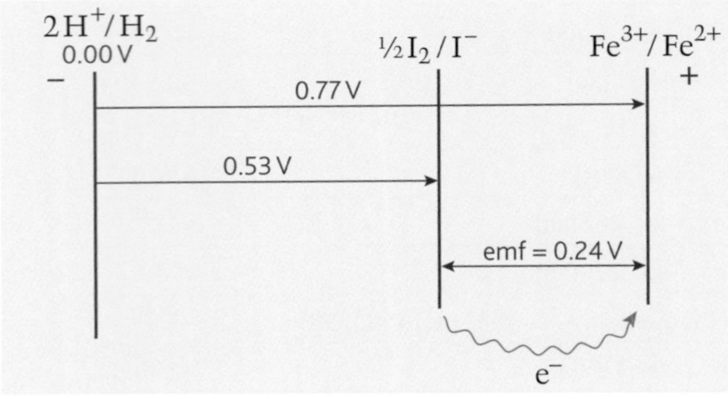

Figure 5 *Working out the emf for: $Fe^{3+}(aq) + I^{-}(aq) \longrightarrow Fe^{2+}(aq) + \frac{1}{2}I_2(aq)$*

This means that:

$$I^- \longrightarrow \tfrac{1}{2}I_2 + e^-$$

$$Fe^{3+} + e^- \longrightarrow Fe^{2+}$$

$$I^- + Fe^{3+} + \cancel{e^-} \longrightarrow \tfrac{1}{2}I_2 + Fe^{2+} + \cancel{e^-}$$

will occur rather than the reverse reaction above and

$$Fe^{2+}(aq) + \tfrac{1}{2}I_2(aq) \longrightarrow Fe^{3+}(aq) + I^-(aq)$$

is *not* feasible. So, iron(III) ions will oxidise iodide ions to iodine.

Summary questions

1 What will be the value of the emf for an $Al^{3+}(aq)/Al(s)$ standard electrode connected to a $Zn^{2+}(aq)/Zn(s)$ standard electrode? Draw a diagram like Figure 3 to illustrate your answer.

2 Use the values of $E^\ominus$ in Table 1 to calculate the emf for the following:

a $Ce^{4+}(aq) + Fe^{2+}(aq) \longrightarrow Ce^{3+}(aq) + Fe^{3+}(aq)$

b $I_2(aq) + 2Br^-(aq) \longrightarrow Br_2(aq) + 2I^-(aq)$

c $MnO_4^-(aq) + 8H^+(aq) + 5I^-(aq) \longrightarrow Mn^{2+}(aq) + 4H_2O(l) + 2\tfrac{1}{2}I_2(aq)$

d $2H^+(aq) + Pb(s) \longrightarrow Pb^{2+}(aq) + H_2(g)$

3 Which of the halogens could possibly oxidise Ag(s) to $Ag^+(aq)$ ions ?

4 a Is the reaction: $Br_2(aq) + 2Cl^-(aq) \longrightarrow Cl_2(aq) + 2Br^-(aq)$ feasible?

b Is the reaction: $Fe^{3+}(aq) + Br^-(aq) \longrightarrow Fe^{2+}(aq) + \tfrac{1}{2}Br_2(aq)$ feasible?

14.4 Electrochemical cells

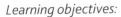

Learning objectives:

- What are the differences between non-rechargeable, rechargeable and fuel cells?
- What are the electrode reactions in a hydrogen–oxygen fuel cell?
- What are the benefits and risks to society associated with each type of cell?

Specification reference: 3.5.3

Modern life would not be the same without batteries – both rechargeable and single use – for laptops, phones MP3 players etc. Nowadays there is a bewildering variety of types and brands advertised with slogans like 'long life' and 'high power'. Batteries are based on the principles of electrochemical cells described in Topic 14.2. Strictly, a battery refers to a number of cells connected together, but in everyday speech, the word has come to mean almost any portable source of electricity. You will need to be able to apply the principles of electrochemical cells, but you will not be expected to learn the details of the construction of the cells described below.

Non-rechargeable cells

Zinc/copper cells

We have a seen, in Topic 14.2, the Daniell cell. This provides an emf of 1.1 V. It was developed by the British chemist John Daniell in the 1830s and was used to provide the electricity for old fashioned telegraphs which sent messages by Morse code. However, it was not practical for portable devices, because of the liquids that it contained. It works on the general principle of electrons being transferred from a more reactive metal to a less reactive one. The voltage can be worked out from the difference between the electrode potentials in the electrochemical series.

Zinc/carbon cells

The electrodes can be made from materials other than metals. In the Leclanché cell, for example (which is named after the Frenchman George Leclanché), the positive electrode is carbon, which acts like the inert platinum electrode in the hydrogen electrode, see Figure 1. The Leclanché cell is the basis of most ordinary disposable batteries. The electrolyte is a paste rather than a liquid.

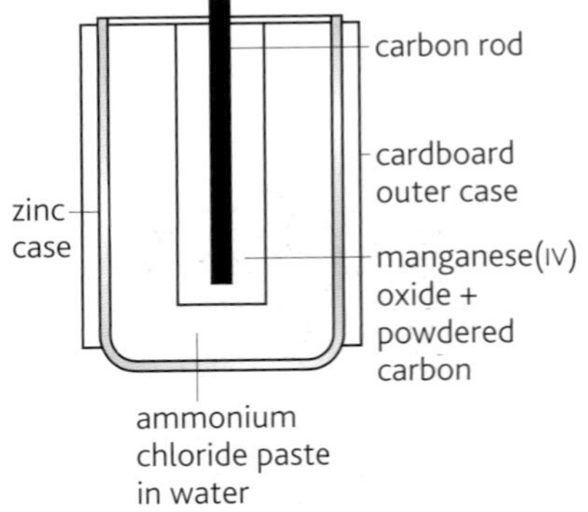

Figure 1 *A Leclanché cell*

The commercial form of this type of cell consists of a zinc canister filled with a paste of ammonium chloride (NH_4Cl) and water – the electrolyte. In the centre is a carbon rod. It is surrounded by a mixture of manganese(IV)oxide and powdered carbon. The half equations are:

$$Zn(s) + 2e \rightleftharpoons Zn^{2+}(aq) \qquad E \approx -0.8\,V$$

$$2NH_4^+(aq) + 2e \rightleftharpoons 2NH_3(g) + H_2(g) \qquad E \approx +0.7\,V$$

Note: these are not $E^\ominus$ values as the conditions are far from standard.

The reactions that take place are:

At the zinc:

$$Zn(s) \longrightarrow Zn^{2+}(aq) + 2e^-$$

(Notice that this is the reverse of the half equation above.)

At the carbon rod:

$$2NH_4^+(aq) + 2e^- \longrightarrow 2NH_3(g) + H_2(g)$$

So the overall reaction as the cell discharges is:

$$2NH_4^+(aq) + Zn(s) \longrightarrow 2NH_3(g) + H_2(g) + Zn^{2+}(aq)$$

emf ≈ 1.5 V with the zinc as the negative terminal

The hydrogen gas is oxidised to water by the manganese(IV) oxide (preventing a build up of pressure), while the ammonia dissolves in the water of the paste.

As the cell discharges, the zinc is used up and the walls of the zinc canister become thin and prone to leakage. The ammonium chloride electrolyte is acidic and can be corrosive. That is why you should remove spent batteries from equipment. This cell is ideal for, say, doorbells, which need a small current intermittently.

AQA Examiner's tip

Detailed knowledge of these cells is not required.

A variant of this cell is the zinc chloride cell. It is similar to the Leclanché but uses zinc chloride as the electrolyte. Such cells are better at supplying high currents than the Leclanché and are marketed as 'extra life' batteries for radios, torches and shavers.

Long life alkaline batteries are also based on the same system, but with an electrolyte of potassium hydroxide. Powdered zinc is used, whose greater surface area allows the battery to supply high currents. The cell is enclosed in a steel container to prevent leakage. These cells are suitable for equipment taking continuous high currents such as personal stereos. In this situation they can last up to 16 times as long as ordinary zinc/carbon batteries, but they are more expensive.

Many other electrode systems are in use, especially for miniature batteries such as those used in watches, hearing aids, cameras and electronic equipment. These include zinc/air, mercury(II) oxide/zinc, silver oxide/zinc, and lithium/manganese(IV) oxide. Which is used for which application depends on the precise requirements of voltage, current, size and cost.

Rechargeable batteries

These can be recharged by reversing the cell reactions. This is done by applying an external voltage to drive the electrons in the opposite direction.

Lead–acid batteries

Lead–acid batteries are rechargeable batteries used to operate the starter motors of cars. They consist of six 2 V cells connected in series to give 12 V. Each cell consists of two plates dipped into a solution of sulfuric acid. The positive plate is made of lead coated with lead(IV) oxide, PbO_2, and the negative plate is made of lead, see Figure 2.

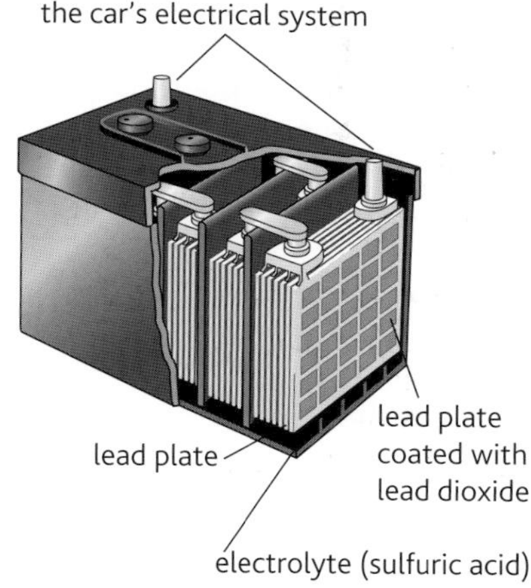

Figure 2 *A lead–acid car battery*

On discharging, the following reactions occur as the battery drives electrons from the lead plate to the lead(IV) oxide coated one:

At the lead plate:

$$Pb(s) + SO_4^{2-}(aq) \longrightarrow PbSO_4(s) + 2e^-$$

At the lead-dioxide-coated plate:

$$PbO_2(s) + 4H^+(aq) + SO_4^{2-}(aq) + 2e^- \longrightarrow PbSO_4(s) + 2H_2O(l)$$

The overall reaction as the cell discharges is:

$$PbO_2(s) + 4H^+(aq) + 2SO_4^{2-}(aq) + Pb(s) \longrightarrow 2PbSO_4(s) + 2H_2O(l)$$

emf ≈ 2 V

Hint

Technically, a battery consists of two or more simple cells connected together. So a 1.5 V zinc–carbon 'battery' is really a cell, while a car battery is a true battery.

Examiner's tip

Make sure that you can use given data to determine the emf of any cell.

These reactions are reversed as the battery is charged up and electrons flow in the reverse direction, driven by the car's generator.

Portable batteries

There are now rechargeable batteries that come in all shapes and sizes.

Nickel/cadmium

These are now available in standard sizes to replace traditional zinc–carbon batteries. Although more expensive to buy, they can be recharged up to 500 times, reducing the effective cost significantly. These cells are called nickel/cadmium and have an alkaline electrolyte. The two half equations are:

$$Cd(OH)_2(s) + 2e^- \rightleftharpoons Cd(s) + 2OH^-(aq)$$

$$NiO(OH)(s) + H_2O(l) + e^- \rightleftharpoons Ni(OH)_2(s) + OH^-(aq)$$

Overall:

$$2NiO(OH)(s) + Cd(s) + 2H_2O(l) \rightleftharpoons 2Ni(OH)_2(s) + Cd(OH)_2(s)$$

$$\text{emf} \approx 1.2\,V$$

The reaction goes from left to right on discharge (electrons flowing from Cd to Ni) and right to left on charging.

Figure 3 *Some of the enormous variety of batteries available today*

Lithium ion

These are used in mobile phones, cameras and laptops. They are light because they are based on lithium rather than heavier metals. They have polymer electrolytes, rather than liquids or pastes which means they cannot leak. A single cell gives a voltage of 3.5–4.0 V, compared with 1.5 V for a zinc/carbon cell. The cell reactions are complex, involving lithium cobalt oxide.

The fuel cell

The vast majority of vehicles today run on hydrocarbon-based fossil fuels – petrol and diesel, for example, in internal combustion engines. The price of these fuels is rising as supplies diminish and there is increasing concern about the effect their emissions have on the environment. Burning hydrocarbons in air produces carbon dioxide (a greenhouse gas) and acidic nitrogen oxides caused by nitrogen and oxygen from the air combining at the high temperatures in the engine. One alternative fuel is hydrogen. This could be burnt in the same way as hydrocarbons, but there is an alternative, the fuel cell. This uses hydrogen and oxygen as 'fuels' to produce electricity to drive an electric motor. The cell is shown schematically in Figure 4.

It consists of two platinum-based electrodes separated by a special polymer electrolyte which allows ions to pass through it. The half equations involved are:

$$2H^+(aq) + 2e^- \rightleftharpoons H_2(g) \qquad E \approx 0.0\,V$$

$$4H^+(aq) + O_2(g) + 4e^- \rightleftharpoons 2H_2O(l) \qquad E \approx 1.2\,V$$

As before, the conditions are not standard.

At the left hand electrode, hydrogen enters and gives up electrons to form H^+ ions. This is the reverse of the first half reaction above.

$$H_2(g) \longrightarrow 2H^+(aq) + 2e^-$$

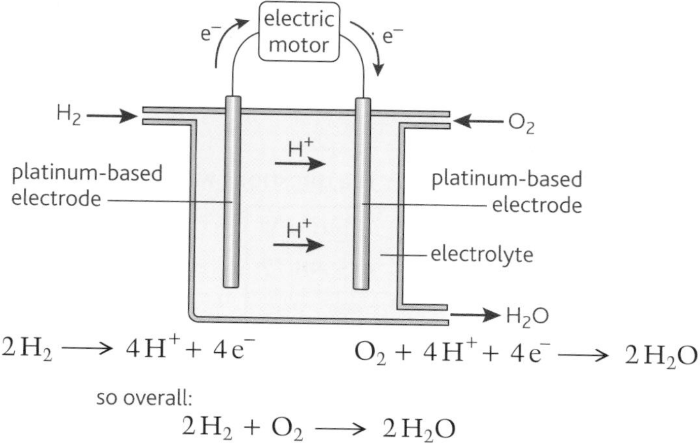

Figure 4 *A hydrogen/oxygen fuel cell*

The hydrogen/oxygen fuel cell does not need to be electrically recharged.

The electrons flow through an electrical circuit where they can power a motor. The H^+ ions flow through the electrolyte to a second electrode. Here they react with oxygen and electrons to form water, which is the only emission from the unit. The half reaction at this electrode is:

$$4H^+(aq) + O_2(g) + 4e^- \longrightarrow 2H_2O(l)$$

To find an overall reaction, we must first multiply $H_2(g) \longrightarrow 2H^+(aq) + 2e^-$ by two so that the electrons will cancel. (This makes no difference to the *E* value.)

$$2H_2(g) \longrightarrow 4H^+(aq) + 4e^-$$

Adding the two half reactions gives:

$$2H_2(g) + O_2(g) \longrightarrow 2H_2O(l) \qquad \text{emf} = 1.2\,V$$

This is the same reaction as burning hydrogen directly in oxygen, except that most of the energy of the reaction is given out as electricity. A little heat is evolved, but the temperature is no more than about 85 °C (358 K) – far below the temperature at which nitrogen oxides form.

As well as uses in road transport, hydrogen fuel cells have been used in manned spacecraft, where the astronauts can drink the water produced.

Figure 5 *A fuel-cell powered vehicle*

The hydrogen economy

At first sight, this type of fuel cell appears to be very 'green' because the only product is water. However we have to consider the source of the hydrogen. At present, most hydrogen is made from crude oil – a non-renewable resource. It could be made by electrolysis of water but most electricity is made by burning fossil fuels, which emit carbon dioxide. Also, hydrogen-powered vehicles will need an infrastructure of hydrogen filling stations to be built, which also raises the issues of storing and transporting a highly flammable gas. For example, in the 1930s two airships which used hydrogen as their lifting gas – the Hindenberg and the R101 – exploded with serious loss of life.

The idea of using hydrogen as a fuel is not new. It was a component of 'town gas', which was supplied to UK homes until replaced by North Sea gas in the early 1970s.

Summary question

1 List the advantages and disadvantages of each cell, described above, with regard to cost, practicality, safety, and the environment.

AQA Examination-style questions

1 Use the data in the table below, where appropriate, to answer the questions which follow.

Standard electrode potentials	$E^\ominus$ / V
$Fe^{3+}(aq) + e^- \longrightarrow Fe^{2+}(aq)$	+0.77
$Cl_2(g) + 2e^- \longrightarrow 2Cl^-(aq)$	+1.36
$2BrO_3^-(aq) + 12H^+(aq) + 10e^- \longrightarrow Br_2(aq) + 6H_2O(l)$	+1.52
$O_3(g) + 2H^+(aq) + 2e^- \longrightarrow O_2(g) + H_2O(l)$	+2.08
$F_2O(g) + 2H^+(aq) + 4e^- \longrightarrow 2F^-(aq) + H_2O(l)$	+2.15

Each of the above can be reversed under suitable conditions.

(a) (i) Identify the most powerful reducing agent in the table.

(ii) Identify the most powerful oxidising agent in the table.

(iii) Identify **all** the species in the table which can be oxidised in acidic solution by $BrO_3^-(aq)$. *(4 marks)*

(b) The cell represented below was set up.

$Pt|Fe^{2+}(aq),\ Fe^{3+}(aq)||BrO_3^-(aq),\ Br_2(aq)|Pt$

(i) Deduce the emf of this cell.

(ii) Write a half-equation for the reaction occurring at the negative electrode when current is taken from this cell.

(iii) Deduce what change in the concentration of $Fe^{3+}(aq)$ would cause an increase in the emf of the cell. Explain your answer. *(6 marks)*

AQA, 2006

2 Where appropriate, use the standard electrode potential data in the table below to answer the questions which follow.

Standard electrode potentials	$E^\ominus$ / V
$Zn^{2+}(aq) + 2e^- \longrightarrow Zn(s)$	–0.76
$V^{3+}(aq) + e^- \longrightarrow V^{2+}(aq)$	–0.26
$SO_4^{2-}(aq) + 2H^+(aq) + 2e^- \longrightarrow SO_3^{2-}(aq) + H_2O(l)$	+0.17
$VO^{2+}(aq) + 2H^+(aq) + e^- \longrightarrow V^{3+}(aq) + H_2O(l)$	+0.34
$Fe^{3+}(aq) + e^- \longrightarrow Fe^{2+}(aq)$	+0.77
$VO_2^+(aq) + 2H^+(aq) + e^- \longrightarrow VO^{2+}(aq) + H_2O(l)$	+1.00
$Cl_2(aq) + 2e^- \longrightarrow 2Cl^-(aq)$	+1.36

(a) From the table above select the species which is the most powerful reducing agent. *(1 mark)*

(b) From the table above select

(i) a species which, in acidic solution, will reduce $VO_2^+(aq)$ to $VO^{2+}(aq)$ but will **not** reduce $VO^{2+}(aq)$ to $V^{3+}(aq)$,

(ii) a species which, in acidic solution, will oxidise $VO^{2+}(aq)$ to $VO_2^+(aq)$. *(2 marks)*

(c) The cell represented below was set up under standard conditions.

$Pt|Fe^{2+}(aq),\ Fe^{3+}(aq)||Tl^{3+}(aq),\ Tl^{+}(aq)|Pt$ Cell emf = + 0.48 V

(i) Deduce the standard electrode potential for the following half-reaction.

$Tl^{3+}(aq) + 2e^- \longrightarrow Tl^{+}(aq)$

(ii) Write an equation for the spontaneous cell reaction. *(3 marks)*

AQA, 2005

3 Use the data below, where appropriate, to answer the following questions.

Standard electrode potentials	$E^\ominus$ / V
$S_2O_8^{2-}(aq) + 2e^- \longrightarrow 2SO_4^{2-}(aq)$	+2.01
$MnO_4^-(aq) + 8H^+(aq) + 5e^- \longrightarrow Mn^{2+}(aq) + 4H_2O(l)$	+1.51
$Cl_2(aq) + 2e^- \longrightarrow 2Cl^-(aq)$	+1.36
$Cr_2O_7^{2-}(aq) + 14H^+(aq) + 6e^- \longrightarrow 2Cr^{3+}(aq) + 7H_2O(l)$	+1.33
$NO_3^-(aq) + 3H^+(aq) + 2e^- \longrightarrow HNO_2(aq) + H_2O(l)$	+0.94
$Fe^{3+}(aq) + e^- \longrightarrow Fe^{2+}(aq)$	+0.77

(a) The concentration of iron(II) ions in aqueous solution can be determined by titrating the solution, after acidification, with a standard solution of potassium manganate(VII).

(i) Explain, by reference to the data given in the table above, why hydrochloric acid should not be used to acidify the solution containing iron(II) ions.

(ii) Explain, by reference to the data given in the table above, why nitric acid should not be used to acidify the solution containing iron(II) ions. *(4 marks)*

(b) (i) Calculate the emf of the cell represented by

$Pt|Mn^{2+}(aq),\ MnO_4^-(aq)||S_2O_8^{2-}(aq),\ SO_4^{2-}(aq)|Pt$

(ii) Deduce an equation for the reaction which occurs when an excess of $S_2O_8^{2-}(aq)$ is added to an aqueous solution of $Mn^{2+}(aq)$ ions. *(3 marks)*

AQA, 2004

4 Use the data below, where appropriate, to answer the questions which follow.

Standard electrode potentials	$E^\ominus$ / V
$2H^+(aq) + 2e^- \longrightarrow H_2(g)$	0.00
$Br_2(aq) + 2e^- \longrightarrow 2Br^-(aq)$	+1.09
$2BrO_3^-(aq) + 12H^+(aq) + 10e^- \longrightarrow Br_2(aq) + 6H_2O(l)$	+1.52

Each of the above can be reversed under suitable conditions.

(a) State the hydrogen ion concentration and the hydrogen gas pressure when, at 298 K, the potential of the hydrogen electrode is 0.00 V. *(2 marks)*

(b) A diagram of a cell using platinum electrodes **X** and **Y** is shown below.

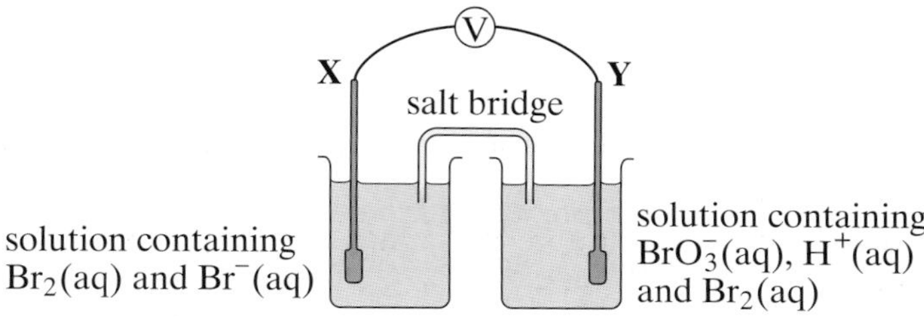

(i) Use the data above to calculate the emf of the above cell under standard conditions.

(ii) Write a half-equation for the reaction occurring at electrode **X** and an overall equation for the cell reaction which occurs when electrodes **X** and **Y** are connected. *(4 marks)*

AQA, 2004

15 The transition metals

15.1 The general properties of transition metals

Learning objectives:

- What are the characteristic properties of the elements titanium to copper?
- How can these be explained in terms of electronic structure?

Specification reference: 3.5.4

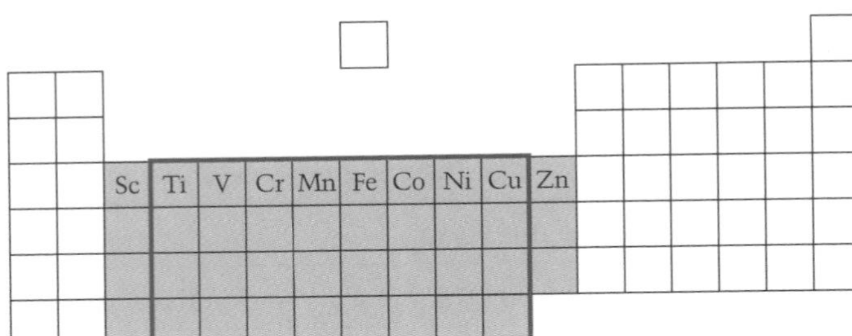

Figure 1 *The d-block elements (shaded green) and the transition metals (outlined in red)*

The elements from titanium to copper lie within the d-block elements (see *AQA AS Chemistry*, Topic 4.1), which are shaded in Figure 1. As we go across a period, electrons are being added to a d sub-level (3d in the case of titanium to copper). The elements from titanium to copper are metals. They are good conductors of heat and electricity. They are hard, strong and shiny, and have high melting and boiling points.

These physical properties, together with fairly low chemical reactivity, make these metals extremely useful. Examples include iron (and its alloy steel) for vehicle bodies and to reinforce concrete, copper for water pipes, and titanium for jet engine parts that must withstand high temperatures.

Electronic configurations in the d-block elements

Figure 2 shows the electron arrangements for the elements in the first d-series.

In general there are two outer 4s electrons and as we go across the period, electrons are added to the *inner* 3d sub level. This explains the overall similarity of these elements. The arrangements of chromium, Cr, and copper, Cu, do not quite fit the pattern. The d sub level is full ($3d^{10}$) in Cu and half full ($3d^5$) in Cr and there is only one electron in the 4s outer level.

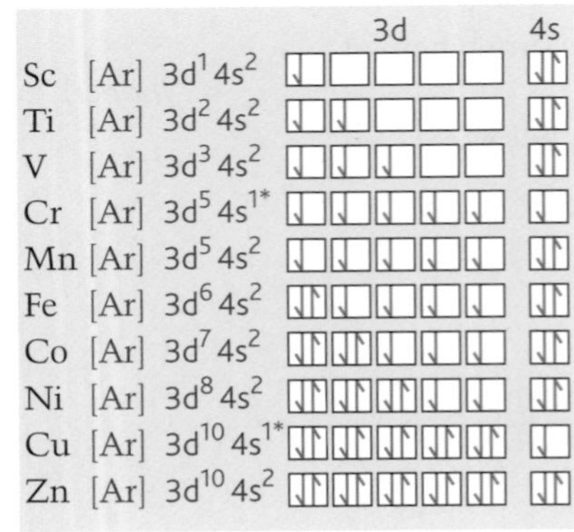

Figure 2 *Electronic arrangements of the elements in the first d-series. [Ar] represents the electron arrangement of argon – $1s^2 2s^2 2p^6 3s^2 3p^6$*

Electronic configurations of the ions of d-block elements

To work out the configuration of the ion of an element, first write down the configuration of the element using the periodic table, from its atomic number.

For example, to find the electron configuration of V^{2+}

Vanadium, V, has an atomic number of 23. Its electron configuration is:

$$1s^2 2s^2 2p^6 3s^2 3p^6 3d^3 4s^2$$

The vanadium ion V^{2+} has lost the two $4s^2$ electrons and has the electron configuration:

$$1s^2 2s^2 2p^6 3s^2 3p^6 3d^3$$

For example, to find the electron configuration of the Cu^{2+} ion

The atomic number of copper is 29. The electron configuration is therefore:

$$1s^2 2s^2 2p^6 3s^2 3p^6 3d^{10} 4s^1$$

The Cu^{2+} ion has lost two electrons, so it has the electron configuration:

$$1s^2 2s^2 2p^6 3s^2 3p^6 3d^9$$

In fact with all transition elements, the 4s electrons are lost first because they are of the highest energy.

AQA Examiner's tip

The electronic configuration of any element can be deduced using the periodic table.

The definition of a transition element

The formal definition of a transition element is that it is one that forms at least one stable ion with a *part* full d-shell of electrons. Scandium only forms Sc^{3+}, which is $3d^0$, in all its compounds, and zinc only forms Zn^{2+} ($3d^{10}$) in all its compounds. They are therefore d-block elements but not transition elements. The transition elements are outlined in red in Figure 1.

Chemical properties of transition metals

The chemistry of transition metals has four main features which are common to all the elements:

- **Variable oxidation states**: Transition metals have more than one oxidation state in their compounds, for example Cu(I) and Cu(II). They can therefore take part in many redox reactions.
- **Colour:** The majority of transition metal ions are coloured, for example Cu^{2+} (aq) is blue.
- **Catalysis**: Catalysts affect the rate of reaction without being used up or chemically changed themselves. Many transition metals, and their compounds, show catalytic activity. For example, iron is the catalyst in the Haber process, vanadium(V) oxide in the Contact process and manganese(IV) oxide in the decomposition of hydrogen peroxide.
- **Complex formation:** Transition elements form complex ions. A complex ion is formed when a transition metal ion is surrounded by ions or other molecules, collectively called ligands, which are bonded to it by co-ordinate bonds. For example, $[Cu(H_2O)_6]^{2+}$ is a complex ion that is formed when copper sulfate dissolves in water.

Figure 3 *Some transition metals in use*

Summary questions

1 The electron arrangement of manganese is:

$$1s^2\ 2s^2\ 2p^6\ 3s^2\ 3p^6\ 3d^5\ 4s^2$$

Write the electron arrangement of:

a a Mn^{2+} ion

b a Mn^{3+} ion

2 The electron arrangement of iron can be written: [Ar] $3d^6\ 4s^2$

a What does the [Ar] represent?

b Which two electrons are lost to form Fe^{2+}?

c Which further electron is lost in forming Fe^{3+}?

15.2 Complex formation and the shape of complex ions

Learning objectives:

- What do the terms 'ligand', 'co-ordinate bond' and 'co-ordination number' mean?
- What are unidentate, bidentate and multidentate ligands?
- How does the size of the ligand affect the shape of the complex ion?
- How does ligand charge determine the charge on the complex ion?

Specification reference: 3.5.4

Synoptic link

You will need to understand covalent and co-ordinate bonding, shapes of simple molecules and ions studied in *AQA AS Chemistry*, Topic 3.9.

The formation of complex ions

All transition metal ions can form co-ordinate bonds by accepting electron pairs from other ions or molecules. The bonds that are formed are **co-ordinate** (dative) bonds. An ion or molecule with a lone pair of electrons that forms a co-ordinate bond with a transition metal is called a **ligand**. Some examples of ligands are: H_2O**:**, **:**NH_3, **:**Cl^-, **:**CN^-.

In some cases, two, four or six ligands bond to a single transition metal ion. The resulting species is called a complex ion**.** The number of co-ordinate bonds to ligands that surround the d-block metal ion is called the **co-ordination number.**

- Ions with co-ordination number six are usually octahedral, for example $[Co(NH_3)_6]^{3+}$.
- Ions with co-ordination number 4 are usually tetrahedral, for example, $[CoCl_4]^{2-}$.

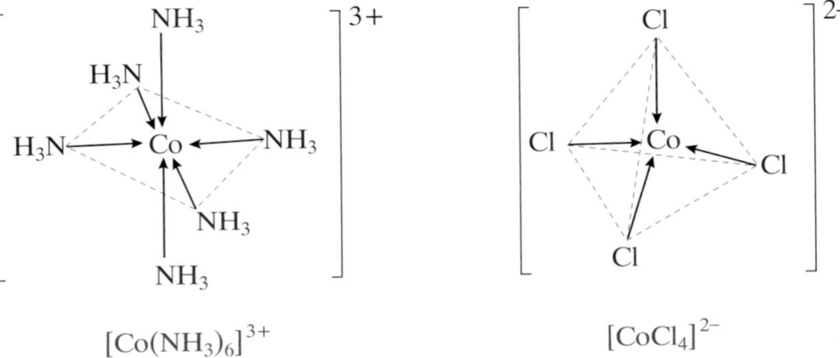

$[Co(NH_3)_6]^{3+}$ $[CoCl_4]^{2-}$

Multidentate ligands – chelation

Some molecules, called **multidentate ligands**, have more than one lone pair which can bond to a transition metal ion. The word 'dentate' comes from the Latin for tooth – they can 'bite' the metal ion more than once.

Bidentate ligands include:

- Ethane-1,2-diamine, sometimes called 1,2-diaminoethane or ethylene diamine.

```
      H   H
      |   |
  H—C—C—H
  H   |   |   H
    \N.  .N/
  H/  :   :  \H
```

Each nitrogen has a lone pair which can form a co-ordinate bond to the metal ion. The name of this ligand is often abbreviated to 'en', for example $[Cr(en)_3]^{3+}$. It is a neutral ligand and the chromium ion has a 3+ charge, so the complex ion also has a 3+ charge.

- Benzene-1,2-diol, sometimes called 1,2-dihydroxybenzene (also a neutral ligand).

AQA Examiner's tip

Both ligand sites of bidentate ligands usually bond to the same metal forming a ring. However, they can act as bridges between two metal ions.

- The ethanedioate (oxalate) ion, $C_2O_4^{2-}$.

An important multidentate ligand is the ion **e**thylene**d**iamine**t**etr**a**cetate, called $EDTA^{4-}$.

This can act as a hexadentate ligand using lone pairs on four oxygen and both nitrogen atoms. Complex ions with polydentate ligands are called **chelates** (pronounced 'key-lates') from the Greek word for claw. Chelates can be used to effectively remove d-block metal ions from solution.

How science works

EDTA can be taken (under medical supervision) as an antidote to poisoning by transition metals. The chelated ions are excreted in the urine.

How science works

Haemoglobin

Haemoglobin is the red pigment in blood. It is responsible for carrying oxygen from the lungs to the cells of the body. The molecule consists of an Fe^{2+} ion with a co-ordination number of six. Four of the co-ordination sites are taken up by a ring system called a 'porphyrin' which acts as a tetradentate ligand. This complex is called 'haem'.

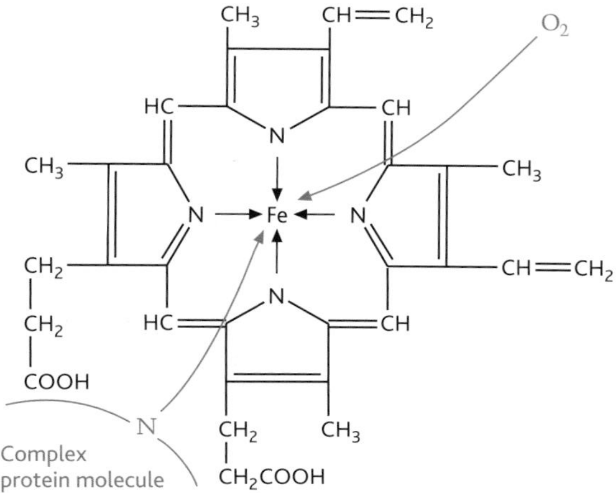

Below the plane of this ring is a fifth nitrogen atom acting as a ligand. This atom is part of a complex protein called 'globin'. The sixth site can accept an oxygen molecule as a ligand. The Fe^{2+} to O_2 bond is weak, as $:O_2$ is not a very good ligand, allowing the oxygen molecule to be easily given up to cells.

Better ligands than oxygen can bond irreversibly to the iron and thus destroy haemoglobin's oxygen-carrying capacity. This explains the poisonous effect of carbon monoxide, which is a better ligand than oxygen. Carbon monoxide is often formed by incomplete combustion in faulty gas heaters and because it binds more strongly to the iron than oxygen, it is possible to suffocate in a room with plentiful oxygen.

Anaemia is a condition which may be caused by a shortage of haemoglobin. The body suffers from a lack of oxygen and the symptoms include fatigue, breathlessness and a pale skin colour. The causes may be loss of blood or deficiency of iron in the diet. The latter may be treated by taking 'iron' tablets which contain iron(II) sulfate.

Shapes of complex ions

As we saw above, the $[Co(NH_3)_6]^{3+}$ ion, with six ligands, is an octahedral shape. Note that an octahedron has six points but *eight* faces. The metal ion, Co^{3+}, has a charge of +3 and as the ligands are all neutral, the complex ion has an overall charge of +3.

The $[CoCl_4]^{2-}$ ion, with four ligands, is tetrahedral. The metal ion, Co^{2+} has a charge of +2 and each of the four ligands $:Cl^-$, has a charge of –1, so the complex ion has an overall charge of –2.

AQA Examiner's tip

The chlorine atom is in Period 3 and so has an extra electron level compared with the nitrogen atom in Period 2.

The reason for this difference in shape is that the chloride ion is a larger ligand than the ammonia molecule and so fewer ligands can fit around the central metal ion.

A few complexes of co-ordination number four adopt a square planar geometry, for example:

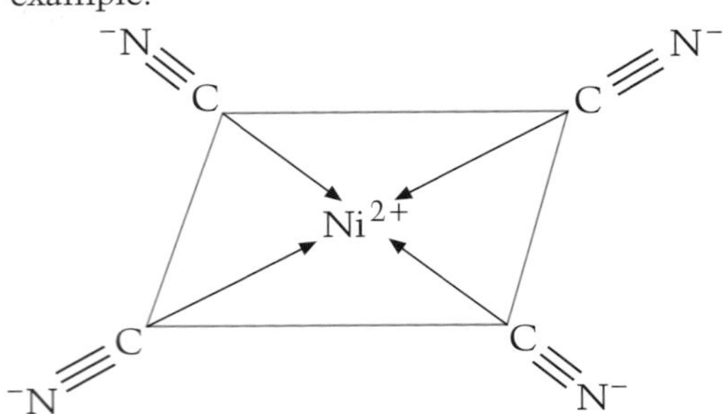

Some complexes are linear, one example being $[Ag(NH_3)_2]^+$:

$$[H_3N \rightarrow Ag \leftarrow NH_3]^+$$

A solution containing this complex ion is called Tollens' reagent and is used in organic chemistry to distinguish aldehydes from ketones, see Topic 5.2. Aldehydes reduce the $[Ag(NH_3)_2]^+$ to Ag (metallic silver), while ketones do not. The silver forms a mirror on the surface of the test tube, hence the name, the 'silver mirror test'.

Complex ions may have a positive charge or a negative charge.

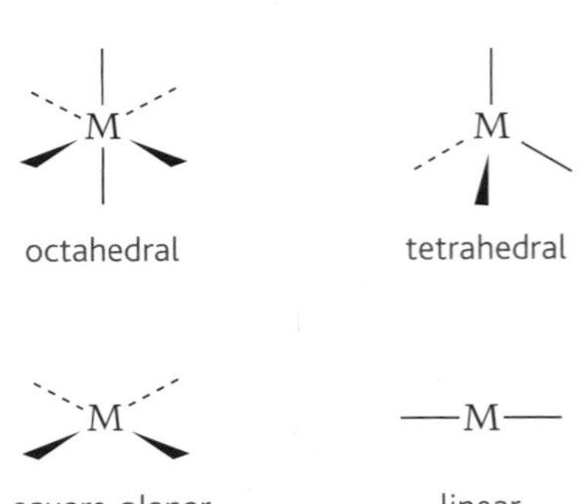

Figure 1 *The four main shapes of transition metal complexes using wedge and dotted bonds*

Representing the shapes of complex ions

Representing three-dimensional shapes on paper can be tricky. Some diagrams in this topic have thin red construction lines to help you to visualise the shapes. These are not bonds. Another way to represent shape is to use wedge bonds and dotted bonds. Wedge bonds come out of the paper and dotted bonds go in, see Figure 1.

How science works

cis-platin

One of the most successful anti-cancer drugs developed in recent years is *cis*-platin. It was discovered following an apparently bizarre experiment in which a solution of ammonium chloride containing bacteria was electrolysed between platinum electrodes and the bacteria failed to multiply.

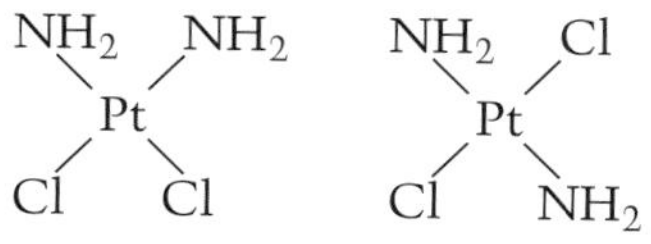

NH_2 NH_2 Pt Cl Cl — *cis*-platin

NH_2 Cl Pt Cl NH_2 — *trans*-platin

This has been most effective in the treatment of testicular (and other) cancers. It is believed to work by bonding to DNA so that it prevents the replication of cancerous cells. Interestingly, the isomeric compound *trans*-platin has no anti-cancer effect.

Cancers are caused by the rapid replication and growth of 'rogue' cells, i.e. ones that should not be in the body. For cells to replicate, the double helix of their DNA must first unwind. *cis*-platin works by preventing this double helix unwinding. In a rogue cell, cis-platin forms co-ordinate bonds with DNA bases, crucially, one on each of the spirals of the DNA double helix. This has the effect of preventing the two spirals unravelling and so the cell cannot replicate and grow. The bonds with the guanine (G) bases of the DNA are co-ordinate ones with nitrogen atoms which have lone pairs. These displace the two ammonia molecules from *cis*-platin. (In fact it appears that the ammonia ligands are first displaced by water molecules, but this is a detail.)

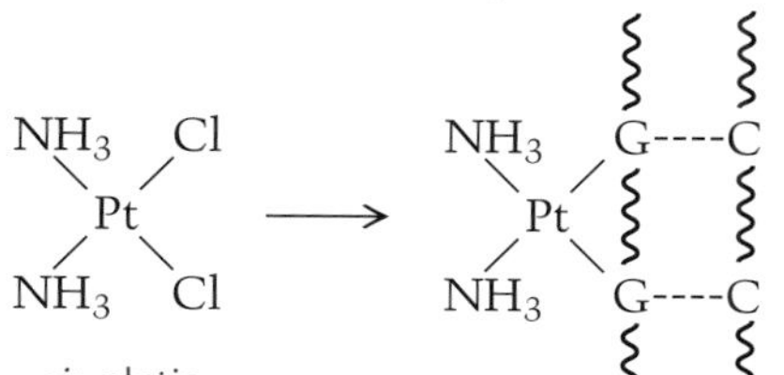

NH_3 Cl Pt NH_3 Cl → NH_3 G----C Pt NH_3 G----C

cis-platin

DNA

Like any drug, *cis*-platin is not without side effects. It will stop the replication of normal cells in the body in the same way as it does 'rogue' ones. It must be used in such a way that the benefits outweigh the risks.

Summary questions

1 a Predict the shapes of the following:
   i $[Cu(H_2O)_6]^{2+}$
   ii $[Cu(NH_3)_6]^{2+}$
   iii $[CuCl_4]^{2-}$

b What is the co-ordination number of the transition metal in each complex in a?

c Explain why the co-ordination numbers are different.

2 Benzene-1,2-dicarboxylate is shown below.

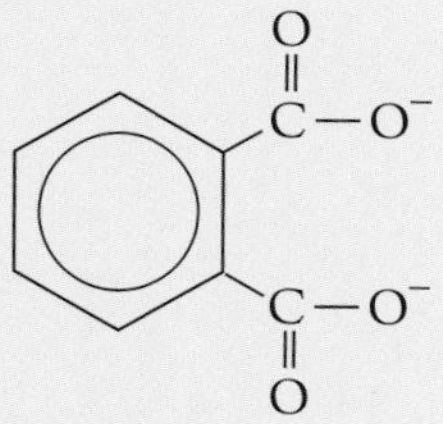

O ‖ C—O^- ; C—O^- ‖ O

a Suggest which atoms are likely to form co-ordinate bonds with a metal ion.

b Mark the lone pairs.

c Is it likely to be a mono-, bi- or hexa-dentate ligand?

15.3 Coloured ions

Learning objectives:

- What is the origin of the colour of a transition metal complex ion?
- What factors determine the colour of a complex ion?

Specification reference: 3.5.4

Most transition metal compounds are coloured. The colour is caused by the compounds absorbing energy that corresponds to light in the visible region of the spectrum. If a solution of a substance looks purple, it is because it absorbs all the light from a beam of white light shone at it except the red and blue. The red and blue light passes through and the solution appears purple, see Figure 1.

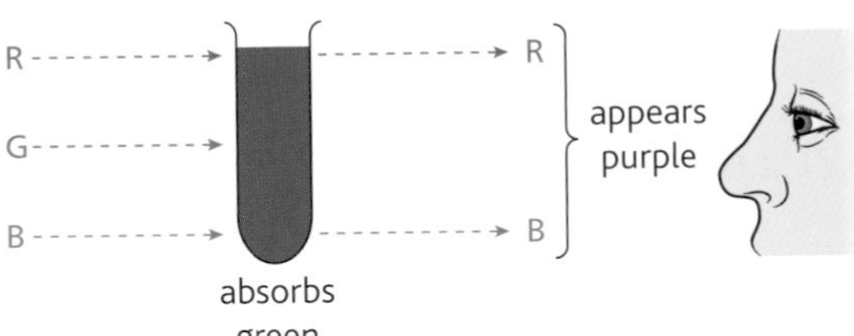

Figure 1 *Solutions look coloured because they absorb some colours and let others pass through*

AQA Examiner's tip

Make sure that you know the factors which give rise to colour changes and are able to illustrate each change by an equation.

Why are transition metal complexes coloured?

This is a simplified explanation, but the general principle is as follows:

- Transition metal compounds are coloured because they have part-filled d-orbitals.
- It is therefore possible for electrons to move from one d-orbital to another.
- In an isolated transition metal atom, all the d-orbitals are of exactly the same energy, but in a compound, the presence of other atoms nearby makes the d-orbitals have slightly different energies.
- When electrons move from one d-orbital to another of a higher energy level, they often absorb energy in the visible region of the spectrum equal to the difference in energy between levels.
- This colour is therefore missing from the spectrum and we see the combination of the colours that are not absorbed.

The frequency of the light is related to the energy difference by the expression $\Delta E = h\nu$, where E is the energy, ν the frequency and h a constant called Planck's constant. The frequency is related to the colour of light. Violet is of high energy and therefore high frequency and red is of low energy (and low frequency).

The colour of a transition metal complex depends on the oxidation state of the metal and also on the ligands (and therefore the shape of the complex ion), so different compounds of the same metal will have different colours. There are some examples in Topic 16.2.

Table 1 shows the colours of four vanadium species each with a different oxidation state. You will not be expected to remember the colours of vanadium ions for examination purposes, but they provide a striking example of the different colours of different oxidation states.

Some more examples how changing the oxidation state of the metal affects the colour of the complex are given in Table 2.

Table 1 *Colours of four vanadium species*

Ox	Species	Colour
5	$VO_2^+(aq)$	yellow
4	$VO^{2+}(aq)$	blue
3	$V^{3+}(aq)$	green
2	$V^{2+}(aq)$	violet

Table 2

Oxidation state of metal	2	3
Iron complexes and colour	$[Fe(H_2O)_6]^{2+}$ green	$[Fe(H_2O)_6]^{3+}$ very pale violet
Chromium complexes and colour	$[Cr(H_2O)_6]^{2+}$ blue	$[Cr(H_2O)_6]^{3+}$ red-violet
Cobalt complexes and colour	$[Co(NH_3)_6]^{2+}$ brown	$[Co(NH_3)_6]^{3+}$ yellow

Finding the formula of a transition metal complex using colorimetry

We can use a colorimeter to find the ratio of metal ions to ligands in a complex, which gives us the formula of the complex. We mix two solutions, one containing the metal ion and one the ligand, in different proportions. When they are mixed in the same ratio as they are in the complex, there is the maximum concentration of complex in the solution. So, the solution will absorb most light.

We will use the blood red complex formed with Fe^{3+} ions and thiocyanate ions (SCN^-) as an example.

If potassium thiocyanate is added to a solution of Fe^{3+}(aq), *one* of the water molecules is replaced by a thiocyanate ion and a blood red complex forms:

$$[Fe(H_2O)_6]^{3+}(aq) + SCN^- \longrightarrow [Fe(SCN)(H_2O)_5{}^{2+}](aq) + H_2O(l)$$

As the concentration of the red complex increases, less and less light will pass through the solution.

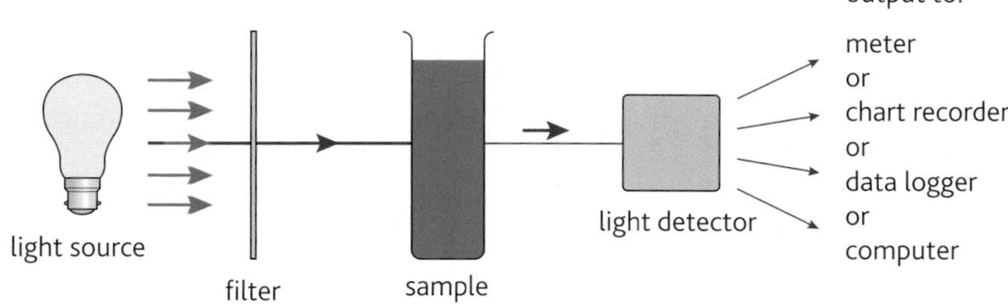

Figure 2 *Using a colorimeter to find a formula*

We start with two solutions of the same concentration, one containing Fe^{3+}(aq) ions, for example iron(III) sulfate, and one containing SCN^-(aq) ions, for example potassium thiocyanate. We mix them in the proportions shown in Table 3, adding water so that all the tubes have the same total volume of solution.

Table 3 *The absorbance of different mixtures of Fe^{3+}(aq) and SCN^-(aq)*

Tube	1	2	3	4	5	6	7	8
Vol. of Fe^{3+}(aq) solution / cm^3	10	10	10	10	10	10	10	10
Vol. of SCN^-(aq) solution / cm^3	2	4	6	8	10	12	14	16
Vol. of water / cm^3	28	26	24	22	20	28	16	14
Absorbance	0.15	0.33	0.48	0.63	0.70	0.70	0.70	0.70

Hint

We usually make the experiment more sensitive by using a coloured filter in the colorimeter. We choose the filter by finding out the colour of light that the red solution absorbs most. Red absorbs light in the blue region of the visible spectrum, so we use a blue filter, see Figure 2, so that only blue light passes into the sample tube.

Each tube is put in the colorimeter and a reading of absorbance taken. A graph of absorbance is plotted against tube number, see Figure 3.

From the graph, the maximum absorbance occurs in tube 5; after this, adding more thiocyanate ions makes no difference. So this tells us the ratio of SCN^- ions to Fe^{3+} ions in the complex. From Table 3, tube 5 has equal amounts of SCN^- ions and Fe^{3+} ions so their ratio in the complex must be 1 : 1. So this confirms the formula is $[FeSCN(H_2O)_5]^{2+}$. (The SCN^- has substituted for one of the water molecules in the complex ion $[Fe(H_2O)_6]^{3+}$.)

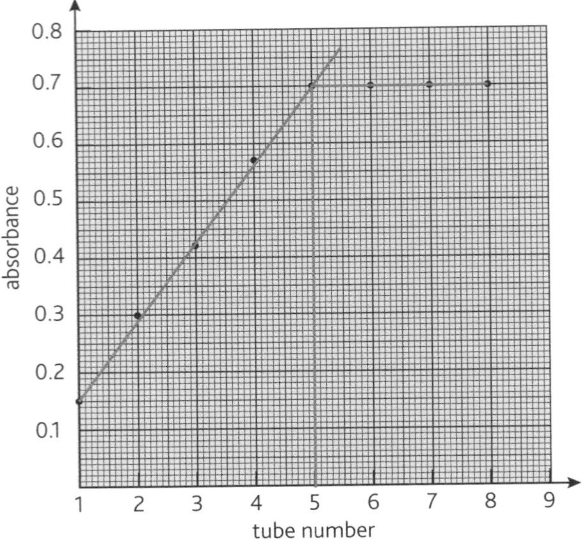

Figure 3 *A graph of absorbance against tube number*

Summary questions

1 a Explain why copper sulfate is coloured, whereas zinc sulfate is colourless.

b A solution of copper sulfate is blue. What colour light passes through this solution?

c What happens to the other colours of the visible spectrum?

2 The graph below shows the absorbance of a series of mixtures containing different proportions of two solutions of the same concentration – one containing Ni^{2+} ions and the other containing a ligand called $EDTA^{4-}$ for short. The two solutions react together to form a coloured complex.

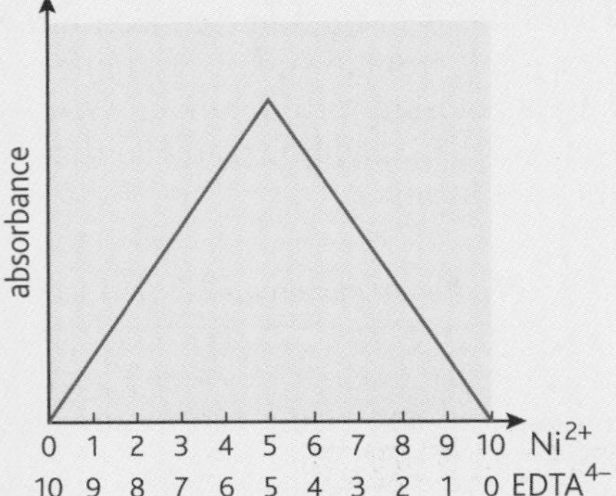

a Which mixture absorbs most light?

b Which mixture contains the highest concentration of the EDTA complex?

c What is the simplest (empirical) formula of the complex?

15.4 Variable oxidation states of transition elements

Learning objectives:

- How can the concentration of iron(II) ions in aqueous solution be found?
- How can chromium(II) ions be oxidised?
- How can cobalt(II) ions be oxidised?
- How can chromate(VI) ions be reduced?

Specification reference: 3.5.4

Group 1 metals lose their outer electron to form only 1+ ions and Group 2 lose their outer two electrons to form only 2+ ions in their compounds. A typical transition metal can use its 3d as well as its 4s electrons in bonding, and this means that it can have a greater variety of oxidation states in different compounds. Table 1 shows this for the first d-series. Zinc and scandium are shown as part of the d-series although they are not transition metals.

Table 1 *Oxidation numbers shown by the elements of the first d-series in their compounds*

Sc	Ti	V	Cr	Mn	Fe	Co	Ni	Cu	Zn
	+I	+I	+I	+I	+I	+I	+I	+I	
	+II	+II	+II	+II	+II	+II	+II	+II	+II
+III	+III	+III	+III	+III	+III	+III	+III	+III	
	+IV	+IV	+IV	+IV	+IV	+IV	+IV		
		+V	+V	+V	+V	+V			
			+VI	+VI	+VI				
				+VII					

The most common oxidation states are shown in red, though they are not all stable.

Except for scandium and zinc all the elements show both the +1 and +2 oxidation states. These are formed by the loss of 4s electrons.

For example, nickel has the electron configuration $1s^22s^22p^63s^23p^63d^84s^2$ and Ni^{2+} is $1s^22s^22p^63s^23p^63d^8$.

Iron has the electron configuration $1s^22s^22p^63s^23p^63d^64s^2$ and $Fe^{2+}$is $1s^22s^22p^63s^23p^63d^6$.

Note: only the lower oxidation states of transition metals actually exist as simple ions, so that, for example, Mn^{2+} ions exist but Mn^{7+} ions do not. In all Mn(VII) compounds, as in MnO_4^-, manganese is covalently bonded, see Figure 1.

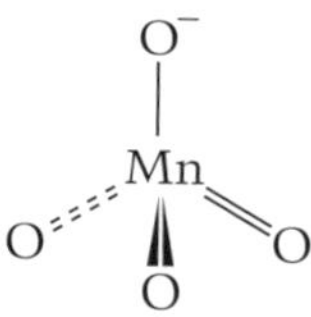

Figure 1 *Bonding in the $[MnO_4]^-$ ion*

Synoptic link

You will need to understand redox equations and volumetric analysis studied in *AQA AS Chemistry*, Topics 10.3 and 2.4.

Redox reactions in transition metal chemistry

Many of the reactions of transition metal compounds are redox reactions, in which the metals are either oxidised or reduced. Iron, for example, shows two stable oxidation states, Fe^{3+} and Fe^{2+}.

Fe^{2+} is the less stable state; it can be oxidised to Fe^{3+} by the oxygen in the air and also by chlorine. For example:

$$\overset{+2}{2Fe^{2+}}(aq) + \overset{0}{Cl_2}(g) \longrightarrow \overset{+3}{2Fe^{3+}}(aq) + \overset{-1}{2Cl^-}(aq)$$

In this reaction, chlorine is the oxidising agent – its oxidation number drops from 0 to –1 (as it gains an electron), while that of the iron increases from +2 to +3 (as it loses an electron). Remember the phrase OIL RIG, oxidation is loss, reduction is gain (of electrons).

AQA Examiner's tip

You need to understand the redox reactions studied in *AQA AS Chemistry*, Chapter 10.

Using half equations

Potassium manganate(VII) reactions

The technique of using half equations is useful for constructing balanced equations in more complex reactions. Potassium manganate(VII) can act as an oxidising agent in acidic solution (one containing $H^+(aq)$ ions) and will, for example, oxidise Fe^{2+} to Fe^{3+}. During the reaction the oxidation number of the manganese falls from +7 to +2.

We must first construct the half equation for the reduction of Mn(VII) to Mn(II):

$$MnO_4^-(aq) \longrightarrow Mn^{2+}(aq)$$

We must first balance the oxygen atoms using H^+ ions:

$$MnO_4^- + 8H^+(aq) \longrightarrow Mn^{2+}(aq) + 4H_2O(l)$$

Then balance for charge using electrons:

$$MnO_4^-(aq) + 5e^- + 8H^+(aq) \longrightarrow Mn^{2+}(aq) + 4H_2O(l)$$

The half equation for the oxidation of iron(II) to iron(III) is straightforward:

$$Fe^{2+}(aq) \longrightarrow Fe^{3+}(aq) + e^-$$

To construct a balanced symbol equation for the reaction of acidified potassium manganate (VII) with $Fe^{2+}(aq)$ we must first multiply the Fe^{2+} / Fe^{3+} half reaction by 5 (so that the numbers of electrons in each half reaction are the same) and then add the two half equations:

$$5Fe^{2+}(aq) \longrightarrow 5Fe^{3+}(aq) + 5e^-$$

$$MnO_4^-(aq) + 5e^- + 8H^+(aq) \longrightarrow Mn^{2+}(aq) + 4H_2O(l)$$

$$5Fe^{2+}(aq) + MnO_4^-(aq) + \cancel{5e^-} + 8H^+(aq) \longrightarrow 5Fe^{3+}(aq) + \cancel{5e^-} + Mn^{2+}(aq) + 4H_2O(l)$$

$$5Fe^{2+}(aq) + MnO_4^-(aq) + 8H^+(aq) \longrightarrow 5Fe^{3+}(aq) + Mn^{2+}(aq) + 4H_2O(l)$$

This technique makes balancing complex redox reactions much easier.

Redox titrations

We may wish to measure the concentration of an oxidising or a reducing agent. One way of doing this is to do a redox titration. This is similar in principle to an acid–base titration in which we find out how much acid is required to react with a certain volume of base (or vice versa).

One example is in the analysis of 'iron tablets' for quality control purposes. 'Iron tablets' contain iron(II) sulfate and may be taken by patients whose diet is short of iron for some reason.

As we have seen above, $Fe^{2+}(aq)$ reacts with manganate(VII) ions (in potassium manganate(VII)) in the ratio 5 : 1. The reaction does not need an indicator, because the colours of the mixture changes as the reaction proceeds, see Table 2.

Using a burette, we gradually add potassium manganate(VII) solution (which contains the $MnO_4^-(aq)$ ions) to a solution containing $Fe^{2+}(aq)$ ions, acidified with excess dilute sulfuric acid. The purple colour disappears as the MnO_4^- ions are converted to pale pink $Mn^{2+}(aq)$ ions to leave a virtually colourless solution. Once we have added just enough $MnO_4^-(aq)$

Hint

The body needs iron compounds to make haemoglobin, the compound that carries oxygen in the blood.

Table 2 *The colours of the ions in the reaction between potassium manganate(VII) and iron(II) sulfate*

Ion	Colour
$Fe^{2+}(aq)$	pale green
$MnO_4^-(aq)$	intense purple
$Fe^{3+}(aq)$	pale violet
$Mn^{2+}(aq)$	pale pink

ions to react with all the Fe^{2+}(aq) ions, one more drop of MnO_4^-(aq) ions will turn the solution purple. This is the end point of the titration.

The apparatus used is shown in Figure 2.

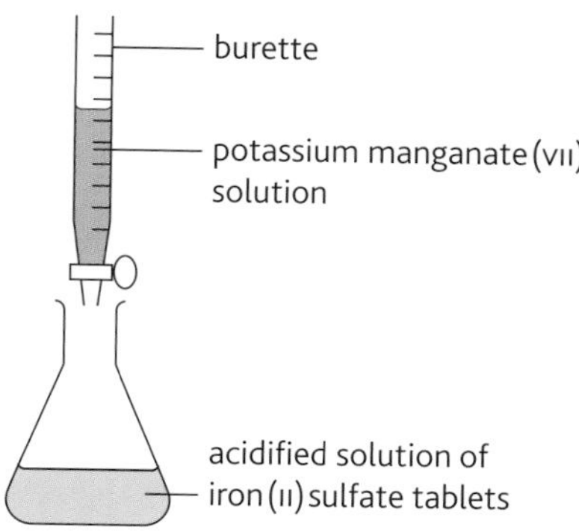

Figure 2 *Apparatus for a titration*

We cannot use hydrochloric acid, as an alternative to sulfuric acid, to supply the H^+(aq) ions in the reaction between potassium manganate(VII) and Fe^{2+}(aq). We can see why this is the case by using $E^\ominus$ values, see Topic 14.3.

Hydrochloric acid contains Cl^- ions. These are oxidised by MnO_4^- ions as shown by the calculation of emf for the reaction below. This would affect the titration, because the manganate(VII) ions must be used only to oxidise Fe^{2+} ions. Manganate(VII) ions do not oxidise sulfate ions.

The relevant half equations with their values of $E^\ominus$ are (see Table 1, Topic 14.3).

$$MnO_4^-(aq) + 5e^- + 8H^+(aq) \rightleftharpoons Mn^{2+}(aq) + 4H_2O(l) \qquad E^\ominus = +1.51\,V$$

$$\tfrac{1}{2}Cl_2 + e \rightleftharpoons Cl^- \qquad E^\ominus = +1.36\,V$$

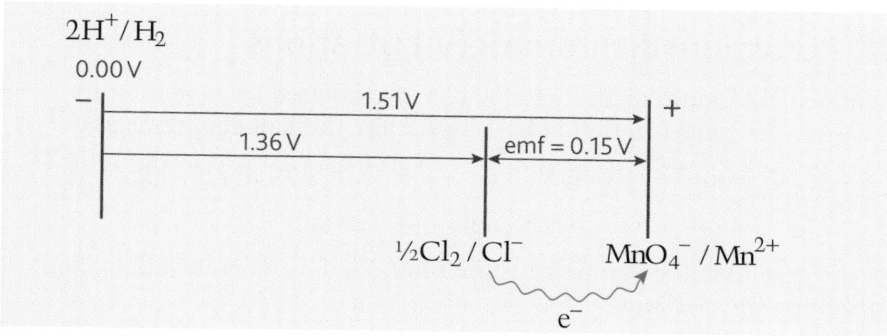

Figure 3 $E^\ominus$ *values show that acidified MnO_4^- ions will oxidise Cl^- ions*

Figure 3 shows that the electron flow is from Cl_2 to MnO_4^-, and the emf is 0.15 V, so the half reaction must be as follows:

$$MnO_4^-(aq) + 5e^- + 8H^+(aq) \longrightarrow Mn^{2+}(aq) + 4H_2O(l)$$

and

$$Cl^- \longrightarrow Cl_2 + e^-$$

Multiplying the lower half equation by 5, to balance the electrons, and adding gives:

$$MnO_4^-(aq) + \cancel{5e^-} + 8H^+(aq) + 5Cl^-(aq) \rightleftharpoons Mn^{2+}(aq) + 4H_2O(l) + 2\tfrac{1}{2}Cl_2(aq) + \cancel{5e^-}$$

Remember to cancel electrons

$$\text{emf} = +0.15\,V$$

This reaction is feasible, so MnO_4^- ions will oxidise Cl^- ions and hydrochloric acid is not suitable for this titration.

Worked example:

A brand of iron tablets has this stated on the pack: 'Each tablet contains 0.200 g of iron(II) sulfate.' The following experiment was done to check this.

One tablet was dissolved in excess sulfuric acid and made up to 250 cm^3 in a volumetric flask. 25.00 cm^3 of this solution was pipetted into a flask and titrated with 0.00100 mol dm^{-3} potassium manganate(VII) solution until the solution just became purple. Taking an average of several titrations, 26.30 cm^3 of potassium manganate(VII) solution was needed.

$$\text{Number of moles potassium manganate(VII) solution} = M \times \frac{V}{1000}$$

where M is the concentration of the solution in mol dm^{-3} and V is the volume of solution used in cm^3.

AQA Examiner's tip

Always show all your working in calculations to enable examiners to award part scores when answers are incomplete or the final answer is wrong.

No. of moles potassium manganate(VII) solution $= 0.00100 \times \frac{26.30}{1000}$

$= 2.63 \times 10^{-5}$ mol

$$5Fe^{2+}(aq) + MnO_4^-(aq) + 8H^+(aq) \longrightarrow 5Fe^{3+}(aq) + Mn^{2+}(aq) + 4H_2O(l)$$

From the equation, 5 mol of Fe^{2+} react with 1 mol of MnO_4^-:

Number of moles of $Fe^{2+} = 5 \times 2.63 \times 10^{-5}$ mol $= 1.315 \times 10^{-4}$ mol

25.00 cm³ of solution contained $\frac{1}{10}$ tablet:

So 1 tablet contains $1.315 \times 10^{-4} \times 10 = 1.315 \times 10^{-3}$ mol Fe^{2+}

Since 1 mol iron(II) sulfate contains 1 mol Fe^{2+}, each tablet contains 1.315×10^{-3} mol $FeSO_4$.

The relative formula mass of $FeSO_4$ is 151.9.

So, each tablet contains $1.315 \times 10^{-3} \times 151.9 = 0.200$ g of iron(II) sulfate as stated on the bottle.

Potassium dichromate(VI) titrations

Acidified potassium dichromate(VI) can also be used in a titration to measure the concentration of Fe^{2+} ions. Here the half equations are:

$$Cr_2O_7^{2-}(aq) + 14H^+(aq) + 6e^- \longrightarrow 2Cr^{3+}(aq) + 7H_2O(l)$$

$$Fe^{2+}(aq) \longrightarrow Fe^{3+}(aq) + e^-$$

AQA Examiner's tip

Note that although chromium is reduced from +6 to +3, the ion $Cr_2O_7^{2-}$ contains two chromium atoms so that six electrons are needed.

So the second half equation must be multiplied by 6 before adding and cancelling the electrons.

$$6Fe^{2+}(aq) \longrightarrow 6Fe^{3+}(aq) + 6e^-$$

$$Cr_2O_7^{2-}(aq) + 14H^+(aq) + 6e^- \longrightarrow 2Cr^{3+}(aq) + 7H_2O(l)$$

$$6Fe^{2+}(aq) + Cr_2O_7^{2-}(aq) + 14H^+(aq) + \cancel{6e^-} \longrightarrow 6Fe^{3+}(aq) + 2Cr^{3+}(aq) + 7H_2O(l) + \cancel{6e^-}$$

$$6Fe^{2+}(aq) + Cr_2O_7^{2-}(aq) + 14H^+(aq) \longrightarrow 6Fe^{3+}(aq) + 2Cr^{3+}(aq) + 7H_2O(l)$$

As before, the $Fe^{2+}(aq)$ solution is placed in the flask with the dichromate in the burette with excess dilute sulfuric acid to provide the H^+ ions.

As it is not possible to see the colour change when a small volume of orange solution is added to a pale green solution, an indicator must be used – sodium diphenylaminesulfonate, which turns from colourless to purple at the end point.

Oxidation of transition metal ions in alkaline solutions

In both the above examples, a high oxidation state of a metal (Mn(VII) and Cr(VI)) are reduced in acidic solution. Oxidation of lower oxidation states of transition metal ions tends to happen in alkaline solution. This is because in alkaline solution, there is a tendency to form negative ions, see below. Since oxidation is electron loss, this is easier from negatively charged species that positively charged or neutral ones.

Typical transition metal species:

- Acid solution: $M(H_2O)_6^{2+}$ positively charged.

- Neutral solution: $M(H_2O)_4(OH)_2$ neutral.
- Alkaline solution: $M(H_2O)_2(OH)_4^{2-}$ negatively charged.

Low oxidation states of transition metals, such as Fe^{2+} are often stabilised against oxidation by air by keeping them in acid solution.

To oxidise a transition metal to a high oxidation state, we often first add alkali, followed by an oxidising agent.

Examples from chromium and cobalt chemistry

Redox chemistry of chromium

Chromium has an extensive redox chemistry, the most important oxidation states being Cr(II) (blue), Cr(III) (green) and Cr(VI) (yellow/orange). In aqueous solution Cr(VI) exists as either the chromate(VI) ion, CrO_4^{2-}, or the dimeric dichromate(VI) ion $Cr_2O_7^{2-}$. The orange dichromate ion is stable in acid solution and the yellow chromate ion in alkalis, as shown by the equilibrium below:

$$\underset{\text{yellow}}{2CrO_4^{2-}(aq)} + 2H^+(aq) \rightleftharpoons \underset{\text{orange}}{Cr_2O_7^{2-}(aq)} + H_2O(l)$$

Chromium(III) is the most stable oxidation state in aqueous solution. Chromium(II) is easily oxidised to chromium(III) by oxygen and can only be prepared in the absence of air. If it is prepared by reduction of chromium(VI) by zinc in acid solution, the hydrogen produced can be used to exclude air.

The half equations are:

$$Cr_2O_7^{2-}(aq) + 14H^+ (aq) + 6e^- \longrightarrow 2Cr^{3+}(aq) + 7H_2O (l)$$

$$Zn(s) \longrightarrow Zn^{2+}(aq) + 2e^-$$

Multiplying the second half equation by 3 (so that the number of electrons cancel) and adding gives:

$$Cr_2O_7^{2-}(aq) + 14H^+(aq) + 3Zn(s) \longrightarrow 2Cr^{3+}(aq) + 7H_2O(l) + 3Zn^{2+}(aq)$$

The half equation for the further reduction of Cr(III) to Cr(II) is:

$$Cr^{3+}(aq) + e^- \longrightarrow Cr^{2+}(aq)$$

So multiplying by 2 to cancel the electrons, and adding to the zinc half equation (above) gives:

$$Zn(s) + 2Cr^{3+}(aq) \longrightarrow Zn^{2+}(aq) + 2Cr^{2+}(aq)$$

The chromium(VI) state is powerfully oxidising and $Cr_2O_7^{2-}/H^+$ is often used as an oxidising agent in organic chemistry.

If sodium hydroxide is added to a solution of a chromium(III) salt, a green precipitate is first formed which dissolves in excess sodium hydroxide to give a green solution containing chromate(III) :

$$[Cr(H_2O)_6]^{3+}(aq) + 3OH^-(aq) \longrightarrow [Cr(OH)_3(H_2O)_3](s) + 3H_2O(l)$$

$$[Cr(OH)_3(H_2O)_3](s) + 3OH^-(aq) \longrightarrow [Cr(OH)_6]^{3-}(aq) + 3H_2O(l)$$

If this solution is then oxidised using hydrogen peroxide, the solution turns yellow as the chromate(VI) ions are formed:

$$2[\overset{+3}{Cr}(OH)_6]^{3-}(aq) + 3H_2O_2(aq) \longrightarrow 2\overset{+6}{Cr}O_4^{2-}(aq) + 2OH^-(aq) + 8H_2O(l)$$

On adding acid, the dichromate ion ($Cr_2O_7^{2-}(aq)$) ion is formed:

$$2CrO_4^{2-}(aq) + 2H^+(aq) \longrightarrow Cr_2O_7^{2-}(aq) + H_2O(l)$$

AQA Examiner's tip

These redox reactions of chromium and cobalt can readily be carried out in the laboratory.

Hint

Some of the zinc will react with the acid to produce hydrogen.

Figure 4 *Flasks showing, from left to right, solutions containing chromium(III), chromate(VI) and dichromate(VI).*

Cobalt compounds

Many M^{2+} ions will be oxidised to M^{3+} in alkaline solution, for example cobalt(II) to cobalt(III). For example:

$$\overset{+2}{2[Co(OH)_6]^{4-}(aq)} + H_2O_2(aq) \longrightarrow \overset{+3}{2[Co(OH)_6]^{3-}(aq)} + 2OH^-(aq)$$

In ammoniacal solution, Co^{2+} ions can be oxidised by oxygen in the air.

If you add an excess of ammonia solution to an aqueous solution containing cobalt(II) ions, you get a brownish complex ion formed, $[Co(NH_3)_6]^{2+}$, containing cobalt(II) ions.

The reactions are as follows:

- First a precipitate is formed by reaction with OH^- ions from the ammonia solution, which is alkaline:

$$[Co(H_2O)_6]^{2+} + 2OH^- \longrightarrow Co(H_2O)_4(OH)_2(s)$$

- Then the precipitate dissolves in excess ammonia:

$$Co(H_2O)_4(OH)_2(s) + 6NH_3(aq) \longrightarrow [Co(NH_3)_6]^{2+} + 2OH^-(aq) + 4H_2O(l)$$

- The resulting complex ion oxidised by oxygen in air (or rapidly by hydrogen peroxide solution) to the yellow cobalt(III) ion, $[Co(NH_3)_6]^{3+}$.

We can use half equations to produce a balanced equation for the redox reaction.

The half equations are:

$$[Co(NH_3)_6]^{2+}(aq) \longrightarrow [Co(NH_3)_6]^{3+}(aq) + e^-$$

$$O_2(g) + 2H_2O(l) + 4e^- \longrightarrow 4OH^-(aq)$$

and multiplying the first equation by 4 and adding these:

$$4[Co(NH_3)_6]^{2+}(aq) \longrightarrow 4[Co(NH_3)_6]^{3+}(aq) + 4e^-$$

$$O_2(g) + 2H_2O(l) + 4e^- \longrightarrow 4OH^-(aq)$$

$$4[Co(NH_3)_6]^{2+}(aq) + O_2(g) + 2H_2O(l) + \cancel{4e^-} \longrightarrow 4[Co(NH_3)_6]^{3+}(aq) + \cancel{4e^-} + 4OH^-(aq)$$

$$4[Co(NH_3)_6]^{2+}(aq) + O_2(g) + 2H_2O(l) \longrightarrow 4[Co(NH_3)_6]^{3+}(aq) + 4OH^-(aq)$$

Summary questions

1 Zinc will reduce VO_2^+ ions to VO^{2+}; VO^{2+} to V^{3+} and V^{3+} ions to V^{2+} ions. The relevant half equations are:

$$Zn(s) \longrightarrow Zn^{2+}(aq) + 2e^-$$

$$VO_2^+(aq) + 2H^+(aq) + e^- \longrightarrow H_2O(l) + VO^{2+}(aq)$$

$$VO^{2+}(aq) + 2H^+(aq) + e^- \longrightarrow H_2O(l) + V^{3+}(aq)$$

$$V^{3+}(aq) + e^- \longrightarrow V^{2+}(aq)$$

a Write the balanced equation for each of the reduction steps.

b V^{2+} has to be protected from air. Suggest a reason for this.

2 A titration to determine the amount of iron(II) sulfate in an iron tablet was carried out. The tablet was dissolved in excess sulfuric acid and made up to 250 cm^3 in a volumetric flask. 25.00 cm^3 of this solution was pipetted into a flask and titrated with 0.001 mol dm^{-3} potassium manganate(VII) solution until the solution just became purple. Taking an average of several titrations, 25.00 cm^3 of potassium manganate(VII) solution was needed. How many grams of iron are in this tablet? A_r Fe = 55.8.

3 The $E^\ominus$ value for $Cr_2O_7^{2-}(aq) + 14H^+(aq) + 6e^- \rightleftharpoons 2Cr^{3+}(aq) + 7H_2O(l)$ is +1.33 V

Use this and the $E^\ominus$ values above and on page 225 to show that acidified $Cr_2O_7^{2-}$ ions can be used in a redox titration with Fe^{2+} when Cl^- ions are present, i.e. that $Cr_2O_7^{2-}$ ions will not oxidise Cl^-.

15.5 Catalysis

Learning objectives:

- What are heterogeneous and homogeneous catalysts?
- How can heterogeneous catalysts be made more efficient?
- How does a homogeneous catalyst work?

Specification reference: 3.5.4

Catalysts affect the rate of a reaction without being chemically changed themselves. We saw in *AQA AS Chemistry*, Topic 8.3 that catalysts play an important part in industry because they allow reactions to proceed at lower temperatures and pressures thus saving valuable resources. We have seen the use of catalysts in organic chemistry in Topic 6.3, for example sulfuric acid in the nitration of benzene and aluminium chloride in Friedel–Crafts acylation. Modern cars have a catalytic converter in the exhaust system which is based on platinum and rhodium. This catalyses the conversion of carbon monoxide, nitrogen oxides and unburnt petrol to carbon dioxide, nitrogen and water.

Many catalysts used in industry are transition metals or their compounds.

Catalysts can be divided into two groups:

- heterogeneous and
- homogeneous.

Heterogeneous catalysts

Heterogeneous catalysts are present in a reaction in a different phase (solid, liquid or gas) than the reactants. They are usually present as solids, while the reactants may be gases or liquids. Their catalytic action occurs on the solid surface.

Hint

Transition metals have partly full d-orbitals which can be used to form weak chemical bonds with the reactants. This has two effects: weakening bonds within the reactant and holding the reactants close together on the metal surface in the correct orientation for reaction.

Making catalysts more efficient

Catalysts are often expensive, so the more efficiently they work, the more the costs can be minimised. Since their activity takes place on the surface we can:

- Increase their surface area: the larger the surface area, the better the efficiency.
- Spread the catalyst onto an inert support medium, or even impregnate it into one. This increases the surface-to-mass ratio so that a little goes a long way. The more expensive catalysts are often used in this way. For example, the catalytic converter in a car (see *AQA AS Chemistry*, Topic 8.3), has finely divided rhodium and platinum on a ceramic material.

Catalysts do not last forever.

- Over time, the surfaces may become covered with unwanted impurities. This is called 'poisoning'. The catalytic converters in cars gradually become poisoned by substances used in fuel additives. Until a few years ago, lead-based additives were used in petrol. The lead poisoned the catalysts and so leaded fuel could not be used in cars with converters.
- The finely divided catalyst may gradually be lost from the support medium.

AQA Examiner's tip

The mechanism of heterogeneous catalytic action is not required but you must understand the factors which determine cost and catalyst efficiency.

Some important examples of heterogeneous catalysts

The Haber process

In *AQA AS Chemistry*, Topic 9.3, we met the Haber process where ammonia is made by the reaction of nitrogen with hydrogen. The catalyst for the process is iron – present as pea-sized lumps to increase the surface area:

$$N_2(g) + 3H_2(g) \xrightleftharpoons{\text{iron catalyst}} 2NH_3(g)$$

The iron catalyst lasts about five years before it becomes poisoned by impurities in the gas stream, such as sulfur compounds, and has to be replaced.

The Contact process

The Contact process produces sulfuric acid – a vital industrial chemical. Around 2 million tonnes are produced each year in the UK and it is involved in the manufacture of many goods.

It is made from sulfur, oxygen and water, the key step being:

$$2SO_2 + O_2 \rightleftharpoons 2SO_3$$

This is catalysed by vanadium(V) oxide, V_2O_5, in two steps as follows:

The vanadium(V) oxide oxidises sulfur dioxide to sulfur trioxide and is itself reduced to vanadium(IV) oxide:

$$SO_2 + V_2O_5 \longrightarrow SO_3 + V_2O_4$$

The vanadium(IV) oxide is then oxidised back to vanadium(V) oxide by oxygen:

$$2V_2O_4 + O_2 \longrightarrow 2V_2O_5$$

The vanadium(V) oxide is regenerated unchanged. Each of the two steps has a lower activation energy (see *AQA AS Chemistry*, Topic 8.1) than the uncatalysed single step and therefore the reaction goes faster.

This is a good example of how the variability of oxidation states of transition metal is useful in catalysis.

Hint

Vanadium(V) oxide is also called vanadium pentoxide.

The manufacture of methanol

Synthesis gas is made from methane, present in natural gas and steam:

$$CH_4(g) + H_2O(g) \longrightarrow CO + 3H_2(g)$$

It is a mixture of carbon monoxide and hydrogen and is used to make methanol:

$$\underset{\text{synthesis gas}}{CO(g) + 2H_2(g)} \longrightarrow \underset{\text{methanol}}{CH_3OH(g)}$$

This reaction may be catalysed by chromium oxide, Cr_2O_3. Today, the most widely used catalyst is a mixture of copper, zinc oxide and aluminium oxide.

Methanol is an important industrial chemical (over 30 million tonnes is made each year world wide) and is used mainly as a starting material for the production of plastics such as Bakelite, Terylene and Perspex.

Homogeneous catalysts

When the catalyst is in the same phase as the reactant, an intermediate species is formed. We saw this, for example in the gas phase, where chlorine free radicals act as catalysts to destroy the ozone layer, see *AQA AS Chemistry*, Topic 14.4. The intermediate here is the ClO· free radical.

A further example of catalysis by transition metals

Peroxodisulfate ions, $S_2O_8^{2-}$, oxidise iodide ions to iodine. This reaction is catalysed by Fe^{2+} ions. The overall reaction is:

$$S_2O_8^{2-}(aq) + 2I^-(aq) \longrightarrow 2SO_4^{2-}(aq) + I_2(aq)$$

The catalysed reaction takes place in two steps. First the peroxodisulfate ions oxidise iron(II) to iron(III):

$$S_2O_8^{2-}(aq) + 2Fe^{2+}(aq) \longrightarrow 2SO_4^{2-}(aq) + 2Fe^{3+}(aq)$$

The Fe^{3+} then oxidises the I^- to I_2, regenerating the Fe^{2+} ions so that none are used up in the reaction:

$$2Fe^{3+}(aq) + 2I^-(aq) \longrightarrow 2Fe^{2+}(aq) + I_2(aq)$$

So iron first gives an electron to the peroxodisulfate and later takes one back from the iodide ions.

Notice that the uncatalysed reaction takes place between two ions of the same charge (both negative), which repel, therefore giving a high activation energy. Both steps of the catalysed reaction involve reaction between pairs of oppositely charged ions. This helps to explain the increase in rate.

The reaction profile would look like Figure 1. Although there are two steps in the catalysed reaction, the overall activation energy is lower than that for the uncatalysed reaction.

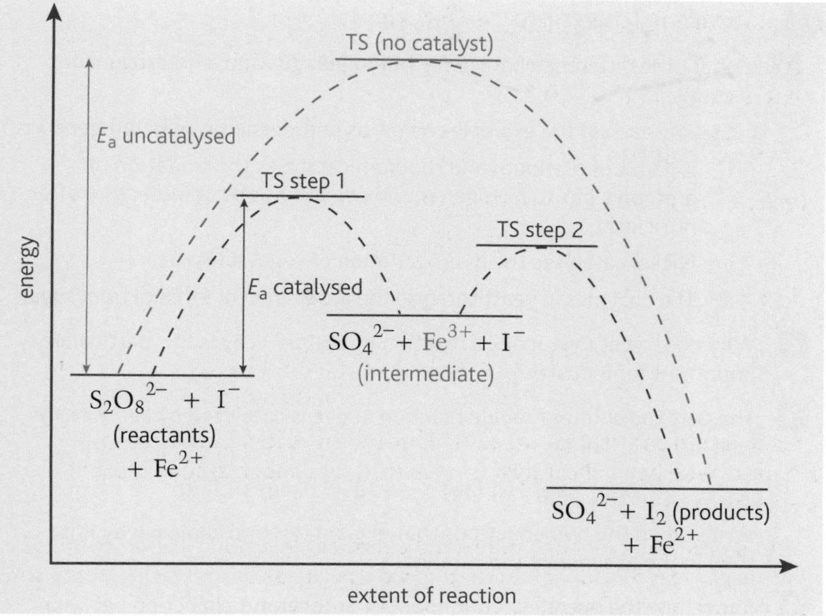

Figure 1 *Possible reaction profile for the iodine/peroxodisulfate reaction. Note E_a for the catalysed reaction is the energy gap between the reactants and the higher of the two transition states (TS step 1)*

Hint

Do not be put off by unfamiliar chemical names (such as peroxodisulfate ions). Make sure you understand the process that they are used to illustrate.

AQA Examiner's tip

Fe^{3+} also acts as a catalyst for this reaction. When this is used, I^- is first oxidised to I_2.

Autocatalysis

An interesting example of catalysis occurs when one of the products of the reaction is a catalyst for the reaction. Such a reaction starts slowly at the uncatalysed rate. As the concentration of one of the products (which is also the catalyst) builds up, the reaction speeds up to the catalysed rate. From then on it behaves like a normal reaction, gradually slowing down as the reactants are used up. This leads to an odd-looking rate curve, see Figure 2.

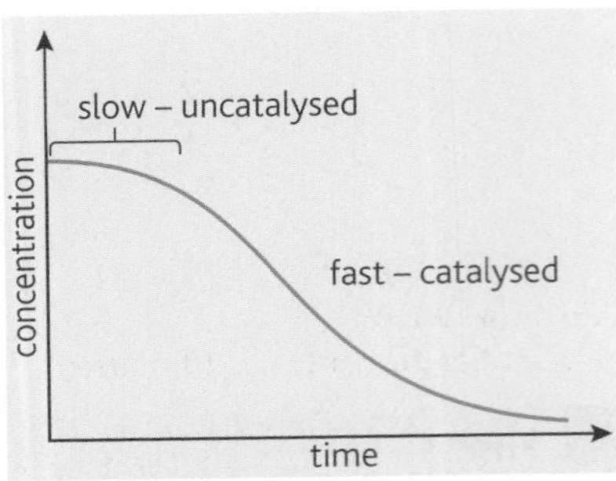

Figure 2 *A concentration/time graph for an autocatalytic reaction*

The oxidation of ethanedioic acid by manganate(VII) ions

One example of an autocatalysed reaction is that between a solution of ethanedioic acid (oxalic acid) and an acidified solution of potassium manganate(VII). It is used as a titration to find the concentration of potassium manganate(VII) solution.

$$2MnO_4^-(aq) + 16H^+(aq) + 5C_2O_4^{2-}(aq) \rightarrow 2Mn^{2+}(aq) + 8H_2O(l) + 10CO_2(g)$$

manganate(VII) ions, hydrogen ions, ethanedioate ions, manganese(II) ions, water, carbon dioxide

The catalyst Mn^{2+} ions are not present at the beginning of the reaction. Once a little Mn^{2+} has formed, it can react with MnO_4^- ions to form Mn^{3+} as an intermediate species, which then reacts with $C_2O_4^{2-}$ ions to reform Mn^{2+}:

$$4Mn^{2+}(aq) + MnO_4^-(aq) + 8H^+(aq) \longrightarrow 5Mn^{3+}(aq) + 4H_2O(l)$$

$$2Mn^{3+}(aq) + C_2O_4^{2-}(aq) \longrightarrow 2CO_2(g) + 2Mn^{2+}(aq)$$

The reaction can easily be followed using a colorimeter to measure the concentration of MnO_4^-, which is purple. The reaction curve looks like the one in Figure 2.

Summary questions

1 a State the difference between a homogeneous and a heterogeneous catalyst.

b Classify each of the examples below as homogeneous or heterogeneous:

i A gauze of platinum and rhodium catalyses the oxidation of ammonia gas to nitrogen monoxide during the manufacture of nitric acid.

ii Nickel catalyses the hydrogenation of vegetable oils.

iii The enzymes in yeast catalyse the production of ethanol from sugar.

2 Why does a catalyst make a reaction go faster? Why is this particularly important for industry?

3 The peroxodisulfate / iodide reaction above is catalysed by Fe^{3+} ions (as well as by Fe^{2+} ions):

$$S_2O_8^{2-}(aq) + 2I^-(aq) \longrightarrow 2SO_4^{2-}(aq) + I_2(aq)$$

Write down the two equations that explain this and explain why it is slow in the absence of the catalyst.

4 Show how the overall equation for the autocatalytic reaction between MnO_4^- and $C_2O_4^{2-}$ can be obtained from the equations for the two catalytic steps.

AQA Examination-style questions

1 (a) The ion $C_2O_4^{2-}$ can act as a bidentate ligand.

(i) Explain the meaning of the term *bidentate ligand*.

(ii) Sketch the structure of the octahedral complex ion formed by Fe^{3+} ions which contains $C_2O_4^{2-}$ as the only ligand. Include the overall charge on the complex ion. *(5 marks)*

(b) The chloride ion can act as a monodentate ligand.

Explain why metal(II) ions do not usually form octahedral complexes when chloride ions are the only ligands. *(1 mark)*

(c) The concentration of $C_2O_4^{2-}$ ions can be determined by titration in acidic solution using a standard solution of potassium manganate(VII). At room temperature, the reaction proceeds very slowly at first but becomes faster after some of the manganate(VIII) ions have reacted.

(i) Suggest why this reaction is very slow at first.

(ii) This is an example of an autocatalytic reaction. State the meaning of the term *autocatalytic* and identify the catalyst.

(iii) Suggest how this catalyst might be involved in the reaction. *(5 marks)*

AQA, 2003

2 In the Haber process for the manufacture of ammonia, the following equilibrium is established in the presence of a heterogeneous catalyst.

$$N_2(g) + 3H_2(g) \rightleftharpoons 2NH_3(g)$$

Identify the heterogeneous catalyst used in this process and state what is meant by the term *heterogeneous*.

A heterogeneous catalyst can become poisoned by impurities in the reactants. Give one substance which poisons the heterogeneous catalyst used in the Haber process and explain how this substance poisons the catalyst. *(5 marks)*

AQA, 2005

3 (a) Octahedral and tetrahedral complex ions are produced by the reaction of transition metal ions with ligands which form co-ordinate bonds with the transition metal ion. Define the term *ligand* and explain what is meant by the term *co-ordinate bond*. *(3 marks)*

(b) (i) Some complex ions can undergo a ligand substitution reaction in which both the co-ordination number of the metal and the colour change in the reaction. Write an equation for one such reaction and state the colours of the complex ions involved.

(ii) Bidentate ligands replace unidentate ligands in a metal complex by a ligand substitution reaction. Write an equation for such a reaction and explain why this reaction occurs. *(8 marks)*

AQA, 2005

4 (a) State what is meant by the term *homogeneous* as applied to a catalyst. *(1 mark)*

(b) (i) State what is meant by the term *autocatalysis*.

(ii) Identify the species which acts as an autocatalyst in the reaction between ethanedioate ions and manganate(VII) ions in acidic solution. *(2 marks)*

(c) When petrol is burned in a car engine, carbon monoxide, carbon dioxide, oxides of nitrogen and water are produced. Catalytic converters are used as part of car exhaust systems so that the emission of toxic gases is greatly reduced.

(i) Write an equation for a reaction which occurs in a catalytic converter between two of the toxic gases. Identify the reducing agent in this reaction.

(ii) Identify a transition metal used in catalytic converters and state how the converter is constructed to maximise the effect of the catalyst. *(5 marks)*

AQA, 2004

16 Reactions of inorganic compounds in aqueous solution

16.1 Lewis acids and bases

Learning objectives:

- What are Lewis acids and bases?
- How can water act as both a Lewis base and a Brønsted–Lowry base?
- What are metal-aqua ions?
- What determines the acidity of metal-aqua ions in aqueous solution?

Specification reference: 3.5.5

Link

You will need to understand the reactions of aqueous ions studied in *AQA AS Chemistry*, Topics 11.3 and 12.1.

You will need to understand Brønsted–Lowry acids and bases studied in this book, Topic 3.1.

Hint

Boron trifluoride has only six electrons in its outer shell and is therefore able to accept an electron pair from ammonia, for example.

The Lewis theory of acidity

We have seen in Topic 3.1 that the Brønsted–Lowry theory of acidity describes acids as proton (H^+ ion) donors; and bases, such as OH^- ions, as proton acceptors.

Another theory (the **Lewis theory**) is also used to describe acids. This theory defines acids as electron pair acceptors; and bases as electron pair donors in the formation of co-ordinate (dative) covalent bonds. For example:

$$BF_3 + :NH_3 \longrightarrow F_3B \leftarrow NH_3$$

boron trifluoride   ammonia

Here boron trifluoride is acting as a Lewis acid (electron pair acceptor) and ammonia as a Lewis base (electron pair donor). The Lewis definition of acids is wider than the Brønsted–Lowry one. Boron trifluoride contains no hydrogen and so cannot be an acid under the Brønsted–Lowry definition. H^+ ions have no electrons at all and so can *only* form bonds by accepting an electron pair.

$$H^+ + {}^-:O{-}H \longrightarrow H{\leftarrow}O{-}H$$

A water molecule has two lone pairs of electrons and it can use one of these to accept a proton (acting as a Lewis base and as a Brønsted–Lowry base) or, for example, to form a co-ordinate bond with a metal ion (acting as a Lewis base).

$$H^+ + H_2\ddot{O}: \longrightarrow [H{\leftarrow}OH_2]^+$$

$$Cu^{2+} + 6\,H_2\ddot{O}: \longrightarrow [Cu(\leftarrow OH_2)_6]^{2+}$$

All Brønsted–Lowry acids are also Lewis acids. Ligands which form bonds to transition metal ions using lone pairs are acting as Lewis bases and the metal ions as Lewis acids.

How science works

Theories of acidity over the years

Acids are a group of compounds with similar properties: neutralising bases, producing hydrogen with the more-reactive metals, releasing carbon dioxide from carbonates, for example. They were probably first recognised as a group by their sour taste. Today, of course, no one would dream of tasting a newly synthesised compound before it had been thoroughly tested for toxicity (which could take some time), but in old chemical papers it is not uncommon to find the taste of new compounds reported along with colour, crystal form, melting point etc.

Many theories of acidity have been proposed, and these have been discarded or modified as new facts have come along. This is how scientific understanding progresses. Theories of acidity include:

Lavoisier (1777) proposed that all acids contain oxygen. This is fine for many acids – nitric, HNO_3, sulfuric, H_2SO_4 and ethanoic (acetic), CH_3COOH, for example, and was a good working theory. However, once the formula of hydrochloric acid, HCl, was worked out, it became clear that this theory could not be correct.

Davy (1816) suggested that all acids contain hydrogen. This looks better – all the above acids fit and the theory has no problem including HCl. It does not explain why the hydrogen is important, though.

Liebig (1838) defined acids as substances containing hydrogen which could be replaced by a metal. This is an improvement on Davy's theory as it explains why not all hydrogen-containing compounds are acidic – there must be something special about that hydrogen that makes it replaceable by a metal. This is a theory that is not far from one we could use today.

Arrhenius (1887) thought of acids as producing hydrogen ions, H^+. This is a development of Liebig's theory. It tells us what exactly is special about the hydrogen – it must be able to become an H^+ ion.

The **Brønsted–Lowry** description of acidity (developed in 1923 by Thomas Lowry and Johannes Brønsted independently) is the most generally useful current theory. This defines an acid as a substance which can donate a proton (an H^+ ion) and a base as a substance which can accept a proton. However, this theory has difficulty with acids that do not contain hydrogen – aluminium chloride, $AlCl_3$, or boron trifluoride, BF_3, for example.

Another theory (the **Lewis theory**) is also used today to describe acids. This theory regards acids as electron pair acceptors and bases as electron pair donors in the formation of co-ordinate covalent bonds.

Antoine Lavoisier (1743–94)

Svante Arrhenius (1859–1927)

Gilbert Lewis (1875–1946)

Hint

When drawing co-ordinate bonds, the arrow ⟶ represents the donated pair of electrons

The acid–base chemistry of aqueous transition metal ions

If we dissolve a salt of a transition metal (such as iron(II) nitrate, $Fe(NO_3)_2$) in water, water molecules cluster around the Fe^{2+} ion so it actually exist as the complex ion $[Fe(H_2O)_6]^{2+}$. Six water molecules act as ligands bonding to the metal ion in an octahedral arrangement. They each use one of their lone pairs of electrons to form a co-ordinate (dative) bond with the metal ion – they are acting as Lewis bases. A similar situation occurs with an iron(III) salt – here the complex formed is $[Fe(H_2O)_6]^{3+}$. These complexes are called **aqua ions**.

Hint

pK_a was discussed in Topic 3.3. It is a measure of the strength of an acid. The *smaller* the value of pK_a, the *stronger* the acid.

However, there is a significant difference in the acidity of these two complexes.

Solutions of Fe^{2+}(aq) are not noticeably acidic, whereas a solution of Fe^{3+}(aq) (pK_a = 2.2) is a stronger acid than ethanoic acid (pK_a = 4.8). Why is Fe^{3+}(aq) acidic at all and why the difference with Fe^{2+}(aq)? This is because the Fe^{3+} ion is both smaller and more highly charged than Fe^{2+} (we say that it has a higher charge density), making it more strongly polarising. So in the $[Fe(H_2O)_6]^{3+}$(aq) ion the iron strongly attracts electrons from the oxygen atoms of the water ligands, thus weakening the O–H bonds in of the water molecules. This complex ion will then readily release an H^+ ion making the solution acidic, see Figure 1. Fe^{2+} is less polarising and hence less O–H bonds break in solution.

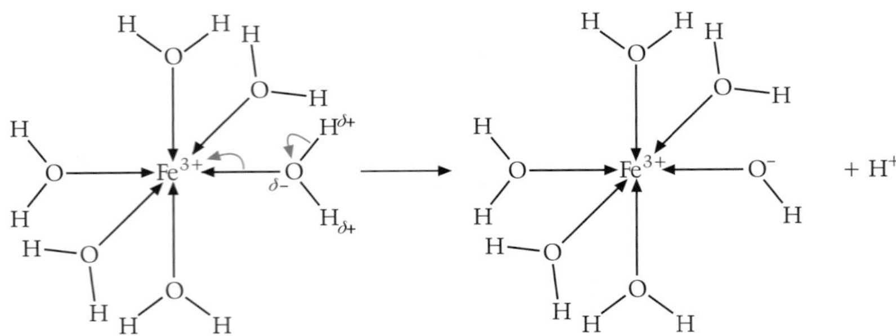

Figure 1 *The acidity of Fe^{3+}(aq) ions*

Written as an equation:

$$[Fe(H_2O)_6]^{3+}(aq) \rightleftharpoons [Fe(H_2O)_5(OH)]^{2+}(aq) + H^+(aq)$$

With transition metals, there is a general rule that aqua-ions of M^{3+} are significantly more acidic than those of M^{2+}.

A similar situation occurs in solutions of Al^{3+}(aq), although aluminium is not, of course a transition metal.

Reactions such as the above are often called **hydrolysis** (reaction with water), because they may also be represented as:

$$[Fe(H_2O)_6]^{3+}(aq) + H_2O(l) \rightleftharpoons [Fe(H_2O)_5(OH)]^{2+}(aq) + H_3O^+(aq)$$

stressing the fact that the $[Fe(H_2O)_6]^{3+}$ ion is donating a proton (H^+) to a water molecule and behaving as Brønsted–Lowry acid.

AQA Examiner's tip

A hydrolysis reaction is one in which O–H bonds are broken and new species are formed.

Some reactions of M^{2+}(aq) and M^{3+}(aq) ions

The above enables us to understand some of the acid–base reactions of transition metal ions in the +2 and +3 oxidation states.

If we add a base (such as OH^-) it will remove protons from the aqueous complex. This takes place in a series of steps as shown below.

In the case of M^{3+}

$$[M(H_2O)_6]^{3+}(aq) + OH^-(aq) \longrightarrow [M(H_2O)_5(OH)]^{2+}(aq) + H_2O(l)$$

$$[M(H_2O)_5(OH)]^{2+}(aq) + OH^-(aq) \longrightarrow [M(H_2O)_4(OH)_2]^{+}(aq) + H_2O(l)$$

$$[M(H_2O)_4(OH)_2]^{+}(aq) + OH^-(aq) \longrightarrow M(H_2O)_3(OH)_3(s) + H_2O(l)$$

$M(H_2O)_3(OH)_3$ is in effect $M(OH)_3$, which is uncharged and insoluble and forms as a precipitate.

In the case of M^{2+}

$$[M(H_2O)_6]^{2+}(aq) + OH^-(aq) \longrightarrow [M(H_2O)_5(OH)]^{+}(aq) + H_2O(l)$$

$$[M(H_2O)_5(OH)]^{+}(aq) + OH^-(aq) \longrightarrow M(H_2O)_4(OH)_2(s) + H_2O(l)$$

The neutral metal hydroxide, $M(H_2O)_4(OH)_2$, is in effect $M(OH)_2$, which is uncharged and insoluble and forms a precipitate.

Link

You will need to understand bond polarity studied in *AQA AS Chemistry*, Topic 3.3, and equilibria in this book, Topic 2.1.

Ammonia, which is basic, has the same effect as OH^- ions in removing protons.

Reactions with the base CO_3^{2-}, the carbonate ion

The greater acidity of the aqueous Fe^{3+} ion explains why iron(III) carbonate does not exist, but iron(II) carbonate does. The carbonate ion is abe to remove protons from$[Fe(H_2O)_6]^{3+}$(aq) to form hydrated iron(III) hydroxide but cannot do so from $[Fe(H_2O)_6]^{2+}$(aq).

$$[Fe(H_2O)_6]^{3+}(aq) + 3CO_3^{2-}(aq) \rightleftharpoons Fe(OH)_3(H_2O)_3(s) + 3HCO_3^-(aq)$$

The overall reaction is:

$$2[Fe(H_2O)_6]^{3+}(aq) + 3CO_3^{2-}(aq) \longrightarrow 2[Fe(H_2O)_3(OH)_3](aq) + 3CO_2(g) + 3H_2O(l)$$

The reaction can be derived as a combination of the following:

$$2H_3O^+(aq) + CO_3^{2-}(aq) \longrightarrow 3H_2O(l) + CO_2(g)$$

with the removal of H_3O^+ displacing the hydrolysis equilibrium below to the right.

$$[Fe(H_2O)_6]^{3+}(aq) + 3H_2O(l) \rightleftharpoons Fe(H_2O)_3(OH)_3(s) + 3H_3O^+(aq)$$

In the case of the aqueous Fe^{2+} ion, which is less acidic than Fe^{3+}(aq), insoluble iron(II) carbonate is formed:

$$[Fe(H_2O)_5]^{2+}(aq) + CO_3^{2-}(aq) \longrightarrow FeCO_3(s) + 6H_2O(l)$$

In general, carbonates of transition metal ions in oxidation state +2 exist, while those of ions in the +3 state do not.

Tests for iron ions

As we have seen, both Fe^{2+} and Fe^{3+} exist in aqueous solution as octahedral hexa-aqua ions. $[Fe(H_2O)_6]^{2+}$ is pale green and $[Fe(H_2O)_6]^{3+}$ is pale brown, and dilute solutions are hard to tell apart. A simple test to distinguish the two is to add dilute alkali, which precipitates the hydroxides whose colours are more obviously different.

$$[Fe(H_2O)_6]^{2+}(aq) + 2OH^-(aq) \longrightarrow \underset{\text{iron(II) hydroxide (green)}}{Fe(H_2O)_4(OH)_2(s)} + 2H_2O(l)$$

$$[Fe(H_2O)_6]^{3+}(aq) + 3OH^-(aq) \longrightarrow \underset{\text{iron(III) hydroxide (brown)}}{Fe(H_2O)_3(OH)_3(s)} + 3H_2O(l)$$

Amphoteric hydroxides

Amphoteric means 'showing both acidic and basic properties'. Aluminium hydroxide is an example of this – it will react with both acids and bases. For example:

$$Al(H_2O)_3(OH)_3 + 3HCl \longrightarrow Al(H_2O)_6^{3+} + 3Cl^-$$

is what we would expect from a normal metal hydroxide – it reacts with acid and is therefore basic.

But aluminium hydroxide also shows acidic properties: it will react with the base sodium hydroxide to give a colourless solution of sodium tetrahydroxoaluminate:

$$Al(H_2O)_3(OH)_3 + OH^- \longrightarrow [Al(OH)_4]^- + 3H_2O$$

Chromium hydroxide, $Cr(OH)_3$, shows similar amphoteric properties:

$$Cr(H_2O)_3(OH)_3 + 3H_3O^+ \rightleftharpoons [Cr(H_2O)_6]^{3+} + 3H_2O$$

$$Cr(H_2O)_3(OH)_3 + 3OH^- \rightleftharpoons [Cr(OH)_6]^{3-} + 3H_2O$$

AQA Examiner's tip

An excess of a strong base, e.g. NaOH, is needed to redissolve the $Al(H_2O)_3(OH)_3$ and $Cr(H_2O)_3(OH)_3$ precipitates.

Anionic transition metal compounds

In most of the transition metal compounds discussed above, the metal exists in a cationic (positive ion) form. In high oxidation states, some metals exist in anionic (negative ion) form. Examples include manganese, which exists as MnO_4^- ions, and chromium which exists as both CrO_4^- and $Cr_2O_7^{2-}$ in aqueous solution. The bonding within these ions is essentially covalent. The structures of the chromate and dichromate ions are shown in Figure 2.

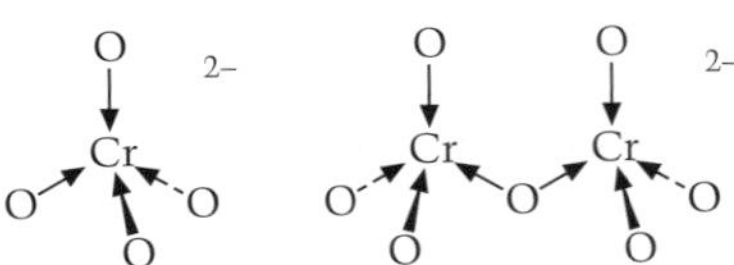

The chromate(VI) ion The dichromate(VI) ion

Figure 2 *Chromate and dichromate ions*

The dichromate ion has an oxygen atom that forms a bridge between two chromiums. The orange $Cr_2O_7^{2-}$ ion is stable in acid solution and the yellow CrO_4^- ion in alkalis as shown by the equilibrium:

$$\underset{\text{yellow}}{2CrO_4^{2-}(aq)} + 2H^+(aq) \rightleftharpoons \underset{\text{orange}}{Cr_2O_7^{2-}(aq)} + H_2O(l)$$

Summary questions

1 What are the oxidation states of the metal atoms in these ions?

a MnO_4^-

b CrO_4^{2-}

c $Cr_2O_7^{2-}$

2 Classify the reaction:

$CrO_4^{2-}(aq) + 2H^+(aq) \rightleftharpoons Cr_2O_7^{2-}(aq) + H_2O(l)$

as redox or acid–base. Explain your answer.

16.2 Ligand substitution reactions

Learning objectives:

- What are the changes in the co-ordination numbers and charges of complexes when different ligands are substituted?
- Why are the complexes formed with multidentate ligands more stable than those with monodentate ligands?

Specification reference: 3.5.5

Link

You will need to understand free energy change and entropy studied in Topic 12.5.

AQA Examiner's tip

Because NH_3 and H_2O ligands are similar in size and both are uncharged, ligand exchange occurs without a change in charge or coordination number.

The water molecules that act as ligands in metal aqua ions can be replaced by other ligands – either because the other ligands form stronger co-ordinate bonds (are better Lewis bases) or because they are present in higher concentration and an equilibrium is displaced.

Replacing water as a ligand

There are a number of possibilities:

- The water molecules may be replaced by other neutral ligands, such as ammonia.
- The water molecules may be replaced by negatively charged ligands, such as chloride ions.
- The water molecules may be replaced by bi- or multidentate ligands – this is called **chelation**.
- Replacement of the water ligands may be complete or partial.

Here are some examples:

In general for an M^{2+} ion, water molecules may be replaced one at a time by ammonia. Both ligands are uncharged and are of similar size, so there is no change in co-ordination number or charge on the ion:

$$[M(H_2O)_6]^{2+} + NH_3 \rightleftharpoons [M(NH_3)(H_2O)_5]^{2+} + H_2O$$
$$[M(NH_3)(H_2O)_5]^{2+} + NH_3 \rightleftharpoons [M(NH_3)_2(H_2O)_4]^{2+} + H_2O$$
$$[M(NH_3)_2(H_2O)_4]^{2+} + NH_3 \rightleftharpoons [M(NH_3)_3(H_2O)_3]^{2+} + H_2O$$
$$[M(NH_3)_3(H_2O)_3]^{2+} + NH_3 \rightleftharpoons [M(NH_3)_4(H_2O)_2]^{2+} + H_2O$$
$$[M(NH_3)_4(H_2O)_2]^{2+} + NH_3 \rightleftharpoons [M(NH_3)_5(H_2O)]^{2+} + H_2O$$
$$[M(NH_3)_5(H_2O)]^{2+} + NH_3 \rightleftharpoons [M(NH_3)_6]^{2+} + H_2O$$

Overall:

$$[M(H_2O)_6]^{2+} + 6NH_3 \rightleftharpoons [M(NH_3)_6]^{2+} + 6H_2O$$

There is a complication, because ammonia is a base as well as a ligand and therefore contains OH^- ions.

$$[M(H_2O)_6]^{2+} + 2OH^-(aq) \longrightarrow M(H_2O)_4(OH)_2(s) + 2H_2O(l)$$
$$M(H_2O)_4(OH)_2(s) + 6NH_3(aq) \rightleftharpoons [M(NH_3)_6]^{2+}(aq) + 4H_2O(l) + 2OH^-(aq)$$

Cobalt(II)

When M is cobalt, Co, the first step is the formation of a blue precipitate of hydrated cobalt (II) hydroxide. This is produced by the loss of a proton from each of two of the six water molecules co-ordinated to the Co^{2+} ion:

$$[Co(H_2O)_6]^{2+} + 2NH_3(aq) \longrightarrow \underset{\text{hydrated cobalt(II) hydroxide}}{[Co(H_2O)_4(OH)_2]}$$

Here ammonia is acting as a base.

Hint

Ammonia is a better ligand than water because the lone pair on the nitrogen atom of ammonia is less strongly held than that on the more electronegative oxygen atom of water. It is therefore more readily donated to the Co^{2+}.

Figure 1 *Solutions of (a) $[Cu(H_2O)_6]^{2+}$ and (b) $[Cu(NH_3)_4(H_2O)_2]^{2+}$*

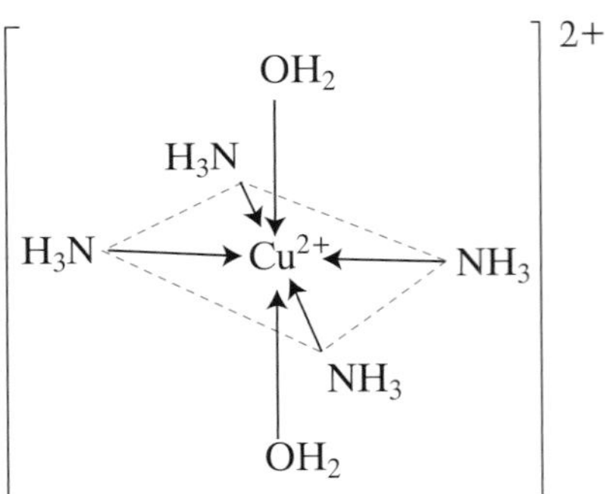

Figure 2 *The shape of the $[Cu(NH_3)_4(H_2O)_2]^{2+}$ ion. The dotted lines are not bonds, they are construction lines to show the square-planar arrangement of the NH_3 ligands*

AQA Examiner's tip

The concentration of chloride ions in saturated NaCl(aq) is insufficient to displace this equilibrium to form $[CuCl_4]^{2-}$.

If we add more of the concentrated ammonia, then both OH^- and all four water ligands are replaced by ammonia. This is for two reasons:

1 Ammonia is a better ligand than water.

2 The high concentration of ammonia displaces equilibria like those above to the right, thus displacing water and OH^-.

Overall:

$$[Co(H_2O)_4(OH)_2](s) + 6NH_3(aq) \rightleftharpoons [Co(NH_3)_6]^{2+}(aq) + 4H_2O(l) + 2OH^-(aq)$$

The blue precipitate dissolves to form a pale yellow solution (which is oxidised by oxygen in air to a brown mixture containing Co(III).

Copper(II)

When aqueous copper ions react with ammonia in aqueous solution, ligand replacement is only partial – only four of the water ligands are replaced. The overall reaction is:

$$[Cu(H_2O)_6]^{2+} + 4NH_3 \rightleftharpoons [Cu(NH_3)_4(H_2O)_2]^{2+} + 4H_2O$$

$[Cu(H_2O)_6]^{2+}$ is pale blue – the well-known colour of copper sulfate solution – while $[Cu(NH_3)_4(H_2O)_2]^{2+}$ is a very deep blue, see Figure 1.

The steps are similar to those above for Co^{2+}. The ammonia first acts as a base removing protons from two of the water molecules in $[Cu(H_2O)_6]^{2+}$to form $[Cu(OH)_2(H_2O)_4](s)$. The first thing we see is a pale blue precipitate of copper hydroxide. When we add more of the concentrated ammonia, the precipitate dissolves to form a deep blue solution containing $[Cu(NH_3)_4(H_2O)_2]^{2+}$ .The ammonia has replaced both OH^- ligands, and two of the H_2O ligands:

$$[Cu(OH)_2(H_2O)_4](s) + 4NH_3(aq) \rightleftharpoons [Cu(NH_3)_4(H_2O)_2]^{2+}(aq) + 2H_2O(l) + 2OH^-(aq)$$

The shape of the $[Cu(NH_3)_4(H_2O)_2]^{2+}$ ion

The $[Cu(NH_3)_4(H_2O)_2]^{2+}$ is octahedral, as expected for a six co-ordinate ion. The four ammonia molecules exist in a square planar arrangement around the metal ion with the two water molecules above and below the plane, see Figure 2.

The Cu—O bonds are longer, and therefore weaker, than the Cu—N bonds, as would be expected, as water is a poorer ligand than ammonia. The octahedron is slightly distorted.

Change in co-ordination number

When we react aqueous copper ions with concentrated hydrochloric acid there is a change in both charge and co-ordination number. Concentrated hydrochloric acid provides a high concentration of Cl^- ligands:

$$[Cu(H_2O)_6]^{2+} + 4Cl^- \rightleftharpoons [CuCl_4]^{2-} + 6H_2O$$

The pale blue colour of the $[Cu(H_2O)_6]^{2+}$ ion is replaced by the yellow $[CuCl_4]$ ion. (Although the solution may look green as some $[Cu(H_2O)_6]^{2+}$ will remain.) Again, the actual replacement takes place in steps. The co-ordination number of the ion is four and the ion is tetrahedral.

$[Cu(H_2O)_6]^{2+}$ is six co-ordinate and $[CuCl_4]^{2-}$ is four co-ordinate, see Figure 3, because Cl^- is larger than H_2O and fewer ligands can physically fit around the central copper ion.

There are some further examples of ligand substitution reactions of other metal ions, both M^{2+} and M^{3+}, summarised in Topic 16.3. They illustrate the principles discussed above.

Chelation

Chelation is the formation of complexes with multidentate ligands. These are ligands with more than one lone pair so that they can form more than one co-ordinate bond. Examples include ethylene diamine, benzene-1,2-diol and $EDTA^{4-}$, see Topic 15.2. These complexes are usually more stable than those with monodentate ligands. This increased stability is mainly due to the entropy change of the reaction.

Ethylene diamine (often represented as 'en' for short) is a bidentate ligand and can be thought of as two ammonia ligands linked by a short hydrocarbon chain. Each en can replace two water molecules:

$$\underset{\text{4 entities}}{[Cu(H_2O)_6]^{2+}(aq) + 3en} \longrightarrow \underset{\text{7 entities}}{[Cu(en)_3]^{2+}(aq) + 6H_2O(l)}$$

In this reaction, *three* molecules of ethylene diamine release *six* of water. The larger number of entities on the right in this reaction means that there is a significant entropy increase as the reaction goes from left to right. This favours the reaction (see Topic 12.5).

A single hexadentate ligand EDTA can displace all six water ligands from $[M(H_2O)_6]^{2+}$.For example:

$$\underset{\text{2 entities}}{[Cu(H_2O)_6]^{2+}(aq) + EDTA^{4-}(aq)} \longrightarrow \underset{\text{7 entities}}{[CuEDTA]^{2-}(aq) + 6H_2O(l)}$$

In this reaction, *one* ion of $EDTA^{4-}$ releases *six* of water. The larger number of entities on the right in this reaction means that there is a significant entropy increase as the reaction goes from left to right. This entropy increase favours the formation of chelates (complexes with polydentate ligands) over complexes with monodentate ligands.

Hint

Practise writing equations for the step-by-step replacement of one ligand with another. They are straightforward but can be tedious, and it is easy to make mistakes with charges. Make sure each step balances for both ligands and charge.

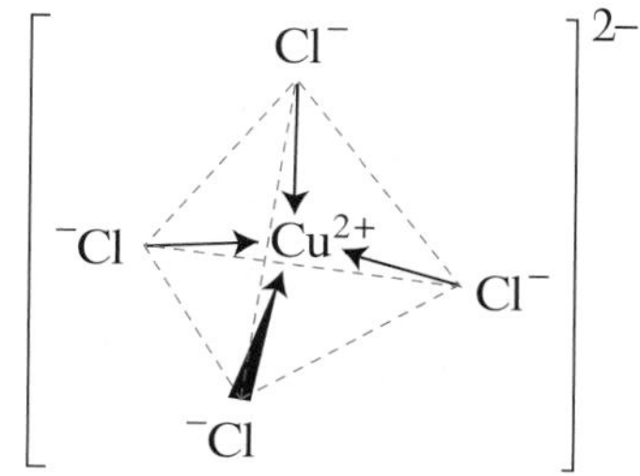

Figure 3 *The shape of the $[CuCl_4]^{2-}$ ion*

Summary questions

1 In the stepwise conversion of $[Cu(H_2O)_6]^{2+}$ to $[CuCl_4]^{2-}$, one of the species formed is neutral. Suggest two possible formulae that it could have.

2 a Draw the shape of $[Cu(H_2O)_6]^{2+}$ and b predict the shape of $[CuBr_4]^{2-}$. Explain your answer.

3 Write equations for the step-by-step replacement of all the water ligands in $[Cu(H_2O)_6]^{2+}$ by en. How many entities are there on each side of each equation? Predict the likely sign of the entropy change for each reaction.

4 When concentrated hydrochloric acid is added to an aqueous solution containing Co(II) ions, the following change takes place:

$[Co(H_2O)_6]^{2+} \longrightarrow [CoCl_4]^{2-}$ and the colour changes from pink to blue.

a Is there any change in the oxidation state of the cobalt?

b Give the shapes of the two ions concerned.

c Suggest two possible reasons for the colour change.

16.3 A summary of acid–base and substitution reactions of some metal ions

Learning objectives:

- What are the products of the reactions between bases and metal aqua ions?

Specification reference: 3.5.5

Link

You will need to understand co-ordinate bonding studied in *AQA AS Chemistry*, Topic 3.2.

The products of many of the reactions of transition metal compounds can be identified by their colours. The tables below show a number of examples of reactions involving different bases.

Figure 1 *Precipitates of (a) iron(II) hydroxide and (b) iron(III) hydroxide*

These tables are no substitute for carrying out these reactions yourself. You should be able to rationalise these observations using the principles explained in Topic 16.2. Note also the colours of the different transition metal species.

In each case the effect of adding the base shown on the left to solutions of aqua ions is shown in the following tables:

Notice that in the case of the M^{2+} ions, precipitates of the metal carbonates form when carbonate ions are added. In the case of the M^{3+} ions, bubbles of carbon dioxide are produced instead. This is a reflection of the greater acidity of $[M(H_2O)_6]^{3+}$ compared with $[M(H_2O)_6]^{2+}$, see Topic 16.1.

Table 1 *$M^{2+}(aq)$*

	$[Fe(H_2O)_6]^{2+}(aq)$ pale green	$[Co(H_2O)_6]^{2+}(aq)$ pink	$[Cu(H_2O)_6]^{2+}(aq)$ pale blue
OH^- little	green gelatinous ppt of $Fe(H_2O)_4(OH)_2$*	blue ppt of $Co(H_2O)_4(OH)_2$	pale blue ppt of $Cu(H_2O)_4(OH)_2$
OH^- excess	green gelatinous ppt of $Fe(H_2O)_4(OH)_2$*	blue ppt of $Co(H_2O)_4(OH)_2$	pale blue ppt of $Cu(H_2O)_4(OH)_2$
NH_3 little	green gelatinous ppt of $Fe(H_2O)_4(OH)_2$*	blue ppt of $Co(H_2O)_4(OH)_2$	pale blue ppt of $Cu(H_2O)_4(OH)_2$
NH_3 excess	green gelatinous ppt of $Fe(H_2O)_4(OH)_2$*	pale yellow-brown solution of $[Co(NH_3)_6]^{2+}$†	deep blue solution of $[Cu(NH_3)_4(H_2O)_2]^{2+}$
CO_3^{2-}	green ppt of $FeCO_3$	pink ppt of $CoCO_3$	blue-green ppt of $CuCO_3$

* Pale green $Fe(H_2O)_4(OH)_2$ is soon oxidised by air to brown $Fe(H_2O)_3(OH)_3$

† Oxidised by air to a dark brown mixture containing Co(III) compounds

Table 2 *$M^{3+}(aq)$*

	$[Fe(H_2O)_6]^{3+}(aq)$ purple/yellow/brown	**$[Al(H_2O)_6]^{3+}(aq)$ colourless**	**$[Cr(H_2O)_6]^{3+}(aq)$ ruby**
OH^- little	brown gelatinous ppt of $Fe(H_2O)_3(OH)_3$	white ppt of $Al(H_2O)_3(OH)_3$	green ppt of $Cr(H_2O)_3(OH)_3$
OH^- excess	brown gelatinous ppt of $Fe(H_2O)_3 (OH)_3$	colourless solution of $[Al(OH)_4]^-$	green solution $[Cr(OH)_6]^{3-}$
NH_3 little	brown gelatinous ppt of $Fe(H_2O)_3 (OH)_3$	white ppt of $Al(H_2O)_3(OH)_3$	green ppt of $Cr(H_2O)_3(OH)_3$
NH_3 excess	brown gelatinous ppt of $Fe((H_2O)_3 OH)_3$	white ppt of $Al(H_2O)_3(OH)_3$	purple solution of $[Cr(NH_3)_6]^{3+}$
CO_3^{2-}	brown gelatinous ppt of $Fe(H_2O)_3 (OH)_3$ + bubbles of CO_2	white ppt of $Al(H_2O)_3 (OH)_3$ + bubbles of CO_2	green ppt of $Cr(OH)_3$ + bubbles of CO_2

Summary questions

1 Why are M^{3+} aqua ions more acidic than M^{2+} aqua ions?

2 Explain why all the compounds of aluminium are colourless.

3 Explain why $[Co(H_2O)_6]^{2+}$ and $[Co(NH_3)_6]^{2+}$ both have a co-ordination number of six and have the same charge.

4 a Write the equations for the reactions of:

  i $[Fe(H_2O)_6]^{3+}(aq)$ with sodium hydroxide solution

  ii $[Cu(H_2O)_6]^{2+}(aq)$ with excess ammonia

 b What colour changes would you expect to see in **a i** and **ii**?

AQA Examination-style questions

1 Consider the reaction scheme below and answer the questions which follow.

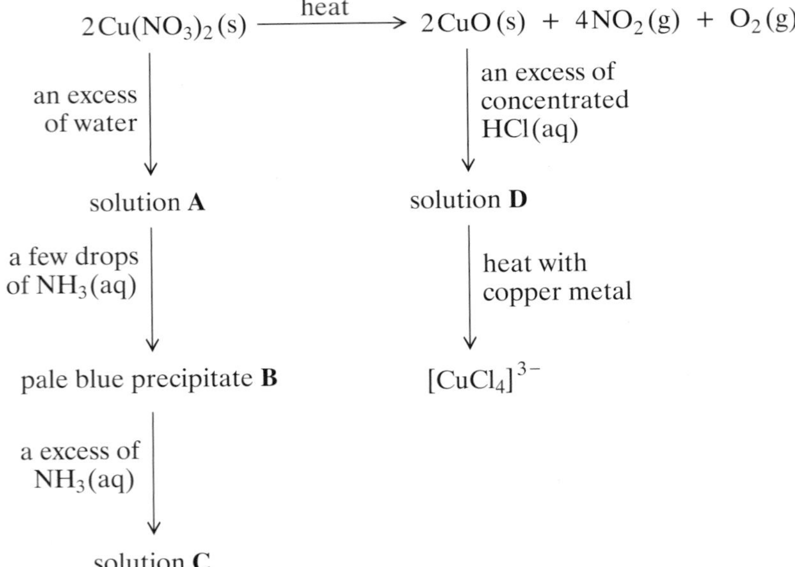

(a) A redox reaction occurs when $Cu(NO_3)_2$ is decomposed by heat. Deduce the oxidation state of nitrogen in $Cu(NO_3)_2$ and in NO_2 and identify the product formed by oxidation in this decomposition. *(3 marks)*

(b) Identify and state the shape of the copper-containing species present in solution **A**. *(2 marks)*

(c) Identify the pale blue precipitate **B** and write an equation, or equations, to show how **B** is formed from the copper-containing species in solution **A**. *(2 marks)*

(d) Identify the copper-containing species present in solution **C**. State the colour of this copper-containing species and write an equation for its formation from precipitate **B**. *(3 marks)*

(e) Identify the copper-containing species present in solution **D**. State the colour and shape of this copper-containing species. *(3 marks)*

(f) The oxidation state of copper in $[CuCl_4]^{3-}$ is +1.

(i) Give the electron arrangement of a Cu^+ ion.

(ii) Deduce the role of copper metal in the formation of $[CuCl_4]^{3-}$ from the copper-containing species in solution **D**. *(2 marks)*

AQA, 2005

2 (a) Give the electronic arrangement of the Co^{2+} ion. *(1 mark)*

(b) Give the formula of the cobalt complex present in an aqueous solution of cobalt(II) sulfate and state its colour. *(2 marks)*

(c) (i) When a large excess of concentrated aqueous ammonia is added to an aqueous solution of cobalt(II) sulfate, a new cobalt(II) complex is formed. Give the formula of the new cobalt(II) complex and state its colour.

(ii) Write an equation for the formation of this new complex. *(3 marks)*

(d) When hydrogen peroxide is added to the mixture formed in part (c), the colour of the solution darkens due to the formation of a different cobalt complex. Identify this different cobalt complex and state the role of hydrogen peroxide in its formation. *(2 marks)*

AQA, 2005

3 (a) Using complex ions formed by Co^{2+} with ligands selected from H_2O, NH_3, Cl^-, $C_2O_4^{2-}$ and $EDTA^{4-}$, give an equation for each of the following.

(i) A ligand substitution reaction which occurs with no change in either the co-ordination number or in the charge on the complex ion.

(ii) A ligand substitution reaction which occurs with both a change in the co-ordination number and in the charge on the complex ion.

(iii) A ligand substitution reaction which occurs with no change in the co-ordination number but a change in the charge on the complex ion.

(iv) A ligand substitution reaction in which there is a large change in entropy. *(8 marks)*

(b) An aqueous solution of iron(II) sulfate is a pale-green colour. When aqueous sodium hydroxide is added to this solution a green precipitate is formed. On standing in air, the green precipitate slowly turns brown.

(i) Give the formula of the complex ion responsible for the pale-green colour.

(ii) Give the formula of the green precipitate.

(iii) Suggest an explanation for the change in the colour of the precipitate. *(4 marks)*

AQA, 2004

4 (a) When aqueous ammonia was added to an aqueous solution of cobalt(II) sulfate, a blue precipitate **M** was formed. Identify the cobalt-containing species present in aqueous cobalt(II) sulfate and the precipitate M. *(2 marks)*

(b) Precipitate **M** dissolved when an excess of concentrated aqueous ammonia was added. The solution formed was pale brown due to the presence of the cobalt-containing species **P**. Identify **P**. *(1 mark)*

(c) On standing in air, the colour of the solution containing **P** slowly darkened as the cobalt-containing species **Q** was formed. State the type of reaction occurring when **P** changes into **Q** and identify the reactant responsible for this change. *(2 marks)*

(d) When potassium iodide was added to the solution containing **Q** and the mixture was acidified, a dark red-brown colour due to the presence of **R** was produced. On addition of starch solution the mixture turned blue-black.
Identify **R** and explain its formation. *(2 marks)*

AQA, 2004

5 (a) State what is observed when aqueous ammonia is added dropwise, until present in excess, to a solution of cobalt(II) chloride, and the mixture obtained is then left to stand in air.

Give the formula of each cobalt-containing species formed. Explain the change which occurs when the mixture is left to stand in air. *(8 marks)*

(b) Explain why separate solutions of iron(II) sulfate and iron(III) sulfate of equal concentration have different pH values.

State what is observed when sodium carbonate is added separately to solutions of these two compounds. Give the formula of each iron-containing species formed. *(9 marks)*

AQA, 2003

AQA Examination-style questions

Unit 5 questions: Energetics, redox and inorganic chemistry

1 Some enthalpy of vaporisation values, $\Delta H^\ominus_v$, and boiling points are given in the table below.

Substance	$\Delta H^\ominus_v$/kJ mol^{-1}	Boiling point/K
$NH_3(l)$	23.4	240
$HF(l)$	32.6	293

(a) State the equation that relates free-energy change, ΔG, to enthalpy change, ΔH, and entropy change, ΔS. *(1 mark)*

(b) Suggest why the free-energy change is equal to zero ($\Delta G = 0$) when a liquid boils. *(1 mark)*

(c) Use data from the table above to calculate the standard entropy change, in J K^{-1} mol^{-1}, when liquid ammonia boils. *(2 marks)*

(d) Explain in terms of intermolecular forces why the enthalpy of vaporisation for liquid hydrogen fluoride is greater than that for liquid ammonia. *(3 marks)*

AQA, 2008

2 Some data required for this question are given in the table below.

Substance	$\Delta H^\ominus_f$/kJ mol^{-1}	$S^\ominus$/J K^{-1} mol^{-1}
$NH_3(g)$	–46.2	193
$N_2(g)$	0	192
$H_2(g)$	0	131

(a) Write an equation to represent the formation of one mole of ammonia from its elements. *(1 mark)*

(b) Using data from the table above calculate the entropy change for the formation of one mole of ammonia from its elements. *(3 marks)*

(c) (i) Use your answer from part (b) and data from the table to calculate the value of the free-energy change, ΔG, for the formation of one mole of ammonia from its elements at 700 K. (If you have been unable to calculate an answer to part (b), you may assume that the entropy change for the formation of one mole of ammonia from its elements is –125 J K^{-1} mol^{-1}. This is not the correct value.)

(ii) Predict in qualitative terms what would happen to the value of ΔG at temperatures lower than 700 K. *(3 marks)*

(d) Suggest one advantage, in industry, of operating this reaction at temperatures higher than 700 K. *(1 mark)*

AQA, 2008

3 (a) The cell shown below can be used to measure the electrode potential of magnesium.

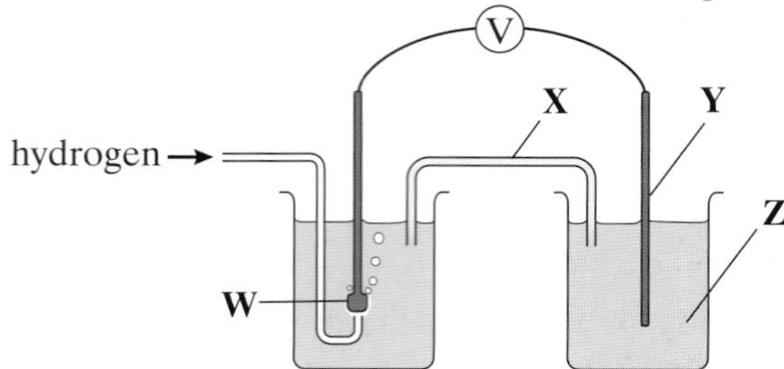

(i) Identify possible chemical substances for **W**, **X**, **Y** and **Z** labelled in the diagram above.

(ii) Give the conventional representation for this cell (conventional cell diagram). *(6 marks)*

(b) An alkaline cell that is used to provide electricity has electrodes which can be represented by the following half-equations. The zinc electrode is the negative electrode.

$$Zn^{2+} + 2e^- \longrightarrow Zn \qquad E = -0.76\,V$$

$$MnO_2 + H_2O + e^- \longrightarrow MnO(OH) + OH^- \qquad E \text{ is to be determined}$$

(i) The e.m.f. of this cell is 1.60 V. Calculate a value for the electrode potential of the manganese oxide electrode.

(ii) Deduce the oxidation state of manganese in MnO(OH)

(iii) Write an equation for the overall cell reaction.

(iv) Identify the oxidising agent and the reducing agent in this alkaline cell.

(v) Give one reason why the e.m.f. of the cell decreases to a very low value after the cell has been used for a long time. *(6 marks)*

(c) A redox reaction occurs when concentrated sulfuric acid reacts with solid potassium bromide.

(i) Write half-equations and an overall equation for this reaction.

(ii) Give one reason why a redox reaction does not occur when concentrated sulfuric acid is mixed with solid potassium chloride.

Write an equation for the reaction that **does** occur. *(5 marks)*

AQA, 2008

4 Iodide ions are oxidised to iodine by peroxodisulfate ions, $S_2O_8^{2-}$. The reaction can be catalysed by Fe^{2+}(aq) ions and by Fe^{3+}(aq) ions.

In an experiment to investigate the uncatalysed reaction, the concentration of iodine was determined at different times. Curve A shown below was obtained.

The experiment was repeated using half the original concentration of iodide ions but keeping other conditions the same. Curve B was obtained.

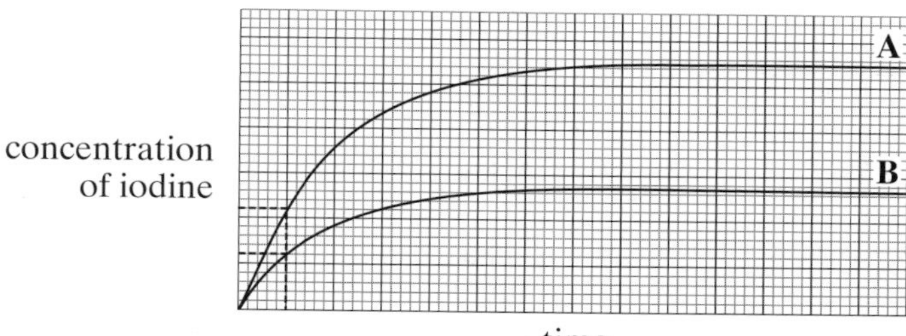

(a) Use these curves and the dotted lines to deduce the order of the reaction with respect to iodide ions. Explain how you deduced the order. *(2 marks)*

(b) On the axes above, sketch a curve to show how the results will change if the experiment leading to curve **B** is repeated under the same conditions of concentration but at a lower temperature. Label this curve **X**. *(2 marks)*

(c) On the axes above, sketch a curve to show how the results will change if the experiment leading to curve **A** is repeated in the presence of a catalyst containing Fe^{2+}(aq) ions. Label this curve **Y**. *(2 marks)*

(d) In the oxidation of iodide ions by peroxodisulfate ions, the Fe^{2+} ions act as a catalyst in a two-step process.

(i) Write an equation for each of the two steps.

(ii) Give two reasons why the Fe^{2+} ions are regarded as a catalyst in this reaction. *(4 marks)*

(e) Silver is used as a heterogeneous catalyst for the exothermic process illustrated by the following equation.

$$H_2C{=}CH_2 + \tfrac{1}{2}O_2 \longrightarrow H_2C{-}CH_2 \text{ (epoxide ring, O bridging both C)}$$

(i) Explain the meaning of the term *heterogeneous* as applied to the silver catalyst.

(ii) Give one reason why silver is a poor heterogeneous catalyst.

(iii) Explain why it is **not** desirable to use a very effective catalyst for this reaction. *(4 marks)*

AQA, 2008

5 The tables below contain some data about aqueous solutions.

	Na^+	Mg^{2+}	Al^{3+}	Cl^-
Enthalpy of hydration, $\Delta H^{\ominus}_{hyd}$/kJ mol^{-1}	–406	–1920	–4690	–364

	NaCl	$MgCl_2$
Enthalpy of solution, $\Delta H^{\ominus}_{sol}$/kJ mol^{-1}	+3.9	–155

(a) Use these data to calculate the lattice enthalpy of dissociation of sodium chloride and of magnesium chloride. *(3 marks)*

(b) Explain why the lattice enthalpy of dissociation of sodium chloride is less than that of magnesium chloride. *(2 marks)*

(c) Suggest why the enthalpy of hydration of aluminium ions is much more exothermic than that for magnesium ions. *(2 marks)*

(d) Aqueous solutions of $AlCl_3$ are acidic.

$$[Al(H_2O)_6]^{3+}(aq) \rightleftharpoons [Al(H_2O)_5(OH)]^{2+}(aq) + H^+(aq)$$

The acid dissociation constant for this reaction, $K_a = 1.26 \times 10^{-5}$ mol dm^{-3}.
Calculate the pH of a 2.0 mol dm^{-3} solution of $AlCl_3$ *(4 marks)*

(e) Write an equation for the reaction that occurs when silicon tetrachloride is added to water. Predict the pH of the resulting solution. *(2 marks)*

AQA, 2008

6 Consider the incomplete Born–Haber cycle and the table of data below.

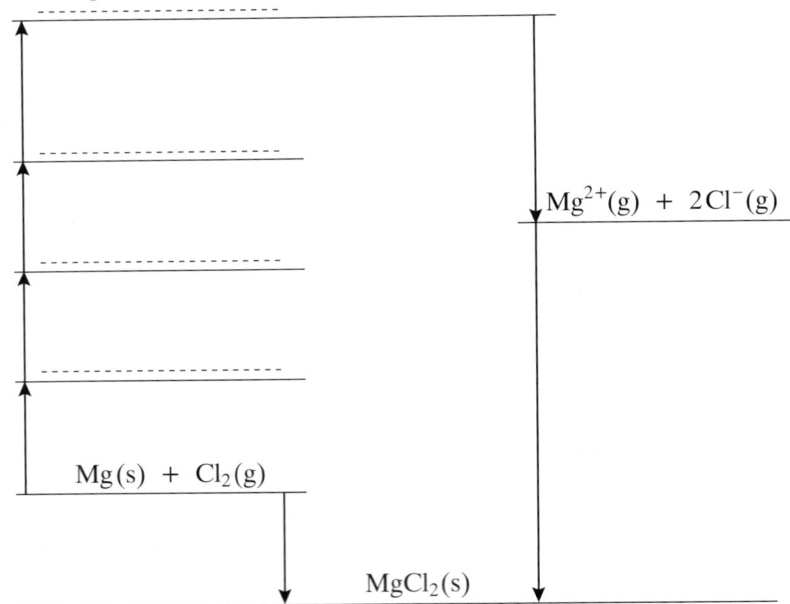

Name of standard enthalpy change	Substance to which enthalpy change refers	Value of enthalpy change /kJ mol^{-1}
Enthalpy of atomisation	chlorine	+121
Enthalpy of atomisation	magnesium	+150
Enthalpy of formation	magnesium chloride	–642
First ionisation enthalpy	magnesium	+736
Electron affinity	chlorine	–364
Enthalpy of lattice formation	magnesium chloride	–2493

(a) Copy and complete the Born–Haber cycle above by writing the appropriate chemical formulae, with state symbols, on the dotted lines. *(4 marks)*

(b) Use the cycle and the values given in the table to calculate the second ionisation enthalpy of magnesium. *(3 marks)*

(c) The standard enthalpies of hydration of the Mg^{2+} and the Cl^- ions are $-1920\,kJ\,mol^{-1}$ and $-364\,kJ\,mol^{-1}$, respectively. Use this information and data from the table in part (a) to calculate the enthalpy of solution of magnesium chloride. *(3 marks)*

(d) The standard enthalpy of solution of ammonium chloride, $NH_4^+Cl^-$, is $+15\,kJ\,mol^{-1}$.

(i) Explain why ammonium chloride dissolves spontaneously in water even though this process is endothermic. *(2 marks)*

(ii) A 2.0 g sample of ammonium chloride is dissolved in 50 g of water. Both substances are initially at 20 °C.

Calculate the temperature change and the final temperature of the solution.

Assume that the specific heat capacity of the solution is $4.2\,J\,K^{-1}\,g^{-1}$. *(5 marks)*

AQA, 2007

7 (a) Give the meaning of the term *electronegativity*. *(2 marks)*

(b) State and explain the trend in electronegativity across Period 3 from Na to Cl. *(3 marks)*

(c) (i) Name the main type of bonding in each of the oxides MgO and P_4O_{10}

(ii) Explain how the type of bonding in P_4O_{10} can be predicted by a consideration of electronegativity. *(3 marks)*

(d) Write equations for the reaction of Na_2O and of SO_2 with water. *(2 marks)*

(e) Write an equation for the reaction of MgO with dilute hydrochloric acid. *(1 mark)*

(f) Write an equation for the reaction of P_4O_{10} with an excess of aqueous sodium hydroxide. *(1 mark)*

AQA, 2007

8 One characteristic property of transition metals is variable oxidation state.

(a) For each of the following processes, write two equations to show how the transition metal catalyst reacts and is reformed. Identify the different oxidation states shown by the transition metal catalyst in each process.

(i) the Contact Process catalysed by vanadium(V) oxide

(ii) the oxidation of ethanedioate ions by acidified potassium manganate(VII), autocatalysed by $Mn^{2+}(aq)$ ions. *(6 marks)*

(b) Cobalt(II) ions cannot easily be oxidised to cobalt(III) ions in water. Suggest why this oxidation can be carried out in aqueous ammonia and identify a suitable oxidising agent. *(3 marks)*

(c) Metal ions $\mathbf{Q}^{2+}$ in acidified aqueous solution can be oxidised by aqueous potassium dichromate(VI).

In a titration, an acidified $25.0\,cm^3$ sample of a $0.140\,mol\,dm^{-3}$ solution of $\mathbf{Q}^{2+}(aq)$ required $29.2\,cm^3$ of a $0.040\,mol\,dm^{-3}$ solution of potassium dichromate(VI) for complete reaction.

Determine the oxidation state of the metal **Q** after reaction with the potassium dichromate(VI). *(6 marks)*

AQA, 2007

9 (a) The compounds CH_3CH_2Cl and CH_3CHCl_2 can be distinguished by comparing their proton nmr spectra.

For each compound, describe its proton nmr spectrum by giving the number of peaks, the integration ratio and the splitting patterns. *(6 marks)*

(b) The following pairs of compounds can be distinguished using the reagents indicated.

Each compound is in a separate aqueous solution. For each one of the compounds, describe what you would observe and write equations for any reactions that occur.

(i) KBr and KI using chlorine water

(ii) $BaCl_2$ and $MgCl_2$ using dilute sulfuric acid

(iii) $CoCl_2$ and $CuCl_2$ using concentrated hydrochloric acid *(9 marks)*

AQA, 2007

Data

Table 1 *Infra-red absorption data*

Bond	Wavenumber / cm^{-1}
N—H (amines)	3300–3500
O—H (alcohols)	3230–3550
C—H	2850–3300
O—H (acids)	2500–3000
C≡N	2220–2260
C=O	1680–1750
C=C	1620–1680
C—O	1000–1300
C—C	750–1100

Table 2 *^{1}H nmr chemical shift data*

Type of proton	δ / ppm
RO**H**	0.5–5.0
$RC\mathbf{H}_3$	0.7–1.2
$RN\mathbf{H}_2$	1.0–4.5
$R_2C\mathbf{H}_2$	1.2–1.4
$R_3C\mathbf{H}$	1.4–1.6
R—C(=O)—C—**H**	2.1–2.6
R—O—C—**H**	3.1–3.9
$RC\mathbf{H}_2Cl$ or Br	3.1–4.2
R—C(=O)—O—C—**H**	3.7–4.1
R(**H**)C=C	4.5–6.0
R—C(=O)—**H**	9.0–10.0
R—C(=O)—O—**H**	10.0–12.0

Table 3 *^{13}C nmr chemical shift data*

Type of carbon	δ / ppm
—**C**—**C**—	5–40
R—**C**—Cl or Br	10–70
R—C(=O)—**C**—	20–50
R—**C**—N	25–60
—**C**—O— alcohols, ethers or esters	50–90
C=**C**	90–150
R—**C**≡N	110–125
benzene ring	110–160
R—**C**(=O)— esters or acids	160–185
R—**C**(=O)— aldehydes or ketones	190–220

The Periodic Table of the Elements

Key

relative atomic mass
atomic symbol
name
atomic (proton) number

1	2											3	4	5	6	7	0
(1)	(2)	(3)	(4)	(5)	(6)	(7)	(8)	(9)	(10)	(11)	(12)	(13)	(14)	(15)	(16)	(17)	(18)
							1.0 **H** hydrogen 1										4.0 **He** helium 2
6.9 **Li** lithium 3	9.0 **Be** beryllium 4											10.8 **B** boron 5	12.0 **C** carbon 6	14.0 **N** nitrogen 7	16.0 **O** oxygen 8	19.0 **F** fluorine 9	20.2 **Ne** neon 10
23.0 **Na** sodium 11	24.3 **Mg** magnesium 12											27.0 **Al** aluminium 13	28.1 **Si** silicon 14	31.0 **P** phosphorus 15	32.1 **S** sulfur 16	35.5 **Cl** chlorine 17	39.9 **Ar** argon 18
39.1 **K** potassium 19	40.1 **Ca** calcium 20	45.0 **Sc** scandium 21	47.9 **Ti** titanium 22	50.9 **V** vanadium 23	52.0 **Cr** chromium 24	54.9 **Mn** manganese 25	55.8 **Fe** iron 26	58.9 **Co** cobalt 27	58.7 **Ni** nickel 28	63.5 **Cu** copper 29	65.4 **Zn** zinc 30	69.7 **Ga** gallium 31	72.6 **Ge** germanium 32	74.9 **As** arsenic 33	79.0 **Se** selenium 34	79.9 **Br** bromine 35	83.8 **Kr** krypton 36
85.5 **Rb** rubidium 37	87.6 **Sr** strontium 38	88.9 **Y** yttrium 39	91.2 **Zr** zirconium 40	92.9 **Nb** niobium 41	95.9 **Mo** molybdenum 42	[98] **Tc** technetium 43	101.1 **Ru** ruthenium 44	102.9 **Rh** rhodium 45	106.4 **Pd** palladium 46	107.9 **Ag** silver 47	112.4 **Cd** cadmium 48	114.8 **In** indium 49	118.7 **Sn** tin 50	121.8 **Sb** antimony 51	127.6 **Te** tellurium 52	126.9 **I** iodine 53	131.3 **Xe** xenon 54
132.9 **Cs** caesium 55	137.3 **Ba** barium 56	138.9 **La*** lanthanum 57	178.5 **Hf** hafnium 72	180.9 **Ta** tantalum 73	183.8 **W** tungsten 74	186.2 **Re** rhenium 75	190.2 **Os** osmium 76	192.2 **Ir** iridium 77	195.1 **Pt** platinum 78	197.0 **Au** gold 79	200.6 **Hg** mercury 80	204.4 **Tl** thallium 81	207.2 **Pb** lead 82	209.0 **Bi** bismuth 83	[209] **Po** polonium 84	[210] **At** astatine 85	[222] **Rn** radon 86
[223] **Fr** francium 87	[226] **Ra** radium 88	[227] **Ac†** actinium 89	[261] **Rf** rutherfordium 104	[262] **Db** dubnium 105	[266] **Sg** seaborgium 106	[264] **Bh** bohrium 107	[277] **Hs** hassium 108	[268] **Mt** meitnerium 109	[271] **Ds** darmstadtium 110	[272] **Rg** roentgenium 111	Elements with atomic numbers 112-116 have been reported but not fully authenticated						

* **58 – 71** Lanthanides	140.1 **Ce** cerium 58	140.9 **Pr** praseodymium 59	144.2 **Nd** neodymium 60	144.9 **Pm** promethium 61	150.4 **Sm** samarium 62	152.0 **Eu** europium 63	157.3 **Gd** gadolinium 64	158.9 **Tb** terbium 65	162.5 **Dy** dysprosium 66	164.9 **Ho** holmium 67	167.3 **Er** erbium 68	168.9 **Tm** thulium 69	173.0 **Yb** ytterbium 70	175.0 **Lu** lutetium 71
† **90 – 103** Actinides	232.0 **Th** thorium 90	231.0 **Pa** protactinium 91	238.0 **U** uranium 92	237.0 **Np** neptunium 93	239.1 **Pu** plutonium 94	243.1 **Am** americium 95	247.1 **Cm** curium 96	247.1 **Bk** berkelium 97	252.1 **Cf** californium 98	[252] **Es** einsteinium 99	[257] **Fm** fermium 100	[258] **Md** mendelevium 101	[259] **No** nobelium 102	[260] **Lr** lawrencium 103

Glossary

A

Acid: Brønsted–Lowry: a proton donor.; Lewis: an electron pair acceptor.

Acid derivative: An organic compound related to a carboxylic acid of formula RCOZ, where Z = —Cl, —NHR, —OR or —OCOR.

Allotropes: Pure elements which can exist in different physical forms in which their atoms are arranged differently. For example diamond, graphite and buckminsterfullerene are allotropes of carbon.

B

Base: Brønsted–Lowry: a proton acceptor; Lewis: an electron pair donor.

Base peak: The peak representing the ion of greatest abundance (the tallest peak) in a mass spectrum.

Buffer: A solution that resists change of pH when small amounts of acid or base are added or on dilution.

C

Carbocation: An organic ion in which one of the carbon atoms has a positive charge.

Chiral: This means 'handed'. A chiral molecule exists in two mirror image forms that are not superimposable.

Chiral centre: An atom to which four different atoms or groups are bonded. The presence of such an atom causes the parent molecule to exist as a pair of non-superimposable mirror images.

Chelation: The process by which a multidentate ligand replaces a monodentate ligand in forming co-ordinate (dative) bonds to a transition metal ion.

Co-ordinate bond: A covalent bond in which both the electrons in the bond come from one of the atoms forming the bond. (Also called a dative bond.)

Co-ordination number: The number of atoms bonded to a metal ion.

D

Delocalisation: Describes the process by which electrons are spread over several atoms and help bond them together.

E

Electrophile: An electron-deficient atom, ion or molecule that takes part in an organic reaction by attacking areas of high electron density in another reactant.

Enantiomer: One of a pair of non-superimposable mirror image isomers

End point: The point in a titration when the volume of reactant added just causes the colour of the indicator to change.

Entropy: A numerical measure of disorder in a chemical system

Equivalence point: The point in a titration at which the reaction is just complete.

F

Fatty acid: A long-chain carboxylic acid.

Fingerprint region: The area of an infra-red spectrum below about 1500 cm^{-1}. It is caused by complex vibrations of the whole molecule and is characteristic of a particular molecule.

H

Hydration: A reaction in which water is added.

Hydrolysis: A reaction of a compound or ion with water.

I

Inductive effect: The electron-releasing effect of alkyl groups such as $—CH_3$ or $—C_2H_5$.

L

Ligand: An atom, ion or molecule that forms a co-ordinate (dative) bond with a transition metal ion using a lone pair of electrons.

M

Molecular ion: In mass spectrometry this is a molecule of the sample which has been ionised by the loss of one electron but which has not broken up during its flight through the instrument.

Monomer: A small molecule that combines with many other monomers to form a polymer.

N

Nucleophile: A negative ion or molecule that is able to donate a pair of electrons and takes part in an organic reaction by attacking an electron-deficient area in another reactant.

O

Order of reaction: In the rate expression, this is the sum of the powers to which the concentrations of all the species involved in the reaction are raised. If rate = $k[A]^a[B]^b$, the overall order of the reaction is $a + b$.

Oxidising agent: A reagent that oxidises (removes electrons from) another species.

P

pH: A scale for measuring acidity and alkalinity. pH = $-\log_{10}[H^+]$ in a solution.

Protonated: Describes an atom, molecule or ion to which a proton (an H^+ ion) has been added.

R

Rate constant: The constant of proportionality in the rate expression.

Rate determining step: The slowest step in the reaction mechanism. It governs the rate of the overall reaction.

Rate expression: A mathematical expression showing how the rate of a chemical reaction depends on the concentrations of various chemical species involved.

Reaction mechanism: The series of simple steps that lead from reactants to products in a chemical reaction.

Reducing agent: A reagent that reduces (adds electrons to) another species.

Strong acid: An acid that is almost fully dissociated into ions in solution.

Triglyceride: An ester formed between glycerol (propane-1,2,3-triol) and three fatty acid molecules.

Weak acid: An acid that is only slightly dissociated into ions in solution.

Answers to summary questions

1.1

1 A reactant – its concentration decreases with time.

2 1.3×10^{-3} mol dm^{-3} s^{-1} to 2 sf

3 The rate of reaction after 300 seconds.

4 That at time 0 seconds, the gradient will be steeper than that at time 600 seconds.

5 The rate of reaction at the beginning is greatest as the concentration of reactants is greatest here and then decreases as reactants are used up.

1.2

1 rate = k[A][B][C]^2

2 a i 1 ii 1 iii 2

b i double ii double iii quadruple

c i 1 ii 5 iii 6 iv 3 v 3

d dm^9 mol^{-3} s^{-1}

3 a the rate constant

b i 2 ii 0 iii 0 iv 1

c 3

d dm^6 mol^{-2} s^{-1}

e a catalyst

4 D It is impossible to tell without experimental data.

1.3

1 a i 1 ii 2

b 3

c 27 mol dm^{-3} s^{-1}

d rate = k[A][B]^2

e No, other species might be involved that have not been investigated.

1.4

1 a B b F (and G) c Step (ii)

2.1

1 a $K_c = \frac{[C]}{[A][B]}$ b $K_c = \frac{[C]}{[A]^2[B]}$ c $K_c = \frac{[C]^2}{[A]^2[B]^2}$

2 a mol^{-1} dm^3

b mol^{-2} dm^6

c mol^{-2} dm^6

3 a 3.46 (no units)

b because it cancels out in the expression for K_c

c further to the left

2.2

1 a 1.01 mol

b 1.067 mol

c 2.067 mol

2.3

1 a i move right ii move left

b i move left ii move right

c i no effect ii move right

2 a It would increase.

b no change c no change

3.1

1 a acid: HNO_3; base: OH^-

b acid: CH_3COOH; base: H_2O

2 1×10^{-10} mol dm^{-3}

3 a H_2O b NH_4^+

c H_3O^+ d HCl

3.2

1 2.00

2 1×10^{-6} mol dm^{-3}

3 1×10^{-5} mol dm^{-3}

4 1.70

5 13.30

3.3

1 chloroethanoic acid

2 They are the same.

3 a 1.94 b 3.10

3.4

1 a

$$2NaOH(aq) + H_2SO_4(aq) \longrightarrow Na_2SO_4(aq) + 2H_2O(l)$$

b 0.50

c 1.5×10^{-3}

d 0.120 mol dm^{-3}

2 a i A ii B

b i B ii A

c Strong, as there is a rapid pH change in the alkaline region at the equivalence point.

3.5

1 b and d

2 b and d

3.6

1 a 5.07 b 4.20

4.1

1 a

```
              H
              |
           H—C—H
              |
           H—C—H
    H   H     |    H   H   H
    |   |     |    |   |   |
H—C—C—C—C—C—C—H
    |   |     |    |   |   |
    H   H     |    H   H   H
           H—C—H
              |
              H
```

b

```
                  H
                  |
               H—C—H
     H   H   H    |    H
     |   |   |    |    |
H—C—C—C—C—C—H
     |   |   |    |    |
     H   |   H    H    H
      H—C—H
         |
         H
```

2 a propan-1-ol b 2-chloropropane c hex-3-ene d ethanol e pentanoic acid

4.2

1 d

2 a *trans*-pent-2-ene or *E*-pent-2-ene

b *cis*-pent-2-ene or *Z*-pent-2-ene

3 b

4 It is the carbon to which the Cl atom is bonded.

4.3

1 a 2-hydroxybutanoic acid

```
    H   H   OH
    |   |   |
H—C—C—C—COOH
    |   |   |
    H   H   H
```

b Yes, the carbon to which the —OH group is bonded has four different groups attached to it.

2 a 2-methyl-2-hydroxypropanoic acid

```
    H   OH
    |   |
H—C—C—COOH
    |   |
    H   CH3
```

b No, it has no carbon to which four different groups are attached.

3 This carbon atom does not have four different groups attached to it.

5.1

1 a pentan-3-one b propanal

2 a A ketone must have a C=O group with two carbon-containing groups attached to it.

b The C=O group can only be on carbon 2, otherwise the compound would be an aldehyde.

c The C=O group must always be on the end of the chain.

3 A hydrogen bond requires a molecule with a hydrogen atom covalently bonded to an atom of fluorine, oxygen or nitrogen. There is no such carbon atom in propanone.

4 The hydrogen atom in an O—H group in a water molecule can hydrogen bond with the oxygen atom in the C=O bond of propanone.

5.2

1 Cl^-

2 a No

b A negatively charged nucleophile will be repelled by the high electron density in the C=C.

c

```
H          H   H   OH
  \        |   |   |
    C=C—C—C—H
  /            |   |
H              H   H
```

3

```
    H   H   H   OH
    |   |   |   |
H—C—C—C—C—H
    |   |   |   |
    H   H   H   H
```

4 The CN^- ions can attack the planar C=O group from above or below. In the case of CH_3CHO this will produce a compound with a chiral centre (four different groups attached to it). This will be a pair of optical isomers. As attack from above or below is equally likely it will be a 50:50 mixture (racemic). In the case of CH_3COCH_3, the product will not have a carbon atom with four groups attached to it. It will not therefore be chiral and will be a single compound.

5.3

1 3-bromobutanoic acid

2

```
     H    H
     |    |     O
Cl—C —C—C//
     |    |    \
     H    H     OH
```

3 The carboxylic acid must be at the end of a chain and therefore in the 1 position.

4 ethyl ethanoate; methyl propanoate

5.4

1 They react with carbonates and hydrogencarbonates to give carbon dioxide; they react with metal oxides to give salts; they react with alkalis to give salts.

2 methanol and ethanoic acid

3 ethanol and methanoic acid

4 They have the same molecular formula but have a different arrangement of their atoms in space.

5.5

Aspirin

1 $(180/240) \times 100 = 75.0\%$

2 a $HOOCC_6H_4OH + CH_3COCl \longrightarrow HOOCC_6H_4OOCCH_3 + HCl$

b HCl

c $(180/216.5) \times 100 = 83.1\%$

1 The carbon of the C=O group is strongly $C^{\delta+}$ because, as well as oxygen, it is also bonded to an electronegative Cl atom which draws electrons away from it.

2 OH^-, because it is negatively charged and contains a lone pair of electrons.

3 Because the nucleophile and the acylating agent join together and then a small molecule is lost.

4

$C_2H_5COCl + NH_3 \longrightarrow C_2H_5CONH_2 + HCl$

$C_2H_5-C^{\delta+}(=O^{\delta-})-Cl^{\delta-} + :NH_3 \longrightarrow C_2H_5-C(-O^-)(-Cl)-N^+H_3$

$C_2H_5-C(=O)-N^+H_3 + Cl^- \longrightarrow CH_3-C(=O)-NH_2 + H^+$

6.1

1 CH

2 a 3

b 4

c The ring structure of benzene has one less double bond than the early structure.

3 Six electrons are spread out over all six carbon atoms in the ring rather than being localised in three distinct double bonds.

6.2

1 van der Waals forces

2 a 1,3-dichlorobenzene b 1-bromo-4-chlorobenzene

3 a

$H_3C-C_6H_4-CH_3$ (1,4-dimethylbenzene)

b

$CH_3-C_6H_4-CH_3$ (1,2-dimethylbenzene)

4 R^+

6.3

1 a electrophilic substitution

b electrophilic substitution

2 2-dinitrobenzene and 1,4-dinitrobenzene

3 Addition reactions would involve the loss of aromatic stability.

4

$C_6H_6 + CH_3CH_2COCl \longrightarrow C_6H_5COCH_2CH_3 + HCl$

$CH_3CH_2C^+O$

7.1

1 secondary

2 ethylpropylamine

3

$H_3C-N(CH_3)-CH_3$

4 a gas

5 It has the same value of M_r as ethylamine, which is a gas.

7.2

1 a $(CH_3)_2NH + HCl \longrightarrow (CH_3)_2NH_2^+ + Cl^-$

b dimethylammonium chloride

2 a It will dissolve, i.e. the oily drops will disappear to give a colourless solution.

b The oily drops will re-appear.

3 Stronger, as it has two electron-releasing alkyl groups.

7.3

Sulfa drugs

1 4-aminobenzoic acid.

1 Because secondary and tertiary amines (and quaternary ammonium salts) may be formed as well.

2 a $CH_3CH_2Cl + 2NH_3 \longrightarrow CH_3CH_2NH_2 + NH_4Cl$

$H_3N: + CH_3-CH_2^{\delta+}-Cl^{\delta-} \longrightarrow CH_3-CH_2-N^+H_3 + Cl^-$

$CH_3-CH_2-N^+H_3 + :NH_3 \longrightarrow CH_3-CH_2-NH_2 + NH_4^+$

b $(C_2H_5)_2NH$; $(C_2H_5)_3N$; $(C_2H_5)_4N^+Cl^-$

8.1

1. 2-aminopropanoic acid
2. Carbon number 2 in alanine has four different groups attached to it.

8.2

1. a amine and carboxylic acid
   b The carboxylic acid is acidic; the amine is basic.
2. two

9.1

1. a, b and d
2. a

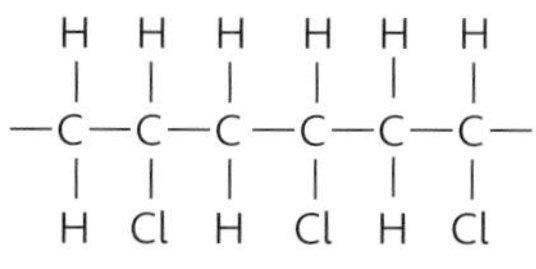

   b polyvinylchloride, PVC
   c poly(chloroethene)
3. $CF_2{=}CF_2$
4. a $CH_2{=}CHCl$

9.2

Disposal of polymers

1. R is $-\!\!\!+CH_2+\!\!\!-_6$; R' is $-\!\!\!+CH_2+\!\!\!-_4$
2. $+\!CO\text{-}R\text{-}CO\text{-}O\text{-}R'\text{-}O\!+_n + nH_2O$
   $\longrightarrow n+\!CO\text{-}R\text{-}COOH + HO\text{-}R'\text{-}O\!+$

Hermann Staudinger

1. 2-methylbuta-1,3-diene
2. Addition since it contains a —C=C— in the structure.

1. a the number of carbon atoms in each monomer
   b 1,10-diaminodecane
   $NH_2(CH_2)_{10}NH_2$
2. They also have CONH linkages.
3. any diol, for example, propane-1,3,-diol
4. a amide (peptide) b ester

10.1

1. a React with HCN.
   b React with methanol (with an acid catalyst).
   c Addition of water (by reaction with concentrated sulfuric acid followed by water).
   d Dehydrate with P_2O_5, for example.
2. a Add water (by reaction with concentrated sulfuric acid followed by water) to produce ethanol, then oxidise with $K_2Cr_2O_7/H_2SO_4$.
   b Reduce (using $NaBH_4$, for example) to propan-2-ol, then react with KBr/H_2SO_4.
3. Step 1: Friedel–Crafts acylation using ethanoyl chloride and aluminium chloride.
   Step 2: Nitration electrophilic substitution using a mixture of concentrated nitric and sulfuric acids.
   Step 3: Reduction (hydrogenation) using Sn/concentrated HCl.

10.2

1. React with sodium hydroxide, acidify and then add silver nitrate solution. A precipitate will form – white for Cl, cream for Br and pale yellow for I. To more clearly distinguish the cream and pale yellow precipitates, add concentrated ammonia – the precipitate will dissolve in the case of Br, but not in the case of I. The white precipitate formed with Cl will dissolve in aqueous ammonia.
2. a Because OH^- ions will form a precipitate with silver nitrate.
   b Using HCl adds Cl^- ions, which will form a precipitate with silver nitrate.
3. a alkene and carboxylic acid
   b $CH_2{=}CHCOOH$
   c $CH_2{=}CHCOOH + Br_2 \longrightarrow CH_2BrCHBrCOOH$
   $CH_2{=}CHCOOH + NaHCO_3 \longrightarrow CH_2{=}CHCOONa + CO_2 + H_2O$

11.1

1. a The molecular ion may fragment, also some ions with two positive charges may be formed.
   b Isotopes such as ^{13}C and ^{2}H cause small peaks of larger *m*/*z* than the molecular ion.
2. a 78 and 80
   b The peak of mass 78 will be three times the abundance of that of 80 because the isotope ^{35}Cl is three times as common as ^{37}Cl.
   c CH_3CO^+
   d 63 and 65
   e $CH_3^{\bullet}$
   f $CH_3COCl^{+\bullet} \longrightarrow CH_3CO^+ + Cl^{\bullet}$

11.2

1. N and O have similar values of A_r (14 and 16 respectively) and, as they have similar sizes and nuclear charges, the O—H and N—H bonds would be expected to be of similar strength.
2. a No
   b There is no peak around 3230–3550 cm^{-1}.

11.3

1. a i 1700 cm^{-1} ii 3000 cm^{-1}
   b i C=O ii C=O iii C=O
   iv O—H v O—H
2. All organic compounds have C—H bonds.
3. The broadening is caused by hydrogen bonding between ethanol molecules in pure ethanol. In the solution, ethanol molecules will be far apart and less likely to hydrogen bond to each other.

11.4

1. a a single peak
   b Both carbon atoms are in exactly the same environment.
2. The upper one is propan-1-ol, as it three peaks because all three carbon atoms are in different environments. The lower one is propan-2-ol, as it has two peaks because there are carbon atoms in just two different environments.

11.5

1 a Isomers have the same molecular formula but different arrangements of atoms in space.

b propan-1-ol: $\overset{A}{CH_3}\overset{B}{CH_2}\overset{C}{CH_2}\overset{D}{OH}$,

propan-2-ol: $\overset{A}{CH_3}\overset{B}{CH}\overset{C}{(OH)}\overset{A}{CH_3}$

c i 4 ii 3

d i A3; B2; C2; D1 ii A6; B1; C1

e i approximately A 1 ppm; B 1.5 ppm; C 3.5 ppm; D 3.5–5.5 ppm

ii approximately A 1 ppm; B 3.5 ppm; C 3.5–5.5 ppm

11.6

1 a A is ethanol, B is methoxymethane.

b A: 4.5 is R—O—H, 3.7 is R—CH_2—O-, 1.2 is R—CH_3

B 3.3 is —O—CH_3

c A: 4.5, 1; 3.7, 2; 1.2, 3.

B: It is not possible to tell.

2

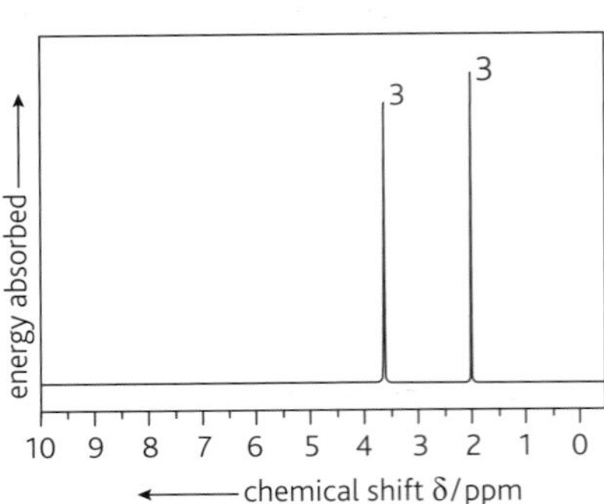

There is no spin-spin coupling because the two CH_3 groups are not on adjacent carbon atoms.

11.7

1 In column chromatography the eluent is a liquid. In gas–liquid chromatography it is a gas.

2 It can separate and help to identify minute traces of substances. For example (among others) substances used in making explosives. [Many other suggestions are also acceptable.]

3 a B b C c A d C

12.1

1 a +788 kJ mol^{-1}

b This is the reverse of the equation for lattice enthalpy formation, so the sign of ΔH is changed.

c The enthalpy change of lattice dissociation.

2 a The electron is attracted by the sodium nucleus, so energy must be put in to remove it.

b The electron is attracted by the chlorine nucleus so energy is given out during this process.

3 a i $Mg(g) \longrightarrow Mg^+(g) + e^-$

ii $Mg^+(g) \longrightarrow Mg^{2+}(g) + e^-$

b The sum of the enthalpies for a(i) and (ii).

12.2

1 a

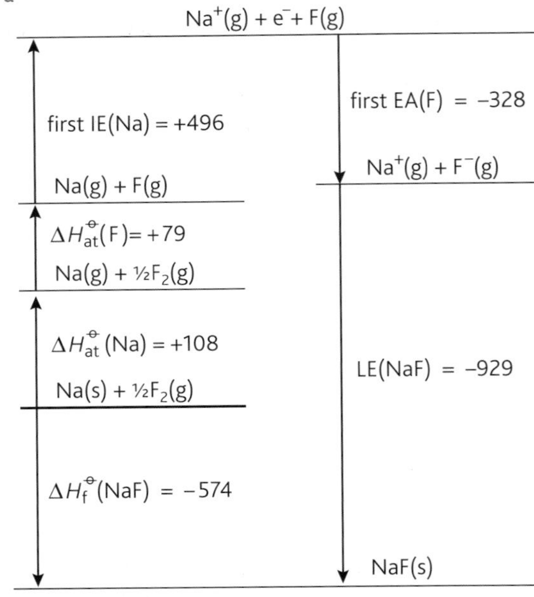

All values in kJ mol^{-1}

b −929 kJ mol^{-1}

12.3

1

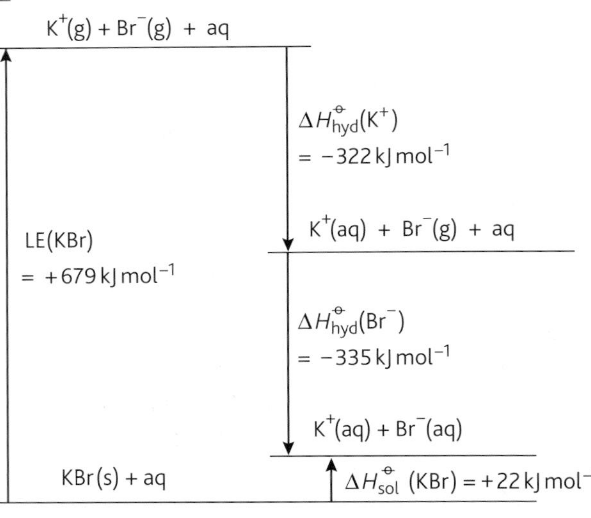

+ 22 kJ mol^{-1}, small because the energy put in to break the lattice is of similar size to that given out when the ions are hydrated.

2 They are small and highly charged positive ions so they strongly polarise negative ions. The calculated value would be greater because there is extra covalent bonding.

12.4

1 a −40 kJ mol^{-1} b −122 kJ mol^{-1}

12.5

1 a i Approximately zero, two solids produce two solids.
ii Significantly positive, a solid produces several moles of gases.
iii Significantly negative, a gas turns into a solid.
iv Significantly positive, a liquid turns into a gas.
b i $-7.8\,J\,K^{-1}\,mol^{-1}$
ii $+876.4\,J\,K^{-1}\,mol^{-1}$
iii $-174.8\,J\,K^{-1}\,mol^{-1}$
iv $+119\,J\,K^{-1}\,mol^{-1}$
The predictions are upheld.

2 a i $+493\,kJ\,mol^{-1}$
ii $-52\,kJ\,mol^{-1}$
iii It is feasible at 6000 K
b 5523 K

3 $-284\,J\,K^{-1}\,mol^{-1}$

13.1

1 They are malleable (can be beaten into sheets) and ductile (can be drawn into wires). They are good conductors of heat.

2 They tend to be brittle; they are poor conductors of heat.

3 a +1 b −1. Oxidation state of oxygen is usually −2.
c $\overset{+2}{Mg}(\overset{-2}{O}\overset{+1}{H})_2$; $+2 + (2 \times -1) = 0$

4 +6

13.2

1 a $Na_2O(s) + H_2O(l) \longrightarrow 2NaOH(aq)$
b i before +1, after +1 ii neither

2 a OH^- ions b greater than 7

3 a acidic
b It is a non-metal.
c $P_4O_6(s) + 6H_2O(l) \longrightarrow 4H_3PO_3(aq)$

13.3

1 a $Na_2O(s) + 2HCl(aq) \longrightarrow 2NaCl(aq) + H_2O(l)$
b $MgO(s) + H_2SO_4(aq) \longrightarrow MgSO_4(aq) + H_2O(l)$
c $Al_2O_3(s) + 6HNO_3(aq) \longrightarrow 3H_2O(l) + 2Al(NO_3)_3(aq)$

2 a $\overset{+4\,-2}{SiO_2}(s) + 2\overset{+1\,-2\,+1}{NaOH}(aq) \longrightarrow \overset{+1\,+4\,-2}{Na_2SiO_3}(aq) + \overset{+1\,-2}{H_2O}(l)$
b No
c No change in oxidation number of any of the elements occurs.

3 $P_4O_{10}(s) + 6H_2O(l) \longrightarrow 4H_3PO_4(aq)$

14.1

1 a +5 b +6 c +2 d +3 e +2

2 $3Zn(s) + Cr_2O_7^{2-}(aq) + 14H^+(aq) \longrightarrow 2Cr^{3+}(aq) + 3Zn^{2+}(aq) + 7H_2O(l)$

14.2

1 a $Ni(s)|Ni^{2+}(aq)\ Ag^+(aq)|Ag(s)$; $E = +1.05\,V$
b Electrons would flow from the nickel electrode to the silver one.
$Ni(s) \longrightarrow Ni^{2+}(aq) + 2e^-$
$Ag^+(aq) + e^- \longrightarrow Ag(s)$
Overall:
$Ni(s) + 2Ag^+(aq) \longrightarrow Ni^{2+}(aq) + 2Ag(s)$

2 a +0.63 V b −0.63 V

14.3

1 0.9 V zinc electrode positive

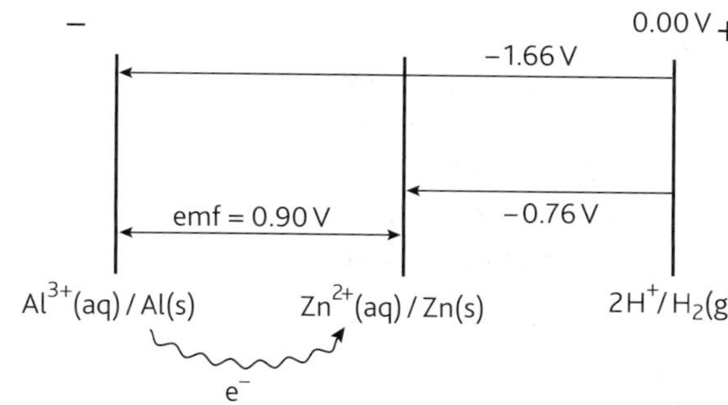

2 a +0.93 V
b −0.53 V
c +0.97 V
d +0.26 V

3 Chlorine and bromine, but not iodine.

4 a No b No

14.4

Answer from main text.

15.1

1 a $1s^2\,2s^2\,2p^6\,3s^2\,3p^6\,3d^5$ b $1s^2\,2s^2\,2p^6\,3s^2\,3p^6\,3d^4$

2 a $1s^2\,2s^2\,2p^6\,3s^2\,3p^6$ b the two 4s electrons
c one of the 3d electrons

15.2

1 a i octahedral ii octahedral iii tetrahedral
b 6, 6, 4
c Cl^- is a larger ligand than either ammonia or water, so fewer ligands can fit around the metal ion.

2 a the two negatively charged oxygen atoms, because they have lone pairs of electrons.
b
O
‖
C — O⁻:

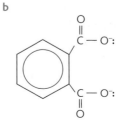

C — O⁻:
‖
O
c bidentate

15.3

1 a The copper ion has part-filled d-orbitals, electrons can move from one d-orbital to another and absorb light. Zinc has full d-orbitals.

b blue

c They are absorbed.

2 a 5:5 b 5:5 c $[NiEDTA]^{2-}$

15.4

1 a $Zn(s) + 2VO_2^+ + 4H^+ \longrightarrow 2H_2O + 2VO^{2+} + Zn^{2+}(aq)$

$Zn(s) + 2VO^{2+}(aq) + 4H^+(aq) \longrightarrow Zn^{2+}(aq) + 2H_2O(l) + 2V^{3+}(aq)$

$Zn(s) + 2V^{3+}(aq) \longrightarrow Zn^{2+}(aq) + 2V^{2+}(aq)$

b This low oxidation state can be oxidised by air.

2 0.0698 g

3 $E^\ominus$ for the reaction:

$Cl_2(g) + 2e^- \longrightarrow 2Cl^-$

is + 1.36 V, but $E^\ominus$ for the reaction of $Cr_2O_7^{2-}$ and Cl^- and is −0.03 V. Therefore the reaction is not feasible. Hence potassium dichromate(VI) will not oxidise chloride ions to chlorine.

15.5

1 a Homogeneous catalysts are in the same phase as the reactants, heterogeneous catalysts are in a different phase from the reactants.

b i heterogeneous ii heterogeneous iii homogeneous

2 It lowers the activation energy. This means that reactions can be carried out at a lower temperature than without the catalyst, thus saving energy and money.

3 First, iron(III) oxidises iodide to iodine, itself being reduced to iron(II):

$2Fe^{3+}(aq) + 2I^-(aq) \longrightarrow 2Fe^{2+}(aq) + I_2(aq)$

Then the peroxodisulfate ions oxidise the iron(II) back to iron(III):

$S_2O_8^{2-}(aq) + 2Fe^{2+}(aq) \longrightarrow 2SO_4^{2-}(aq) + 2Fe^{3+}(aq)$

Catalyst is needed since the reaction is slow. The reaction is slow since both ions are negative ions. These ions will repel each other, reducing the chance of effective collisions.

4 $4Mn^{2+}(aq) + MnO_4^-(aq) + 8H^+(aq) \longrightarrow 5Mn^{3+}(aq) + 4H_2O(l)$

$2Mn^{3+}(aq) + C_2O_4^{2-}(aq) \longrightarrow 2CO_2(g) + 2Mn^{2+}(aq)$

Multiply the top equation by 2 and the lower one by 5 to give the same number of Mn^{3+} ions:

$8Mn^{2+}(aq) + 2MnO_4^-(aq) + 16H^+(aq) \longrightarrow 10Mn^{3+}(aq) + 8H_2O(l)$

$10Mn^{3+}(aq) + 5C_2O_4^{2-}(aq) \longrightarrow 10CO_2(g) + 10Mn^{2+}(aq)$

Then combine the two equations and cancel any species that appear on both sides:

$2MnO_4^-(aq) + 16H^+(aq) + 5C_2O_4^{2-}(aq) \longrightarrow 2Mn^{2+}(aq) + 8H_2O(l) + 10CO_2(g)$

16.1

1 a +7 b +6 c +6

2 Acid–base. It is not redox as the chromium is in the +6 state before and after. One of the oxygen atoms accepts two protons H^+ ions.

16.2

1 $Cu(H_2O)_4Cl_2$ or $Cu(H_2O)_2Cl_2$

2 a

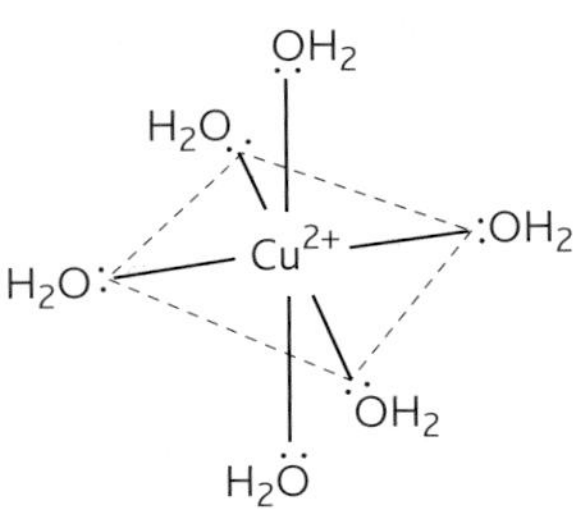

b Bromide ions are bigger than water molecules, so fewer can fit around the copper ion. The shape is tetrahedral.

3 $[Cu(H_2O)_6]^{2+}(aq) + en \longrightarrow [Cu(H_2O)_4(en)]^{2+}(aq) + 2H_2O(l)$

$[CuH_2O_4(en)]^{2+}(aq) + en \longrightarrow [Cu(H_2O)_2(en)_2]^{2+}(aq) + 2H_2O(l)$

$[Cu(H_2O)_2(en)_2]^{2+}(aq) + en \longrightarrow [Cu(en)_3]^{2+}(aq) + 2H_2O(l)$

At each step two entities produce three, therefore the entropy change of each step is likely to be positive.

4 a No, it remains at +2.

b $[Co(H_2O)_6]^{2+}$ is octahedral and $[CoCl_4]^{2-}$ is tetrahedral.

c The ligands have changed as has the co-ordination number.

16.3

1 They are smaller and more highly charged and therefore more strongly polarising. They can thus weaken one of the O—H bonds in one of the water molecules that surround them, thus releasing a H^+ ion.

2 Aluminium is not a transition metal. It has no part-filled d-orbitals. It is electrons moving between part-filled d-orbitals that absorb light and make most transition metal compounds coloured.

3 Both NH_3 and H_2O are of similar size and are neutral ligands.

4 a i $[Fe(H_2O)_6]^{3+}(aq) + 3OH^-(aq) \longrightarrow Fe(H_2O)_3(OH)_3(s) + 3H_2O(l)$

ii $[Cu(H_2O)_6]^{2+}(aq) + 4NH_3(aq) \longrightarrow [Cu(NH_3)_4(H_2O)_2]^{2+}(aq) + 4H_2O(l)$

b i The pale violet solution changes to a reddish brown solid.

ii The pale blue solution turns to dark blue.

Index

D

E

F

G

H

I

K

L

M